changing the way the world learns

To get extra value from this book for no additional cost, go to:

http://www.thomson.com/wadsworth.html

thomson.com is the World Wide Web site for Wadsworth/ITP and is your direct source to dozens of on-line resources. *thomson.com* helps you find out about supplements, experiment with demonstration software, search for a job, and send e-mail to many of our authors. You can even preview new publications and exciting new technologies.

thomson.com: *It's where you'll find us in the future.*

About the Authors

Peggy D. Bennett and Douglas R. Bartholomew are former elementary music teachers who now teach in university settings. Continuing contact (as teachers and observers) with children and elementary teachers in workshops and school settings has contributed greatly to the perspectives presented in this book. Work with undergraduate music and education majors, as well as with graduate music and classroom teachers, has provided a rich background from which the authors draw questions and conclusions about singing in the education of children.

Both authors have published articles in professional journals on a variety of topics, have been elected to leadership positions in their respective state music education organizations, have taught workshops and courses for teachers in the United States, Canada, and Japan, and are charter members of the not-for-profit organization Music EdVentures.

Peggy D. Bennett *(Ph.D., University of North Texas)* is Professor of Music and Director of Music Education at Texas Christian University in Fort Worth and was previously Professor and Head of Music Education at The University of Texas at Arlington. Author of numerous pedagogical and research articles, Bennett is also an active clinician for educational conferences, universities, and school districts. Honors have included UTA's Chancellor's Council Award for Excellence in Teaching and Outstanding Alumna recognition from both the University of North Texas and Ball State University.

Douglas R. Bartholomew *(Ph.D., Case Western Reserve University)* is Associate Professor of Music Education at Montana State University at Bozeman. Bartholomew received the 1985 award for Outstanding Dissertation in Music Education given jointly by the Music Educators National Conference and the Council for Research in Music Education. He organizes the Montana Elementary Music Forum, which sponsors seminars each summer in Bozeman, and his written work has been published in books, journals, and newsletters.

SongWorks 1

Singing in the Education of Children

Peggy D. Bennett
Texas Christian University

Douglas R. Bartholomew
Montana State University at Bozeman

Wadsworth Publishing Company
I(T)P® An International Thomson Publishing Company

Belmont, CA • Albany, NY • Bonn • Boston • Cincinnati • Detroit • Johannesburg
London • Madrid • Melbourne • Mexico City • New York • Paris • San Francisco
Singapore • Tokyo • Toronto • Washington

Editorial Assistant: Lori Mikuls

Senior Project Editor: Debby Kramer

Production: Greg Hubit Bookworks

Print Buyer: Barbara Britton

Permissions Editor: Robert Kauser

Designer: Christy Butterfield

Copy Editor: Carole Crouse

Cover Designer: Seventeenth Street Studios / Randall Goodall

Compositor: TBH/Typecast

Printer: Courier Companies / Kendallville

For more information, contact Wadsworth Publishing Company, 10 Davis Drive, Belmont,
CA 94002, or electronically at http://www.thomson.com/wadsworth.html

International Thomson Publishing Europe
Berkshire House 168-173
High Holborn
London, WC1V 7AA, England

International Thomson Editores
Campos Eliseos 385, Piso 7
Col. Polanco
11560 México D.F. México

Thomas Nelson Australia
102 Dodds Street
South Melbourne 3205
Victoria, Australia

International Thomson Publishing Asia
221 Henderson Road
#05-10 Henderson Building
Singapore 0315

Nelson Canada
1120 Birchmount Road
Scarborough, Ontario
Canada M1K 5G4

International Thomson Publishing Japan
Hirakawacho Kyowa Building, 3F
2-2-1 Hirakawacho
Chiyoda-ku, Tokyo 102, Japan

International Thomson Publishing GmbH
Königswinterer Strasse 418
53227 Bonn, Germany

International Thomson Publishing Southern Africa
Building 18, Constantia Park
240 Old Pretoria Road
Halfway House, 1685 South Africa

SongWorks is a registered service mark.

ISBN: 0-534-51327-1

Contents

Foreword

We have reached a point in America where singing is at risk. This most natural act—once commonly practiced by Americans of all ages—is not as common anymore. This foreword and this book are about what can be done to Get America Singing . . . Again!

Singing uses an instrument that we all carry with us wherever we go. In the very first months of life we all exercise our vocal cords by crying, cooing, or just experimenting with the up and down siren-like pitch possibilities of our voice. The child quickly finds out that his or her voice gives power—the ability to attract attention of parents when one needs something. As we get older we join with others in making our voices work together in chants and simple songs; and we start to experience the joy of community vocalization.

Singing, like any bodily muscle action, must be exercised to stay fit or improve. When children are subjected to a society that has become increasingly passive, they are inclined to fit in. When watching TV substitutes for activity or creative play, the child loses a great deal. When too many people start to say things like "I can't carry a tune in a bushel basket" or "I'm a non-singer," we know we are in trouble.

What we gain from singing together as children or adults is immense. Group singing can instantly create a sense of community in a room full of people who have never even met. Singing can quickly alter someone's comfort level—it can turn fear or unhappiness into a much happier state. Songs also carry very important cultural and historical messages, and like stories, songs help children learn the do's and don'ts of society's norms. Singing gives us all the power to recreate our lives—the opportunity for personal enrichment and group identity.

This book will help you find a place for singing in your life. It will teach you important techniques for finding your own voice and for working with others. It will enlarge your personal song bag, and it will help restore the importance of singing in American life and American schools. Enjoy the process. Feel the power of music.

Will Schmid

Preface

Why Did We Write This Book?

Gaining confidence in our own voices and developing a devotion to singing in education came slowly to both of us. We did not begin our musical lives as singers. Growing up in Indiana and Nebraska, we spent most of our time performing in high school and university bands and orchestras, not choruses. Not until we became elementary music educators did we begin to realize the importance, the value, and the joy of singing. As we encouraged our students to sing, we ourselves gained courage as singers. But, you may ask, is singing really all that necessary in today's world?

In recent years, music has made its way into nearly every nook and cranny of our daily lives. Music is in the movies we watch, in the stores we shop, in the television programs and commercials we see, and on radios that awake us. We can buy recordings of nearly every kind of music—music for every purpose, taste, and age. Because music, in great amounts and diversity, is all around us, we rarely need to sing to have music. With so much music made and performed for us, why would we write a book that encourages people, even those with limited musical skills, to sing?

School curricula are increasingly crowded. Teachers are expected to teach, and students are expected to learn, everything—from health enhancement to critical thinking, from social skills to computation, and from appreciating cultural commonalities to understanding cultural diversity. There is so much to do in so little time. If hurried children and harried teachers already have too much to do, why would we be asking them to do more by including singing in their classes?

The answer to these questions is simple: *because song works.*

Song works as a way of creating community. When we sing together, we contribute our voices to the community of singers; yet the unique qualities of individual voices are maintained, even as they mingle and blend with others. Song works as a symbol of individuals working cooperatively within groups, a symbol of being ourselves within a larger social organization.

Song works as a direct, personal music experience. When we sing, we feel the energy of the music in our muscles, we hear it with our ears, and we shape it with our minds and voices. *When we sing, we become the music.*

Song works as a means of expression. Love, sadness, wonder, loyalty, and humor are just a few of the feelings that can be conveyed through song. Song gives voice to our thoughts, feelings, and ideas.

Song works to stimulate thinking. Singing can help students feel comfortable with their surroundings, and therefore it can offer a context for thought. When we sing, we experience language. Words, images, stories, and syntax are presented in songs. By finding patterns, adding verses, sequencing events, or interpreting meaning, we discover that song also provides the content for thought.

To assist teachers in learning how song can work for you and your students, we offer a variety of strategies for helping students enjoy the musical experience, express themselves through music, and think as they sing. *The purpose of this book, then, is to present singing as a fundamentally valuable, inherently social, personally enjoyable, and richly educational experience to which all teachers and students have access.*

What Do We Hope to Accomplish?

Our aim was to write a book in a dynamic, inquisitive style that approximates "good teaching." At its best, teaching is an interactive, corresponding process, and that ideal is emphasized in both the content and the format of this book. To elicit your interaction, we ask you questions, give you things to do, inform you about additional resources, and expect you to reflect on practices (past, present, and future) that influence your own singing in the education of children. As we wrote *Song-Works 1*, we envisioned a book that would

- inspire in you an "I can do it!" attitude toward singing and toward the teaching of singing activities;

- be entertaining yet poignant, easily readable yet challenging;

- build confidence in and stimulate curiosity about teaching, learning, and music;

- illustrate "best practices" as we have observed them in masterful teachers;

- help both preservice and in-service teachers find specific ways to lead children in music activities and also provide thoughtful commentary on the general issues related to those activities;

- focus on a set of principles rather than on a specific methodology to guide you in the ways you see and respond to children, teaching, and music;

- strike a balance between principles and practice, between music theory and music performance, between asking and telling, and between showing specific procedures and fostering creative independence;

- provide a limited core of songs from which you can transfer and extrapolate the teaching strategies and behaviors illustrated;

- stimulate your continuing pursuit of knowledge, skills, and understanding about the teaching and learning processes;

- speak directly to you as a professional, whether novice or veteran, who seeks to cultivate characteristics of good teaching;

- feature music in an intriguing, nonthreatening way—as a context for learning and as a subject to be studied through active listening and music making;

- touch each of you in ways that create personal connections to the book's contents.

What Kind of Book Is This?

SongWorks 1 is not a typical college textbook, nor was it intended to be. Our years of experience in teaching children, teaching university students, and teaching teachers inspired us to write a book that would help teachers teach, but would not necessarily organize a course for teachers. Rather than focusing on the question "What should the content of this course include?" we were instead guided by the question "What are important topics and ideas for teachers to know and think about in working with children?"

Also, we were not interested in writing a traditional teachers' manual. Many teachers' manuals for working with music and children seek to answer the question, "What do teachers need to know about music in order to teach children about music?" We chose to consider instead "What best practices have we seen that would help teachers and children benefit from singing experiences?" Given its unique content, we believe *SongWorks 1* fills a void—in the genres of both professional books and textbooks for teachers.

For years, we taught our music education courses using no textbook. Though the available textbooks were filled with valuable information and written by respected colleagues, they did not fit our way of teaching and did not provide the material we considered critical for our students to know. *SongWorks 1* began to take shape as a synthesis of the topics, handouts, skills, activities, issues, discussions, questions, and readings that amalgamated the contents of our courses. More than just a collection of our experiences in these categories, however, our writings evolved into a book that aims to capture the essence of music education for children—the heart and spirit that ideally permeate all singing activities and teaching strategies.

Who Is *SongWorks 1* For?

SongWorks 1 is geared toward both classroom and music specialists and toward both preservice and in-service teachers. This inclusive approach provides a solid basis for further music education, for both children and adults.

The activities of *SongWorks 1* are intended for elementary-age students—primary ages (kindergarten through Grade 3) and intermediate ages (Grades 4 through 6). The application of this content, however, could extend to both younger and older students, and the discussions of teaching behaviors apply to many, if not all, instructional settings.

How Is *SongWorks 1* Organized?

Chapters: Although there is reasoning behind the sequence in which chapters in this book are presented, you need not read or study the chapters in sequence. When the text refers to an unfamiliar term or concept, you will find ample explanation in another section or in the Glossary. Chapters and the sections within each chapter are organized to provide busy teachers and students with brief yet relatively complete treatment of a topic.

Principles: We have utilized a principle approach to the contents of this text. Because the book is framed around the Principles of Teaching and Learning as stated in Chapter 2 and because the practices and discussions are intended to illustrate those tenets, citations of specific principles appear in the margins throughout the text. A reproducible display of the principles of *SongWorks 1* appears on the inside back cover of this book.

Scenarios: Sprinkled throughout *SongWorks 1* are scenarios of classroom experiences that are based on true stories and potential school situations. Scenarios use the power of storytelling to give personal glimpses of life in a classroom of children and offer memorable anecdotes that give a context for the topics being discussed.

Folk songs: Chapter 9 includes approximately forty folk songs and approximately ninety-five accompanying games that give a context for practicing the principles laced throughout the book. Each folk-song game is described and analyzed in detail. Such thorough treatment provides models for leading children in playful activities and for reflecting upon and assessing the learning opportunities apparent in varieties of singing experiences. In essence, the pedagogical practices of *SongWorks 1* are illustrated in the folk-song games mentioned throughout the book and described in Chapter 9. And in turn, these folk-song games provide the groundwork for additional music experiences.

As stated earlier, *SongWorks 1* does not attempt to cover all topics and activities that are appropriate and desirable in music classes for children and music classes for future teachers. Giving important topics such as the use of classroom instruments, guided listening to concert music, and presentation of culturally diverse song material the thorough and careful treatment that they deserve, and that we have given to the topics that are presented in this text, is beyond the scope of *SongWorks 1*.

Rather than provide an expansive collection of songs, we have selected a core of songs and have given them extensive development with activities that have been classroom- and time-tested throughout North America. The play activities that accompany the folk songs provide illustrations of how to interact, play, and think within a context of singing. Anthologies of children's songs and music series texts are readily accessible to provide a broad spectrum of musical experiences, activities, and performance options.

The songs and activities of *SongWorks 1* are not a broad representation of cultures, periods, and styles but contexts for activities that acknowledge, appreciate, and respect similarities and differences among individuals. Such acknowledgment, appreciation, and respect are, of course, at the heart of the multicultural movement in North America and are the foundational principles on which the ideas and activities of this book are built.

Our wish is that in reading this book, considering the ideas and questions, implementing the practices, and reflecting on the principles, you will find that song works for you and your students.

Acknowledgments

A book such as *SongWorks 1* begins long before any words are written. As students of our students, we have felt both the exhilaration of teaching something well and the ache of knowing we needed to improve. Perhaps more than our teachers, our students have shaped our thinking and forged the set of principles by which we teach. Whether they were preschool, elementary, university, or graduate students, it is to our students that we feel most indebted for the lessons we have learned.

At the beginning of our careers, we each had the good fortune to meet Mary Helen Richards. Our association with Mary Helen's work, Education Through Music™, lasted from 1971 to 1991, first as students in her courses, next as apprentices who traveled with her, and then as colleagues teaching courses and developing materials. We believe that the influences of Mary Helen's gusto for teaching and thinking, her compassion for children of all ages, and her determination to maintain a musical approach to music education are evident throughout this book.

Joining us in this venture of *SongWorks 1* are friends with whom we have taught, laughed, and studied for over twenty years. Our collaborators, Fleurette Sweeney, Anna Langness, and Betty Hoffmann are the delightful teachers who were models for many of our principles and practices. Fleurette has given us unflagging encouragement and support throughout our careers, and she always seems to have more when we need it. Anna's inspired teaching has, in turn, inspired us to share her amazing gift for working with children and adults, and our own students have been the direct recipients of Anna's classroom expertise. We are especially indebted to Anna for her inspiration in writing Chapter 5 of this volume. For earlier versions of this book, Betty has doubled as cheerleader and copy editor. Her commitment to teachers and children *and* her extraordinary training in grammar have given her the strength to read every word, answer every question, and ponder every discussion that you will read here. We know of no one else who would voluntarily be this meticulous with our work, and Betty's participation in this project has been invaluable. The spirits and the wisdom of Fleurette, Anna, and Betty grace the pages of this book.

Special appreciation goes to Dr. Marty Stover of the College of St. Catherine in St. Paul, Minnesota, and Fleurette Sweeney of the University of British Columbia for their willingness to field-test each version of this book at their respective institutions and to share their own and their students' feedback on its contents.

Seeking and accepting feedback from a variety of reviewers contributes to the quality of any manuscript. The first version of this book was printed in 1992 and was titled *SongWorks: Valuing Singing in Education.* We are grateful to those reviewers who provided feedback and encouragement on our early efforts with this text:

Susan Kenney, Brigham Young University, Provo, Utah

Janet Montgomery, The University of Colorado–Boulder

Ann Small, Stetson University, Deland, Florida

Marilyn Winter and Judy Suvak, two experienced music teachers in Montana, generously read that first manuscript through the eyes of practicing elementary teachers and offered supportive feedback. Freelance editor Marnie Pavelich was especially helpful and meticulous in reading our work and helping us fine-tune our writing as we revised the 1994 version, *SongWorks 1: Singing in the Education of Children.* Respected colleagues offered substantive reviews of the 1994 and 1995 versions, and we appreciate their careful and thorough assessments of the book:

Nancy Boone, Middle Tennessee State University, Murfreesboro, Tennessee

Janice Cusano, Indiana University–Bloomington

Susan Kenney, Brigham Young University, Provo, Utah

Ellen McCullough–Brabson, University of New Mexico–Albuquerque

Diane Persellin, Trinity University, San Antonio, Texas

Martha Riley, Purdue University, Lafayette, Indiana

Maribeth Yoder-White, University of North Carolina–Greensboro

Several practicing elementary classroom and music teachers read and critiqued portions of the folk-song games of Chapter 9; their helpful feedback was invaluable and greatly appreciated. Readers were Ann Shaner, Montana; Ruth Ann Darnall, British Columbia; Carla Vennes, British Columbia; Reneé Westlake, Montana; Anna Langness, Colorado; Vicky Suarez, Texas; Fleurette Sweeney, British Columbia; and Beth Cain, Texas.

To our spouses, Harley Quick and Patty Bartholomew, a "thank you" does not come close to expressing the magnitude of our heartfelt appreciation. Working on this project has required sacrificing much of our valued time with them. The continual patience and support they have shown us are powerful reminders of the quality of life we enjoy with them.

Singing in Education

1

Why Do We Value Singing?

SCENARIO — SINGING AS A FAMILY

Driving across the plains, every member of the family was anxious to arrive at their destination. They ran out of conversation at the same time they ran out of patience with each other. Suddenly, one child began singing *She'll Be Comin' 'Round the Mountain* in a quiet, dull voice. Though they had not sung this song together in years, one by one each family member joined the boisterous sing-along. Between verses, there was often a momentary pause while they tried to think of what words came next. When a family member would remember the next verse and begin singing in the spirit of "I've got it!" all would laugh and continue singing. Without realizing it, the family was rejuvenated and reconnected as the time flew by.

SCENARIO — SINGING AS A CHILD

A preschool child, sitting on the kitchen floor with his toys while his mother was fixing dinner, sang what he knew of *Home on the Range* to accompany his play. "Oh, home on the range, where the deer and the cantaloupe play . . . Oh, home on the range, where the deer and the cantaloupe play . . . Oh, home on the range, where the deer and the cantaloupe play."

"It's antelope, dear. 'Where the deer and the antelope play,'" corrected the mother gently. "Mommy, can I have a cookie?" "Not this soon before dinner."

Turning back to his toys and oblivious of his mother's correction, he continued his play, singing, "Oh, home on the range, where the deer and the cantaloupe play . . . Oh, home on the range, where the deer and the cantaloupe play . . . Oh, home on the range, where the deer and the cantaloupe play."

SCENARIO   SINGING AS A PATRIOT

A convention of business women and men included opening ceremonies with music provided by local high school musicians. On the minds of everyone as the flag was presented was the recent beginning of military conflict. Nearly everyone in the audience knew someone who was affected by the troop deployment to a far-off land.

After an introduction by the school orchestra, the high school chorus began to sing *The Star-Spangled Banner*. At first, only the choir was singing; but within seconds, voices from the audience could be heard joining in. Some had not participated in singing the national anthem in many years; they usually just listened. By the last phrase of the song, everyone in the huge room was singing, some feeling their voices catching in their throats. The conductor's release for the final chord was met not by applause but by silence as all in the room realized the emotional impact of the moment.

SCENARIO   SINGING AS A PARENT

He never sang in the class of women. Although he was taking the college course for credit and planned to be a teacher, singing was too personal, too embarrassing, too difficult for him to reveal in a university course filled with women who seemed to participate so freely.

Not until the tenth week of class did he speak for the first time. To the surprise of everyone, he volunteered a response to the teacher's question "Does anyone have a connection for us before we begin class? Has an 'ah-HA' happened to you since last we saw each other?"

"I usually read a story to my two-year-old daughter each night before she goes to sleep," he began as quiet attentiveness surrounded him. "Last night, she shocked me by asking, 'Daddy, would you sing me a song?' I figured after all this time in class, I should know a song to sing to her, so I did." There was a softness in the looks he received from his classmates. "What song did you sing?" asked a woman seated near him. "*Twinkle, Twinkle, Little Star*," he answered, seeming somewhat embarrassed to say it, ". . . about twelve times!" Chuckles greeted his recognition that his daughter wanted him to "do it again!"

After a brief pause, just before the attention left him, he added with a grin, "I guess I need to learn some more songs!"

SCENARIO   SINGING AS CONSOLATION

Live national television coverage glued a country to the unfolding events in a town in west Texas. A small child, not a year old, had fallen down an abandoned well shaft. The entire community was mobilized in efforts to get to her and extricate her from the shaft. Rescuers worried about falling temperatures as well as possible injuries and dehydration.

Reality forced them to acknowledge that she would remain in the shaft at least overnight. Calls were placed and received from all over the country in efforts to save the little child. Her frantic young parents looked on, helpless.

After many hours, in an attempt to discern her state of health, a small microphone was lowered into the shaft. As rescuers and parents listened intently to hear her cries, they were met instead with a touching sound. Her mother looked up to the expectant crowd of caring adults with tears in her eyes and a voice shaking with emotion, "She is singing *Winnie the Pooh*."

PRINCIPLE 7

These marginal citations refer the reader to the Principles of Teaching and Learning stated on pages 31–41.

If singing can foster positive human inter-action, maybe that is reason enough for us to engage in it.

What is it about singing that has the power to touch us so deeply? Songs of every era, of every style, of every type feel powerful to those who listen to or sing them. The songs we sing can be complex or simple; they can be happy or sorrowful. We sing to express joy and pain, wonder and reflection, togetherness and solitude.

Even though we may agree that singing is good for people, the way in which we approach and treat singing can either support or diminish that benefit. Therefore, an important topic addressed in this book is how to sing with others. Singing can foster positive social interaction and personal development, but it does not do so automatically.

To reap the benefits of singing in the classroom, we must pay attention to the context and approach we use to

- develop students' sense of trust and acceptance;
- build students' vocal skills and their attitudes about voices;
- demonstrate our attitudes and responses to students' efforts;
- articulate the reasons we give for singing.

What Is Singing?

What does it mean to be a singer? Few of us would stand up in a group of people and announce, "I can sing!" or "I am a singer!" More people feel comfortable apologizing, "I can't sing!" Why is it that so many people are reluctant to recognize and proclaim themselves as singers even though they *can* sing and *do* sing? In its simplest form, singing is like talking with elongated vowels. One child commented, "Singing is like cursive, talking is like printing." If we can talk, we can sing. Yet, just as in any other activity, including talking, each of us may be at a different level of development and accomplishment, and singing does require us to use our voices with greater precision than talking does.

Imagine a continuum of singers. At the extreme right are those who have achieved greatness by gaining nearly complete control of their vocal facility. These singers would be the Olympic gold medalists of voice, those who have conditioned and refined their voices in the extreme, maintained their skill, and earned lasting recognition. Some names that come to mind for this area of the continuum are Luciano Pavarotti, Leontyne Price, Ella Fitzgerald, Bobby McFerrin, and Barbra Streisand. Few of us would place ourselves on the far right of this spectrum.

At the other end of the continuum are people who have little or no vocal facility, who are able to do little more than talk-sing. This extreme lack of vocal facility can be the result of an injury to the vocal mechanism, brain damage, or simple lack of experimentation with vocal production. Again, few of us can honestly say we fit into this category of singer.

Most of us find ourselves somewhere in the middle. Where we place ourselves on this continuum at any given moment depends on a number of factors that affect our singing voices and how we feel about our singing (Bennett 1986a). How do these factors affect the quality and confidence of your singing?

- Your level of fatigue
- The relative high or low range in which a song is sung
- Singing alone
- Whether or not others can hear you sing
- How warmed up your voice may be for singing
- Your familiarity with the words and melody of the song

- With whom and with how many people you are singing
- Where you are singing: in a shower or on a concert stage
- Your sense of being evaluated or judged by others
- Your feelings of embarrassment at singing

Singing is a priceless activity and a right that belongs to everyone. Voices vary in levels of achievement, maintenance, and fitness. Recognition of the physical, mental, and attitudinal aspects of singing helps us to nurture singers and preserve their right to sing. (See Chapter 4 for further discussion on voices.)

Vocal abilities can be appreciated from the same perspective as walking and running abilities. If we compare speaking to walking and singing to running, we realize that running and singing require extra effort, endurance, breathing, and conditioning. Vocal endurance and agility, then, are more matters of practice and conditioning than of inherent talent. Music teachers, especially, should not expect all students to be vocal "runners" when they have had little opportunity or guidance to move out of the "toddling" and "shuffling" stages of vocal activity. Seeing students as emergent vocal athletes may broaden our opinions of their skills and potentials (Bennett 1986a; Langness 1991a; Thurman 1991).

Singing is not something reserved for the gifted few, and with rare exceptions, it is an activity in which all people can engage. Singing in its natural, unselfconscious form is the subject of this book.

Singing and Pleasure

SCENARIO   THE JOY OF SINGING

As you sit in your car at a stop light, some movement inside the car behind you catches your attention. As you look in your rearview mirror, you see someone singing with mouth wide open and showing intense involvement with exaggerated facial expressions, shoulder swaying, and hand gestures.

You smile as you watch this display of pleasure and abandonment in singing.

Taking an athletic approach to voices and to singing frees us from the outdated view that one is born a singer (or not) and mandates that we be aware of the stunting effect that critical attitudes and words can have on developing singers.

▶ Did you picture a teenage boy or girl in this scenario?

▶ Did you picture a young child?

▶ Did you picture an adult singing to his or her companion?

▶ Did you picture an elderly man or woman?

▶ Would you take equal pleasure at each of these visions?

Ideally, all of us at any age should feel free to sing with absolute abandon and pleasure, to break into song "at the drop of a hat." Most parents and teachers have experienced the joy of hearing a child leap into spontaneous song. Singing either a familiar song or one created on the spot, children seem more capable than any of us of knowing and experiencing the value of singing for the sheer pleasure of singing.

▶ When was the last time you recall singing for the sheer pleasure of singing?

▶ Do you remember where you were at the time and what you were doing?

▶ Do you remember why you were singing?

▶ Whom were you with and what were you feeling?

PRINCIPLE 7

Singing is not just for the expression of pleasure, but it is often associated with pleasing circumstances. Singing enables us to express the pleasure we feel, and it is often a catalyst for those feelings. Singing can shape us by bringing feelings of pleasure into experiences that, by themselves, might be neutral. Simply hearing someone else sing can give us pleasure.

Singing should find a valued place in our schools and in our daily lives, if only for the pleasure it brings. To set the tone of a classroom, a social event, or a work experience is an important reason for singing. Unfortunately, singing does not bring pleasure automatically: Witness those who do not enjoy singing or who consider singing superfluous. Part of the challenge this book presents is to help people discover how to harness the potential pleasure of singing.

Singing and Our Feelings

Although singing can be pleasurable and can express pleasure, its expressive potential is broader than that. Through the ages, people have used song to accompany worship, wonder, and romance. Through hymns and chants, people have been able to pray, give thanks, and express their wonder and awe. Patriotic songs give expression to feelings of civic pride and identity. Love songs have brought comfort and consolation, instilled hope, and both quieted and fired passions. Songs can function like lightning rods for the feelings associated with love and courtship as well as with heartbreak and disappointment.

Songs become associated with emotions, memories, and feelings, in part because they seem able to clarify them. Besides giving pleasure, singing can serve as a vehicle for the expression of our feelings, something words often fail to do. Songs can validate our feelings, give them focus, and by placing them in a public forum, let us see them in a new perspective.

Although the relationship of song to feelings is an important reason to value singing, it may not be clear why singing belongs in the classroom. Part of the reason for singing in the education of children lies in the role that feelings play in learning and classroom interactions.

Singing provides ways to cultivate feelings of empathy and kinship and of civic pride and individual confidence. Singing provides opportunities to clarify feelings of joy and disappointment, of kindness and resentment, and of respect for oneself and others.

Singing and Social Experiences

Singing is a rich and complex activity, involving high degrees of social interaction, language, and thinking, as well as opportunities for movement and dramatic expression. Singing reminds us that we do live in a world with other people; it is an act that connects people. The social dimension of song is clearly an important and fundamental part of its value. *SongWorks 1* is dedicated to the belief that the socializing potential of song can be an effective tool in shaping healthy classroom environments. This potential includes the powerful influence that singing can have on the development of students' attitudes toward and skills for working together.

SCENARIO

THE POWER OF SONG

Sammy has yet to fit into the class comfortably. He does not speak and only rarely makes eye contact with teachers or with fellow students.

One day, however, when the class is playing *I'm Going Downtown*, Sammy begins paying more attention. He watches closely as the line of children travels around the circle, adding a new child to the group with each new turn. Quietly, Sammy watches

the process. "We're going downtown. We're going downtown. We're going down to Cleveland to show our friends around."

Soon, Sammy sees Georgia bend down in front of him and ask him, "Would you like to come to town with us, Sammy?" Sammy looks at Georgia, pauses slightly, and responds, "Yes, I'd like to come along." Georgia reaches out her hand to help Sammy stand and takes him to the end of the line. Although she wisely makes no comment, his teacher smiles warmly and feels a great sense of relief and celebration. This is Sammy's first time to participate freely in a class activity.

What might it be about the singing, the song, or the activity that encouraged Sammy to participate? Sammy may have responded to the pleasure of the song or to the emotional safety of the activity.

▶ Under what circumstances do you feel free to sing or otherwise make a contribution in a group?

▶ Can you recall a time when a song helped you relax and be more comfortable with a group?

Singing is usually regarded as a musical experience, but it is fundamentally a social experience. A social bond commonly develops among people who sing together. They share the sounds of their voices with each other; they listen to each other; and they coordinate their efforts with others in the group. Singing together can be a model for cooperative effort, as each participant makes a unique contribution and, at the same time, adjusts to the needs of the group.

Songs have played a role in establishing the identity of social groups as diverse as the nationalist movement of pre–World War II Germany and the United States antiwar movement of the 1960s. The sense of civic pride that comes from hearing one's national anthem also is an indication of song's social dimension.

Singing is a communicative act, because it puts part of oneself into a public dimension. The social dimension of solo singing becomes apparent when the singer sings to someone else, in a concert, game, lullaby, or serenade. The singer shares the sound of his or her voice, the song, and the interpretation with other people. It may come as a surprise that singing alone, with no one else present, also has a social aspect. Sitting under a tree at sunset, enjoying the end of the day, and marveling at the mystery of life might be an occasion to sing a favorite song quietly to oneself. Although it may not be obvious or true that singing in this situation is directed to another person, the song has understandable words and employs intelligible musical structures, demonstrating its social fabric and our kinship to the world in which we live.

PRINCIPLE 7

Through singing, we can learn to support and trust other people. Because many songs involve wordplay, movement, or games, there are ample opportunities to share and interact. Singing together can help people make individual contributions to a group and learn how to respond to the contributions of others. Singing songs of other cultures can give us an intellectual appreciation for differences in people and places, and singing with others can give us opportunities to cultivate habits and skills necessary to cope in our own lives with individual differences.

Singing and Language

Songs tell stories, portray events, state opinions, describe people and places, and, in general, do all the kinds of things we expect from language. The connection between

Part of the value of song lies in its intimate relationship with language.

song and language, treated briefly here, is important and will be discussed in depth in several places throughout this book.

Songs are language experiences. Think about a song you know that tells a story, one from your childhood perhaps. How are the stories in songs similar to stories without songs? How are they different? Think of the words of a song you like. Some people focus more on the words of songs than on the music. When they talk about a song they like, they are often talking only about the words. Is that true for you? Think about *The Star Spangled Banner*.

A significant amount of the beauty, effect, and appeal of a song resides in the power of its language.

▶ How do the words and the music combine for the effect the song has on you?

▶ Which is the more important contributing factor: the words or the music?

▶ Ask yourself the same questions about a song on the radio that you like.

▶ How are the words of songs like poetry?

▶ Do you find yourself listening for rhyme, poetic meter, and rhythm?

Music, Singing, and Thinking

Singing is sometimes considered a mindless activity, because it may take our minds off things and because we may do it with little conscious effort. Singing does involve thought, however, especially when we are fully engaged in it, physically, affectively, and cognitively. When we coordinate actions with a song, for example, we are thinking. To start and stop our walking while singing requires us to listen ahead in time, to anticipate the beginning, and to predict the ending of the song.

Moving in synchrony with music requires us to sequence, time, and coordinate sound, muscle, and intention.

Although simply repeating a song may involve very little thought, songs provide opportunities to create actions, verses, and interpretations. Finding words that will describe actions, fitting words into songs, creating new ways to move, suggesting new rhymes, and imagining contexts that help explain what a song is about—all take thought.

Songs provide contexts for thinking.

▪ Identifying and comparing rhythmic and melodic patterns

▪ Symbolizing sound in movement, words, and notation

▪ Comparing and ordering sounds by length or pitch height

▪ Making distinctions in phrase length, finding moments of musical emphasis and closure

▪ Learning to defend decisions with evidence based on our shared experience of sound

Very often, it is the way we engage in singing that stimulates thought. Singing can be a mindless, seemingly reflexive activity. What people are asked to do while they sing, what they are asked to listen for, what challenges they are to respond to can turn the singing experience into a focused, concentrated activity.

Singing and Vocal Development

▶ How often, how much, and in how many ways do you use your voice?

▶ How has a person's use of his or her voice affected your ability to listen?

▶ Have you ever had laryngitis or been unable to speak for a length of time?

▶ Imagine the distance that could grow between people if they were unable to speak. Imagine the effort they would have to exert to make up for this lack.

Vocal development does not occupy an important place in most discussions of educational aims and objectives, but there is little doubt that voice is a basic tool of human interaction. Issues surrounding vocal development will be addressed further in Chapter 4. For now, however, it is important to recognize that singing with children provides opportunities to address attitudes about voices, singing, and speaking, to let voices develop flexibility, to become aware of the vocalization process, and to practice good vocal habits.

Singing, Children, and Music

A case has been outlined for valuing singing in classrooms, and important relationships have been identified between singing and its potential benefits: singing and pleasure, singing and feeling or expression, singing and social interaction, singing and language, singing and movement, singing and thinking. At this point, you may be wondering about the relationship between song and music. The discussion so far has been as much about music as about song. There are several reasons, however, for focusing just on the benefits and values of song.

This book is not broadly about the value of singing, nor is it limited to the value of music. *It is about the value of singing with children, singing in classrooms, and singing in education.* Children are born singers, and singing is a natural avenue for structuring their musical experiences.

Singing is a child's most direct form of musical experience. Singing does not need any external aid or media; it lets children as well as adults be responsible for the production of the music. *In a sense, when we sing, we become the music.* This immediacy is becoming less and less available in other musical experiences, in which the music is performed for us by professional musicians or is mediated by electronic means. Mature and polished performances by gifted people will always be welcome; yet singing promotes a personal involvement for children that may be missing in other musical experiences. When we sing with children, we are not participating in an oversimplified or reduced musical experience. Singing is a complete musical experience.

Singing is a basic musical experience. One can argue about whether singing or instrumental music came first historically, but there is little doubt that much of the history of musical experience grows out of the human desire or need to sing. Whether singing originated in poetry, ritual, or a form of emotional expression, much musical experience is founded upon, has developed from, and continues to develop out of the singing experience. When we sing with children, we have a chance to connect to these basic musical drives.

Finally, as we have already noted, singing is an integrated experience, involving language, music, movement, and other singers. Children are not only born singers, they are born speakers, movers, and thinkers as well. Singing reflects those qualities. The social interaction present in singing situations is certainly present in other musical experiences but usually not in the same degree; singing experiences tend to highlight this social dimension of music. Language, a fundamental part of the singing experience, is only indirectly a part of other musical experiences. Singing is a language experience, a social experience, and a movement experience *as well as* a musical experience.

Do We Teach *Only* Songs?

Unaccompanied singing gets little recognition in today's recording and instrumental music environment; yet there is richness in this type of singing. Unaccompanied

Although there are other kinds of musical experience, singing does not lack any element essential to the musical experience.

PRINCIPLE 4

singing need not replace other musical experiences, but it should not get lost amid the intensity and production of much of today's music. The natural and free expression of unaccompanied song as a reflection of what we know and feel should be preserved and recognized in education, throughout childhood, adolescence, and adulthood.

Singing is a way for people to participate directly in the act of music making. A person's quality of life can be enriched by singing, even when that person also performs on a musical instrument or listens to recorded music. Music can be instrumental, vocal, or computer generated; it can be live or recorded.

Playing instruments and listening to recorded music are two basic types of musical experience to which children should have access; they are important components of a total music curriculum.

The place to begin music education, however, especially with younger students, is with singing. Singing provides a foundation for the growth and flourishing of instrumental and recording-based musical experiences. This strong belief in the importance of singing does not reject or ignore the important roles of recorded and instrumental music. In many places throughout this text, the terms "song" and "singing" can be replaced with the more general term "music," and the strategies and procedures found here can be effectively extended to experiences with instruments and recordings. The following chart on the pros and cons of using recorded music—specifically recordings that accompany children's singing and playing—and classroom instruments is intended to provide information so that readers may choose appropriate activities.

RECORDED MUSIC

Pros
- Young children as well as adults can draw great satisfaction from listening to music that does not rely upon themselves as the sound source.
- Recorded music provides access to sounds and compositions that we may not have the opportunity to create ourselves or to experience in a live setting.
- Recordings can offer us experiences with ensemble performances even though we are alone.
- Recorded music can be repeated as often as we like, and we can become completely familiar with musical characteristics that we may not know how to identify.
- Recorded music can accompany our singing, dancing, moving, and playing.

Cons
- Recordings of singing games and dances can diminish opportunities for creative, spontaneous music making and idea contributions on the part of the listener-participator.
- The tempi and ranges of song recordings tend not to be flexible and may not be ideal for vocal and motor participation. This is especially true for young children.
- Sometimes recorded music is tailored to adults' concepts of attractiveness, pedagogical applications, and cleverness. Recordings that appeal to adults do not necessarily satisfy the imagination and curiosity of young children.

INSTRUMENTS

Pros
- Instruments can be combined effectively with singing to offer additional musical interest, variety, and sophistication.
- Classroom instruments can be motivating tools for students. Students like to hold them, play them, and explore their sound-making possibilities.
- Instruments can be used to extend music-study activities and to apply students' knowledge of devices for musical composition and accompaniment.

Cons
- Depending on which instruments are used and how they are used, performance on classroom instruments can require motor skills that some students may not have. This is especially true for young children.
- Students' intrigue with playing instruments can supersede their interest in making musical sounds. Aiming for music making rather than noisemaking can be a difficult challenge in some classes.
- Instruments can be costly additions to an already strained music budget.

Singing and Playing

Many songs and singing experiences have overt play characteristics. Some songs are designed for students to make up actions; others ask students to act out stories. Some are chase games; others are word games. Some songs are so clearly focused on our feelings by the stories they tell that it is difficult to think of them in the context of play. Other songs have such a powerful play and movement dimension that they seem to have very little to do with language or thought. Most, if not all, songs and singing experiences, however, can have a playful dimension involving imagination, interaction, and intrigue. The following section examines the play, movement, and language dimensions of song and explores some of the issues these dimensions raise for classroom use.

What Is Play?

What does it mean to play? Think of how you feel when you are playing. For some of us, the model for play is competitive sports. To others, play may mean performing on a musical instrument. It may also mean going for a drive, doing craft activities, watching a movie, or playing a board game. In education, the concept of play has not always held the respect that it does today. School was once for work, not play. School and learning were serious business, and play was what children did at recess or after school.

In the 1950s, scholars introduced the idea that play had a very important and vital role in the education of children. Though some educators, parents, and taxpayers may still have reservations about play activities during school hours, many recognize that play is not the opposite of work: Play *is* children's work. And much learning can take place when children are involved in guided play (Garvey 1977; Piers 1972).

▶ If play means being immersed in an enjoyable activity for which there is no punishment and in which you can make choices to shape your destiny, think back to the last time you really played. Can you recall your feelings and attitudes during and after playing?

▶ Did you play any song games as a child? Name one game you played that had a song to accompany it. Can you recall the setting and the feelings you had about playing the game?

▶ Collect and list your ideas about what happens when we play and why play can be a valuable tool in learning.

▶ In what specific ways can we be intellectually stimulated during song activities? List the song activities and the relevant thinking that you have experienced.

Before the advent of television, singing games were more prominent in the American cultural heritage than they are today. Children played games like *The Farmer in the Dell* and *Pop! Goes the Weasel* for fun and enjoyed the chances to be "it"—to chase, elude, surprise, choose, and be chosen. Unlike other games, however, singing activities incorporate the act of singing with the act of playing. In singing activities, the song functions to time, structure, describe, stimulate, and embellish the play.

WAYS IN WHICH SONGS SHAPE PLAY

1. Timing events in the activity: when one can start running, when someone needs to be chosen.
   Ex.: *Three Blind Mice* and *I'm Going Downtown*

2. Structuring interactions. Identifying roles, and stimulating conversations among participants.
   Ex.: *Muffin Man* and *London Bridge*

3. Describing actions and activities with language. Naming body parts and motion; identifying directions and movements.
   Ex.: *Circle Left* and *Sing with Me*

4. Setting a tone and mood that is attractive and full of joyful participation: suggestions for spirited movement and interactions.
   Ex.: *Rig-a-Jig-Jig* and *Uncle Joe*

Think of your classroom goals as you consider these elements for study and skill development within a song. Can you see that singing activities can be played for the simple enjoyment of the play but can also provide models for achieving specific educational goals?

In their simplest descriptions, singing activities offer children a way of playing together that is led by their own singing. Song activities generally involve varying degrees of movement, language, social interaction, and intellectual stimulation. Because learners are engaged in so many different ways as they play and sing, maximum involvement of the whole child or the whole being can occur. Opportunities for and practice of sensory integration and coordination can occur over and over through various turns of a singing game or through playing various games.

Auditory, visual, and motor engagement through song activities provides a fertile setting for integration and coordination of our senses.

As they play *Ring Around the Rosy*, students sing, listen, and watch as they walk or skip in a circle. When the cadence "all fall down" is sung, students coordinate what they are singing and hearing with how they are moving and what they are seeing as they fall to the floor. Notice how the visual (seeing), auditory (hearing), and kinesthetic (movement) modes are operating and combining as children play this and other singing games. The power and potential of singing activities become clear when educational goals are achieved at the same time that intrigue and enjoyment are maintained.

Learning How to Play

Although the importance of playing and singing in education is emphasized here, a sense of play and comfort with playing can vary greatly from class to class. Teachers have become increasingly vocal in recent years about their students not knowing how to play.

SCENARIO   LACK OF PLAYING SKILLS

An experienced and accomplished music teacher was becoming increasingly frustrated with the behavior problems that arose in her classes whenever she attempted to engage students in a singing game. For several weeks, Mrs. Suvak pondered what to do about this. "Should I just have them stay in their seats?" she wondered. Even as she considered this option, she knew that many students were intrigued and motivated during the activities. And she believed firmly in the substantial benefits of singing-game activities that fostered students' social, movement, language, and thinking skills.

One day, Mrs. Suvak needed to speak with a classroom teacher who happened to be on recess duty. As the two talked, she watched her students at play. "As I watched my students, I was appalled at the limited kinds of play I saw. Students were either hitting each other, running up to groups and screaming, playing football or basketball (and chastising the ones who 'messed up'), or grabbing other students' belongings and running off. I did not get the sense that these students knew how to play in any other ways. I knew then the answer to my question. Rather than abandon my plans for play in music class, I needed to teach these students *how* to play."

PRINCIPLE 1

When students do not know how to play in groups, they may act silly, not follow rules, and complain that the activity is "baby stuff." If that is the case with your students, you may need to move in small increments toward freedom and activity in the

---

POINTS TO CONSIDER IN TEACHING STUDENTS HOW TO PLAY

- The enthusiasm with which you introduce an activity: Be matter-of-fact and low key, or animated and motivating, depending on the student population.

- The amount of movement or the formation that takes students away from their chairs or seating assignment: Begin from chairs with a few students up and moving at a time, or immerse all students in the activity to avoid self-consciousness.

- The opportunities for students' decisions in shaping major features of an activity: Allow students to decide in which direction to go or which one of three ideas to try, rather than how to play a game.

- The complexity and diversity of tasks required of students as they sing: Students can stand and sing rather than walk and sing; offer intellectual challenges to older students ("Sing the names that have only three syllables").

- The degree to which you expect students to become involved in an activity when they do not know the purpose or the intent of their playing: "This activity challenges us to listen and to be precise with our movement. We call that auditory-motor coordination." "Hand signs help us focus our singing, our listening skills, and our kinesthetic, or motor, skills. Musicians are always challenged to use this type of coordination."

play you offer. The initial steps can be characterized by limiting and monitoring various aspects of your teaching approach; and if students have not seen and heard *you* play and sing, you may want to prepare them with lighthearted humor for experiencing this side of your teaching persona: "You haven't seen me like this before, have you?" "I enjoyed getting a turn in this game, too." "I'm just learning how to work with these activities, so I hope you'll help me out."

With younger and older students, it may be wise to scale down the magnitude of play in an activity. Especially with older students, identifying the skills involved, the challenges they must meet, and the relationships to other interests and sports can help them trust your motives in asking them to participate in something that may initially embarrass them.

Remember that the goal in planning singing activities for our students is their successful participation in those activities. Spending some time thinking about what constitutes play and what playing means to a person's participation can prepare us for appreciating our students' ways of playing. More on how to construct appropriate, playful activities can be found in "Making Activities Context Appropriate" in Chapter 9.

We must watch our students and construct ways of playing with songs that appeal to and capture their imaginations and that match their need to appreciate and understand why we are playing.

Playing and Competition

PRINCIPLE 2

Whether or not to incorporate competitive activities in the classroom is a problem. The nature of competition means that there is generally one winner and many losers (Kohn 1992, 1986). Some of us question the validity of competition in the classroom and the long-term effects of competition on our students even though we recognize the short-term motivational potential. Others regard competition in the classroom as simply a way to expose students to "real life." Whether the level of competition is the "who can get there first?" challenge of a chasing game or the "we were the best!" contest between classes for special privileges and treats, competition is rarely a simple issue for the students it affects. See "Rethinking Competition" in Chapter 8 for further discussion of this topic.

> The subtle, long-term messages for the student who always loses and for the student who always wins can easily grow out of our control, no matter what gems of wisdom we espouse to soften them. (Bennett 1992b)

▶ What are the effects of pitting students against one another, whether for purposes of the sport of a game, the control of behaviors, or the development of esprit de corps for a class or group?

▶ What is the relationship between these effects and the educational goals we have for our students?

The games and activities in this book either lack or minimize competition among students as they play. In games such as *Uncle Joe, Three Blind Mice,* and *A-Hunting We Will Go,* the activity centers on a race. By modeling an appreciation of the strategies and the efforts involved in the race, however, rather than focusing just on who won, the teacher guides students to consider other dimensions of the contest.

- "Wow! Did you see how fast she was going? Good effort!"
- "We sure captured some foxes that time; we must have surprised them by our slyness!"
- "What a race!"

Maximizing the number of students involved is a primary goal in education. When we reward the fastest students with *more* turns, we minimize the number of students who will get turns, and we give more opportunities for improvement to those who least need it. Our challenge, therefore, is to look for ways to rotate turns. In racing and chasing activities, two options for accomplishing this are choosing the last one caught for the next turn and having the student who does *not* win get the next turn.

Our students may not come to or enter games with an open and accepting view of a competitive act. It is up to us, therefore, to shape their understandings and show them alternative ways of viewing physical, intellectual, social, and musical challenges that involve others.

Spirited participation can result when the element of competition is introduced into an activity. We must help students acknowledge and experience the satisfaction and enjoyment, however, that can come from group co-operative efforts and alternatives to competitive participation.

Playing, Singing, and Social Interaction

What follows are three versions of activities for *Paw-Paw Patch*. Each version differs in the amount of social interaction and the amount of teacher direction apparent. Note the levels of freedom and structure, as well as teacher-choice and student-choice for each version of this song activity.

1. "Let's sing all four verses of the song *Paw-Paw Patch*: 'Where, oh, where is pretty little Susie? . . . Come on, boys, let's go find her. . . . Come on, girls, let's go find her. . . . Pickin' up paw-paws, put 'em in a basket. . . .' Check your posture, think about the words to the song, and get your voices ready. Let's listen for good singing."

2. "By the count of six, without talking or bumping, get yourselves into groups of six people. Ready. One, two, three, four, five, six." "Now, how many verses do we know to the song *Paw-Paw Patch*? Decide among yourselves, and be ready to tell us the first few words to each verse. You'll have one minute to decide."

   "Within your group, think of a way that you will act out the words and meanings of each verse of the song. You will want to practice your ideas while you sing the song to make sure you can sing as you act. You'll have five minutes to collaborate, and then we'll have a progress report. When you hear me begin singing the song, join the singing. That will get us all focused to share our ideas."

3. "Everyone get into groups of six." "Now let's sing all the verses to *Paw-Paw Patch*." "In your group, make up actions for each verse, then we'll share ideas!"

▶ Have you done similar types of activities with your students?

▶ Do you remember one activity with more fondness than the others?

▶ Which activity do you think your students would remember best and why?

▶ Which of these activities would you prefer to use with your students? If you answered, "It depends," explain why.

To assess the various elements and the degrees of impact that these activities may have on your students, you may find it helpful to think of a continuum. Using your own speculation and experience, where would you place each of the following items as you consider Versions 1, 2, and 3 above?

CONTINUUM OF EXPERIENCE

Minimum	Maximum

1. Degree of social interaction between and among students
2. Noise level in the classroom
3. Enthusiasm or excitement level of students
4. Impression of activity on students' memories
5. Relaxation and freedom in students' singing
6. Freedom and control set up by the directions

You are the person in the best position to decide the extent to which your students would benefit from changing the degrees of social interaction involved in any activity, at any given class time.

When we change the degrees of social interaction within activities, the activity and the students can become more settled and more controlled or more animated and more alive. Each of these changes may be more desirable at one time than another. Adding activity to a song probably means that less-structured study can occur during the activity and that more student behaviors that need your supervision will surface.

TYPES AND DEGREES OF SOCIAL INTERACTION IN SINGING GAMES

Watch
"Look at Mark as you sing his name (his idea, for his turn)."
"Watch Jim as he shows us his idea (his map, how to move)."
Here We Are Together; Looby Loo; Punchinella

Listen
"Listen to Kim's voice as she starts the song (tells us her idea)."
"Can you hear the voices of other students as you sing your song?"
Mulberry Bush; Circle Left; Rig-a-Jig-Jig

Touch
"Hold the hand of the person next to you as we skip (walk, hop) in a circle."
"Take your partner's hand as you take a turn."
Rig-a-Jig-Jig; Muffin Man; Looby Loo

Speak
"Describe your idea (what you are thinking)."
"Talk with your partner and decide what you think the answer is."
How to play a game, what the words to a song mean, what musical information and symbols mean

Partner
"Think of a way to show your idea (scissors, hand signs, motions) with your partner."
"Show your partner what you have figured out and let your partner show you his or her ideas."
"Let's watch this set of partners as they show us their idea."
Johnny, Get Your Hair Cut; Hot Cross Buns; maps, song dots, song scores

One Person
"Ask Carol if she would like to join us."
"Invite Nathan to come to town (on the train, join our family) with us."
"Let's watch and listen to Jeannie. What will she have us do?"
The Farmer in the Dell; Mulberry Bush; Looby Loo

Small Group
"Come up with a way to act out the song."
"Show us your ideas for solving the puzzle (a group motion, how to read this)."
"Let's see what we observe as this group shares its ideas."
Scotland's Burning; Row, Row, Row, Your Boat; Did You Ever See a Lassie?

Whole Group
"Let's see if we can keep our circle round for the whole song."
"Describe what you saw when we all tried that idea."
Circle games, all singing activities

Cooperative efforts between and among our students can foster many lifelong skills and ways of valuing others.

PRINCIPLE 1

PRINCIPLE 2

Why, then, would increasing social interaction for activities be worth your efforts? Social interaction that is structured, paced, modeled, and organized during singing activities can provide opportunities for critically important social skills to develop in students of any age. Depending on the singing activity and classroom goals, students can work individually, with partners, or in varying sizes of small groups to meet simple song-game challenges: "Think of a motion," "Think of a rhyming word," "Think of new words that fit this pattern," "Think of how you can show the rhythm of that part of the song," and so on.

POTENTIAL BENEFITS OF COOPERATIVE SOCIAL INTERACTION

Acceptance	of others' ideas and contributions
Adaptability	to others' ways of showing and expressing ideas
Patience and Tolerance	for the ways in which others contribute and participate that may be different from our own
Respect	for similarities and differences among people and their ideas
Curiosity	about how others think and solve problems
Alternatives	for responding to a wide range of social situations: verbally, physically, and nonverbally
Insight	into the presence and the importance of varying roles that people play in order to have a successful and satisfying activity

---

Playing and Turns

Interacting with others means that we must learn to take turns and give turns. Taking a turn places us in a position of responsibility, though we may think of it simply as a position of leadership. When we work, sing, or talk with others, our responsibilities include listening, watching, and reflecting as well as letting others lead.

PRINCIPLE 2

Consider the following types of turns and note the level of responsibility and the type of opportunity each kind of turn involves: *singing* turns, *talking* turns, *listening* turns, *watching* turns, *leading* turns, *following* turns, *song-starter* turns, and *game-starter* turns. Turns can be very important, especially to young children. Fairness, sensitivity, and delight in taking turns and giving turns are life skills that can be practiced at any age within a singing activity. Through various opportunities to take turns with differing responsibilities, we can learn important insights about ourselves and others.

What can we learn from taking turns and giving turns?

- We may be more suited for some types of turns than for others.

- We may enjoy some turns and not others.

- Our reactions to different turns can vary from day to day and activity to activity.

- We may need more time to observe others before we are ready to take some types of turns.

- When we know what type of turn we are taking, we can be more clear and more confident about our "job" for that turn.

Students can be turn-givers by choosing someone to offer an idea, by choosing someone to take his or her turn, or by choosing a song- or game-starter. Here are three suggestions for teaching turn-taking and turn-giving (Bennett 1985).

- Minimize using turns as rewards or enticements to behave.
- Broaden the scope of turns to include all the roles of an activity, not just being "it."
- Think of a turn as a specific job for the student to do. Comfort, security, and focus can come with this specificity.

► Think of a real-life occasion when you had a "turn" that you did not want. How did you handle the situation?

► Did others know by your reaction that you did not want the turn?

► If you had preferred that people not know you were disappointed, how else could you have responded?

► How would you have preferred people respond to you when you didn't want a turn?

► Now think of the reverse situation. You wanted very much to receive a turn at something and did not receive it. Ask yourself the same questions.

Acting in a way that does not reveal how we are feeling is not necessarily deceptive; sometimes it can be diplomatic or kind. Knowing when and why we might want to conceal rather than reveal our disappointments (or vice versa) can give us alternatives for our reactions. (For further discussion of this idea, see "Being Honest" in Chapter 7.) Our students might benefit from our insightful attitudes regarding reactions to and preferences for turns, and we may be able to help them see how their reactions influence others. When we hear, "But, teacher I didn't *get* a turn!" we can use the opportunity as a teachable moment, introducing students to various types of turns.

- "Today we have time for only four playing turns of *Circle Left.*"
- "Charlie, I'd like you to take three watching turns from my chair to tell us what you observe as we play the game."
- "Who will take a turn as the song-starter for Jessica's turn to start the game?"
- "Robert, I don't know whether you were able to notice, but there were students who worked very hard at their *following* turns. Take one more *leading* turn so you can watch us follow you."
- "We'll have three more playing turns today for this game. Let's see whom the song will choose."

Playing, Singing, and Moving

Many songs suggest actions. *The Farmer in the Dell, Ring Around the Rosy,* and *Mulberry Bush* are examples of activities in which the actions are shaped by, paced by, and organized around a song. The connection between music and movement, however, is more profound than that. Movement is a natural response to music.

The most obvious evidence of the connection between movement and music is our natural tendency to move when we are in musical situations. We tap our feet, snap our fingers, sway, or nod our heads as we feel the rhythmic impulses of music to which we are listening. When situations permit, we march, skip, and dance to music.

Conductors, of course, use movement to guide ensembles. In these examples, the shared characteristic of rhythm is evident in both the music and the movement.

Rhythm results from change. The rhythm of music results from contrasts in sound and silence as well as changing sounds, pitches, patterns, directions, dynamics, and lengths. Movement also generates rhythm through changing directions, speeds, actions, and contrasts in repose and motion. The connection between movement and rhythm is so strong that we could almost consider the terms equivalent, and the connection between movement and music can be seen in the words we use to describe music.

- Melodies jump and skip.
- We hold and sustain sounds.
- Rhythms are smooth or jerky.
- Songs can have a bounce to them.
- Tempo indications refer to walking rates (*andante*) and liveliness (*allegro*).

Song and movement are natural companions. Because of the close correspondence of music and movement, our response to song includes the kinesthetic, or motor, domain. In other words, actions are a natural complement to singing. Actions can be stationary, *axial* movements (clapping, tapping, swinging, nodding, touching, or bending), or they can be *locomotor* movements (hopping, walking, skipping, or running). (See table on next page.)

As you have probably experienced, combining movement with singing can heighten students' motivation to participate, *and* it can diminish students' motivation to participate. It can be focusing, and it can be distracting. It can be controlling, and it can be freeing. It can energize singing, and it can overwhelm singers. To best apply movement with singing, we must each be attentive to, responsible for, and cognizant of the needs of our students at any given time in their study. For more information on how contexts can affect movement choices, see "Making Activities Context Appropriate" in Chapter 9.

PRINCIPLE 5

Playing, Singing, and Language

Song is the combination of words and music. Singing a song is an experience in language. Think about these experiences in learning a song:

- We learn vocabulary and stories.
- We pronounce words and patterns of language.
- We highlight the expressive, poetic component of language.
- In a game activity, we use and practice language skills: issuing invitations, responding in whole sentences, and substituting nouns, verbs, and adjectives.

Sometimes it is difficult to tell the difference between song and language. Some actors capitalize on the closeness of this relation by singing in a "speaking way." Others speak with such drama and expression that they seem to be singing. We can hear the melodies of foreign languages even when we do not understand the words. When people for whom English is not a first language speak English, we may have difficulty understanding their speech precisely because they use different speech rhythms and melodies. And, as in music, speaking can show such contrasting feelings as anger and tenderness or determination and sadness by using the same words but changing the expressive qualities.

BENEFITS OF COMBINING MOVEMENT WITH SINGING

Coordination of auditory and motor skills at specific moments
> *Did You Ever See a Lassie? Looby Loo*

Controlled movement through focused listening over time
> *Here We Are Together* (move-and-stop game); *Rig-a-Jig-Jig; Come and Follow Me*

Experiences participating at different levels of involvement (axial or locomotor movements)
> *Circle Left; Here We Are Together*

Opportunities to make free, expressive movement choices
> *Did You Ever See a Lassie?; Old Grumbler*

Practice in following prescribed movement ideas
> *Rig-a-Jig-Jig; Mulberry Bush; Circle Left;* tapping rhythms, beats, dances

---

Spoken language has all the characteristics of song. The easiest way to demonstrate this is to mimic meaningful speech by babbling. Babies seem to capture much of the melody of language in their babbling. Their vocalizations are rhythmic, and their voices rise and fall in pitch and loudness. Double-talk, the use of real English words but in a nonsensical order, gives additional evidence of this point. When we get the melody of speech right, we may not have to say real words to communicate our meaning.

Imagine a greeting you might use when hearing from someone you have not seen for many years. Listen to how your voice sounds when you say, "You're in Montana now?" Notice that your voice changes in pitch at the end of the question. If your voice does not rise in pitch, the comment no longer sounds like a question. Some people habitually use significant changes of pitch in their speech. Others use only a narrow range. Try speaking on a single pitch, not letting your voice rise and fall in its normal fashion, giving the impression of a robot. The contrast between normal and robot speech highlights the *melodic content* of our language.

Like song, language uses contrasts in *loud* and *soft* for a variety of expressive purposes. English words have natural accent patterns that can be identified by ear. We also give emphasis to certain words by saying them louder, and we shape our speaking, as we do our singing, by making subtle adjustments in accent and stress.

Our language is full of *rhythm*. We can speak slowly or quickly, with even divisions between syllables or in a jerky fashion. Poetry uses rhythmic devices that are almost identical to those used in music: repeating rhythms and regularly occurring accents, which result in a feeling of beat and meter.

The *structures* of language and song are also similar. Both have surface structures and deep structures. The surface structures are the sounding elements, the words and the tones. The deep structures reflect mental activity: organizations of the surface based on certain rules. In language, the rules have to do with grammar. In music, they have to do with tonality and meter. In both song and language, smaller elements are combined to form larger units. Words and tones, respectively, can form sentences and phrases, which can then form paragraphs and songs.

In song, the musical characteristics of language are simply extended. The *melodies* of language are emphasized, the *rhythms* are controlled, and the *structure* (the play of repetition and contrast) tends to be simplified. Some of us find ourselves having a different emotional reaction to words if we sing instead of say them.

Songs also provide varied opportunities for language play. Whether for rhyming, naming actions, dramatizing, or simply singing names, the language in songs is meant to be savored and enjoyed. In many songs, the language is meant to be manipulated.

PRINCIPLE 7

Singing Names   Our names are important to us. Songs can be personalized by the use of names, and singing a student's name in a song is a way of recognizing the student. By making the name special, we send the message that the student is important.

Songs that use students' names, sometimes called name games, include *Here We Are Together, I'm Going Downtown, Circle Left,* and *Daddy Loves the Bear,* but names can be used in many songs. Name games are particularly valuable when students do not know each other, but name games are also very helpful in setting a warm, comfortable tone and in building a sense of trust and acceptance among classmates.

Describing Actions   Notice how active these titles and first lines of songs are. They all tell us to do something: *Sing with Me, Circle Left, I'm Going Downtown, A-Hunting We Will Go, Johnny, Get Your Hair Cut, Skip to My Lou, Did You Ever See a Lassie Go This Way and That? Here We Go 'Round the Mulberry Bush.* These and many other songs were created to accompany and guide the actions and movements of games. Because the actions and movements of the games change, the words change, also. When students suggest words to accompany the actions created in songs, they practice using descriptive language, they put into their own words what they are doing, and they get the pleasure and satisfaction of hearing their ideas sung. Sometimes, part of the fun of making up actions is being able to say how to sing them.

Rhyming Words   The poetic nature of many song texts provides opportunities to explore rhymes. Sometimes there are rhyming words in songs, and sometimes the purpose of a song activity is to make up new rhymes. *Whistle, Daughter, Whistle* and *Mad Man* are both rhyming games that let students make up new verses based on the rhyming pattern of the song.

Playing, Singing, Language, and Drama

The connections among song, language, and drama have a long history in ritual and opera. Even today, musicals and movies combine these elements in a variety of ways. Songs that tell stories can be acted out, and songs that describe events, however briefly, can be the subject of short dramatic experiences. Getting into small groups to choose parts, explore actions, and decide how to show what the words of the song suggest can give new life to a song. The traditional game that goes with *The Farmer in the Dell* is a small dramatic structure by itself. *Old Grumbler, Uncle Joe, Scotland's Burning, Cockles and Mussels,* and *Mary Had a Little Lamb* all suggest characters, actions, and events that can be the bases of small plays. For example, after learning the song and the verses, students can act out the story of *Mary Had a Little Lamb.* The drama can take place in several ways. Students can volunteer to act out the lamb or Mary for the class. Small groups can be assigned to act out one verse. Small groups can be assigned to create a scene (without movement, a still life) from one verse that depicts part of the story. (See Chapter 9 for suggestions on the use of drama with these songs.)

Creating New Verses   Many songs allow for the addition of new words. Sometimes only one new phrase is inserted, as in the action songs. In the name and rhyming songs, a single word might be changed. Songs can also be used as the basis for a completely new set of lyrics. New stories can be told using the tunes of familiar songs. Classroom operas can evolve from a familiar song and story.

The inclination to use a familiar song as the basis for a new set of words is strong. Satirists often change the words of familiar songs to lampoon politicians or other public figures. The result is a parody. Do you remember *On Top of Spaghetti*? It is a parody of *On Top of Old Smokey:* "On top of spaghetti, all covered with cheese / I lost my poor meatball when somebody sneezed." Do you recall any of the parodies of songs you learned in childhood? *The Battle Hymn of the Republic* ("Mine eyes have seen the glory of the burning of the school") has been parodied in schools many times, and so has *Row, Row, Row, Your Boat* (". . . throw your teacher overboard and listen to her scream"). The tune for *The Star-Spangled Banner* was not composed just for that anthem. The words were written in tribute to the United States, but the tune was an old British drinking song (Hitchcock 1974, 36). Putting new words in a song is one way of making the song new, letting it take on new meaning, even if that is distasteful to us. People have recycled songs in this way for hundreds of years.

Changing the words of a song, whether to tell a new story, to describe a change of action, or to sing about particular students, should be done with care. Listen carefully to how new words fit a song (see the next section). When we want to personalize a song by using it to practice specific skills such as rhyming, counting, sequencing, or motor coordinations, it can be important for us to remember the background and history of that song. As is obvious from the discussions of song backgrounds found in Chapter 9, it can be difficult if not impossible to determine the original words and tune of a song. A song can be viewed as a cultural artifact, reflecting the attitudes, hopes, concerns, and life situations of the people who found value in the song. The values of using songs to tell the stories of our own students and classrooms are in tension with the values of retaining a more original form of a song. These two sets of values illustrate the need for balance to maintain the musical and cultural contexts that reflect the diversity of our human history and to use these same songs to help our students understand themselves—their own attitudes, hopes, concerns, and life situations.

Being Aware of Language Accent

Changing the words of a song, by the inclusion of names, the substitution of action descriptions, or the creation of new verses, requires listening skills. To be accurate in making language modifications like these, we attend to how much time is allowed for words in the song and plan for the placement of accents in both the song and the language.

When language is used in a song indiscriminately, without attention to natural flow and inflection, the benefits of language study are no longer as effective. Instead, it may become more difficult to hear syllable division and word accent, because a tension and an incompatibility between the music and the language now exists. The following exercises utilizing the song *Here We Are Together* (see Chapter 9) illustrate this point.

▶ Sing the song *Here We Are Together.* When the place for names comes in the song, sing, "There's Gina with Jeremy, and Jeremy with Ben."

Many names, such as Gina, Jeremy, and Ben, fit the song with little effort. Each of these names, however, has a different number of syllables, and consequently, the rhythm is adjusted slightly in each case. Names with two syllables and the accent on the first syllable, as in "Gina," fit the rhythm of this song easily.

► Sing the names again and notice the differences in how "Gina" and "Jeremy" fit the melody.

► Notice that the last two syllables of "Jeremy" are quicker but that the first syllable feels as if it occurs on a strong moment of the song.

"Ben," which has a single syllable, requires a different kind of adjustment. When the song has two different tones and only one syllable on which to sing them, a **slur** occurs. Listen to how your voice slides and drops when you sing "Ben." Slurs occur when we sing one syllable with two or more tones. Still, "Ben" starts on the same accented tone that "Jeremy" and "Gina" started.

When names have accents on syllables other than the first one, the adjustments become a bit more complicated.

► Sing, "There's Elaine with Maria, and Maria with Elizabeth" and listen to what your voice does.

► Did you hear the slur on the second syllable of "Elaine"?

► Did you also notice that the first syllable of "Elaine" seemed to come a little earlier than you expected, or at least earlier than when you sang "Gina"?

The first syllables of the names Gina, Jeremy, and Ben are set on the higher tones of the melody patterns and on a strong rhythmic place, the beat. For the names Elaine, Maria, and Elizabeth, it is the second syllable that is set on the higher tones. Try placing the first syllable of "Maria" on the higher tone. Do you hear how it changes the pronunciation of the name?

Because the accent of "Elaine" is on the second syllable, the "-laine" occurs at the same place in the song as would the first syllable of "Gina." The accented syllables should be placed on musically accented parts of the song. These accented parts of the song are sometimes called **beats**. Consequently, the "E-," first syllable of "Elaine," occurs before the beat. This is an example of an **anacrusis,** an unaccented sound followed by an accent at the beginning of a phrase or a musical unit.

It is not always obvious how words should be set to songs. Some people pronounce the name Marianne, for example, with an accented first syllable and others pronounce it with an accented third syllable: MARianne, MariANNE. If the third syllable is accented, then that syllable should be placed on the accented part of the song, on the higher tones in *Here We Are Together.* In this case, the anacrusis would consist of two unaccented sounds, "Ma-" and "ri-" for "Ma-ri-ANNE."

Sometimes we do not notice where the accents are, or we are unable to hear them. Practice will help us hear the accents more accurately. Paying close attention to the sound of the language is also important to avoid distorting the words. Distortion of language can result from giving syllables uncharacteristic accents and emphases. Important words should come in important places in the song. The care we take with the placement of words in the song reflects our interest in developing listening and language skills. Because changing the language in song can change the music, attending to these changes by focusing on them and becoming more sensitive to them develops skills and understandings basic to music and language.

The words of a song can be distorted by the way in which we sing them. To experience this, sing *London Bridge* and purposely overemphasize each syllable. The effect may seem heavy and labored. You might feel the tendency to slow down to fit these additional accents into the musical flow. Sing the song again, and emphasize slightly

When setting new words to songs, it is important to be sensitive to potential pronunciation problems and to try to match the natural accents of the language with those of the song.

Attention to the way in which we sing words not only permits the exploration and study of language and music but also allows the experience to become more expressive, more balanced, and, in short, more beautiful.

only "bridge," "down," and "La-(dy)." Singing a song with fewer accents may feel lighter and more flowing.

Use of heavy movement like stomping or jumping while singing can also distort language by affecting the flow of song. Doing these types of heavy movements once in a while will not harm anyone's development. Habitual indulgence in an approach to singing that distorts the natural flow of language and music, however, can encourage bad habits and will ultimately be detrimental to the quality of developing musicianship.

Being a Music Maker

Teaching songs to children and singing songs with children means that we are the models through which children learn songs. Some of us are confident of our musical competence in leading singing and music activities; some of us are not. It is easy to presume that those with a music background, who have studied music for years, are the ones who are confident in teaching music to children and that those who have no formal music studies or training are not confident. Such a presumption is not necessarily true.

Preservice and in-service *music* teachers who have been trained as instrumentalists may not have had experience developing their vocal skills and competence. In contrast, some preservice and in-service *nonmusic* teachers have always seen themselves as singers and have no hesitation about leading groups in singing. Some who have extensive vocal training may not know how to modify or apply their skills appropriately to lead children in singing. To prepare you for the upcoming sections, dealing with how you see yourself as a musician and music maker, consider this self-inventory of your own music background.

MUSIC-MAKER INVENTORY

On a scale of 1 to 5 (5 is the highest ranking), rate your levels of confidence or experience.

_____ I enjoy singing.

_____ I can sing.

_____ I can teach a song to others.

_____ I can lead others in singing.

_____ I listen to music.

_____ I can name the symbols of music notation.

_____ I sight-read music, *with* an instrument.

_____ I can sight-sing (read) music.

_____ I have performed music for others as a soloist.

_____ I have performed music for others as a member of a group.

Even those of you who ranked your confidence and experience in each of these categories with the rating of 1 or 2 will not be overwhelmed by the approaches described in the following chapters. Instead, the strategies presented intend to inspire you with confidence and develop your competence as you enjoy your role in teaching and singing with children.

What Is a Musician?

Do you think of yourself as a musician? If you were asked to name some musicians, what people would come to mind? First, you might think of professional musicians, people who make their living making music. Whatever the style of music they are associated with, these people have devoted their lives to sharing music through recordings and live performances. Some of them are well known because of popular hits or TV appearances. Some of them are known only because of their positions and reputations as noted teachers in special music schools devoted to the preparation of professional musicians. Still others are known only to small groups of people, often performing anonymously or without obvious recognition, in all kinds of situations, from movie sound tracks and commercials to large orchestral ensembles.

In thinking of musicians, you might have thought about the people in your community, people that you know personally, who make their living at music. Secondary and elementary music teachers might have come to mind. Piano teachers, church organists, choir directors, and local nightclub performers are others who may not have anything like a national or even a regional reputation but who clearly are seen by their friends and neighbors as musicians.

Another category you might have considered is the amateur musician. The community band and choir members, the family member who plays piano for fun and relaxation, the friend who plays guitar around campfires, all actively participate in music making, even though they do not make a living at it.

When asked to think of the musicians you know, you might not have thought to list people who sing only in the shower or with the radio. You might not have considered those whose only participation in music is to buy recordings and listen to their stereo systems. Are they musicians, too? We sometimes reserve the term "musician" for someone who has highly developed music skills and engages in professional music activities. A problem with this narrow use of the term arises, however, when it excludes other people from participating in music activities.

If musicians are those who make their living by *making* music, and the "-ian" suffix would suggest that that is the meaning of the word, then most of us are not or cannot be musicians. In our culture, this way of looking at musicians creates a split, a separation between the artists and the audience, a gap that can be difficult to bridge. In the music practices of some cultures, the gap that distinguishes those who *do* from those who *watch* and *listen* is noticeably absent. David McAllester sees the musical life of the Venda of South Africa as a "music educator's dream become reality" (1985, 1). Among the Venda, McAllester observes, one achieves full stature as a human by demonstrating musical skills. In short, everyone is a musician.

A balance between the acceptance that "musician" is generally reserved for professional activities and the desire that everyone see himself or herself as musically active can be attained by adopting a new term. A term that is inclusive, yet does not necessarily imply professional stature in music performance, is "music maker." Music making can appropriately describe music performance at any age and at any level of expertise.

What Is Music Listening?

Listening to music is a form of musical activity, though not all forms of listening are active. It can be surprising to notice how much music is present in our daily lives: on the radio and on television, in the supermarket, and in waiting rooms. Sometimes we cannot escape it. Rarely are we asked, or even given the option, to pay close attention to any of this music—the music is simply there. The music may affect us and may make waiting a little less tiresome, but it is hardly intended to elicit critical or analytical judgments about the sounds, even when we have nothing to do but listen.

Much of the time, background music is supposed to maintain a subtle, more or less unnoticed profile. And we often go along, letting the music operate on us "at a distance," without attending to the melody, the singer, the accompaniment, or even the mood. Is it possible that we buy more food, that we are more cheerful, or that we make our way through aisles faster when peppy music is being played in the grocery store?

Even in more standard musical events, like concerts, our attention may wander from the music as we think our own thoughts: about our companion, our previous day's accomplishments, or our next day's activity. This type of *passive listening* contrasts with listening that characterizes musical involvement: active listening. *Active listening* is not simply receptive. Active listening tries to comprehend, understand, categorize, recall, predict, recognize, characterize, describe, identify, imagine, associate, evaluate, and compare. This is the kind of listening that a musician, of whatever caliber, engages in, whether singing, performing, practicing, or just listening. Active listening, an important element in all music making, should be practiced when teaching songs and encouraged when children are singing.

PRINCIPLE 4

Making Music and Reading Music

Although reading music is a basic skill for most musicians, those who are church choir members, barbershop singers, parlor pianists, and self-taught guitarists can be very accomplished performers yet not be able to read music. Many of our popular musical styles rely very little on music notation or the ability to read music.

Teaching music by ear, without the use of notation, is a procedure used commonly in many situations. This *rote* approach, which has been used successfully by teachers who can read music as well as by those who cannot, has been a useful, albeit limited, strategy for teaching music at all levels for many generations. Rote teaching is done through teacher modeling and student observation and imitation (Bartholomew 1994b).

Reading music notation is not required for active participation in music, even in our own highly literate, technological culture. In fact, technology itself has made immediate, sophisticated performance of music readily available to the unskilled, illiterate musician. If reading music is not required of many professionals, why would we require it of less intensive music participants?

Reading music can be valuable, efficient, and desirable. By itself, however, it is not a helpful criterion for identifying a musician. Reading music is neither necessary to nor sufficient for being a musician. Lack of music-reading skills limits the extent to which we can independently investigate unfamiliar material and literature. The relative importance and impact of this lack can vary greatly from person to person, setting to setting, and culture to culture. Teachers can make music with students—by teaching songs, guiding aural and vocal skills, stimulating interest in music—and accomplish all these tasks effectively, without recourse to music reading.

What Is Music Performance?

Let's return to our initial image of a musician. We often associate musicians with public performance. A common site for this performance is a stage, a place reserved for special engagements, set apart from normal affairs. This physical separation from the audience distances the performer from the mundane. Thinking about performance in ways that separate the musician from the audience has consequences for what we think being a musician is, for what we think being a singer is, and for what we think teaching music is all about (Small 1977).

Performance does not need to have a professional air. To perform is to act, to do something. We often think of a performance as doing something in front of other people, but these other people need not be a paying audience or a special gathering. When your students sing and play *Did You Ever See a Lassie?* in any of the versions described in this book, they are performing. As Alfred Schutz (1964) has pointed out, music is a social act: *We make music together.*

We usually sing with other people, but even when we sing for no one but ourselves, the song (its language, history, meaning, and genesis) presupposes other people. When we sing a song, we involve ourselves with other people. In other words, when we sing, we do so with an audience, with and for other people. In an elementary classroom, the teacher and the children are their own audience.

Our typical view of performance also emphasizes the rehearsed and carefully prepared nature of the act. Nonmusic specialists are sometimes surprised when someone with extensive music training declines to perform extemporaneously with the comment "I've nothing prepared." Performances that involve the coordination of dancers, stage managers, speakers, and musicians, that demand the planned interaction of many people, that comprise complex musical interactions, can hardly be spontaneous. These characteristics do not need to define our notion of performance, however. We perform whenever we sing. When we sing for the fun of it, because we like a song, because we like how it makes us feel, we are performing. Performing can be spontaneous.

Although we are not expecting to be on stage every time we sing, we can listen and attend to our music making, leaving room for practice and improvement. You might liken musical performance to meal preparation. Nearly any meal requires a certain amount of preparation. Sometimes it involves only buying, cleaning, slicing, and putting things out on a plate. At other times, mixing and cooking come into play. A gourmet meal involves a great amount of preparation, and a part of the enjoyment of such a meal can be the recognition of the effort required.

A concert is like a gourmet meal because it takes a great deal of preparation. A concert is also like a gourmet meal because it is not the usual daily fare. Most of us are not the performers at a concert—we consume the music and admire the chef. Classroom singing, on the other hand, is for everybody, every day, and can involve as little as the selection of an appropriate song and the desired focus procedures. And it is true that, just as someone might like to pick an apple right off the tree to eat, we can perform music by singing anytime the spirit moves us.

Performing is a fundamental and inescapable aspect of musical activity. Even though the word "performance" may conjure up images of concerts, rehearsals, and a gap between performers and audiences, the fundamental component of performing is *making* music. Prowess, preparation, and audience are secondary. Thinking of musical activity as making music can seem less threatening than thinking of it as performing.

Making music with others is performing. Making music together—performing together—is the heart of classroom music instruction.

PRINCIPLE 7

Making Music and Teaching Music

Have you ever taught someone to ride a bicycle or make chocolate chip cookies or throw a ball? Most of us have taught such things, but did we consider ourselves experts at what we were teaching? Did we need to do wheelies, to be a gourmet, to pitch like Nolan Ryan, or to know the chemistry and physics involved in those activities?

Prior experience is probably necessary to teach them, but *extensive* experience may not be. The same statement can be true of leading music activities.

The prior experience necessary to lead singing is being able to sing a song that we like or that moves us. That's all. We do not need to know about harmony or the history of music, to sing like Ella Fitzgerald, or to have a degree in music to sing with students. Singing with our students may feel like riding a wobbly old bike. Although we may be unsure of our vocal coordination, singing with our students communicates information to them that will be important to their musical lives.

When we sing with our students, we demonstrate our personal relationship with music. We show them by example that participation in music is not limited to professionals and aficionados. Using the analogy of teaching bicycle riding, if we fix up our bicycle, find out how it works, practice riding without hands, learn the physics of balance and mechanical action, and think about how learning and knowledge take place, that information is bound to improve our teaching. But is it not more important for us to put the student on the bike and run alongside him or her?

Knowing how our voice works, developing greater vocal flexibility, learning about the construction of melody, and thinking about what a person needs to learn in order to sing a song are bound to help our knowledge base and, perhaps, our confidence level. But those tasks do not take the place of, and may not even be necessary to, singing alongside our students.

The point here is to put singing with students in its proper place as a musically valuable activity, not to trivialize other aspects of music education. Singing with students, sharing with them what music can do, and demonstrating our personal relationship with music is not teaching music in the traditional sense, but it *is* teaching music activity—*it is teaching and leading music making*. The basis of teaching music activities is making music with students. Can you help students become musically active? Can you help students become music makers? If you think of being a music maker in the context of activity (singing and listening), you can begin to answer those questions for yourself.

- When you share your musical life with students by singing with them, letting them see that we need not make a living at music to reap its rewards, you are enriching children's lives through music making.
- When you sing with students and help them develop their vocal flexibility, you are teaching music-making skills through singing.
- When you challenge the listening skills of your students and help them develop their ability to attend to sound, you are teaching music-making skills through listening.

Teaching music *begins* with making music, but it generally involves much more than that. Making music by singing with students is the beginning of music instruction and is a necessary foundation on which to build. As knowledge and understanding develop, as listening skills become sharper, as voices develop greater flexibility, the musical experience can deepen and broaden. Teaching music, besides providing a foundation, can also stimulate the development of listening skills and vocal awareness as well as musical knowledge, understanding, and skills in order to make this deepening and broadening possible.

Making the distinction between teaching music and leading music activities creates an interesting problem. We want all teachers to see themselves as music makers and leaders of music activities. Nearly every music education association and many music teachers have taken the position, however, that only music specialists, those with degrees and certification in music, can and should teach music. Although this is a legitimate position, it can exclude other teachers from being encouraged to use

---

WHAT DO WE NEED TO KNOW? TEACHING MUSIC ACTIVITIES AND TEACHING MUSIC

Teaching Music Activities

1. Knowledge of activities appropriate to the interests, developmental levels, and classroom contexts of a variety of students

2. Knowledge of how students might respond during activities and what alternatives we have for reacting to them

3. Knowledge of potential musical and extramusical benefits to students as a result of participation in activities

4. Development of listening and singing skills that provide accurate production and monitoring of the music being experienced

5. Believing in one's own capabilities for beginning, leading, and developing singing and movement activities for children

Added to these items is the ideal of a sensitivity to levels of quality in making music.

Teaching Music

1. Knowledge of notation (meters, keys, rhythms, pitches, clefs, measures)

2. Knowledge of the internal structures of music (beats, scales, harmonies, phrases)

3. Knowledge of, and sometimes skills in, instruments (voice, keyboard, recorder, band and orchestra instruments, pitched and nonpitched classroom instruments, autoharp, guitar)

4. Knowledge of appropriate scopes and sequences for teaching music information to children

5. Knowledge of characteristics of music learning and skill development in children

Added to these items is the ideal of a sensitivity to levels of quality in making music and exposure to the alternative methods and resources available.

(Bennett 1992a)

music in their classes. Just what is it that nonmusic specialists are not supposed to be doing? What is it that only music specialists are qualified to teach?

We want all teachers to feel confident enough and compelled enough to offer their students music activities. If you do teach your students song activities, can we call you a music teacher? Well, yes and no. You may be leading music activities, yet you may not *feel* qualified or *be* qualified to teach an entire music curriculum for a range of age groups as music teachers are certified to do.

Even if you are not hired to be the music teacher, by making music with your students, you are providing them with the basics of a good music education.

Restricting the term "music teacher" so that the definition makes any teacher feel that he or she should not be leading students in music activities is contrary to our principles in *SongWorks 1*. Therefore, to be accurate about what you do *if you are not a certified music teacher,* we recommend saying that you are a music maker with your students. Being a music maker is a goal everyone can achieve. And the fact that you engage in and lead your students in music making gives the experience of teaching an extraordinary enrichment.

Chapter Epilogue

Singing is a valuable activity. Although some of us may be uncomfortable proclaiming ourselves as singers, we all have a right to sing and to be music makers. Singing brings pleasure, expresses feelings, fosters social interaction, and stimulates language. Singing and playing provide an engaging context for thinking, learning social skills, coordinating movement, exploring language, dramatizing imaginations, and integrating skills and knowledge. Some children may not have learned the skills necessary for spirited whole-group cooperation and interaction, and therefore they deserve to be taught how to play. Whether our goal is to teach music or to lead children in music activities, singing with children enriches their lives and ours.

Principles of Teaching and Learning

2

The Principles of *SongWorks 1*

Principles are important to us because they shape boundaries and supply tracks for our choices and behaviors as teachers. Principles are the common threads that bind together our teaching behaviors, practices, and methods. Our principles form the foundation on which we base our actions and build our teaching identities. Therefore, our principles function as a basis for making judgments, comparisons, and decisions (Farnsworth 1909; Mursell 1956; Swanwick 1988).

To illustrate how a principle can shape our classroom attitudes and behaviors, consider the potential classroom effects of this belief: "As a teacher, I am responsible for everything that happens in my classroom." If you use this principle as a basis of your approach to your responsibilities, roles, and goals as a teacher, several effects may result:

PRINCIPLE 5

- You may be meticulous about stating and monitoring all details surrounding the procedures, rules, and general organizations of your classroom.
- You may see yourself as the authority who determines and controls what does and does not happen to your students—academically, socially, emotionally, and physically.
- You may personally identify with the compliments and criticisms given to individuals in your classroom for their behaviors and achievements.
- You may feel personally threatened or defeated when students do not meet the expectations you have set for them.

▶ Would each of these effects be equally acceptable to you?

▶ Would some effects be detrimental to the ways in which you want to see yourself as a teacher?

▶ How would you modify the principle after considering its potential effects?

By identifying and recognizing the principles under which we are operating, we can become more aware of ourselves as teachers. We can provide more consistency in our actions and reactions to students, colleagues, parents, and administrators. We also can become more articulate in stating our positions, describing the beliefs behind our actions, and providing rationales for our classroom choices. When we know our principles, we can also become more selective consumers of educational trends, popular methodologies, and workshop offerings.

SongWorks 1 is based on principles of teaching and learning, individual responsibility and social interaction, and human growth and freedom. Rather than relying on any particular methodology, a set of accepted practices, or a detached, neutral position, we have attempted to base this text on general assumptions and beliefs that have guided our own educational practice. These principles, which derive from our beliefs, are grounded in our experiences, our reflections, and our careful examination of the research and commentary of others. The discussions of classroom practices, music activities, educational goals, and musical information that are found throughout this text are guided by those principles.

The remainder of this chapter outlines seven principles, gives a description of and a rationale for each, and considers the challenges or difficulties posed by each. Our intention is not that every reader adopt our principles. We recognize that a principle can be given very different interpretations, which can, in turn, drastically affect choices based on that principle. We recognize that sometimes principles conflict to create a difficulty in choosing a course of action. We also recognize that different situations, contexts, personalities, requirements, and expectations may elicit different principles. In fact, among the reasons to focus on the principles we have proposed here is to challenge readers to consider their own principles and beliefs carefully, as well as to highlight the role of principles in guiding educational decision making. We want to support teachers in becoming aware of and thoughtful about their own principles.

Being a teacher means constant acting, reacting, and responding. A principle can serve as an internal lighthouse that guides us toward actions that match our values and beliefs. A principle can also illuminate our path to being the teacher and person we want to be and draw us toward informed choices that are proactive rather than reactive (Covey 1989). As illustrations, imagine the following possible classroom situations.

> *Knowing our principles makes us better teachers. Because we know on what foundations our behaviors are based, we seek congruency with those foundations in all that we do, say, and think as we work with our students.*

> *Knowing what our principles are can help us know how we want to react rather than simply know how we are reacting.*

SCENARIO | PRACTICING OUR PRINCIPLES 1

You feel extremely irritated about a student's behavior. After trying many strategies, you have completely lost patience and feel resentful that this student is not willing to cooperate with you.

Because you believe that anger and sarcasm do not effectively change classroom behaviors, you decide to delay your response to the student until you can offer a constructive one, one that is not born of anger and frustration.

SCENARIO | PRACTICING OUR PRINCIPLES 2

You think to yourself, "This activity worked *great* in the workshop I attended, and I really like the song." Watching your students, however, you realize that the activity is completely teacher-prescribed and teacher-directed. Students are simply going through the motions and are not engaged.

Because you believe that students learn better when they feel involved and feel a sense of ownership for the activity, you decide to adjust the lesson to allow for more student choices next time.

Adopting and maintaining a set of principles is a process. As situations change and as we grow, we may feel compelled to adjust our principles. A shift in beliefs, a new understanding, or a change in our work environment may necessitate this adjustment. What once seemed to be the very basis of our teaching may seem inappropriate or naive later in our careers. The following principles were chosen because they have sufficiently broad application, reflect common teaching situations, and reflect the authors' basic beliefs about teaching. Revisions of and additions to this list are appropriate. Principles grow from inside a person and, therefore, must be considered individually.

Principle 1

> **Students have the right to be treated with respect and dignity for their ideas, skills, and stages of development.**

SCENARIO

MESSAGES TO STUDENTS

One of your goals in your new year of school is to let students know how you appreciate them and their ideas. You want to give the message "I see that you're here, and I am interested in you." Taking stock of how well you reached this goal after the first week of classes, you think back to the comments you made to your students. You recognize some comments that met your goal and some that did not.

"Jenny, your rhyme today had a neat little twist in the way it contrasted words that are close in sound but very different in meaning."

"Angie, you didn't spell any of the long-vowel words correctly. Do you remember the silent 'e' rule?"

"Good morning, Eddie. You look ready to sing today."

"Aaron, what do you have to say that is so important? *I'm* talking now!"

"What brightly colored shoes you have on today! Would you like us to sing about them?"

"You think the Muffin Man made cornmeal muffins?"

"I noticed that you heard all the repetitions of the rhythm today, Karyn, even though the song fooled you on the melodic repetitions."

"How can you expect other students to like you if you keep squeezing their hands? You need to take a 'time out' and think about this."

"Let's see if we can make ourselves look just like Harold when we get to the end of the song."

A student's sense of dignity comes from being recognized and being treated as a valuable person who is capable of having independent thoughts and making independent decisions. Respecting a student is our way of showing that we honor each individual's right to personal dignity and of reinforcing students' self-esteem and esteem for others (Marzano 1992).

Many factors in an educational setting can compromise a student's sense of dignity and self-worth. Being in groups, taking tests, following rules, doing "what the teacher says," being compared with others, and trying to make friends are all important parts of the schooling process. Each of these factors, however, can take its toll on one's sense of acceptance and worth. Therefore, we must be conscious of and sensitive to the affirmations that we give students as they continually adjust to the systems of education within our classrooms and schools. We recognize that our intent to respect

PRINCIPLES OF TEACHING AND LEARNING

1

Students have the right to be treated with respect and dignity
for their ideas, skills, and stages of development.

2

Students deserve an engaging learning environment
in which they feel safe enough to demonstrate freely
their understandings and skills through
various types of participation.

3

Student learning is the responsibility
of both teachers and students.

4

Learning is holistic and constructive.

5

A teacher's attitudes, behaviors, and
methodologies should be compatible.

6

Accurate and constructive feedback
helps students become independent learners.

7

Quality of life is enriched through music and singing.

students can take many shapes, and we believe that the resolve to be respectful and accepting of learners as people should permeate teaching at all ages and stages.

CHALLENGES IN PRACTICING PRINCIPLE 1

- To search for ways to show respect for students
- To respect students despite the differences we see in class, culture, habit, belief, and opinion; in other words, to respect the differences among and between people
- To communicate and model respect for students even when they respect neither others nor themselves
- To assess student achievement meaningfully while still valuing both the student and the achievement
- To find ways for students to make independent decisions within a group
- To address behavior problems effectively without belittling students
- To appreciate that because people are in different stages of development, their skills and understandings will differ

Principle 2

> **Students deserve an engaging learning environment in which they feel safe enough to demonstrate freely their understandings and skills through various types of participation.**

SCENARIO

ENGAGEMENT AND CONFIDENCE

Whenever Bryan begins a math assignment, he seems to need to start from scratch. He does not trust that he knows how to solve math problems, does not believe that he can solve them, and does not know where to start on them. Once he gets started, he does fine on repetitive tasks, but he takes little initiative or pleasure in working with numbers. When asked to tell how he might begin on a certain problem, he replies with resignation, "I don't know."

Sarah likes to see how things work. She loves trying to fix small household appliances, eagerly taking them apart, looking at the connections, examining all the parts, trying to guess what could be amiss. She has little knowledge about electricity and mechanics, has only small success in getting the parts back together correctly, and less success in actually fixing anything, but she is gradually learning what to expect when she first opens something. Sarah confidently describes the process she goes through when confronting a new challenge: "First I look for the screws that hold it together and undo them. After I get it apart, I look for something broken or disconnected."

Bryan has more knowledge and skills in math than Sarah does in engineering, but Sarah clearly has more interest and confidence in what she is doing. Consequently, even with a poorer success record, Sarah attacks her challenges and is able to tap into what she does know about how things work. She is even able to rise above her abilities at times and fix things without really knowing what she is doing. Bryan, on the other hand, knows what he needs to know to solve the problems but does not seem able to tap into this reservoir of knowledge. He frets over assignments without making headway on the problems.

▶ What keeps Bryan from releasing his potential, from accessing the knowledge he has and applying it in problem-solving situations?

▶ Why is Sarah, unaware of her limitations, able to approach problems in new or unfamiliar settings with confidence that she can solve them?

Responsive, interactive education aims for maximum generation of students' ideas. To be engaged means to be "hooked up," to be "in gear," to play an active role in what is taking place. When learners are only going through the motions of an activity rather than engaging in active, thoughtful participation, their motivation may be more one of obligation than of interest. They may see the activity more as the teacher's plan than as their activity. Participating simply out of a sense of compliance can diminish any student's potential for learning.

Because responsive, interactive education treats student responses as integral and considers them crucial to effective pacing and guidance in the teaching process, it relies heavily on students' revealing what they are thinking. Therefore, emotional safety is imperative for freedom to respond with honesty and creativity. When we put ourselves in the learners' shoes and feel threatened with embarrassment, harsh evaluation, or humiliation, we become sensitive to some of the ways in which students commonly react to such threats:

- Our brains may downshift so that we cannot tell or show what we *do* know (Hart 1983).

- We may become less motivated to participate in the task.

- We may choose to give a silly answer rather than risk giving a wrong one.

- We may feel we have no investment in learning or retaining the information being presented.

- Our ability to study may be overwhelmed and superseded by our emotional response to the threat of the situation.

When we are comfortable in the learning situation, we may be more willing to risk the discomfort that is sometimes necessary to explore new concepts in the learning process.

We apparently record the feelings we have about a learning task at the same time we record the content we learn as a result of the task. In cases of math anxiety, for example, math learning is tagged with negative feelings that hinder learning. On the other hand, when we are fascinated by and interested in the solution of a mathematical puzzle, we often call it a game. Although some teachers believe that all learning should be fun, especially music learning, terms such as "enjoyable," "interesting," "challenging," and "satisfying" better capture the engagement and comfort associated with efficient learning. Not all topics and tasks will be fun for us or for our students, but we can take the initiative to construct experiences that minimize tedium and monotony. Teachers should be cognizant of the affective settings in which we expect students to learn. Maximum learning occurs when students are engaged, stimulated, and emotionally safe. Therefore, learning is centered in the whole child—socially, emotionally, intellectually, musically, and physically (Eisner 1994).

CHALLENGES IN PRACTICING PRINCIPLE 2

- To focus and guide active learning, balancing the desire for students to make choices and contributions with the requirements of time, space, patience, multiple agendas, and goals

- To manage the activity level so that students are engaged but not out of control, they participate but not without focus, and they feel a sense of ownership and responsibility for the activity

- To be sensitive to different levels of students' confidence
- To respond to student contributions in ways that support and encourage the students who are contributing as well as those who are not yet contributing

Principle 3

Student learning is the responsibility of both teachers and students.

SCENARIO

CREDIT AND BLAME

"Gosh, that lesson went well today," the teacher thought as he reflected on the fifth-grade class that had just left his room. "All my planning paid off. I was able to take those kids through that sequence much faster than I predicted. Of course, I didn't give them time to get sidetracked or goof off; I sure put them through their paces! Now that we've covered all that material, I can go on to the next unit. After today's lesson, I'm sure the kids have got it."

On another day, the same teacher has just finished teaching the same class of fifth-grade students. The teacher's self-talk this day is quite different. "Ugh! What was wrong with those kids today? They just didn't get it. No matter what I did, they reacted like slugs. These kids can be so slow sometimes!"

▶ How are the adages "teachers can teach, but students don't have to learn" and "teachers cannot teach any faster than students can learn" relevant to the Credit-and-Blame scenario?

▶ What mistaken conclusions was the teacher in this scenario drawing about himself and his students?

Neither teachers nor students can be held fully accountable for the learning that does and does not occur in a classroom. Students, whether or not they are conscious of it, have a powerful effect on the quality of teaching they are afforded. The degrees to which students at any age exhibit interest, enthusiasm, apathy, cooperation, initiative, curiosity, belligerence, and investments in learning have a strong impact on our abilities to teach them.

Learning is certainly a personal, maybe an intimate experience, and ultimately a student is responsible for his or her own learning. But learning takes place in a context, and that context can either help or hinder learning. When students must rely upon teachers, in classrooms and in schools, the issue of responsibility becomes clouded. A student who is not interested in learning can be forced to attend a school and can, as a result of that context, make surprising gains in understanding and achievement. His achievement may be partly the result of his own mental, physical, and attitudinal equipment, but it also may be due to the way a teacher engaged him in the learning situation.

In contrast, an eager student who ambitiously seeks out an apprenticeship with a master craftsman may end up confused about her goals. She may be turned off by a sense of craft that emphasizes technique to the exclusion of artistry and expression. Of course, this student's responsibility for her learning and progress needs to embrace more than just her own goals and objectives.

By accepting the role of teacher, we must assume a great deal of the responsibility for student learning. Ideally, this responsibility is shared by student and teacher, and each acknowledges the role of the other in the learning enterprise. The degrees to which teachers at any level of experience offer organization, preparation, intrigue, acceptance, tolerance, understanding, compassion, and knowledge of the subject matter have a strong impact on students' abilities to learn. As co-participators in the learning process, teachers find themselves in such varied roles as facilitators, provokers, nurturers, managers, catalysts, prompters, and coaches. Sometimes we feel limited by the range of *our* skills and knowledge, and yet, we can take heart that the achievements of our students can reach beyond those limitations. Study, then, becomes a joint investigation that is a catalyst for challenges, self-discoveries, and development of skills and understandings (Bennett 1987).

CHALLENGES IN PRACTICING PRINCIPLE 3

- To find teaching strategies that balance the responsibilities of both teacher and students

- To recognize when different roles are called for and to switch easily among them, whether nurturing, managing, provoking, guiding, or facilitating

- To work with students in ways that do not overwhelm them with our own curiosity, stifle them with our self-imposed limitations, or confuse them with a lack of interest in learning something new

- To let students take responsibility for their own learning, realizing that we cannot learn for them, but continuing to support their efforts through encouragement, direction, evaluation, and our choices of materials, methods, and goals

- To maintain a love for learning, a sense of honest self-appraisal, and a curiosity and wonder about the world, knowledge, and development

Principle 4

Learning is holistic and constructive.

SCENARIO

CONSTRUCTING AN UNDERSTANDING

It was early-morning band practice and students were in various stages of warming up, wiping sleep from their eyes, getting their instruments assembled, and arriving late. A couple of the early students, both trombonists, started playing their music backward, starting from the very last note. Mr. Bayliss, the music teacher, noticed this and wrote on the board, "Egad! A base tone denotes a bad age."

Several students, including the trombonists, noticed and asked what it meant. "Well," replied Mr. Bayliss, "what were Phillip and Ed doing with the music?" At that point, most of the students were curious about what was going on. "We were playing it backward," was the response. Mr. Bayliss then pointed at the board and said, "Go ahead and read that backward." There were a few puzzled looks and a try or two of saying, "Age, bad, a . . ." Mr. Bayliss reminded them that Phillip and Ed had been playing the notes backward, one at a time. It was quiet for a moment as the students looked at the board, and Mr. Bayliss realized this might be the right moment to start the rehearsal. "All right, open your warm-up books to page 12, and let's get started."

The band began playing long tones up the scale, and Julie, a percussionist, suddenly blurted out, "Oh, it's the same thing forward as backward!" The band stopped

and looked at Julie. She pointed at the board and repeated, "It says the same thing whether you read it forward or backward." Mr. Bayliss nodded, pleased that she could figure it out and satisfied that now that the answer to this puzzle was given, there would be no more interruptions.

As the band finished the warm-ups and Mr. Bayliss was giving instructions for the next piece, a trumpeter, with a grin from ear to ear, raised his hand. When called on, he said, "It's the same thing, forward or backward, isn't it?" Mr. Bayliss smiled at this delayed reaction but agreed readily. Julie looked confused. "I just said that," was her immediate contribution, but the trumpeter didn't seem to hear.

As the rehearsal went on, other students would, one by one, come to the realization that, indeed, the sequence of letters was the same whether you started from the beginning or the end. Mr. Bayliss, who almost wished he had not bothered writing this palindrome on the board because of all the interruptions, could tell by the looks on faces and the urgent body language when a student finally solved the puzzle. Each time, the student would comment, as if the first to mention it, "It's the same forward and backward." As more students solved the problem, Julie's confusion because they hadn't figured it out when she first mentioned it turned into a private joke with Mr. Bayliss. She became tickled at hearing other students restate what was to her the obvious. Her discovery had not seemed to help any other student see the puzzle; each student had to see it for himself or herself before the instruction made sense.

At the end of rehearsal, Sara slowly put her clarinet away, looking at the board almost continuously. At last she grinned, turned to Julie and said, "Julie, look at the board. It says the same thing forward as backward." Julie just turned to Mr. Bayliss and laughed. Mr. Bayliss winked back. He had just learned something about the difference between learning and being told answers.

When we encounter something to learn, we bring to it the composite of our past experiences and understandings. Already in place, therefore, is a scaffolding, a schema by which we can make sense of and give meaning to that which we experience. Sometimes learning is easy because we bring to it a rich background of connections to previous events in our lives. At other times, however, learning is a struggle because connections with our previous experiences are not apparent, and we must put forth effort to find those connections or to forge new ones. The ways in which and the extent to which we learn are partly dependent on our individual abilities to see and make connections—to construct meaning.

Learning takes place in a broad context of growth and interaction, a holistic setting. It does not occur in a vacuum. This context includes various details, perspectives, backgrounds, frameworks, structures, and relationships that may be neither a part of our awareness nor a part of our plans. Sometimes, in our efforts to simplify, we manipulate the complexity of a task by changing its context. The reduction of context, however (making things simple by isolating them from the perspectives and backgrounds in which they are normally found), can sometimes make easy tasks surprisingly difficult. Context can also make surprisingly complex tasks easy. We construct meaning out of the experiences we have in the world, not just from the elements of a lesson, the words of a lecture, or the pages of a book.

Learning is an active process of assembling the pieces of experience into more and more complete accounts of that experience, a constructive process. Based on what we already know and the contents of new experiences, we construct a theory, or in Piaget's terms, we invent our understanding of how the world works (Gardner 1991, 1981; Piaget 1973). Teachers provide new experiences for students, and, in all those experiences, it is the *students* who are the active agents of their own learning (Brooks and Brooks 1993; Dewey 1956; Eisner 1994).

- Teachers have students recall and reflect on patterns in their experience.

- Teachers confront students with unexpected consequences, leading them to rethink their understandings.

- Teachers urge students to explain their experience.

- Teachers provide opportunities for students to symbolize or represent their experience.

Without students' natural curiosity, engagement, reflection, confusion, and perception, learning cannot occur.

But what framework do we use to look at our students in constructive, holistic ways? Sometimes we are tempted to neglect holistic properties and overcompartmentalize students and other people. In candid reflection, we may find that we have generalized one facet of another's being, using one selected part to create a false whole. Although such categorizing may serve to guide us in our treatment of and reactions to others, it can also impede the processes of teaching, learning, and understanding.

WHO IS A WHOLE CHILD?

Who and what is a "whole child"? As I posed this question to myself, the metaphor of a hologram came to mind in terms which Peter Senge described in his book, *The Fifth Discipline*. With this metaphor in mind we can begin to look at the component "pieces" of the whole child and know that the whole inheres in each piece "from a different point of view."

"If you cut a photograph in half, each part shows only part of the whole image. But if you divide a hologram (a three dimensional image created by interacting light sources), each part shows the whole image intact. Similarly, as you continue to divide up a hologram, no matter how small the divisions, each piece still shows the whole image. . . . But the component "pieces" of the hologram are not identical. Each represents the whole image from a different point of view . . ." (p. 212).

A whole child is a unique, individual person with a body: who, through that body, relates to nature, people, and things.

A whole child is a person who perceives: who sees, hears, touches, smells, and tastes.

A whole child is a person who moves: who, through movement, develops an awareness of time, space, and gravity.

A whole child is a social person: a person in relationship with others and a person who relates with others.

A whole child is an emotional person: who loves and hates; laughs and cries; fears and trusts; hopes and grieves; is angry and peaceful; joyful and sad.

A whole child is a person who thinks: a person who makes judgments: more than, less than; longer than, shorter than; bigger than, smaller than; higher than, lower than; the same as, different from. In other words, a whole child is a person who seriates; a person who notices sequence and puts things in sequence; a person who notices patterns and creates patterns; a person who plans; a person who solves problems and puzzles; a person who wonders. A whole child is a person who notices cause and effect in nature, people, and things.

A whole child is a person who wills: who makes choices and decisions for action.

A whole child is a person of language: who talks and sings, who communicates what she or he perceives, feels, understands, decides, and wonders.

A whole child is a person who reflects: who sees with an "inner" eye, hears with an "inner" ear, feels with an "inner" touch, moves with an "inner" movement. A whole child is a person who thinks about his or her experiences.

A whole child is a person who imagines: a creative person who, in interaction with the world of nature, things, and people, creates the unique expression of who he or she is and who he or she will become.

A whole child is an aesthetic person: who perceives beauty in nature, things, and people.

A whole child is a person who remembers: who has a story.

Even as we look at the separate, interrelated "parts" of a whole child, we know full well that we are describing an abstraction. No "whole child" exists apart from the individual children with whom we interact day by day in our classrooms.

(Fleurette Sweeney, Vancouver, B.C., 1992)

Reminding ourselves to view each student as a "whole child" can sound like a worthy goal. In "Who Is a Whole Child?" Fleurette Sweeney provides a unique portrayal of the ways in which our viewing others as whole beings can foster compassion and understanding.

CHALLENGES IN PRACTICING PRINCIPLE 4

- To find teaching strategies that progress logically from large contexts (songs, stories, games) to smaller units (tones, intervals, patterns)

- To understand the elements of our curricula in sufficient depth that we can see the relations between the parts and the wholes, how they work together, and, especially, how the parts depend upon their respective wholes

- To be able to guide study from broad understandings to specific and determinative facts

- To recognize and trust that students construct their understandings in spite of how hard we work at presenting appropriate information and guiding their explorations

- To realize that the understanding of things that students construct may not agree with conventional adult perspectives. This may occur when students categorize information differently or when they see and emphasize different patterns and relationships in their perceptions

Principle 5

A teacher's attitudes, behaviors, and methodologies should be compatible.

SCENARIO

MATCHING PLANS TO EXPECTATIONS AND STUDENTS

It was October and Mr. Olly was planning to teach the song *Drunken Sailor* to his fifth-grade music class. Mr. Olly knew that learning *Drunken Sailor* would be preparation for the part-singing activities with this song that he had planned for a later time. This particular group of students tended to be rowdy, easily excitable, and difficult to keep still; Mr. Olly frequently lost his patience with them.

He felt certain that students would like the song and the jiglike actions he had learned at a summer workshop, but Mr. Olly also knew that these students have difficulty controlling themselves. Another concern was that the energetic movements would likely produce some vocal qualities that would contradict the kind of part singing he had in mind for this song. "How much movement can I use in the lesson without the students getting out of hand?" he wondered to himself as he planned his lesson.

Opting for quiet imagery, Mr. Olly decided to introduce the song by having students explore the setting and describe the characters that might be involved. In this way, he could use student contributions and still have them practice singing with a buoyant, energized, and breathy tone.

Mr. Olly's plan centered on having a sailor singing the refrain, "Weigh, hey, and up she rises. . . ," while walking to work. He planned to sing this part of the song in quiet tones, while walking around the room, using his voice and actions to further demonstrate the mood of stillness and quiet anticipation that he wanted to create. Mr. Olly would then ask students to suggest images about the time of day, the smells and sights around the harbor, the people the sailor might see, the kinds of boats, and the sailor's purpose. "Why is he going to work today? Why so early? Where has he been? Is he alone?"

To make sure he would remember how to create the scene, Mr. Olly wrote the following in his plan book: "It is morning and the sun is just coming up over the horizon. Seagulls soar over the water's edge looking for food. A cool mist fills the spaces between shops and homes. The only sounds are the lapping of waves on the beach, the creaking of boats as they sit in steadily rising tide, and a lone sailor humming this song as he makes his way to his ship."

As Mr. Olly reviewed his plans, he felt relieved that he was not going to teach the song with lots of movement. The benefits of movement for his students were clear in his mind: It releases energy, it relaxes muscles in their necks and shoulders for more efficient breathing and vocal production, and it takes their minds off the fact that they are singing, so they sing less self-consciously.

But there would be time to do the movement lesson later, Mr. Olly reflected, as his mind drifted back to a harbor, a sunrise, and a sailor humming as he walks across a pier.

Sometimes the song materials and teaching strategies we choose are counterproductive to our goals. Unknowingly, we may introduce elements into our classes that are incompatible with our principles and, therefore, incompatible with the academic, social, and musical expectations we have for our students. This is especially common when there are fundamental tensions between principles, beliefs, goals, desires, needs, and practices.

Tensions can sometimes exist between the principles we espouse. Being aware of these tensions can help us be prepared to decide when one principle should take precedence in a given situation. "Practicing what we preach" may not be enough, because tensions can exist between the things we preach and the various practices we employ. Sometimes tensions need to be resolved, either by dropping a practice that conflicts with a principle or by modifying or synthesizing principles. At other times, however, the tensions between principles and practices need only to be considered and managed. Compatibility among principles and between principles and practices is a goal for ourselves and our students. How might incompatibilities show up in our teaching?

- We can value students' freedom to respond and their spontaneous suggestions for shaping activities, yet have rigid rules and punishments for spontaneous classroom behaviors.

- We can value and desire students' full participation in and enjoyment of singing, yet voice narrow standards about what good singing is and present songs that do not appeal to students because of our commitment to a narrow view of art music.

- We can value students' engagement in the learning process, yet use methods that offer little opportunity for students' input.

CHALLENGES IN PRACTICING PRINCIPLE 5

- To monitor the quality of our verbal and nonverbal treatment of students

- To assess carefully our methods for leading students to new information and skills

- To be informed about and sensitive to our selection of song literature and activities

- To consider our short- and long-term expectations for students' behaviors and achievements

Through continual, conscious assessment of and reflection on our practices, we gain assurance that our practices reflect the principles in which we believe.

Accurate and constructive feedback helps students become independent learners.

When students are given constructive and descriptive feedback about their responses, they gain information by which they can learn to continue, discontinue, adapt, or elaborate on their current behaviors and understandings. Constructive feedback relies neither on exuberant praise nor on harsh criticism to communicate assessments of students' responses. Rather, constructive feedback offers observations, which can also be followed with encouragement, correction, compliments, or simple recognition.

★ **SCENARIO**

CONSTRUCTIVE FEEDBACK

"Why does Jimmy continue to pester Sally? I've told him umpteen times to stop." These were the thoughts going through Mrs. Anderson's mind as she listened to her class sing *Old Dan Tucker* and move to the beat. She found herself feeling angry that she had to speak to him one more time about his behavior.

Unsure of what to say that would finally stop his pestering, Mrs. Anderson bought some time by having students suggest different actions to perform on the beat. As they sang and moved, Mrs. Anderson watched Jimmy. She saw that as he was pestering Sally, his movements came close to matching the beat.

After the song ended, Mrs. Anderson spoke directly to Jimmy in a matter-of-fact tone. "Jimmy, you are close to doing the beat accurately. Bothering Sally only confuses both of you. Everyone feel the beat by tapping your little fingers right in front of your faces for this turn. Jimmy, watch your fingers closely, and I bet you'll get it this time!"

There is a complex web of relationships between and among various kinds of feedback. Verbal and nonverbal, positive and negative, intrinsic and extrinsic, and general and specific are some of the oppositions with which we must work. Winning, losing, being "number one," failing, and getting an "A" are some of the cultural values that function in our classrooms. These oppositions and values deserve our thought, especially in preparing us to give the kind of feedback that will be most effective to our students' independence in learning.

Although students become adept at reading their teachers' meanings within the context of each teacher's classroom behaviors, the critical role that feedback plays in teaching and learning warrants attention from even the most experienced among us. (See Chapter 7 for further discussion on feedback.)

CHALLENGES IN PRACTICING PRINCIPLE 6

Shifting the emphasis of our feedback from complaints and compliments to simple observations and encouragement can offer substantial variety, support, and information to students about their responses.

- To recognize different types of feedback—their purposes and respective advantages and disadvantages

- To be aware of the effects that various types of feedback can have on learning and on different students

- To notice sufficient detail in student achievement, performances, and contributions to make constructive and descriptive comments

- To see how our beliefs and practices concerning praise, competition, rewards, and achievement affect what our students perceive to be the value of what we are teaching

- To rethink our positions on praise, competition, rewards, and achievement in view of what we want to accomplish in schools

Principle 7

Quality of life is enriched through music and singing.

SCENARIO   THE POWER OF SINGING

Miss Nelson took a deep breath and began to sing. She had just settled a fight between several students, a fight that had begun on the playground, was continuing at the start of her class, and had definite racial overtones. She wasn't sure she had fixed anything, but at least the students involved weren't shouting or trying to hit each other. There were hard looks on their faces, and the other children were understandably upset both by the tension in the room and by the animosity expressed.

Miss Nelson calmly began to sing: "Round, round the wild birds fly. Poor little bird in a cage, don't cry. Hide your eyes and soon you'll be with the wild birds flying free. Who's standing back of you, can you say? If you guess the name, you can fly away!" Without saying anything, she moved slowly around the room, noticing the relief in some students' eyes as they began to see things get back to normal. Starting the song a second time, she continued to move quietly around the room, not offering any explanations. Her students knew this song and liked the guessing game they played with it, but Miss Nelson did not ask any of them to sing or guess her name. As she began the song a third time, a few students joined her in singing. Because Miss Nelson sang with her class frequently, this was a natural thing for them to do.

Miss Nelson stopped behind Kim, a student who had not been involved in the fight, and repeated the last line, "If you guess my name, you can fly away." Kim looked at her in confusion. Normally the students would have their eyes closed and would have to guess. Miss Nelson looked at Kim expectantly and repeated the last line of the song. Kim said hesitantly, "Miss Nelson." "That's right," the teacher responded and started singing and moving again. More students joined the singing and another student had a chance to answer the question.

As she sang the song a sixth time, Miss Nelson noticed that a couple of the students involved in the fight were singing, so she engineered her movements to stop behind one of them at the end of the song. After the student answered, "Miss Nelson," the teacher began singing and moving, and almost all students sang with her. The sound of their voices was calming, peaceful, and beautiful. She knew better than to think that the hurt feelings were healed, but Miss Nelson was relieved that students' attention had been directed elsewhere.

Could one of the fighting students take her place walking around the room? Miss Nelson stopped behind one and asked, "Peter, would you like the song to take you through this enchanted forest, where birds can talk?" Peter got up and started moving with the song. He stopped behind a student, repeated the last line by himself, and listened as the student looked at him and said, "Peter." Miss Nelson asked Peter to invite this student to take his place moving around the room.

Breathing a sigh of relief at Peter's participation, Miss Nelson made a mental note of the change in her students: All were singing; they were looking at each other with quiet eagerness and saying others' names; they were making invitations as they had practiced in other activities; and even the students who had been fighting were relaxing. "Maybe I will be able to get something done this afternoon, after all," Miss Nelson thought.

- Music is a distinctive feature of human life.
- Music brings vitality, grace, and charm to our lives.
- Music provides opportunities for reflection and contemplation.
- Music rouses and stimulates just as it refreshes and soothes.

The musical experience requires disciplined thought (Howard 1992), cherishes human interaction (Higgins 1991), and otherwise celebrates the potential of human life. Each person has the right and the qualifications to be a music maker. Singing and listening are basic aspects of musical activity and human living. It is through listening that we are moved, challenged, calmed, recharged, and charmed by music. By singing, we can participate directly in musical experience, from profoundly expressive musical works to songs of innocent simplicity. Through song, we are able to express ourselves musically. Although the purposes and qualities of those expressions can vary greatly, the main effect of this principle is in crafting practices that nurture students in musical development and that support all people in considering themselves singers.

Throughout history, singing has been considered a satisfying social experience. The connections that can be made through singing are increasingly important to balance and to bridge the global, technological, multicultural, and ecological concerns in our world. We believe singing can be a powerful tool in making those connections.

CHALLENGES IN PRACTICING PRINCIPLE 7

- To help people develop healthy vocal habits and attitudes
- To choose musical materials and activities that support vocal development and that reflect musical impulses and positive human aspirations
- To maintain the link between musical experiences and the quality of life
- To recognize the role singing plays and has played in human interactions
- To see singing not just as a way of teaching music but also as a human expression that has direct and concrete connections to physical, linguistic, social, affective, and cognitive development

Singing provides a bond for similar and disparate groups. Singing affirms and reaffirms ideas, connections, and emotions. Singing provides nonverbal, global expressions of acceptance, recognition, and respect.

Chapter Epilogue

Through the seven principles presented in this chapter, a foundation is laid for singing in classrooms. This foundation encourages engagement, interaction, and integration. In view of the relationships between music and play and between development and play, one might characterize such a foundation as playful. An approach to teaching music based on a playful foundation such as this needs both clarification and elaboration. Teachers who want to utilize this kind of foundation will need to examine how they will guide and direct activities that encourage student engagement and cooperation. They will need to develop ways of responding to student contributions and achievements that respect the dignity of the student and encourage further contributions. They will need to explore the various components of musical experiences they are providing to realize the movement, linguistic, educational, and musical potential therein.

One source for the authors' beliefs in the value of song was the exploration, examination, and utilization of activities that involved students in singing games and other movement-oriented singing experiences. The play that took place in these

Teachers should regard the singing activities described as examples of a playful foundation for learning and are encouraged to apply the principles at work in these activities to other materials and environments.

activities became a model of engaging, interactive, and holistic learning experiences. *Throughout this book, activities are described in a variety of ways, not because they are to be taken as the only ways in which these principles can be put into action, but because they illustrate important themes of these principles.* Indeed, it is important to see these activities as examples of a playful foundation, a foundation that recognizes student and teacher responsibilities, freedom and structure, leading and following, individual work and cooperation, action and thought in the learning process.

Teaching and Singing Songs 3

Teaching Songs to Children

Not so long ago, we would not have been considered qualified to teach songs or music to children, especially if we were music teachers, unless we could play the piano proficiently. Since the 1960s, however, when the approach of Hungarian educator Zoltán Kodály became popular in the United States, teachers of music have more readily recognized the benefits of unaccompanied singing. Kodály believed that voices are best accompanied by other voices and that we learn to sing better in tune when we match a voice to another voice rather than to an instrument (Choksy 1988).

It is not uncommon these days to see music rooms with no piano or to meet successful music teachers who are not adept at keyboard skills. Although our classes and our school programs may be enhanced by piano accompaniment, it is not *essential*, nor is it recommended, for daily activities in teaching and singing with children. We need no instruments or equipment to do an excellent job of teaching song activities to our students. All we really need is ourselves and our students.

Although musical instruments and sound-production equipment can add flavor and enjoyment in some situations, neither is essential to good singing or good teaching.

Choosing Songs to Sing

▶ What songs do you remember enjoying from your childhood?

▶ What songs cause you to react, "Oh, I love that song!"?

▶ Are there some songs that receive an "Oh, good!" response when your students know they are about to sing them?

▶ What makes us enjoy, like, and value certain songs?

What gives a song its power? Is it the melody? Clearly, some melodies have a special attraction. Have you noticed that some songs get stuck in your head and you seem unable to stop them from repeating, over and over and over? Occasionally, just the melody gets stuck, and we find ourselves humming a song, even though we cannot recall the words.

Do the words give a song its power? The expressions used in songs to tell stories, portray characters, or convey feelings can often stick in our minds. They focus our thinking about a topic or a feeling. Many children and adults savor the language they have learned in song.

Given the great variety of songs and the many ways in which they can be used, how do we choose "good" songs? The context in which the song is used and how one attends to the song are both of fundamental importance. The criteria for selecting a song for a classroom activity fall into three major categories: technical considerations, cultural considerations, and level of interest.

Technical Considerations

The relative complexity of a song can be determined by examining its linguistic and musical structure. Songs can be useful devices by which to learn new words, but it will be more difficult to learn the words of a song if all the words are new. Complex clauses and long sentences make songs difficult in the same way they make texts difficult.

Musical structure also plays a part in selecting a song. A song with a range of more than an octave can be more challenging vocally than one with a range of a fifth. A song with a contour that has many changes of direction and a variety of leaps from tone to tone can present difficulties to someone trying to learn it. The number of different tones and the number of different durations also affect how difficult a song will be to learn. Length, number of verses, and predictability of structure should be considered in selecting a song to teach children. One way to evaluate the complexity of a song is to look for repetition. The more repetitions you can find in words, rhythms, or melody, the simpler the song.

Is it true that the simpler the song, the more appropriate it is for younger students? Not necessarily. Simple is not always better. Songs lacking complexity may not be of interest to anyone. Choosing a song on the basis of technical considerations alone is a bit like planning a meal on the basis of nutritional content alone. Unless you and your students feel satisfied with a diet of musical "vitamin pills," you will want to look at other criteria.

Cultural Considerations

Songs are the creations of cultures. Many of the world's folk songs grew out of cultural traditions and are rich in history, context, and purpose. Folk songs tell the stories of peoples, and they have been used to celebrate heroes, events, and memories. When we sing these songs, we have a chance to revisit, examine, and discuss the contexts from which they grew.

Sensitivity to cultural issues is important. By singing songs that have strong cultural roots, we gain a recognition that other people have created songs that sound different from our own. Acknowledging differences in songs can be a step in recognizing and valuing cultural differences, but simply singing a Japanese song, for example, will have little effect on our awareness of the Japanese culture. Multicultural awareness involves knowing about and respecting individual differences and cultural differences, not just knowing a diverse repertoire of songs. A respect for individual differences can be developed by the manner in which songs are presented and studied, and it can be nurtured through various kinds of interactions between classmates.

The subject matter of a song plays an important role in the selection process, especially with contemporary songs and songs of older folk material. With growing societal concern about use and abuse of alcohol, singing *Drunken Sailor,* even if we change the words to "seasick sailor," can cause a pedagogical problem. Singing a song about death, such as *Old Grumbler* or *Aunt Rhody,* whether in a serious or a whimsi-

PRINCIPLE 7

Cultural and multicultural awareness has more to do with the development of social skills than with the choice of songs.

cal vein, can be a sensitive issue. Songs with overt spiritual content can also pose a problem. It is important to be clear about the purpose we have in choosing to sing a song, whatever its content, and it is important to consider the impact that the content of a song can have on our students.

Authenticity in performance of songs is of major concern to some music educators. Knowing the historical perspectives, cultural values, social behaviors, and performance practices from which a song originated can be valuable. This knowledge can guide the presentation and use of songs with today's students by suggesting a story, an activity, or a context in which to situate the song. Knowledge of a song's background can also help us to avoid the use of songs that present offensive stereotypes of people of various races or nationalities. The texts of some songs, whose more traditional versions reflect cultural values with which we may disagree, such as racism or sexism, have been changed so that the song is less provocative. But changing texts to avoid references to difficult issues, such as death or injustice, can take the bite and vinegar out of a song. When we know the history of a song, we can use the song as a springboard for a discussion of problematic views and behaviors, we can avoid the song because of its troubling past, or we can use the song knowing that important cultural issues are hidden by its present adapted text.

When we do not know the history or background of a song, our lack of knowledge limits us in our use of the song. We may also be less prepared for adult objections to it. Songs must be chosen and shared in classrooms, however, even when such background information is not available. Ignorance of a song's history is not sufficient reason to dismiss it from our own or our students' repertoires. If the text is not patently offensive, if it speaks to student interests or humor, if it has the sparks of human intelligence or honesty, and if it is musically satisfying, then maybe the song's authenticity can remain an open question.

We want our students to forge connections with songs that have cultural and musical value. We want to help students develop meaningful and personal relationships with the songs we teach them. And we want to use songs that broaden our students' musical lives and connect them to other people living and singing in human community throughout the world.

The point is to create a meaningful context in which a song can have a purpose for a group of people. In the classroom, the challenge is to create situations in which students can find meaning—their own meaning, not someones else's—in a song. This requires balancing the tensions between the past and present of a song, the traditional and the adapted, our personal beliefs and those of other people, and styles that are comfortably familiar and those that are surprisingly different.

Songs are powerful. That is why they have been used to express spiritual and other deeply felt human emotions. Songs can provide opportunities to build bridges across the gulfs of understanding that separate child from child and culture from culture. Like any power tool, songs need to be used with care.

Level of Interest

Possibly most important in choosing songs to sing is the level of interest a song has for the singers. When we are so interested in singing a song that we are willing to repeat it over and over, it matters little how complex the song is or how difficult the subject matter.

Linguistic Interest   Many songs tell stories about people, places, and events. They employ language for sound effects: rhymes, nonsense syllables, and many words in a small space of song. Children's songs are often about animals and other elements in the natural world. And, of course, many songs express our feelings: love, mystery,

---

PRINCIPLE 5

The re-creation of songs by holding to standards of authentic context and performance practice is less important than the sensitive use of songs with the students in our classrooms.

awe, grief, consolation, joy. The language of a song is clearly an element in how interesting a song can be. When the language of the song captures a person's imagination, it is likely that the song will be of interest to that person.

Musical Interest   Some educators have created songs with simplified melodic and rhythmic material for pedagogical reasons, assuming that simplified songs are easier for students to learn and thus for teachers to teach. Others have wanted to limit the repertory of songs to the tonal and rhythmic relationships around which their aural skills and notation curricula are based. Still others have seemed to rate the difficulty or complexity of a song by its notation: the simpler the notation, the simpler the song.

Clearly, the complexity of a song is a criterion in its selection for a given situation. But who finds a song of simplified tonal or rhythmic content very interesting? Songs made up of just two or three different tones often have less musical interest than songs using a greater number of tones. The same is true for songs of limited rhythmic content. Songs with minimal rhythmic variety rarely display much vitality or suppleness and can often distort the rhythm and accent of the lyrics.

PRINCIPLE 5

The musical interest of a song is often described by words like beauty, elegance, charm, spirit, vitality, and power. These are obviously difficult words to define. If we look for songs that we think are beautiful and spirited, we will find songs that are more than just ordinary and more than just cute and that seem to be more than just commercial jingles or gimmicks. Our sense of beauty may not be someone else's, but neither is it likely to be the final word on beauty. Beautiful and spirited songs, however, seem to beg us to sing them and seem to be of more than just momentary value.

Interest in the Activity   Although musical and linguistic issues are important, perhaps a more fundamental issue is how we teach a song and capture the imaginations of students. When a song provides a context for a student's personal expression or choice, the song will have more meaning and be more interesting to students. When the sound that students make as they sing is buoyant, pleasing, and apparently effortless, there is a greater chance that they will be interested in singing. In contrast, when singing is coarse and strained, interest will likely wane.

PRINCIPLE 2

"Well, we have five minutes left before the bell rings. All we can do is sing a song to make the time go faster." As that statement illustrates, using songs in a trivial manner makes songs trivial. Songs used only as means to other ends, that are not valued in themselves, become limited in value. The reason we sing is critical to our ability and disposition to attend to the song.

Knowing a Repertoire of Songs

Have you ever started teaching a new song to a group and found that, because the song was new to you, you could not recall the tune or the words to begin? Incidents like that can be frustrating and embarrassing, but they occur to most of us who teach and lead singing. One way to avoid forgetting a song is to practice singing it over and over until you can sing it automatically. As you will see, too, knowing some things about the song can help you get started on the right track as you begin to teach it. A great deal of repetition and the ability to sing the song without prompts will help prepare you for teaching a new song to your students. You will be most effective as a song leader if you develop a varied list of songs that you know well, a repertoire for classroom singing.

- Knowing a repertoire of songs will give you confidence as you lead singing activities.

- Knowing a repertoire of songs will give you alternatives in singing with your students.

- Knowing a repertoire of songs will help you respond appropriately to students' singing needs.

Songs can provide opportunities for social, cultural, linguistic, physical, and intellectual development. Sometimes adults find it difficult to appreciate the songs and musical experiences that children find valuable. What musical experiences do children typically value?

- Music they make themselves

- Music that involves them in satisfying emotional, intellectual, and physical experiences—in experiences they want to repeat

- Music presented in a context that is rich in musical, linguistic, and social structure

To help our students learn to value songs, we must choose valuable songs. Four suggested criteria are listed here to help you in this selection process. Specific information on how to make these judgments is sprinkled throughout this and following chapters.

1. Choose songs that children can sing well and can eventually sing independently and confidently. Consider the difficulty of the words and the music.

2. Choose songs that are valuable and enjoyable from a musical point of view. Ask yourself, "Will my students want to sing this song years from now? Do they enjoy it now?"

3. Choose songs that will provide a variety of musical experiences. Consider different modes of student involvement (movement, language play, listening challenges), different styles (children's songs, ballads, work songs, story songs, patriotic songs), and diverse cultures (Asian, African, European, Hispanic, and the various subdivisions of each). See the following chart for representative examples of songs from these categories.

4. Choose songs that relate to the interests of students. Is the language interesting? Is the movement satisfying, and does it fit the song? Are the social interactions valuable for the students?

A BASIC REPERTOIRE OF SONGS

- Folk songs just for singing:
  Oh, Susanna; Skip to My Lou; Home on the Range; On Top of Old Smokey; She'll Be Comin' 'Round the Mountain; Old Dan Tucker; There's a Hole in My Bucket
- Greeting and closing songs:
  The More We Get Together; Hello Everybody; Sing with Me
- Action songs requiring little or no change in seating and format:
  If You're Happy and You Know It; Row, Row, Row Your Boat; This Old Man
- Song games involving whole-group movement and play:
  The Farmer in the Dell; Looby Loo; Punchinella, A-Hunting We Will Go; Rig-a-Jig-Jig

(continued)

A BASIC REPERTOIRE OF SONGS (continued)

- Songs involving simple language exploration through rhyming and word substitution:

  This Old Man; When I Was One; Mulberry Bush; Whistle, Daughter, Whistle; Down by the Bay; Jenny Jenkins; Daddy Loves the Bear; Mad Man

- Patriotic songs, state songs, and songs of national pride:

  America the Beautiful; The Star-Spangled Banner; O Canada; My Home's in Montana; The Eyes of Texas; Back Home Again in Indiana; Deep in the Heart of Texas

- Seasonal songs:

  Love Somebody; Deck the Halls; Over the River and Through the Wood; Ground Hog; Skin and Bones

- Sea chanteys and work songs:

  Drunken Sailor; Haul Away, Joe; Shenandoah; Drill, Ye Tarriers, Drill; Pick a Bale of Cotton

- Ballads and songs that tell stories:

  Scarborough Fair; Barbara Allen; Don Gato; Frankie and Johnny; Cockles and Mussels

- Animal songs:

  There Was an Old Lady Who Swallowed a Fly; Froggie Went a-Courtin'; Old MacDonald

- Songs of the American West:

  Home on the Range; Goodbye, Old Paint; Sweet Betsy from Pike; Tom Dooley

- Spirituals and songs of African Americans:

  Swing Low, Sweet Chariot; Wade in the Water; This Train; Gonna Sing When the Spirit Says Sing; Get on Board, Little Children; Over My Head

- Songs for part singing:

  (See "Teaching Part Singing and Part Listening" in this chapter.)

- Songs from television, movies, and Broadway:

  My Favorite Things; 76 Trombones; Under the Sea; Whistle While You Work; Sesame Street; Just the Bare Necessities; Can You Feel the Love Tonight?

- Songs of Native Americans:

  Cheyenne Melody; The Owl Sings (Yuma); *Shoorah* (Salish)

- Songs of the Middle East:

  Shalom Haverim (Israel); *My Homeland* (Lebanon); *Gathering Olives* (traditional Arab); *Black Cat* (Iraq)

- Songs of Asia:

  Sakura (Japan); *Wild Birds* (Japan); *Hao Peng You* (Looking for a Friend, China)

- Songs of Africa:

  Funga Alafia (Liberia); *Sansa Kroma* (Akan); *Siyahamba* (Zulu)

- Songs of Mexico and Hispanic Americans:

  DeColores; El Coqui

Songs from the preceding chart and additional songs for a variety of categories may be found in song collections listed in Appendix A.

Each of the songs in the chart is material for further musical experience and study. Take the time necessary to develop your students' repertory of songs. Once you have built a repertory of songs for yourself and your students, you can use those songs to study the elements and the sounds of music. Almost all the songs chosen for

SongWorks 1 and found in Chapter 9 are English-based folk songs that capture some of the spirit of the North American heritage and present the natural rhythms, inflections, and pronunciations of the English language.

Approaches to Teaching Songs

Imagine yourself driving in your car. You hear one of your favorite songs on the radio and begin singing along. As you sing, you are surprised to realize that you know all the words. You ponder, "How did I learn this song?" As you consider the following questions, remember that on the radio, each time a song is aired, it is played through from beginning to end.

- ▶ How did you learn the song?
- ▶ Did you just pick it up as it went along?
- ▶ How much of it did you learn the first time you heard it?
- ▶ Did you learn certain words or phrases first?
- ▶ How many times had you heard the song before you knew it and liked it?
- ▶ Did you like the song after hearing it the first time, or did you like it more with each repetition?

PRINCIPLE 4

Reflecting on how we learn songs outside school can help us understand how we learn music. Typically, we get acquainted with a piece of music by hearing it as a whole, from beginning to end. Whether they are lullabies sung to babies, popular songs on the radio, marches, or symphonies, the most common musical experiences involve the playing of musical pieces from beginning to end, as a whole, whether the audience knows the music or not. Presenting music in this way lets the music speak for itself.

The *whole-song approach* is at the forefront of the teaching strategies presented in this text. It is the completeness of a whole that gives meaning, context, and perspective to its parts. When you use the whole-song approach, students can learn a song by processing it in the ways that will be most helpful to them.

Consider an alternative approach to hearing and learning songs: the *part approach*. You would hear the first phrase of a song several times to make sure you knew it before going on to the next phrase. You would proceed phrase by phrase, part by part, until you learned the whole song. Then you would go back and put all the pieces together. It may seem that the part approach would help you learn the words to a song more quickly or learn the tune more accurately than the whole-song approach. That is not necessarily the case. Let's look at some of the assumptions the part approach makes.

The Part Approach

When we choose to teach a song by singing it one phrase at a time, we are assuming that our students will be able to sing the song along with us more quickly when it is taught in bite-size pieces. This way of teaching suggests, therefore, that it is more important to have students sing along with us, immediately and accurately, than it is to preserve the overall quality of the musical experience shaped by the structure of the song.

The part approach also assumes that students will learn musical material more quickly than with the whole-song approach. Typical out-of-school situations turn this around and work on the assumption that it is better to present musical material as a whole and that listeners will learn the music soon enough. The radio disc jockey recognizes the potential impact of a song and presents it as a whole. That challenges us to learn the song as best we can, perhaps by requesting to hear it again. The conductor of an ensemble does the same thing in a concert situation. The music performance is placed in front us, and we are given the responsibility of trying to keep up with the whole piece.

Teaching a song in parts, commonly done through *echoing,* assumes that nothing musical is lost in the process. Clearly, that is not true. When a song is broken up into parts (phrases, measures, and word groups), the sense of musical flow and of the whole can be marred, disjointed, and disrupted. To illustrate this phenomenon, sing both the teacher's and the students' parts in the following example. Notice the diminishing sense, especially on the part of the students, of the wholeness of the song.

A PART APPROACH TO TEACHING A SONG

Teacher	Students
Here is a new song. Echo me.	
Oh, give me a home	
	Oh, give me a home
Where the buffalo roam,	
	Where the buffalo roam,
Where the deer and the antelope play,	
	Where the deer and the antelope play,
Where seldom is heard	
	Where seldom is heard
A discouraging word,	
	A discouraging word,
And the skies are not cloudy all day.	
	And the skies are not cloudy all day.

PRINCIPLE 4

We do not typically enjoy our favorite music when it is subjected to modifications like these. Why would we assume that our students would not be similarly affected when we teach songs using the part approach? Compare the musicality of, as well as the auditory and vocal tasks required in, both whole-song and part approaches. Relying strictly on this kind of echoing to teach a new song does not let students practice listening for clues to understanding in the larger dimensions of the song.

When we read a story to a young child, we do not "teach" the first page before going on to the second. We recognize (a) that the second page and the following pages will help the child understand the first page, (b) that the first page makes the child want to go on to the second, and (c) that the child did not have to know everything about the first page to understand the rest of the story.

The Whole-Song Approach

In everyday situations, we learn music by hearing it again and again, and we pay attention enough to learn the music because we want to learn it: We like the music and want to hear it again.

Singing the whole song for students is an effective way to teach them a new song. Encouraging students to listen as we sing helps them to focus and to listen with a purpose. We can be confident that students are taking in the song even though they are not immediately singing the whole song. As we lead singing in the initial stages of a

How quickly we learn a song may be of less importance than how often we want to hear it.

game activity so that students can hear the song as they coordinate their movements, we can relax about the inaccuracies and incompleteness we may hear in their singing. As they do when they learn songs from the radio, students cue in to certain parts of the song, often learning more interesting parts first and filling in the remaining pieces later, sometimes needing special help with some passages.

Teaching a song and an activity at the same time can be especially helpful for older students. In some cases, students in intermediate and higher grades are freer to learn and to sing a song when the focus of attention is not on their vocal participation in the new song but on a game activity. Students need not learn a song before they enter into a song activity. Many students can learn the song effectively and efficiently as they participate in an activity. In fact, when learning the song becomes a time-consuming, tedious prerequisite to learning a game, students may have already lost interest in the activity.

The following scenario illustrates how using a part approach can supplement a presentation of the whole song. Only those parts of the song that require focus, re-hearsal, or adjustment need to be singled out. The students are focused on the teacher's accurate performance of the parts, and the parts are quickly put back into the context from which they came.

COMBINING THE WHOLE-SONG AND PART APPROACHES TO TEACHING A SONG

Teacher	Students
Here is a new song. Listen as I sing it; then tell me what it is about.	
Oh, give me a home Where the buffalo roam, Where the deer and the antelope play, Where seldom is heard A discouraging word, And the skies are not cloudy all day.	
What do you think the song is about?	[Students answer with various ideas.] It's not about New Jersey!
Right. The song says "Where the buffalo roam, where the deer and the antelope play." What else does the song say?	There aren't any clouds.
That's the last line. Does the song say there aren't any clouds at all?	It's just not cloudy all day
Yes. Now listen to the whole song. You may sing whatever parts of the song you remember.	[Students sing in various places with the teacher.]
Do you have any questions about a word or words before we sing it again?	What is a discouraging word?
Listen to that part of the song. What do you think it means? "And seldom is heard a discouraging word, and the sky is not cloudy all day."	Does it mean that ranchers don't get grumpy and tell each other off?
Well, it means something similar to that. Herding cattle is hard work, and when cowboys work together without saying discouraging things like "You sure don't rope cows very well!" their work gets done faster. The same thing is true for working together in third grade, isn't it?	
Let's antiphon the song this time. You fill in any section of the song that I leave out.	[Students antiphon, hearing the whole song but singing only the parts that the teacher does not sing.]

Does the echo or part approach have a place in teaching songs and music? Yes. There are times when echoing is necessary and useful for focusing on certain parts of a song. When you want to correct a word, rhythm, or melodic pattern, echoing can be an appropriate and effective way to limit information and to focus on the confused part of the song.

An important challenge here is to look for ways to make corrections and to study song content within the context of the whole song. We believe that preserving musical quality in this way also preserves students' attraction for the songs that we are teaching them.

Introducing a New Song

Exploring the possible meanings of songs by considering their words can bring them to life. It is important to know what we are singing, even when that knowledge may not match the original meaning. Although some songs give teachers opportunities to supply important cultural and historical contexts (spirituals, patriotic songs, pioneer songs), any song can come alive as students bring their own meanings to it. Discussing the words and possible settings of songs helps students personalize and contextualize them, encourages students to investigate other interpretations, and provides for collaboration in sharing various ideas (Bennett, 1996). Making songs meaningful seems especially important to students for whom English is not a primary language.

As students share what they hear and imagine as they listen to a song, give them opportunities to develop their ideas.

- "Tell us more about why you think that."
- "What made you imagine that?"
- "Have you ever been to (seen) a place like that? What was it like?"

Making Songs Meaningful

The musical meaning of a song is more than just what the words are about. Melodies soothe and rouse. The musical flow of a song, the kind of balance in its construction, the impact of its melodic character—all contribute to the musical meaning a song can have for someone.

Songs can be personalized and made meaningful by incorporating students' names (*Johnny, Get Your Hair Cut, Sing with Me*), students' actions, ideas, or new words (*Circle Left, Punchinella, A-Hunting We Will Go*), and simple decisions that students make about the activity. (See the section on "Offering Students Choices" in Chapter 7.)

Encouraging Listening

Most teachers want students to listen. But how do we construct listening experiences so that students are focused and purposeful in their listening? Compare these two listening tasks:

- "Listen to this new song."
- "Listen to this new song, and I will ask you what it's about."

In which task would students most actively listen *for* something? At all times as we teach songs, we should encourage listening, but active listening does not occur simply because we say, "Listen." Giving students something to listen for, a challenge for listening, or a puzzle to solve motivates them and captures their attention for songs. After saying, "Here's a new song," you can include a listening task for your students by adding these challenges:

PRINCIPLE 7

Making songs meaningful for students is important to their enjoyment, their memory, and their performance of songs. Meaning is most lasting and most understandable when it comes from the students' own collaborative experiences that are guided by the teacher's supportive and inquisitive questioning.

PRINCIPLE 2

- "After I have finished singing, I'll ask you what you heard."
- "When I have finished, tell me what word or words you heard."
- "After you listen to the song, tell us what you think it is about."
- "As you listen, imagine where you might hear a song like this."
- "As you listen, close your eyes and imagine what you might be seeing (smelling, hearing, feeling) as you sing this song."
- "Listen to this song, and I will ask you if there are any words that are new to you."

Starting a Song

Imagine a choir, orchestra, or band conductor who does *not* take a preparatory stance to let students know the music is about to begin, who begins conducting *without* a preparatory gesture, and who sings or plays so loudly that he or she is not listening and cannot hear what the group is doing.

Can you predict what effects these behaviors may have on the quality of musical performance given by the group this conductor is leading? The conductor shows a lack of attention to and respect for the piece of music and the performers. Not only are these behaviors not acceptable practices for conductors of ensembles, they also illustrate important points to consider for all of us who lead singing.

Witnessing its absence has made it clear that all teachers who lead students in singing need to know and use a song-starting procedure. For some, starting a song is a simple task, easy to master. For others, it is a challenge that warrants repeated practice and monitoring.

Teaching students how to start a song can also be gratifying. They learn to lead songs with precision and clarity. If a student has trouble modeling the song-starting sequence that follows, simply offer him or her a song-starting turn by saying, "Class, listen for Mary's voice and sing with her," or "Barry, give us a 'ready, sing.'"

PRINCIPLE 3

Although teachers may use a similar procedure intuitively, a four-step sequence is identified here for use in starting songs (Bennett 1984). The four steps are *focus*, *pitch*, *gesture*, and *listen*.

Focus   To aid students in making a concerted effort to sing a song, we need to ensure their verbal and nonverbal preparation. "Is your song ready?" "Let's sing for Sarah's turn." "Here comes the song." "Eyes here." "Voices ready." These phrases can draw students' attention to the expectation of the song and of singing. Accompanied by the teacher's subtle look and posture of anticipation, such phrases can give the necessary focus for the whole group's participation in singing. The focus is on the song and being ready to sing.

Pitch   To sing a song together, a group must hear the tone on which they will be singing, the starting pitch, *before* they begin to sing. Being given a starting pitch before singing prepares students' ear-throat coordination, allowing them to match the starting pitch. Without adequate preparation, students cannot be expected to sing the first words of the song with the song leader. And without the opportunity to hear the starting pitch, they cannot be expected to know the pitch on which to sing.

To give the initial pitch, simply *sing* "Ready," "Ready, sing," "Sing," "Here we go," or "Begin" on the first tone of the song. *The directive word or words must be sung rather than spoken to adequately prepare the singers.*

Vocal variety and renewed auditory interest can be achieved by changing the starting pitch during repetitions of a song. With younger or less experienced singers, changing starting pitches too frequently can be confusing. On the other hand, staying in one key for too long can introduce a subtle but frustrating element in the classroom:

Some beginning teachers and nonmusic specialists think there is a specific pitch that should be chosen as a starting pitch for songs. When children are singing unaccompanied during an activity, many different starting pitches can be appropriate.

It can be out of students' ranges or it can border on auditory monotony. Changing starting pitches can be challenging and enlivening. The following suggestions may be helpful in finding a starting pitch appropriate for students' voices.

- If a song starts high in its range, choose a starting pitch high in your vocal range.
- If a song starts low in its range, choose a starting pitch in a comfortable place in your voice.
- If a song starts in the middle of its range, choose a starting pitch that feels somewhat high in your vocal range.

For most of us, but especially for those in the early stages of vocal awareness, choosing a starting pitch that is higher or more lifted than our usual speaking voice is recommended. Then, by listening to students' singing, you can decide whether or not the starting pitch needs to be raised or lowered for the next singing of the song. As you listen to students sing, ask yourself, "Are their voices able to sing the lowest tones of the song?" "Are they able to easily sing the highest tones?" When you hear students' voices dropping out for the lowest notes or straining to sing the highest notes, you will want to adjust the starting pitch accordingly for the next repetition of the song.

Here is a procedure that has worked well for some teachers just beginning to implement the song-starting sequence. Practice this sequence with several songs: *Looby Loo, Mary Had a Little Lamb,* and *London Bridge.*

1. Sing the first few words of the song aloud or in your inner hearing.
2. Sing the first pitch aloud.
3. Then, sing "ready" on that same pitch.

Those of you who perform this sequence easily and automatically may find it difficult to imagine the need for such small steps and for backing up from the first note of the song to sing "ready." For those who are just beginning to build confidence in leading group singing, however, an initial, systematic procedure can be helpful.

Gesture   Important during and following the "ready" pitch are the gestures or motions that let a group know when to begin singing. Most common motions are a head nod, a hand gesture, or the first step or movement of an activity. Without a visual cue, students must wait for you to begin singing before they will be able to join the song. A simple head movement is all that is needed and is probably the most efficient cue you can use.

After a slight pause following the "ready" pitch, take a *gentle* breath and lift your head to signal preparation for the **downbeat** (the first accented beat of the song). Then lower your head and simultaneously begin to sing. Some songs begin with one or more unaccented sounds that precede the downbeat. These unaccented sounds are called pickups or **anacruses.** If a song begins with an anacrusis, sing the pickup word or words as you lift your head, just before the downbeat. Practice using the song-starting procedure with songs that begin with an anacrusis: *The Farmer in the Dell, Rig-a-Jig-Jig,* and *Muffin Man.*

It is natural to inhale in coordination with song-starting gestures. Be cautious, however, about modeling tension in the breath and gesture. Any throat sound made while inhaling can indicate tension and can cause inefficiency in breathing and vocal production for both teacher and students. Emphasis is placed on the breath being a relaxed "letting in" of air. For further information on these topics, see Chapter 4, "Learning About Voices."

Experiment with the song-starting gesture and help students notice the importance of the cues you are giving them. Without any gestures or pitch cues, simply

Help students appreciate the sense of ensemble that results when all members of a group know when and how they are to begin and end a piece of music together.

PRINCIPLE 3

begin singing a song and have the class join in when they can. Ask students to notice how soon they were able to join you in singing when you gave them no visual or vocal cues. If you are using an instrument or a recording to accompany students' singing, you will need to adapt these song-starting procedures. Students will still need to know when and on what pitch to start singing. How will you give the starting tone and gesture when singing with recordings or with an instrument?

Listen   This last step in starting a song may be the most challenging. Listening is crucial to any singing. Often, our own enjoyment of singing takes precedence over our duty to listen to students' voices. Because children's voices can seldom compete with a full, mature voice, some students may stop singing to listen to their teacher. And when a teacher takes full responsibility for keeping the song going, the students may feel no urgency or motivation to learn the song or to participate in the singing. In many cases, students take part more fully in singing when the teacher's voice is barely audible.

Once a familiar song is started and students are participating in the singing, you should relax your hold on being the lead singer. Listening to students as they sing can give many important clues about their vocal ranges, their vocal production, and their confidence with the words, melody, and rhythm of a song. For many of us, being a sensitive listener to students as they sing requires discipline.

Reintroducing Familiar Songs

In introducing and reintroducing songs, aim to be predictable enough that your students can decipher what you are doing, yet unpredictable enough to capture their attention and offer an element of intrigue for the song and for the study.

After you have introduced a song and your students have sung it, you can study its elements with a variety of extending activities. Depending on how well your students learned the song when it was first introduced and what your goals are for studying the song, reintroduction may need to include several turns of singing the whole song to get the words, rhythms, and melody back "into" the students.

To engage students most productively in investigating new or familiar songs, you can let them "teach" by collecting what they already know. Drawing on the collective expertise of class members by asking questions and letting them describe and explain what they recall and recognize serves to share the responsibility for teaching. This method of soliciting students' responses also demonstrates interest, respect, and acceptance of students' abilities to teach themselves.

Presenting Secret Songs

PRINCIPLE 2

What makes a puzzle or a secret so fascinating? Perhaps it is that there is a question to answer, an intrigue to be explored, or a problem to solve. Presenting a secret song means intriguing students by giving clues about a song the teacher has in mind.

WAYS OF REINTRODUCING A SONG

1. **No introduction**
   Simply begin singing and welcome students to sing along.

2. **Recall of information (collaborative recall)**
   "What can you remember about the new song we learned in our last music class?"
   "Who can tell us a word or words that you remember from the song?"
   "Who can sing a part of the song that you remember?"

3. **Secret-song presentation**
   Present the song as a secret in any one of the ways listed in the discussion on Secret Songs.

Properly used, the secret-song strategy can be an excellent tool for song study and analysis. The proportion of time invested in the secret-song activity can vary greatly, depending on the lesson focus, the clues given, the degree of challenge that the presentation clues set up, and the value that you and your students place on problem solving and guessing time. Secret songs can be used to introduce a lesson or a segment of a lesson.

How to Present a Secret Song

For the secret-song procedure to be effective, students must already know the song. After selecting a familiar song (*Row, Row, Row Your Boat*), you may try this sample first experience in presenting a secret song to students of any age.

SCENARIO   **PRESENTING A SECRET SONG**

"I have a secret song in my hands. I am going to sing the song in my head and let my hand tap it as I sing it. If you think you know what it is, don't tell anyone. Keep it a secret. Hold your hands still and your lips closed so you can listen." Ms. Rouse began tapping the rhythm to the song *Row, Row, Row Your Boat* on her palm, making sure to tap as musically as possible to capture the flow and spirit of the song. Some students began singing and tapping with her.

Wanting to emphasize students' challenge to listen, Ms. Rouse responded by saying, "Oops! Some of you forgot that you were only listening for the secret. Put it back inside you and listen again.

"Raise your hand if you think you know what song was in my hands or if you heard a song in your head." Several children raised their hands eagerly. Ms. Rouse continued the challenge by asking children to check their ideas. "Let's listen again, and if you think you know the song, sing the song in your inner hearing and check to see if it fits what my hands are singing. Be sure to check the song all the way through." Ms. Rouse tapped the song again. With each repetition of the secret song, she sang a "ready, sing" preparation, then put the song in her inner hearing as she tapped.

"Are you able to match the words to the song you are hearing with the song my hand is tapping? You can let your lips sing the words to your song as you listen to my hand tapping. That will give you some extra help matching the sounds of your idea to the song I am tapping." Children moved their lips to the words of the song they were hearing and listened as the teacher tapped the secret song again.

"Let's see what some of your ideas are. Raise your hand if you have an idea for what song you heard in my hands." Each individual with a raised hand was asked to share his or her idea, even after the correct answer was given. Because Ms. Rouse wanted the children to continue listening and checking, she gave no indication which answers were correct or incorrect.

"Well, we have some differing opinions. Let's check some ideas. Joey thinks the secret song is *Looby Loo*. Let's sing that song and check it with my song." Ms. Rouse gave the students a starting pitch and encouraged them to sing the song, then to lip-sing *Looby Loo* as they listened and watched her hands tapping the song. The group sang and checked each of the songs offered by the students. After each singing of a song idea, students put the song in their inner hearing as they listened to the teacher tap *Row, Row, Row Your Boat*.

As Ms. Rouse continued to keep her song secret, she listened and watched for students' decisions on whether the song fit what her hands were tapping. Study continued as time and student focus permitted.

"You all think the secret song is *Row, Row, Row Your Boat*? Are you sure? You'd better check it once more. Sing that song in your inner hearing. Here comes the secret song again."

PRINCIPLE 1

PRINCIPLE 2

▶ Why might it be worth your time to allow each student to say what he or she thinks the secret song is?

▶ What happens for a student when he or she is encouraged to voice an opinion, even if it is the same as someone else's?

The emphasis in exploring secret songs is on allowing students to say what they think, know, or hear and on simply accepting their answers without overt evaluation.

Acting with mild surprise or intrigue at *each* answer to "What is the secret song?" maintains the attitude of the secret and sets the tone for playful study. Accept words from a song in addition to titles of songs. You may probe further by asking, "The song about the rabbit? Do you remember any words of the song?" By not giving away or accepting the first correct answer, the teacher intends to encourage students to check, explore, and recheck their ideas. (See "Eliciting and Accepting Students' Responses" in Chapter 7.) This strategy also allows those who have not yet figured out the puzzle to have more opportunities to do so through repeated hearings of the song yet with new clues given by class members' responses.

Presentation Modes for Secret Songs

The specific way in which the secret song is presented can fall into one of three categories or combinations of these: nonnotation, nonconventional notation, and conventional notation. Because the rhythm is dictated by the word combinations of a song, it is much more song-specific than beat. Unless you are purposely demonstrating the difference between rhythm and beat, use the rhythm pattern rather than the beat to present a secret song. (See the Glossary for any unfamiliar terms in this chart.)

PRESENTATION MODES FOR SECRET SONGS

Nonnotation Presentations
1. Tap or chin the rhythm.
2. Show the melody by moving a flat hand up and down with the interval relationships.
3. Use Curwen hand signs..
4. Perform the rhythm on a nonpitched instrument (wood block, drum, rhythm sticks).
5. Perform the rhythm on a pitched instrument (xylophone, piano, tone bell), using only one note (no melody).
6. Perform the song on a pitched instrument, including rhythm and melody.
7. Act out the game activity or the meaning of the words of a song.
8. Offer verbal puzzles: "I'm thinking of a song about something that is always above us . . . That we can never touch . . . That we can only see at certain times." (*Twinkle, Twinkle, Little Star*)

Nonconventional Notation Presentations
1. A prepared song map showing the structure or selected places (repeated phrases, cadence movement, or rhythm) in the song.
2. An ideograph.
3. Song dots showing phrases and/or relative spacing of faster and slower notes.
4. A melody graph.
5. A drawing of the meaning or special words in the song. This can be shown all at once or drawn in phases as clues (drawing a lane, then a man, then a muffin to show *Muffin Man*).

Conventional Notation Presentations
1. The solfège score.
2. The rhythm score.
3. The beat score with rests as clues.
4. Melody only on staff (no rhythms).
5. Melody and rhythms on staff.

Giving Clues to Secret Songs

PRINCIPLE 2

Giving and getting slight clues during the process of figuring out a secret song can be an enjoyable experience for you and your students. In some classes, clue-giving has become a game in itself as students creatively and musically select strategic ways to offer more information about the secret song.

For example, when you have presented the secret song *Row, Row, Row Your Boat* by tapping it and a student has whispered the correct answer to you, encourage him or her give a visual clue for the class. The student may decide to act out "row" each time it is sung as you continue to tap the rhythm pattern. Of course, that clue will probably give away the secret immediately. If, however, the student decides to act out "stream," "merrily," or "dream" when your tapping comes to those words, the intrigue and the motivation to continue listening may build.

You can make clue-giving progressive by adding clues one at a time to your (or a student's) initial presentation of the secret song. Clue-giving can also be a group activity that challenges a group to select a secret song, decide on the clues, coordinate all clues with the inner singing and hearing of the song, and present them to the class.

Students can become very skillful in offering visual and auditory clues.

- They *coordinate* their clues with a specific phrase or individual sound from the song.
- They *pace* their demonstrations to match the song and other students' clues.
- They repeatedly *listen* to the secret song in their inner hearing.

Although the *play* of clue-giving for secret songs may appear to be simply fun, the rewards in student achievement through creativity, cooperation, motivation, sound analysis, refined listening, auditory tracking, dramatic interpretation, and collaborative efforts can justify the time invested in this activity.

Teaching Part Singing and Part Listening

Part singing refers to singing in harmony. As opposed to **unison singing,** in which everyone sings the same pitch at the same time, part singing may have groups singing the same song at different times, two different songs, a repeated pattern in one group and a song in the other, or a melody with accompanying lines that blend in harmony.

PRINCIPLE 5

Before beginning a part-singing activity, it is important to consider *why* you are offering children this experience. Youth-camp singing in a bus or around a fire, wherein one group tries to outshout the other, is not what we are after for a musical experience. Instead, we have three musical goals for part singing:

- *Making music* by experiencing two (or more) -part harmony
- *Singing interdependently* by performing a melody while a different melody is being sung
- *Listening* to the other parts while singing a different song or part

Part singing that emphasizes listening and musical qualities will encourage *interdependent* singing. Individuals will be singing in relation to other singers, not in opposition to them. If attention is not paid to the quality of singing and focused listening, poor part-singing habits often result.

▶ Have you had an experience in part singing? Reflect on and describe the level of satisfaction you remember from that experience.

Partner Songs, Rounds, and Ostinati

There are three primary ways to introduce part singing to our students: partner songs, rounds, and ostinati. *Partner songs* are two songs (or more) that sound pleasant when they are sung at the same time. Most pentatonic songs work well as partner songs with other pentatonic songs. Pentatonic songs contain only DO, RE, MI, SO, and LA. (FA and TI are absent or in unimportant positions.) A *round* is a song sung by two or more groups starting at different times. A *canon* is similar to a round, but it has a devised ending. A round has no established ending. An *ostinato* is a pattern that repeats throughout a song, as an accompaniment. Ostinato patterns can be purely rhythmic (no melody) or melodic (rhythm and pitch) and can be described as getting stuck on a phrase.

▶ Some teachers believe the easiest way to introduce part singing is through partner songs. Do you agree? What have you noticed?

▶ Why might partner songs be easier for children to sing and to listen to than either rounds or ostinati?

Which songs will work well as partner songs? Which ostinato will work and which will not? Which songs will work as rounds? The answers to these questions are found in experience, exploration, and information. Sometimes you will not know how a part-singing activity will sound until you try it, so allow your students to experiment with the possibilities. The following tips may help prepare for leading part singing and part listening.

Partner Songs (See box on next page.)

1. Check the beginning tones for each song or part. Are they all the same? If not, practice hearing and singing each starting tone so that you can help a group begin on the proper tone. Challenge students to hear and sing the starting tones for each partner song. (See chart on Sample Partner Songs.)

2. Is the song that you are singing pentatonic? A pentatonic song partners well with another pentatonic song.

3. Check for anacruses (see Chapter 6). If a song begins with an anacrusis, be aware that one group may need to begin slightly ahead of the other for partner songs.

4. One song may need to be sung much more slowly than normal in order to match the tempo of the partner song.

5. Partner songs seem to be most compatible when they have the same meter signature.

Rounds

1. Check the beginning tones for each song entrance. Practice hearing and singing each starting tone so that you can help a group begin on the proper tone.

2. Is the song that you are singing pentatonic? Pentatonic songs generally work well as rounds.

3. There are several ways to indicate where the second group should enter: Give them a gesture, specify a word to listen for, name a certain number of beats to wait. Avoid entrances that do not occur on the beat.

SAMPLE PARTNER SONGS

Partner songs that have echo structure, diatonic tonality, and duple beat divisions
   Mary's Wearing Her Red Dress
   Mary Had a Little Lamb
   Johnny, Get Your Hair Cut
   Muffin Man
   London Bridge

Partner songs that have short-short-long or balanced structure, pentatonic tonality, and duple beat divisions
   Circle Left
   Daddy Loves the Bear
   Hot Cross Buns
   I'm Going Downtown
   Scotland's Burning

Partner songs that have short-short-long or balanced structure, pentatonic tonality, and triple beat divisions
   A-Hunting We Will Go
   The Farmer in the Dell
   Sally Go 'Round the Sun
   Looby Loo

Partner songs that have short-short-long or balanced structure, diatonic tonality, and duple beat divisions
   Bluebird
   Old Brass Wagon
   Paw-Paw Patch
   Polly Put the Kettle On
   Roll That Brown Jug Down to Town
   Skip to My Lou
   Sing with Me

---

4. Rounds are often designated in music books, and the entrances are usually marked by numbers above the staff. Listening to a recording of groups singing rounds can help students appreciate the concept and the results of this strategy for part singing.

Sample Rounds   Suggestions for material to use in singing rounds include any pentatonic songs listed under Sample Partner Songs. Rounds and canons can be found in every past and current music series textbook for the elementary grades (publishers include Macmillan, Silver-Burdett, American Book Company, Holt Rinehart & Winston, and Allyn & Bacon) and in many collections of songs for children.

   Pentatonic: *Scotland's Burning, Circle Left, The Farmer in the Dell, Old House*

   Nonpentatonic: *Music Alone Shall Live, Viva La Musica, Let Us Sing Together*

Ostinati

1. Check the beginning tones for the song and the ostinato pattern. Are they all the same? If not, practice hearing and singing each starting tone so that you can help a group begin on the proper tone.

2. Is the song pentatonic? Pentatonic songs work well with a wide variety of pentatonic ostinati.

3. Check for anacruses that begin the song or the phrase used as an ostinato. If an anacrusis is present, be aware that one group may need to begin slightly ahead of the other.

4. If it can be repeated easily, an ostinato can be selected and performed by using the cadence chunk of a diatonic song, any chunk of a pentatonic song, or any phrase of a round. (See "Phrases and Song Chunks," in Chapter 6).

Sample Ostinati   Suggestions include any phrase or chunk from the pentatonic songs listed in Sample Partner Songs or Sample Rounds.

SONG	OSTINATO PATTERN
Circle Left	Shake those fingers down
I'm Going Downtown	To show my friends around
A-Hunting We Will Go	And then we'll let him go
Uncle Joe	Don't mind the weather

The following procedure may help your students to be successful in singing ostinati with songs.

1. Group 1 and Group 2 sing the song *A-Hunting We Will Go.*

2. When the singers come to the cadence chunk "and then we'll let him go," challenge Group 2 to get "stuck" on that chunk, repeating it over and over, as Group 1 sings the song again. Challenge students in Group 2 to listen to Group 1 to know when to stop singing.

Ostinati can be performed on classroom instruments as well as sung. Rhythm ostinati can be performed with rhythm instruments (sticks, simple shakers, claves, drums, and tone blocks), body percussion (clapping, snapping, clicking, tapping), and nontraditional sound-making devices (zippers, keys, coins, forks, pots, whisk brooms, combs). Melodic ostinati can be performed on tone bells, barred instruments (xylophones, metallophones, glockenspiels), and other pitched instruments (recorders, piano, kalimbas). To focus listening is a challenge when using instruments, but, just as in part singing, listening challenges can give musical shape to the experience and structure the behaviors of the students.

Challenge your students to suggest songs to try as partners, patterns to try as ostinati, and songs to try as rounds. Then allow them to make decisions about how interesting or compatible the songs sounded.

Beginning Part Singing and Part Listening

To be successful in accomplishing the first two goals of part singing—making music and singing interdependently—children must know the selected song very well and be able to sing it without your help.

▶ Have students had adequate repetitions of the song so that they can sing it without you?

▶ Do they sing with an energetic yet light sound?

Once students know the song well, emphasize the third goal of part singing—listening.

Young students do not necessarily have the same musical expectations as adults for something sounding "good." Be sure to allow and accept their explorations of songs and sounds.

1. The class sings a familiar song—for example, *Hot Cross Buns.*

2. As students repeat the song, challenge, "This time I am going to sing something different. Let's see if you can sing your song, listen to me, and not get mixed up."

3. As students sing *Hot Cross Buns*, sing *Scotland's Burning* at the same time. Be sure not to oversing. Sing energetically enough that they can hear you but lightly enough that they must listen.

PRINCIPLE 2

4. When the songs end, ask students to describe what they heard. "What was I singing?" "What did you hear?" Accept all answers without indicating agreement or disagreement.

PRINCIPLE 3

5. "Let's do the same thing and you can check out your ideas as you sing and listen this time. Be sure to sing *and* listen."

6. "What song did you hear?" "Could you hear *every* word I sang?" "Yes, I was singing *Scotland's Burning*." These questions encourage children to listen as they sing. Several repetitions may be necessary for children to adjust to listening and singing.

7. "Let's see if I can offer you a puzzle. I may sing different words to part of the song this time. When we finish singing, I'll ask you if you heard any new words." Change the words for one place in the song, for example, sing "smoke" instead of "fire," "singing" instead of "burning," or "milkshakes" instead of "water." Again, the emphasis is on motivating students to listen as they sing by setting up achievable, interesting challenges. This step of the process can be elaborated into a variety of versions of the song, as long as the play engages students' attention. Other puzzles to encourage listening could include simple changes made by repeating a part of the song, leaving out part of the song, or clapping a portion of the song.

8. Gradually, ask students in different parts of the room to sing *Scotland's Burning* with you. "Let's have Mark, Michelle, Jim, and Willie sing with me this time. Be sure you can hear our song all the way through as you sing yours." As you add more students to *Scotland's Burning*, continue to challenge students to listen. Remove your voice as soon as students can sing on their own. These same or similar steps can be followed in introducing ostinati and rounds.

When they achieve musicality, help students relish the beauty of the sound they are creating. Perhaps more than in any other singing venture, quality and sensitivity to volume can easily deteriorate during part-singing activities. By suggesting that they sing with more energy rather than singing louder, you will remind students to support their voices with breath energy rather than to sing with a louder, heavier sound.

PRINCIPLE 1

PRINCIPLE 2

Challenge sections to match other sections in volume. "Let's see if you can listen to the other section for the entire time you are singing. Sing so you can hear the other group." Approach part singing as a cooperative effort, not a competition. Using terms such as "section" and "part" rather than "team" and "group" may help to avoid the idea of competition in singing and may help to give a sense of ensemble from the earliest part-singing experiences.

Encouraging Part Listening

A common practice is to divide students equally between or among parts for part singing, but this practice need not be a priority. By focusing on imbalanced parts, students must try harder to hear each part. Whether you are singing rounds, ostinati, or partner songs, the following divisions can be enjoyable, challenging, and educational.

PART 1	PART 2
Teacher	Class
Teacher + a few students	Remainder of class
Row 3	Rows 1 and 2
One partner	Other partner
Half of class	Other half of class
Students wearing jeans	Students not wearing jeans

PRINCIPLE 2

Questions and additional challenges can enrich students' appreciation of, skills in, and understanding of the part-singing experience. Sample challenges for listening and describing can include the following:

- Students describe the effects of various part-singing combinations. They practice using appropriate musical terminology to describe their ideas: consonance, dissonance, dynamics, contrast, unison, and so on.

- Students listen for places in their parts where they sing the same word or tones. They get stuck on that word or tone, sustaining that one pitch or singing the rest of the words on that single pitch to complete the song.

- Students switch songs or parts when they sing a certain word or when the teacher or another student gives them a signal (clap, gesture).

LEADING SINGING: SIX SIMPLE REMINDERS

Range:	Choose a starting pitch that is somewhat higher than the pitch of your speaking voice. Use the focus-pitch-gesture-listen sequence for starting a song. As you listen to students sing, decide if the pitch you have chosen is too high or too low for their range. Make any necessary adjustments for the next singing of the song.
Singing:	Use a light, lifted singing voice. Breath energy will help keep your voice light and airy (in contrast to heavy and raucous) as a good model for children's voices. Be careful not to overpower students' voices as you sing with them.
Tempo:	Be aware of the tempo that best maintains the spirit of the song. Choose a tempo that is neither too fast for clear enunciation nor too slow for efficient vocal production.
Movement:	Movement to a song should *accompany,* not *govern,* the musical flow. Be cautious about movement that is heavy or mechanical, causing the song to sound the same way.
Language:	Choose songs that preserve rather than distort natural pronunciations, inflections, and rhythms of the English language. When inserting words into a song, be sure to listen for the least distorting way to set the words to the music.
Communication:	Be aware of the message your eyes, facial expression, posture, and gestures give to students as you lead them in singing. Do you appear interested in what students are doing? Do you appear interested in what *you* are doing? Are you communicating the allure of the song to capture students' attention and to help them value the music?

(Adapted from Bennett 1990b)

- Students offer suggestions for tempo and dynamic variations. Use appropriate symbols and terms, if the context warrants it, to describe students' arrangement of the part-singing experience. Aim for musicality and beauty, and help students recognize these dimensions of their music making.

- Students use neutral syllables (*oo, ah, mm, bum, dee,* and so on) for one part to contrast with words. Also sing neutral syllables with both parts so that students can hear the harmony (the combinations of sounds) more clearly.

Chapter Epilogue

Each time you plan to sing a song with students, keep in mind the purpose for the song, the monitoring process by which you will observe students' responses, the repetitions of the song that you will provide for students, and the vitality with which you present the song and lead the activity. The following four perspectives will guide your success in teaching and singing songs.

- Purpose: Give students a challenge or focus so that they attend to the song. Give them something to listen for or a problem to solve that requires listening. Reasons to sing the song again include the opportunity to sing a student's name, to have more turns, to use student contributions, to listen more closely to patterns, and to reexperience the enjoyment of singing.

PRINCIPLE 6

- Monitor: Keep track of how the students are doing. Are they singing the correct words, melody, rhythm? Are they matching their movements to the music? What are you hearing in their voices? Are they able to sing the song independently of you or other students?

PRINCIPLE 2

- Repetition and variation: We need to hear songs more than once to learn them, and there is always more to learn about a given song. If a song does not stand repeating, it may not be a very good song. Movement activities, opportunities for student contributions, and study challenges are ways to provide for the repetition that is sometimes needed to learn a song well, without introducing a numbing monotony.

    Consider the amount of information that children must process when a song activity is presented to them: words, tune, actions, challenges, and so on. With more information, simpler challenges may be appropriate. For example, *If You're Happy and You Know It* can easily be extended for younger children by keeping all the words the same, except for those that describe the changing action—"Clap your hands," "Nod your head," and so on. This challenge maintains sameness yet introduces difference in the changing motion. Slight variations may intrigue and challenge younger children, but older children often appreciate greater variation. In both cases, however, the suitability of the task depends on the children, their experience, and the purpose of the activity.

    Select variations and challenges that support or are at least compatible with the musical experience. Note that when it is the adult who is responsible for leading an activity, the adult's need for change can take precedence over the child's desire to keep it the same. Be sensitive to the children's level of experience and ability.

Sometimes singing a song, enjoying a song, and making music is the purpose. Singing a song and participating in musical activity can be a beautiful and fulfilling experience. Too much variation can distract us from this purpose and experience.

PRINCIPLE 2

Vitality: By now, it is clear that we believe that an effective and constructive way to teach songs is to maintain the vitality of the singing and song-study experiences. Students become intrigued about the songs they are being asked to sing and study. Their attention is captured and their curiosity is cultivated through playful strategies for engaging their participation and imagination. These goals are of paramount importance for keeping music alive for our students.

Learning about Voices

4

Developing Vocal Awareness

Have you ever thought about your voice? Most of us use our voices every day of our lives, yet we spend little time thinking about them. In fact, it may not be until you have lost your voice that you become aware of it. Commonly referred to as *laryngitis*, losing your voice can serve as a reminder to appreciate your voice and to maintain your vocal health. You can begin the journey of vocal discovery and awareness by listening to voices in all varieties of settings, situations, and contexts. Track what you hear and how you react to what you hear in voices.

▶ List the varieties of ways in which you use your voice during a day. Include the simple, personal activities as well as those that might be more obvious.

▶ Do you notice that your voice does not always sound the same? Are you aware of how your voice sounds in any given situation?

▶ Can you think of a situation in which your voice did not work the way you wanted it to? Or has your voice ever not sounded the way you wanted it to?

▶ Are there times when you can control your voice? Are there times when you cannot?

▶ When are you most confident with your voice?

▶ Do some people have voices that make you want to avoid them? Describe their voices.

▶ Do some people have voices that draw you to them? Describe their voices.

▶ Have you ever correctly detected a person's mood or physical well-being by hearing his or her voice?

▶ Have you ever incorrectly detected a person's mood or physical well-being by hearing his or her voice?

If you want efficient and expressive (or interesting) use of your voice, you cannot take it for granted. By finding out even a little bit about how the voice works and by learning how to care for it, you can maximize the potential of this wonderfully flexible and resilient instrument.

Vocal awareness is critically important for teachers. The ways in which we use our voices and the ways in which we respond to voices shape our classroom environments and our professional interactions. There are three primary reasons that teachers' vocal awareness is important: our position as *vocal models*, the *effects* of our voices on listeners, and our *vocal health*.

Vocal Models

Have you noticed yourself beginning to sound like the person with whom you are speaking? For some of us, it is easy to adopt unknowingly the vocal sounds and speech patterns of those with whom we are communicating. Whether we know it or not and whether we want to be or not, each of us is a *vocal model* for those around us, including our students.

PRINCIPLE 3

For teachers and parents, the idea of being a vocal model is especially important. Recognizing the importance of this role suggests that we maintain proper vocal health and proper vocal use. Speaking and singing with adequate breath energy, appropriate vocal placement, and relative variations in pitch, pace, and volume give us a solid foundation on which to stand as vocal models.

Vocal Effect

We use our voices to produce certain effects on or reactions in our listeners. By moderating the pace, pitch, volume, and inflection of the voice, we communicate not only through our words but also through the sounds of our voices.

PRINCIPLE 2

- ▶ Would you use your voice differently if you were reading a story to your second-grade class than if you were having a conference with your principal?
- ▶ Is the voice you use to silence a cafeteria full of children different from the voice you use to greet your students at the door of your classroom?
- ▶ If you were to console a child who was upset, how would your voice sound?
- ▶ If you were to demand the attention of a child who was being defiant, how would your voice sound?

Although the voice does not change each time it is used in a different way, the effect it has on others can change. Becoming aware of the effects our voices have on others and the effects that others' voices have on us is a first step toward vocal awareness and control.

Vocal Health

Depending on the extent to which you rely on your voice during daily routines, developing laryngitis or other vocal problems can have a profound impact on your quality of life and even your livelihood. Imagine a clerk, a bank teller, a telephone receptionist, or a teacher having chronic hoarseness or laryngitis. Our voices are expected to produce under a variety of demands, conditions, and functions. We expect our voices to carry us through numerous endurance tests, sometimes with little or no thought to the conditioning that is essential to proper health and performance. Constant use of our voices, hour after hour, day after day, could qualify us to be vocal marathoners. Such constant and extensive vocal use demands the best preventive practices.

If your teaching position requires you to talk or sing constantly, take opportunities during the day to give your voice a rest. There are times before class, during class, and after class when, with proper planning, you can rest your voice and recuperate from vocal fatigue. Listening rather than talking during lunchtime and during singing activities can provide needed relief. Informing students or colleagues that you are resting your voice can help them appreciate your quietness or silence. When you take care of yourself in this way, you also help others learn how to take care of their own vocal health.

What <u>Is</u> a Voice?

Not long ago, elementary schoolchildren were taught that they had two *vocal cords* that stretched like rubber bands across their voice box. The vibrations of those band-like cords caused vocal sound. For some, the image of those rubber bands twanging around inside their throats conjured up the possibility of one of them stretching to the breaking point. What if a vocal cord broke?

When technological development made it possible to use the laryngoscope to view the throat, voice scientists discovered how voices work. We do not have vocal *cords;* instead, we have what can be described better as **vocal folds:** folds of tissue that are connected to the left and right sides of the *larynx,* the organ of the voice, or the voice box. These folds separate when we inhale (to allow air to flow through the passage) and come together when we speak or sing. A complex set of internal and external muscles, exhaled air, and the rippling, wavelike motions of the vocal folds combine to produce vibrations that are the sound waves of our voice. So, from this perspective, a voice is a combination of muscle and breath flow.

In the sound-making process, the two folds collide during the rippling. You may have heard that when an orchestra tunes, each instrument tries to match the oboe's "A" pitch. That "A" vibrates at 440 cycles per second and is called "A440." The number of times our vocal folds collide to produce a pitch is the same as the number of vibrations per second. So, when we sing A440, the A above middle C on the piano, our vocal folds are colliding 440 times per second. The intensity of this process varies with the amount of pressure used in bringing the folds together.

Can you imagine what would happen to your hands if they collided (rubbed or clapped) 440 times per second for a period of time (Thurman and Welch 1991)? For vocal folds to endure, they must be lubricated properly. A thin coating of mucus flows over the folds and acts as a lubricant to protect the tissue. The effectiveness of the thin, watery mucus depends on adequate hydration, which comes from drinking adequate amounts of liquid, especially water. Dehydration causes the mucus to become thick and sticky and can result in inflammation and irritation of the tissue. Hoarseness or laryngitis can result.

For the sound that we call a voice to result from the activity of the vocal folds, there must be a *resonating chamber,* just like the hollowed and shaped body of a guitar. Although to some extent, the whole body serves as a resonating chamber for the voice, the primary vessel for producing a particular vocal quality is the vocal tract: the larynx, throat, and mouth. The sound is made stronger or weaker according to the qualities of this tract. The physical differences among individuals' bodies define this resonating chamber and contribute to the uniqueness of each person's voice quality.

In addition to the physical factors of muscle, breath, lubrication, and resonation, voices include regional accents, dialects, and colloquialisms. As you might have seen in the movie and play *My Fair Lady,* it is possible for some people to recognize a person's place of origin by listening to his or her speech patterns. Have you heard an interview on the radio or television in which the person speaking had an accent or a speech pattern that you recognize?

As Morton Cooper stated in his 1984 book, *Change Your Voice, Change Your Life,* our voices are as unique to us as our fingerprints. The combination of physical factors and speech patterns gives that uniqueness. Through years of using our voices in certain ways, we develop a range of vocal habits. Without compromising the identity of our voices, we want to take a look at the relative helpfulness of those vocal habits.

Developing Good Vocal Habits

The Habitual Voice

At any age, we can develop vocal habits that are constructive or destructive to vocal health. Sometimes early participation in activities such as cheerleading, theater, or debate can lead to vocal habits of which we are not aware. Sometimes vocal habits come from trying to sound a certain way: like a parent, a favorite actor, or a teacher. Certain physical ailments can contribute to vocal habits: continual throat clearing, chronic coughing, or asthmatic conditions.

Aiming for natural vocal production is not as simple as it might seem. The term "natural" applied to vocal production suggests speaking and singing with ease, making an effortless sound, and doing something that feels natural precisely because we do not feel it. Finding and using your *natural voice*, however, can become complicated when you use those criteria, because your *habitual voice* may not be your natural one. How can you know the difference? Even though distinguishing between your natural and your habitual voice may be difficult, if you are aware of your vocal habits, then you can at least monitor your helpful and harmful practices (Cooper 1984).

Monitoring vocal habits is critical to teachers. Our voices are our most important tool in our classrooms. Imagine getting through a teaching day *without* the use of your voice! Identifying the practices that can interfere with proper vocal use and production can enhance our voices and, for some of us, save our careers. To that end, the following suggestions are offered to build healthy habits and to avoid harmful ones.

Vocal Warm-ups

Just as gentle stretches prepare our muscles for jogging, an aerobic workout, or any other physical exercise, vocal warm-ups prepare our voices for talking and singing. Vocal warm-ups can be helpful to all of us for several reasons.

- They can be done by teachers and students, in groups or individually.
- They can be done in preparation for a day of speaking or a class of singing.
- They can be done in the middle of a class or as an exercise when students' vocal production indicates that voices need relaxation, stretching, or attention to coordination.
- They can be done to relieve tensions in our bodies and our voices, to remedy vocal fatigue or vocal overuse.
- They can be done to give our vocal habits a tune-up in the middle of a day.

Experiment with the following vocal warm-ups and exercises. To get the proper benefit from them, do them gently, with attention to slow, smooth movements and continued deep, relaxed breathing throughout.

BODY RELAXATION

1. Standing or sitting, gently roll your head toward one shoulder without lifting either shoulder. Then slowly move your head in an arc, rolling it toward the

chest and toward the other shoulder. Repeat this gentle forward head roll several times, letting your chin fall slowly to your chest. Avoid pushing your head back.

2. Lift and lower your arms slowly, to your sides and in front, inhaling as you lift, exhaling as you lower your arms.

3. Rotate your shoulders by circling them forward, up, back, and forward again. After a few rotations, reverse the direction, aiming for flexibility and freedom of movement.

4. With feet about shoulder-width apart and knees slightly bent, pull your stomach in and round your back as you bend forward from the waist. Relax your upper body in a "rag doll" position, then slowly lift your upper body, gradually lengthening your spine until your sense of tallness extends from your toes through the top of your head.

BREATH STREAM AND BREATH ENERGY

1. Let air in as if you are yawning, relaxing your face, nostrils, and throat as you do so. For some, the phrase "take a breath" rather than "let the air in" implies too forceful an activity and may involve constricting the throat.

2. Sigh with a breathy quality, letting the air flow from you in a gentle, sustained stream. Feel the breath energy that you are generating.

3. Add a hiss or "ss" sound to your sigh as you release and sustain the airflow. You can also add a rolled "r" or a tongue flutter to help check your ability to sustain your released airflow.

4. Add your voice to the breath stream by gently sighing and saying "oo," "ah," or "hoo," and let it glide on your airflow. Notice how your breath carries your voice as you practice breath energy with these *sigh glides*. After doing the initial sigh glides, let your voice fall then rise in pitch. Explore and experiment with your sigh glides by gently extending your voice to higher and lower parts of its range (Thurman and Welch 1991).

5. Now add words and continue your sigh glides: "Well," "Hi," "What are you doing?" and so on. Aim to maintain the breath energy, relaxation, posture, and airflow to carry your voice that you established in other breath-stream exercises. Sense your voice as it glides up and down while you say these words and phrases.

VOCAL PRODUCTION

1. Experiment with a balance of muscle and breath in vocal production. Consider a continuum that at one end is purely muscle and at the other is purely breath. Neither total muscle nor total breath creates sound. As you move vocal production from the muscle side toward the center, you will gradually add breath to the muscle effort. Likewise, moving toward the center from the breath side gradually adds slight vocal sounds to the air flow. Ideally, we project vocal sounds that have a balance of breath and muscle (Thurman and Welch 1991).

Continuum of Breath and Muscle

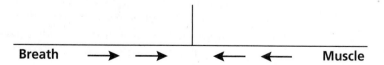

Knowing the continuum of breath and muscle balance and being able to shift your vocal production along the continuum are valuable in monitoring healthy vocal production. Especially in times of vocal fatigue or stress, moving toward the breathy side of the continuum can rescue your voice.

2. Give yourself a "voice lift" (Cooper 1984). Practice lifting the placement of your voice by experimenting with the "mm-hm" response that generally signals agreement. Place one hand on your chest and the other in the area of your cheeks and nose. As you say "mm-hm" several times, can you feel the resonance of your voice shift from your chest to your face? You may need to sustain the sound on each syllable to feel the placement shift. The higher placement, when you can feel your voice resonance in your cheeks and nose, is the **lifted voice,** sometimes called the **head voice** or the *upper register.* The lower placement is called the **chest voice** or the *lower register.*

3. Using a lifted voice supported by breath energy, begin speaking greetings, poems, or words to songs to establish healthy habits for vocal production. Aim for a breathy sound rather than a nasal sound. This may seem like extra effort and may not feel easy or efficient. If that is the case, the reason may be not that you are producing sound improperly but that these are new, and consequently effortful, habits of vocal production. It may also be that you are not accustomed to using breath energy to carry your voice, so that this additional support may feel like effort to you in the beginning. If you are not accustomed to using your voice in this higher placement, you may also initially respond negatively to the way it sounds to you.

Releasing Tension

Tension builds in our voices as we sing and speak. For that reason, consider doing activities that will release tension and will give your vocal muscles a chance to recover from the physical strain placed on them. The warm-ups described earlier can be used to release tension in the middle of the day, at the end of the day, or whenever you feel vocal strain. Use activities like these also to cool the voice down after extensive use.

Voice Education for Students

PRINCIPLE 1

Many of us avoid mentioning anything about voices rather than risk saying or doing something that could make a child or *anyone* feel embarrassed. Everyone has heard stories of the adult whose singing life was stunted in childhood by an insulting remark or an action that signaled "You can't sing." Some of us can claim to be the main character in one of those stories.

A voice is not something we can see. Unlike a piano, a clarinet, or a drum, we cannot hold one out in front of us and say, "This needs some polish," "It may be time to buy a new one," or "This thing sure isn't working right." Our voices are inside us. Because our voices represent how we communicate, how we are identified, and how we are unique from everyone else, our voices seem as if they *are* us.

When something is said about our voice, we may feel as if it is being said about us. Our voices are so personal to us that there may be no easy way to separate them from our selves. This separation is exactly what we are after, however, in working toward voice education. Differentiating between self and voice can help us treat voices as

AIMING FOR VOCAL HEALTH

POSTURE

Cultivate
- A tall alignment of the body for both sitting and standing by lengthening the spine.
- A lifted rib cage, shoulders down, jaw not too high or too low.

Avoid
- Any tension created by a straight, rigid posture.
- A sunken chest with shoulders forward and jaw hyperextended.

BREATH ENERGY AND MUSCLE

Cultivate
- Supporting your voice with breath energy and airflow.
- The balance of breath and muscle in vocal production.
- Using more breath when your voice is tired.

Avoid
- Forcing your voice with muscle and inadequate breath.
- Loud whispering with an already hoarse voice.
- Speaking in quiet tones with a lack of breath energy—for example, talking on the phone with a fatigued sound.

VOICE USE

Cultivate
- Variety in pitch, placement, pace, loudness.
- Teaching strategies that allow vocal rest. Use nonverbal attention-getters, and schedule periods of silence.
- Warm-ups before extended voice use: sigh glides, breathing, hissing, tongue flutters, or buzzing with lips.

Avoid
- Excessive coughing, raucous laughter, throat clearing.
- Shouting or talking over loud backgrounds: recess, cafeteria, music ensembles.
- Overuse in singing or speaking: too loud, too soft, too high, too low, too long.

GENERAL HEALTH

Cultivate
- Drinking adequate amounts of water: 8 glasses daily; urine should be pale. Do not rely on thirst for drinking liquids.
- Proper nutrition and exercise.

Avoid
- Antihistamines and conditions that dry your voice and your environment.
- Smoking.
- Large amounts of alcohol and caffeine: These are diuretics that dehydrate your body.
- Touching your face with your hands: Germs and viruses are easily spread to the mouth, eyes, and nose.

instruments that deserve our care, our attention, our purposeful development, and, sometimes, our humor. We can maintain the distinction between our students and their voices by the way we talk about their voices. Imagine your reactions if each of the statements at the top of the following page were directed to you.

Is there ever a good reason to say to another person, especially a child, "You can't sing!"? We think not (Bennett 1991b). But how do you talk about voices and work with voices without embarrassing students and without inhibiting their motivation to sing?

PRINCIPLE 2

PRINCIPLE 6

PRINCIPLE 5

PRINCIPLE 1

COMMENTING ON VOICES	
Person Focus	**Voice Focus**
"You sound a little tired today."	"Your voice sounds a little tired today."
"You don't seem to be able to sing those notes."	"Those notes seem to be difficult for your voice to sing."
"You need to be quiet now."	"Your voices need to be quiet now."
"Are you ready to sing?"	"Is your voice ready to sing?"
"I didn't know you could do that!"	"I didn't know your voice could do that!"
"Give us a challenge."	"Give our voices a challenge."
"See what you can do."	"See what your voice can do."
"You sounded better today."	"Your voice sounded better today."

Issues in Voice Education

Depending on the singing backgrounds of your students and your own experience with and confidence about singing, you may encounter a wide variety of responses in voice education activities. The following suggestions may help guide you in providing satisfying and enjoyable voice education for your students. Remember, you are the expert in your classroom, and you become an expert by being an active observer of and listener to your students' needs. The most effective strategies will be those that are compatible with your principles. Looking back at Chapter 2 and the discussions of principles, consider how your principles will guide your work with students' voices.

High and Low

The terms "high" and "low," staples in music education, can be confusing to children. The highness and lowness of pitch in music actually refers to the relative placement of notes on the staff; it is a visual image and a metaphorical description of the pitch continuum. There is nothing about our vocal production of high or low sounds that makes them higher or lower; they are actually faster and slower vibrations (Bennett, 1986a).

Thinking "That's a high note I have to sing there; I'd better reach for it" can be counterproductive vocally because reaching for high notes and low notes can induce tension and strain. The effort used to reach high or low tones can cause the vocal mechanism to constrict, so that a person *can't* sing them. Gestures that show outward and downward movement as voices rise in pitch can help to counteract this tendency (Langness 1991b). Images of lightness, energy, and buoyancy can help reduce the effort it takes to sing.

In everyday language, we say, "Turn up the radio," "Turn down the television," and "Lower your voice." High and low are often confused with loud and soft. Be aware of this confusion as you work with voices, and be consistent in use of the terms "high" and "low." Help students clarify these terms by having their voices demonstrate high, quiet sounds as well as low, loud sounds.

Volunteering for Turns and Practice Turns

Although we generally think that allowing students to volunteer for a turn is a courtesy, volunteering can sometimes be more intimidating than being called upon. Peer awareness often makes students, especially older ones, hesitant to volunteer for classroom tasks and activities. In voice education activities, calling on a student matter-of-factly, as if a response is expected rather than requested or demanded, can let a student "off the hook" in front of his or her peers. "Michael, let's hear your voice do that." "Let's listen as Amy takes a turn with her voice."

Before we risk showing others something we can do, many of us like to have a practice turn. Offering students practice turns during their vocal explorations can encourage them to respond and can enliven the activity. All students can take practice turns at once, or the class can take practice turns by sections. Other alternatives for practice turns involve closing eyes and facing away from the group.

Laughter and Voice Education

Voice exploration activities can elicit much laughter and delight. We often react with laughter when we hear an unusual sound, are surprised by a voice, or feel slightly embarrassed. When we are listening to and studying voices, however, this natural tendency to laugh can be a serious interference. Langness (1991a) recommends enlisting the students' help in monitoring their urge to laugh. Rather than scolding students for laughing, you can help them understand and use alternative ways to express their delight. "Why is it so comical for us to use and hear our voices like this? Sometimes, maybe we are just surprised or embarrassed. However, during voice study, if we laugh, a person may think we are laughing at him or her, and we don't want to do that."

Langness offers some specific ways to address the problem of laughter without making a rule that restricts students' responses.

> Let's monitor our urges to laugh. Think about what you can do to keep from laughing. I prefer that there would be no laughter. I could make a strict rule that there can be no laughter, but I know that someone will totally surprise us with a wonderful singing sound and we'll instantly laugh and cheer. So, if we laugh, I'll want to know, "What made us laugh that time?" You may discover some ways to control laughter. Let me know what works. (1991a, 43)

Let students know that with such intense listening to each voice during turns, laughing can cause us to miss a person's vocal contribution. We want students to concentrate on noticing how voices are working, on getting a certain sound from our voices, and on describing what our voices are doing. When we laugh, our voice muscles contract so much that it makes a big change in our vocal set.

Gestures

Arm and hand gestures can sometimes help voices make smooth transitions during vocal production. These gestures can show the movement of the voice or contribute to the freedom of vocal production. Gestures can suggest pitch, intensity, and direction of vocal *glissandos* (sliding through pitches in an upward or a downward direction) and sigh glides, and they can help students free their sound by letting outward gestures create the image of carrying their voice (Langness 1991a). To use gestures only to reflect rise and fall in pitch may limit their positive effect on students' voices. Think of gestures that go out, in, and around to reflect and elicit use of breath energy, rather than thinking of gestures solely as means to demonstrate the up and down motions of melodic contour.

Gestures are not always helpful. They can constrict neck and shoulder muscles, restrict breathing, and cause unwanted tensions. Notice when gestures for vocal glissandos or other activities may hinder your students' vocal production and when they may help.

What We Feel

Part of vocal awareness and discovery is noting the changes that occur in the voice when it produces various sounds. Rather than telling students what they should be feeling, it is important to encourage students to sense and describe what they are feeling in the vocal mechanism. Many of us are so accustomed to asking, "How do you feel?" that changing our wording to "What did you feel?" takes some practice. When students are asked, "How did that feel for your voice?" they will often answer, "Fine." If we consistently ask, "*What* did you feel in your voice?" we can help students begin to attend to how their voices are working. Beginning vocabulary may include terms such as little/big, loud/soft, easy/hard, quiet/noisy, and high/low.

Collection versus Correction

When we ask students what they feel and hear in their voices, we are collecting information from them that gives us a perspective on their vocal production. Those of us who have studied voice by taking private lessons and singing in choirs may be tempted to correct the terminology or the images that we hear in students' responses. Correction of responses can be counterproductive to vocal exploration and awareness. We want students to continue to explore, listen to, and describe voices.

> They [students] grow in their awareness of the sounds they hear; they realize that not everyone hears the same things or describes sound in the same way; and they expand their vocabulary of words and gestures for describing sound. (Langness 1991a, 42)

Observation versus Evaluation

How accustomed are you to making observations without evaluation? Emphasizing "what we hear" in voices rather than "what we like" about voices may take some practice. How we phrase questions is critical to students' learning to make observations rather than evaluations.

ELICITING OBSERVATION RATHER THAN EVALUATION

Elicits Evaluation	**Elicits Observation**
1. "How did his voice sound?"	1. "Describe what you heard in his voice."
2. "What did you think about her voice?"	2. "Tell us something you heard in her voice."
3. "How did that feel to you?"	3. "What did you feel that time?"

Constructive Terminology

The VoiceCare Network, a not-for-profit organization devoted to vocal health and development, encourages teachers to avoid using terms to describe voices that could be counterproductive to healthy, efficient vocal use. Terms such as "work," "try," "control," and "make" suggest effort, and their use in vocal education needs reevaluation. Terms such as "let," "allow," and "challenge" imply less aggressive efforts. Consider how you might rephrase these statements: "*Try* harder!" "*Make* your voice do that." "I need to hear your voices *working*." "You need to *control* that pitch" (Thurman and Welch 1991).

Matching Pitch

Matching pitch is matching the sound of your voice to the pitch produced by another person or an instrument. Although many of us match pitch with little effort or awareness, some children and adults find accomplishing this task to be a great challenge.

Pitch matching is not the isolated, clearly defined skill it may seem. There are physical and psychological dimensions to this skill. For almost everyone, pitch matching is dependent on context. Some match pitch effortlessly when singing in a group but are clueless when they are expected to match a single tone played on the piano. Others can match a pitch sung by a friend but cannot do it under testing conditions with a teacher. Successful pitch matching depends on the people we are with, the reasons we are trying to match pitch, and the specific requirements of the task. Changes in any one of those factors can have either a positive or a negative effect on a person's ability to match pitch (Goetze and Yoshiyuki 1988).

To match a given pitch, we must listen to the pitch, hear it in our inner hearing, let our vocal mechanism adjust to the appropriate placement, and coordinate breath and muscle to produce the pitch. Unless there is serious hearing damage (which is rare), matching pitch is more a function of ear–throat awareness and coordination than a function of the ear or the voice alone. For many adults and children, difficulty in matching pitch stems from a problem with this coordination. Remedial pitch-matching activities, therefore, should focus on freeing the voice from tension (both physical and psychological) and triggering the breath energy and ear–muscle coordinations required. Above all, people need to continue to use their voices to develop the vocal control necessary to matching pitch under varied conditions.

PRINCIPLE 1

PRINCIPLE 4

Exercises and teaching strategies that contribute to the freedom and coordination necessary to match pitch are those described in sections on vocal warm-ups, gestures, constructive terminology, phases for vocal awareness, and ways to discover voices. Avoid the narrowly focused expectation that a student should match a single, modeled pitch. More often than not, the command to "sing this pitch" creates tension and, therefore, constricts the vocal mechanism while at the same time doing little to help the voice gain the coordination and freedom necessary to sing the pitch. Phrases of songs, sigh glides, glissandos, speaking-voice imitations, and gestures can be spontaneous exercises that support voices in matching pitch.

Male Voices: Child and Adult

Sometimes young children have an easier time matching the speaking and singing voice of another child than that of an adult (Green 1990). An adult male's voice is normally an *octave* lower than an adult female's or a child's voice. When children try to sing with a man, they may have a difficult time learning a new song and finding what pitch to match. The lack of opportunity to sing with adult males is a major factor in this difficulty. When men sing in the children's register (an octave above the normal adult male register), children match pitch better than when the adult sings in a normal male register (Yarborough, Morrison, Karrick, and Dunn 1995). Children who have had extensive singing experience do not have as much trouble matching pitch with an adult male voice as do those who have not had much experience.

SCENARIO   CHILD AND ADULT MALE VOICES

Mrs. Thompson decided to try an experiment. "Boys and girls, I have invited Mr. Fowler to come in to class today to demonstrate some things about male voices. Most of you have seen Mr. Fowler in the halls and know that he is our new assistant principal.

"I have told Mr. Fowler that some of you boys are a bit confused about whether or not your voices should sound like a man's voice or a girl's voice. As I have explained before, up to a certain age—often around 13 to 15—boys' and girls' singing voices sound very much the same. It's not that boys sound like girls or that girls sound like boys; they all sound very similar, they have young voices.

"Listen to Mr. Fowler and me as we sing *Hot Cross Buns.* Tell me what you hear in our voices." The two adults sang together, and when they finished, students were asked to raise their hands if they could describe something they heard. "You sounded different." "He sang louder than you did." "You were higher."

"Yes, it can be easy to hear the differences between women's and men's voices, but it's not so easy to hear the difference in younger voices. Boys and girls, listen to Mr. Fowler try to make his voice match mine." The two adults sang, and Mr. Fowler tried to sing in falsetto voice. Many students laughed, but Mrs. Thompson quickly focused them on how much his voice has changed since he was a child. "In some ways, men have two voices they can use, their normal voice and their falsetto voice. Can you think of any singers who use their falsetto voice?"

As the experiment continued, the two adults sang together, trying to match each other's voice; then students explored matching Mr. Fowler's voice, one at a time, then in groups. Before Mr. Fowler left their class, he assured the boys that their voices would change in time and encouraged them not to worry about this natural process as it happened to them. "It can be harmful to your voice to try to sing too low, trying to sound like a man, before your voice has changed. So let this process occur naturally and you won't risk vocal strain from trying to make your voice do something it's not ready to do."

If you are a man, here are some things you can do to help students hear and match the pitches of a song you are teaching.

- Have a child start a song.
- Sing in a lighter, quieter voice than normal.
- Sing in falsetto voice.
- Use a pitched instrument, such as a piano or a recorder, to give pitches to children.

The option that is most effective for you will depend on your vocal facility. Ideally, whether you are male or female, you will help children know the differences between adult male voices and theirs by training them to listen and adjust their voices. Singing with them on a consistent basis gives them opportunities to hear the differences and make the necessary adjustments.

PHASES FOR VOCAL AWARENESS

1. Students *experiment* with the quality and range possibilities of their voices.
2. Students *describe* how their voices feel, where they feel their voices, and how their voices sound as they experiment.
3. Students *match* quality and range of the teacher and other students in singing or speaking activities.
4. Students *decide* which labels best fit a given vocal production of their own and others' voices (for instance, "high," "medium," or "low"; "loud," "medium," or "quiet").
5. Students *produce* a particular sound according to a given label ("high," "soft," "smooth," and so on).
6. Students *produce* a specific pitch to match one given by another voice or instrument.

(Bennett 1986a, 34)

A Sequence for Vocal Awareness

A first step toward vocal awareness and education is to listen to voices and describe what we hear and what we feel. Though there are several potential variations, a possible sequence for stages of vocal development was suggested in "A Responsibility to Young Voices" (Bennett 1986a). These phases for vocal awareness engage students in exercises that ask them to experiment with, describe, match, and label a wide variety of vocal sounds. All these prior activities work together to prepare students for producing specific pitches that match a voice or an instrument (matching pitch).

Specific ways in which these exercises can be explored are found in the following chart for working with voices.

WORKING WITH VOICES

Objectives	Student Tasks	Challenges and Commentary
Listen to the varieties of sounds that voices make in regular speech, and describe them without evaluation.	Students say their names, one at a time, as the turn passes around the circle. Students can close their eyes as they listen, knowing when it is their turn to speak by listening for the sound coming around the circle.	"Tell us what you notice about some of the differences we hear in voices. Avoid saying what you liked or didn't like. Just think of a way to describe them." Vocabulary suggestions include: fast/slow, high/low, loud/soft, and other descriptions that students offer.
Explore what speaking voices can do.	Students use a familiar poem or saying ("I just love to eat hamburgers") as each takes a turn using his or her voice in a new or unusual way.	"What did you learn about what voices can do as you heard all of our different ways of speaking? Let's collect ideas on the board so we can see the words and thoughts people use to describe voices."
Explore what voices can do, and describe what is felt as voices produce sigh glides and glissandos.	Using "oo" or "ah," students experience and experiment with various vocal glissandos. This activity can include a student giving his or her own vocal idea or echoing a student's or a teacher's glissandos.	"Did you feel your voice as you performed that glissando? Describe what you felt. Because our voices are different from each other, some glissandos may be easy for some of our voices and challenging for others. Notice which ones challenged your voice."
Gain vocal control by matching quality and range of a speaking voice.	Students experiment with new ways to use their speaking voices on a familiar phrase (Ex.: "Old Dan Tucker was a mighty man") as the turn passes around the circle, as students volunteer, or as you gesture to a student to take a turn. After each offering, the class or individuals can imitate (echo).	"Our voices exercised in different ways to imitate our classmates. Tell us something you noticed about your voice when it was matching someone else's." "Have you noticed that some people's voices caused ours to speak faster (slower, quieter, higher) than normal? Who can give me an example of this? These are such good exercises for our ears and our voices."

(continued)

WORKING WITH VOICES (continued)

Objectives	Student Tasks	Challenges and Commentary
Gain vocal control by matching the pitch and action of vocal glissandos.	Students give vocal glissandos as others match their examples. The echo response can come from the whole group, a small group, a partner, or an individual.	"Michelle, was that your high, medium, or low voice?"Low." "Jonathan, when you echoed Michelle, did that voice *feel* low to you? Sometimes another person's low voice is our high or medium voice, so it's important for us all to know what we consider the high, medium, and low ranges for *our* voices." "Was your voice able to do that? Did Jenny's voice sound just like Susan's? When did Jenny's voice start sounding different from Susan's?"
Gain vocal control and demonstrate understanding by giving an appropriate vocal response to specific requests and terms.	Students use a familiar phrase ("skip to my lou, my darling") to speak or sing in their high/medium/low, quiet/medium/loud, and fast/medium/slow voices.	"David, your voice matched exactly what my voice did. Your ears detected the sound and helped your voice know what sound to make. Tell us what you did or felt so that your voice knew what to do."
Match pitch by singing the same tones given by a vocal model.	Students sing a familiar song or phrase as they attempt to match the exact pitch of the teacher or another student. Responses can be given within the whole group, in small groups, with partners, or individually.	"Did you hear how Martha and Patty were on the same pitch? How can you tell when they are and aren't matching pitch?"

Giving Feedback about Voices

Imagine that you have just spoken your own name in a vocal awareness exercise and your teacher is going to respond. Which would you prefer she say?

- "That was a *lovely* voice!"
- "We couldn't hear you. Speak louder."
- "Thank you."
- "That's it!"
- "That was *wonderful*!"
- "OK."
- "You spoke with such energy!"

PRINCIPLE 6

Do you prefer any of these reactions? Would any of them have been fine with you? Can you see how both overreacting and underreacting can have an impact on any further motivation to participate? What we say in response to our students' speaking and singing voices deserves consideration. Do we respond with whatever comes to mind? Do we respond with one of the few appropriate phrases we know? Do we respond with quotes that we saw in a workshop or read in a book? (See Chapters 7 and 8 for further discussion on the use of feedback in the classroom.)

Langness's research (1992) revealed fifteen categories for teachers' verbal responses as they taught singing to children. In the following chart, response categories and examples of teacher feedback are directly quoted from that study. These data were collected from observations of teachers and students in public school music classrooms. Consider the possible feelings, responses, and information that students may receive from these statements. Are there some types of verbal responses that you have neglected to use with your students? Are there some verbal responses that you would not use with students? Why or why not?

Types of Verbal Responses	Sample Quotes
1. Repeated student answers	
2. Acceptance/Acknowledgment of response	"OK." "All right."
3. Agreement/Affirmation	"I noticed that, too." "I think that was better, too."
4. Praise (enthusiastic, exaggerated description)	"Oh, that sound *beautiful*!" "Terrific!"
5. Positive evaluations	"That sounds *much* nicer." "That's correct!"
6a. Encouragement (referring to effort)	"There you go." "Nice job."
6b. Encouragement through negative assurances	"She was too high, now that's not a sin . . ." "If your voice is not high, that does *not* mean that there's something wrong with you."
7. Teacher approval	"I like the way Joe is sitting straight in singing position." "I approve of that, a lot!"
8. Teacher disapproval	"Stop, class. [Waits] Stop and tune in." "No. I'd like to have you singing in the best way, (student's name)."
9a. Descriptive of musical behaviors (Knowledge of Results/Performance)	"He was singing on pitch with me." "You start out beautifully and then you start to get too low."
9b. Descriptive in approximations	"Better. You're pretty close." "That was better. It was a little higher."
9c. Descriptive with qualifiers	"Some of you aren't getting quite high enough." "Most of you landed up on the top."
9d. Descriptive through humor (somewhat sarcastic)	"OK. If you do this and smile at me, that's fine, I love to see your smiles, but if you go . . . [good-natured humor] "You sound just like me and it's awful today."
10a. Question: to elicit student descriptions	"What did you feel?" "How much voice, how much air?"
10b. Questions: to elicit student self-evaluation/assessment/awareness	"How did you do it better?" "Did you hear yourself any clearer?"
10c. Questions: to seek clarification, expansion, or continuation of student answer	"On each of the notes or just on some of the notes?" "You think it was better. Why?"
10d. Questions: to lead student(s) to the "correct" answer	"What's that, speaking or singing?" "Could you hear it change? I heard it change. Did you hear it change?"

(continued)

(continued)

Types of Verbal Responses	Sample Quotes
10e. Questions: to elicit student suggestions for revised task	"So what would you suggest? How can they fix that?" "I wonder if you could sing with more energy?"
11. Request or suggest repetition of task (with reason for request)	"Would you sing that one more time? I could hardly hear you." "Let's listen one more time."
12. Corrective for repeated task	"Keep it up there." "Loosen the mouth."
13. Revised task	"OK, let's see if we can find a different singing place . . ." "I wonder if you could make them all consistent?"
14. Normative	"I can hear that you're higher than last year, and so it's going to get better."
15. Summative	"OK. I think it was better, too." (Followed student summation) "Boy! This is working hard, isn't it? I see concentrated faces. I see you really listening and trying to do what I'm asking. That's wonderful."

(Langness 1992, 222–225)

Note the distinctions between the various categories of feedback. Being aware of these diverse categories can help us to see how our responses to students may affect their emerging vocal awareness, skills, and education.

Chapter Epilogue

Our voices are perhaps our most basic means of communication. They are expressions of who we are as much as of what we think. They deserve our care and attention. To harness the power of singing, we must reflect on our attitudes about voices, learn about voice production, and develop skills that promote healthy vocal attitudes and habits in our students.

Engaging Listening

5

Listening is an essential component of all musical activities. Performers, composers, audiences, music students, and music teachers all listen to music as part of their respective interests and responsibilities. This chapter is devoted to presenting a variety of techniques and guidelines for developing students' listening skills by engaging them in music-making activities.

Listening skills provide a sound basis for future musical development. The double meaning of "sound basis" is intentional. Developing solid skills in recognizing, discriminating, categorizing, and synthesizing relationships in sound is essential to solid development in music. A fundamental goal of this chapter then is to present ways to engage students' listening and to help them develop skills in working with sound. Throughout Chapter 5, the term "sound skills" will remind us about the importance of *listening* in sound musical development.

Listening Skills and Singing Skills

Teaching music activities to children and leading children in singing do not require us to be vocalists of the calibre we might hear in a solo recital. The relief we may feel at that realization, however, does not excuse us from our responsibilities to be the best musical models we can be for children's music performance, singing. As we learn and sing songs, we can develop sound skills.

How do we develop sound skills? Practice, practice, practice. You have heard this encouragement before, right? To develop singing skills and listening skills, there is no substitute for *doing* singing and listening activities. For those who have music training and for those who do not, vocal facility comes from being informed about our voices, performing exercises that extend our understanding and skills, and being willing to use our vocal and listening skills regularly. Students and teachers may practice their singing and listening skills with any song by using the study techniques described in this chapter. We can build and practice our sound skills by figuring out the melody, rhythm, and structure of each song we sing, and by performing and listening to songs in a variety of ways. If you encounter music terms in this chapter with which you are unfamiliar, please refer to the discussion of terms in Chapter 6 or to the definitions in the Glossary.

Having responsibility for leading others inspires us to become aware of our role as musical models and to notice the techniques through which we can become better musicians.

PRINCIPLE 3

PRINCIPLE 4

85

When we begin to study sound through singing, one danger is allowing the song to become too mechanical, overly technical, or unmusical. *As we engage students' listening, therefore, our goals are to preserve context and musicality for the song.* Although these goals sound simple enough, they can be especially challenging unless we have strategies to highlight musical phrases or elements *while* we are singing. It is through singing that we can preserve context and through the study techniques that we can maintain musicality.

The study techniques of *chinning, inner hearing, antiphonning,* and *movement* help us to achieve our goals for listening. Through these techniques, we can refine our listening skills as we are making music, preserving the "wholeness" of the song by singing. The study of notation through music maps, song dots, ideographs, and form books can focus students' listening skills by combining sound and symbols for singing and by preserving the musical shape and the musical expectations that are built into a song.

Performance Modes

Listening skills can be sharpened and honed in a variety of performance modes. Chinning, inner hearing, antiphonning, and movement are ways to engage children in and challenge them to develop listening skills while they are singing. Each has its own specific strengths and character, but all share certain features:

- They provide opportunities to observe student achievement and performance.
- They focus listening on specific parts or phrases of a song without altering the flow of the music.
- They offer means by which students may lead, adjust challenges, and share their own ideas with others.

Because students and teachers vary the tasks, these performance modes provide ample opportunities for practicing and reinforcing listening skills without the feeling of simple drill. As you consider and practice each of these study techniques, examine how it challenges students' listening skills, how it engages the students, and what skills it requires.

Chinning

The term "chinning" originated in the Maritime Provinces of Canada (Creighton 1962). The folk equivalent of scat singing, chinning (cheek music or diddling) was used to provide dance music when no instrument was available. *Chinning* a song or a melody simply means singing it on "doo" or some other consonant-vowel syllable (Richards 1980; Richards and Langness 1982). Although we probably all chin when we do not recall the words to a song, chinning can be an important and effective ped-

---

PRIMARY GOALS OF CHINNING

- To neutralize the effect of vowels and consonants on melody so that pitches and tones can be heard more clearly
- To provide a masking effect for portions of a song when only certain phrases or chunks are highlighted for study
- To maintain the rhythmic, melodic, and structural elements of a song while omitting the words

SAMPLE APPLICATIONS OF CHINNING	
Recalling a song	"Let's chin the song *Oh, Susannah* on the syllable 'dee.' As you chin, think of what words you remember from the song."
Listening for repeated tones	"Chin the melody pattern on 'loo' each time you sing "circle left." Do you hear any tones that repeat?"
Listening for a selected melody pattern	"We're going to find all the SO₁ SO₁ DO DO patterns in *Scotland's Burning*. Let's sing the pattern before we begin the song [Sing SO₁ DO]. Let's chin the song on 'too' as we listen for SO₁ DO—it will make them easier to hear."
Listening for a selected rhythm pattern	"The secret pattern we're listening for is 'ba ba ba ba ba' [four sixteenths and a quarter note]. Let's chin that." [Chin pattern in rhythm.] "For practice, let's chin it and put it in our feet. Now our elbows. Now let's find it in the song. Chin *This Old Man* and listen for that pattern."
Highlighting selected phrases	"Sing only the DO RE SO₁ SO₁ MI DO patterns in *Did You Ever See a Lassie*? If the melody does not match, just chin it on 'loo.' "

agogical tool. As a legitimate performance mode, chinning allows students to sing a melody or to speak a word or set of words without interference from the sounds or meanings of those words. In this way, chinning becomes a tool for careful, focused listening and helps students hear sound relationships in their simplest form. Chinning also helps students hear repeated notes and repeated patterns without the added confusion of words.

Students can chin whole songs, parts of songs, or anything spoken, such as names and word patterns. Chinning can be the performance mode for the whole song, or it can be combined with other study techniques, such as tapping, inner hearing, or antiphonning. The performance mode for chinning is vocal, since chinning is performed only by singing or speaking.

Here are some sample statements by which to introduce chinning to your students.

- "Let's sing the song again except, instead of singing the words, sing 'doo' for every sound in the song."

- "When we sing 'la' or 'doo' to every sound that the words of a song make, we call that chinning. Although it has nothing to do with our chin moving, the word is a very old one that describes singing without words."

- "How would George Washington's name sound if we chinned it (speaking, not singing)? How would we chin Booker T. Washington's name? How would your *whole* name sound if you chinned it?"

- "Let's sing that song again, but this time chin the cadence phrase. Can you alternate singing and chinning the phrases of the song?"

Inner Hearing

Inner hearing is the skill of hearing words, melodies, and sounds inside our heads without those sounds being externally present. Inner hearing is a skill necessary to reading, to matching pitch, and to rehearsing silently. Without inner hearing, we would never be aware of more than one sound at a time. Without inner hearing, reading could never be more than naming letters, and music reading could never be more than naming notes. It is very important that our students develop this mental

---

PRIMARY GOALS OF INNER HEARING

- To internalize sounds so that we can hear those sounds even when they are not externally present

- To provide a means through which we can read symbols and hear the sounds they represent without needing to produce or perform those sounds

- To maintain the rhythmic, melodic, and structural elements of a song while omitting the words

---

PRINCIPLE 4

activity. Inner hearing helps students recall previously experienced music, recognize music as the same in different performances, and distinguish between different musical pieces. In short, it may be difficult to learn *anything* if one's inner hearing is not working properly.

To teach yourself or your students to activate inner hearing, you may find this sequence helpful:

▶ Sing the song *Happy Birthday.*

▶ Sing the song by moving your lips but keeping the song inside your head, in your inner hearing. Can you hear the song inside your head?

SAMPLE APPLICATIONS OF INNER HEARING

Introducing inner hearing	"As we sing *The Farmer in the Dell,* let's put the song in our inner hearing when we get to the last 'the farmer in the dell.' We'll move our lips to the words, but the song will sound only inside our heads."
	For some adults and children, the "lips only" approach is a necessary step to activate inner hearing.
Gesture game	"When you see me gesture with this hand, we'll sing the song; but when you see me change hands, we'll put the song in our inner hearing, until I use the other hand again."
Focusing on tonal patterns	"Let's make our hand signs for the SO MI DO when we hear it in *Ten in the Bed,* but let's sing the song inside our heads for that pattern."
	"What will *Hot Cross Buns* sound like if we sing only the MI RE DO patterns and put the remainder of the song in our inner hearing? Let's see!"
Focusing on rhythm patterns	"Sing only the DUTADETA DU DE [pretty little Susie] rhythms in *Paw-Paw Patch.* Everything else we'll put in our inner hearing."
	"Sing the rhythm of the song with your hands, but put the song in your inner hearing."
Focusing on steady beat	"As we sing *Skip to My Lou* in our inner hearing, let's tap the beat of the song. Listen to see if we all start and stop our actions at the same time."
Study time	"As you study this secret song, use your inner hearing to check it with the song you think it might be."
	"Study this score, and in your inner hearing, predict how you think some places may sound."
Noise management	"Although we can get very excited in this game as we cheer our friends' efforts, we don't want to disturb the classes next to us. So all cheering and yelling need to be in your inner hearing. You may cheer with your body, sitting in your space, but not with your voice. Let's practice that before we begin the game."

▶ Sing the song by keeping it in your inner hearing, not moving your lips. Can you still hear the song inside your head?

The ability to inner-hear makes discrimination, recognition, and recall of music possible. It lets us imagine and create music in our minds. Inner hearing connects individual sounds to create flowing musical phrases and is a contributing factor in the perception of tonality and meter. Inner hearing, the ability to think sound, is a fundamental cognitive skill in music.

Prepare students for using their inner hearing with statements like these:

- "This time as we sing the song *If You're Happy and You Know It*, let's put the word 'hands' inside our heads. Can you do that? It can be tricky to remember. Let's try it. Good luck!"

- "Let's put the ending of the song *Mary Had a Little Lamb* inside our heads, in our inner hearing, when we get there. What is the end of the song? [Its fleece was white as snow.] You can move your lips to the words [avoid exaggerating], but don't let the sound come outside your head. Here we go."

Antiphonning

Antiphonning is a way of performing a song in which a leader and responders alternate performing successive parts of the song; it is a kind of fill-in-the-blank activity for singing a song. The leader takes the first turn and sings a part of a song. The responder begins singing whenever the leader stops and continues until the leader re-enters the song.

The term comes from a style of performance in which vocal or instrumental ensembles alternate phrases and sections of music (antiphony). Antiphonning takes advantage of our seemingly natural tendency to complete a familiar song, melody, phrase, or saying (Richards 1980; Richards and Langness 1982). The traditional knock that goes with the "shave and a haircut" rhythm is an example of this need for completion. Who among us can resist knocking back the reply, "two bits"?

When we antiphon, our mental and vocal challenge is to follow the parts of the song that the leader performs so that we may be ready immediately to begin when it is our turn. Antiphonning also develops inner hearing skills, because this mental tracking is a form of inner hearing. When antiphonning, students must "think" the whole song, not just parts of it. Antiphonning provides the chance to correct mistaken words, inaccuracies in melody, or variations in rhythm by drawing students' attention to certain patterns, words, repetitions, or other elements of the song. To add auditory information and to listen for improved accuracy, we can control which parts the students perform and which they hear us perform.

The leader can indicate turns by gesturing. Gestures help introduce antiphonning to students: "When my hands point to me, it is my turn to sing. When they point to you, it is your turn. Watch to see when it is your turn to sing or listen." Gestures are not necessary, however. The absence of gestures forces the responders to listen even

PRINCIPLE 4

PRIMARY GOALS OF ANTIPHONNING

- To be prepared to respond when it is our turn (music responsiveness)
- To preserve the flow of the song as leaders and responders perform their parts (musicality)
- To engage learners in studying, performing, and enjoying the music experience

more closely to know when to begin: "No clues this time. Your ears will tell you when to sing and when to listen. More concentration is needed now." Antiphonning can also be done with eyes closed: "Who would like a turn antiphonning me with eyes closed? We'll have no visual clues, so our ears are really challenged to concentrate."

Anna Langness presented the session "Antiphonning: A Means to Skill Development and Assessment" at the 1993 State Conference of the Colorado Music Educators Association. In her handout for this session, Langness stated, "Antiphonning preserves the 'wholeness' of the song: therefore, preserving the musical expectations of progression from one part to the next and the relationships of the parts to the whole."

SAMPLE APPLICATIONS OF ANTIPHONNING

Introducing antiphonning
"As I sing this familiar song, fill in any parts I leave out. We call this skill *antiphonning.*"

Sing a song the students know, and leave out the final phrase or chunk. Then, challenge students to fill in phrase endings or whole phrases.

Using gestures
"You'll get some clues this time that will show you when it's your turn to sing. Are your eyes, ears, and voices ready?"

Sing a familiar song, gracefully gesturing to yourself as you sing, then giving a welcoming gesture to students when it is their turn to sing.

Watching for clues
"No gestures this time. Your listening will really need to be concentrated! Your challenge will be to focus so closely on the song that you come right in when I stop singing."

Students are encouraged to activate their observations of subtle facial and postural clues even though you may try not to give any clues.

Ears only
"We're really going to give our listening a workout this time. What will happen to our singing and our antiphonning if we close our eyes? Can we do it? Will it work? Let's try it, then make some observations."

Practicing inner hearing
"Let's antiphon with ourselves as we put some words in our inner hearing. Which words of the song should we sing inside our heads?"

Student leaders for class
"Let's have a volunteer to lead the group in antiphonning our song. Leaders may decide whether or not to use gestures. Class, be ready to antiphon."

Student partners
"Find a partner and take some practice time antiphonning the song. Take turns being leader and follower."

Leading a small group
"In your groups of four or five, each of you takes a turn being the leader for antiphonning. Your group will be supportive and responsive as you develop and practice this important music skill."

Circular antiphonning
"As we sit in our circle, Joey will begin the song and pass it to Fred. The song will keep going that direction, and if the person before you has the cadence, take a moment, then begin the song again. Your turn to sing the song comes to you whenever the person before you stops singing."

Voice games
"After all our vocal exploration, we know how to use our voices in varieties of ways. As Tobey leads us, let's antiphon her voice quality as she *speaks* the song."

Antiphon-speaking a song to encourage vocal exploration can also be used to challenge students to antiphon the opposite vocal quality of the leader in dynamics, tempo, and articulation.

SAMPLE APPLICATIONS OF ANTIPHONNING (continued)

Conducting antiphonning	"As we sing this song, Brooke will be our conductor. If she gestures with her right arm, this side will sing; the other group will sing if she gestures with her left arm."
	"This may be a big challenge! Charity may conduct to *this* side, or to *that* side, or to *both* sides at the same time, or to *herself* only to sing."
Mixing rhythm and text	"I'll tap the words, and when you antiphon me, you'll sing them." [Be sure to give a starting pitch.]
	"Rodney will sing the words, but you'll tap them and sing them in your inner hearing when you antiphon."
Rhythm antiphonning	"Let's sing the words in our inner hearing as we antiphon-tap the song."
	Students can suggest various ways to perform the rhythm as they antiphon, creating interesting combinations of sounds as they aim for precision in rhythm.

Mixing text and rhythm syllables

"Antiphon me, please. We'll sing *Looby Loo*."

[T singing]	Here we go Looby Loo
[S singing]	Here we go Looby Lie
[T singing]	Here we go Looby Loo　　DUDADI DUDADI DU.
[T singing]	DUDADI DU DI DU
[T singing]	DUDADI DU DI DU
[S singing]	DUDADI DU DI DU DUDADI DUDADI DU.

Syllables may be introduced and learned simply as another way to sing the song. Antiphonning allows and supports varied practice of the new syllables.

Mixing text and tone syllables

"Antiphon me, please."

[T singing]	Circle left, do-oh, do-oh
[S singing]	Circle left, do-oh, do-oh
[T singing]	Circle left, do-oh, do-oh　　MI MI RE RE DO
	(Repeat as needed)
[T singing]	SO₁ DO DO do-oh, do-oh
[T singing]	SO₁ DO DO do-oh, do-oh
[S singing]	SO₁ DO DO do-oh, do-oh　　MI MI RE RE DO

Antiphon-dotting and singing	"My chalk is going to tap the song *Did You Ever See a Lassie?* on the board. Antiphon the song when my chalk stops; when it comes back in, remember, your turn is momentarily over." [Give a starting pitch.]
	"Carrie will let her chalk begin the song, and Andy will antiphon Carrie's chalk. Let's listen as they antiphon the song with their chalk. Will we hear every syllable of every word?"
Mystery singers circle	"Let's make our standing circle very close so that our shoulders are touching. Our eyes will be closed as we sing the song, and you'll sing *only* when I [or a student] am touching your shoulder. This is our time for quiet listening as we enjoy the voices in our class."
Partner songs	"As group 1 sings *Mary Had a Little Lamb,* group 2 will sing *London Bridge*. As you sing your partner song, listen carefully to the other song. Whenever you see me give you this gesture, switch to the other group's song. We may also change back, so be ready. This activity takes lots of skill in singing and in listening!"

Some ideas in the following chart are adapted from Langness's handout. See the Glossary or Chapter 6 for any unfamiliar terms in the chart. Practice antiphonning the songs *A-Hunting We Will Go* and *The Farmer in the Dell,* alone or in a group. If you are alone, you may perform the responder's part by tapping, inner hearing, or chinning. Note that words are grouped according to language phrases.

LEADER	RESPONDERS
A-hunting	we will go.
A-hunting	we will go.
We'll catch a little fox and put him in a box	and then we'll let him go.
The farmer	in the dell.
The farmer	in the dell.
Hi-ho the derry-o	the farmer in the dell.

Because a goal of antiphonning is to perform the song as if only one person is singing, smooth, musical transitions between the leader and the responders are emphasized. Help children value singing and hearing songs as musical wholes, flowing from beginning to end. Model musical, rather than disjunct, divisions within a song. Phrases, phrase combinations, and half phrases provide structures by which antiphonning can best be experienced and practiced. For example, sing "Hi-ho the

---

SIZE OF DIVISIONS FOR ANTIPHONNING

LEADER	RESPONDERS
Phrases	
Twinkle, twinkle, little star	How I wonder what you are
Up above the world so high	Like a diamond in the sky
Twinkle, twinkle, little star	How I wonder what you are
Phrase Combinations	
Twinkle, twinkle, little star, How I wonder what you are	Up above the world so high, Like a diamond in the sky
Twinkle, twinkle, little star, How I wonder what you are	
Half Phrases	
Twinkle, twinkle	Little star
How I wonder	What you are
Up above	The world so high
Like a diamond	In the sky
Twinkle, twinkle	Little star
How I wonder	What you are
Mixtures of Sizes	
Twinkle, twinkle	Little star
How I wonder what you are. Up above	The world so high
Like	A diamond in the sky
Twinkle, twinkle, little star, How I wonder	What you are

derry-o" rather than "Hi-ho the der-." Challenge students to perform the song as if they were in a musical ensemble rather than in a musical race.

Keep in mind that the goal of antiphonning is for the leader and the responders to be so attuned that the song sounds as if one singer is performing it intact. No doubt, you will also experience antiphonning in smaller parts—words and word units of songs—especially once students get the chance to be leaders. Note how antiphonning the song in smaller parts can present additional challenges to musical flow.

SMALLER PARTS

LEADER	RESPONDERS
Twinkle	Twinkle
Little star	How I wonder
What	You are
Up	Above the world
So high	Like
A diamond	In the sky
Twinkle	Twinkle
Little	Star
How	I wonder
What	You are

When the parts are smaller than half phrases, the flow of the song can be lost because the parts are so brief. Other than for an enjoyable challenge on occasion, the word-by-word option for antiphonning should be minimized.

To introduce antiphonning, the following statements may be used.

PRINCIPLE 4

- "Let's take turns singing the song. I'll start, and my hands will let you know when it's your turn to sing."
- "Listen for the whole song, even though you won't be singing the whole song aloud. I'll start, and you finish what I begin."
- "I'll begin singing the song, and you fill in the parts I leave out."
- Tap the song with the thumb and forefinger of one hand, and antiphon with the same movement of the other hand. After students listen to the whole song being performed this way, ask, "Did you hear the whole song? I'll sing with my right hand and you sing when my left hand taps."

Movement

Singing and moving are almost inseparable activities. The act of singing, as well as any act of music making, involves movement, even the simple movement of moving the lips and vocal mechanism. Movement, therefore, is an essential ingredient in performing songs, and it is also an essential ingredient in developing song skills.

Moving to songs can involve general, free, expressive actions coordinated with the flow of the whole song or specific sections within the whole song; it can involve prescribed, specific demonstrations of sound patterns; or it can involve combinations of these. Therefore, movement can be seen and used as both an expressive mode and a demonstrative mode for experiencing and studying music.

Performance modes for movement while singing can be the whole-body, locomotor movements of skipping, walking, hopping, jumping, crawling, or running.

PRIMARY GOALS OF MOVEMENT

- To connect listening and moving so that movement becomes a performance mode for the flow of music as well as for specific musical elements

- To provide a highlighter for portions of a song when only certain phrases or chunks are to be studied

- To maintain the rhythmic, melodic, and structural elements of a song while omitting the words

---

Movement can also involve the finer motor, axial skills of stomping, patting (thighs), snapping, tapping (fingertips on palm), or clapping. The fine motor activities listed here work well as demonstration modes for refined listening and performing.

These statements may be used to introduce movement as a sound skill technique:

- "This time as we sing the song, let's sing with our hands as well as our voices. Hold one hand like this (palm up), and use the fingertips of your other hand to tap the sounds of the words. Get your hands and your voices ready."

- "Were you able to 'row your boat' that time right with the music? Did you let your song tell your oars when to row? Listen as you sing and let the song tell you when to move."

When the *ear* is engaged in the coordination, movement to music is distinguished from amusical movement (clapping as applause, tapping as pounding, walking as stamping). Constantly remind students to listen as they move and sing, letting the song tell them how and when to move. Be cautious so that when you clap or tap a song (or move in any other way), you are modeling musical movement by "singing the song in your hands." "Teachers must always care about being the best musical model we can be; and, we must help students develop the skills of musical movement" (Bennett 1988b).

APPLICATIONS OF MOVEMENT

Cadence points	Starting and stopping movement (walking, skipping, jumping) with the beginning and ending of the song. "Let's see if we can begin moving when we begin singing and stop our movement right when the song stops."
Coordinating movement with sound	Coordinating a selected movement with a part of a song. "Our challenge is to remember to shake our arms when we sing the words 'a-rig-a-jig-jig,' and skip when we sing 'away we go.'"
Showing the rhythm	Showing the rhythm of the words (in various body parts) to all or parts of a song. "Let's tap the words with our hands each time we sing 'the muffin man' in our song." "Let's tap the ending (cadence) of the song on our hand. What words will we tap?"
Feeling the beat	Feeling the beat in our legs (hands, head, eyes) as we sing. "Let's show the music in our hands as we feel the beat and sing the song."
Showing the melody	Showing the melodic contour with hand signs. "Each time you hear the SO₁ LA₁ DO pattern, show what you hear by using your hand signs."

Notation Modes

Conventional music notation is a complex, sophisticated system for writing the sounds that we want others to hear or perform. Seeing the staves, clefs, meter signatures, key signatures, measures, bar lines, notes, rhythms, sharps, flats, repeat signs, double bars, ledger lines, slurs, ties, and other music symbols used to notate even the simplest song can overwhelm a person who is trying to study the song score.

This section outlines alternative notation systems that engage listening in the process of writing and reading music. In music maps, song dots, ideographs, and form books, the aspects of a song that are most obvious and require the least amount of explanation are the first notated. Mapping and song dotting lend themselves easily to students' early experiences with writing music because they preserve free, individual movement to the flow of a song and allow students to write music while performing it.

In all four notation modes, all the parts of a song are kept intact, and melodic, rhythmic, and structural elements are not initially isolated. Music mapping, song dotting, ideographing, and form books will help you see how you can engage your students' listening so they can discover and enjoy the acts of writing and reading music.

Music Mapping

A music **map** is a line that represents the flow or movement of music (Richards 1984). Drawn while a song or an instrumental work is being sung or heard, a map is a kinesthetic symbol as well as a visual one. In its simplest interpretation, a map shows the beginning and ending of sound and the flow of sound that happens in between. Whether intentional or not, portions of a map may also resemble movement to specific aspects of rhythm, beat, melody, or structure. Mapping uses a symbol (a line) that needs no prerequisite skills in notating and reading sound patterns. Making and reading maps involve and integrate auditory, motor, and visual modes and focus on the structure and flow of a song. (Detailed discussion and sample lessons for teaching mapping can be found in *SongWorks 2.*) Follow the two sample maps presented in Figure 5-1 as you sing the songs they notate.

A First Mapping Procedure
A map begins, continues, and ends simultaneously with the song. Although teachers can make lead maps that intentionally represent specific elements in the music, students should be given the freedom to feel the flow of sound rather than be instructed to show certain music elements when making maps.

With some classes, a first mapping experience works best if students have the opportunity to watch several maps being made by the teacher or classmates. When a song is well known to students, they are ready to map. Remember to give a starting pitch so that students will be able to begin mapping simultaneously with the beginning of the song.

Examples of three student maps are shown in Figure 5-2. Each was made to the song *Come and Follow Me.* They illustrate how maps for the same song can vary in appearance. The more experience students have in making and following maps, the more clarified their maps tend to become.

▶ Which map seems to be the most energetic?

▶ Which map suggests a beat feeling to you?

▶ Which map is easiest for you to follow?

▶ Which map do you think captures the flow of the walking game?

FIGURE 5-1

Two sample maps

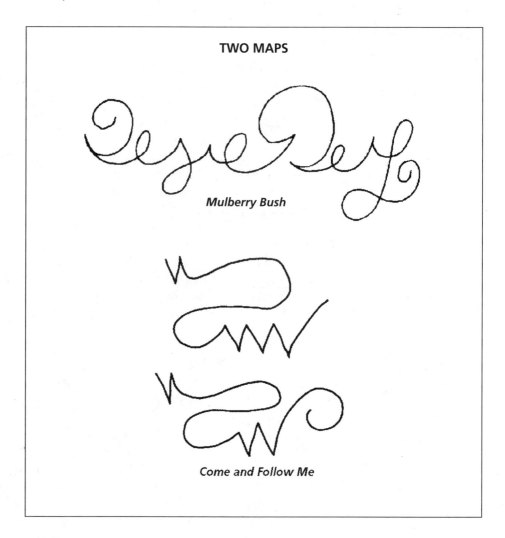

TWO MAPS

Mulberry Bush

Come and Follow Me

PRINCIPLE 4

A PROCEDURE FOR MAPPING 1

Map   Three or four students come to the chalkboard. "Hold your chalk on the board, and when the song begins, let your chalk sing by making a line for the song. Feel the song in your hand and let it move your chalk. Stop your chalk at the end of the song, the cadence." Mapping can also be modeled by the teacher making three or four different maps at the board.

Study   After the maps are made, students notice the similarities and differences in maps. "A map shows how we each felt the song. It doesn't need to look like anyone else's map, because it is our personal movement to the song."

"Ed's map has loops. Does it loop all the way through the song?" "Michelle's map has a big curve in the middle. What words are we singing on the curve?"

In some classes, reading and following maps naturally evolves during the study time; in other classes, studying maps without reading them can be beneficial.

Map   After the class has spent a short amount of time noticing the similarities, differences, and designs in maps, three or four more students come to the board to make new maps. "I wonder how these people will show us the movement they feel for the song."

FIGURE 5-2

Come and Follow Me:
*Three examples of
student maps*

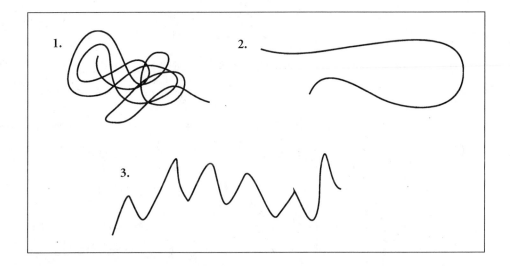

A PROCEDURE FOR MAPPING 2

Read   Challenge students to read their maps by tracing them with their fingers. "I wonder if these students could read their maps this time. We know the maps were made with the song; can we read them with the song? Good luck! Let's all sing for them to read."

Share   Students who had no trouble making a map could encounter difficulty following it. "Try following again before you decide you can't read it." "I wonder if one of your friends could read your map with the song. Choose someone to try it."

Qualitative judgments that refer to liking or noticing the beauty of certain maps can cause some students to try to make maps that please the teacher rather than explore their own sense of musical flow. You might also want to avoid the term "draw" when referring to maps. This image may give some students the idea that they are to draw a picture.

PRINCIPLE 6

For some children, reading skills can be substantially different from writing skills. Following maps should be presented as a challenge, not a test. Comments such as "Maybe your finger could go slower (or faster) next time" or "Where is that place in your map that seems to be such a puzzle for your finger?" can gently guide a child to success in reading his or her map.

Another Mapping Procedure

Maps can be made by using a wide felt-tip marker and a large piece of blank paper. If children are capable of managing their behavior, a sitting circle on the floor can be ideal for mapping. Children may also be seated on the floor in scatter formation or at desks.

Students can explore and study their maps in several ways.

- Watch and sing while an individual follows his or her map.
- Make another map of the song, practicing the new map in the air or with a finger on paper before making it.
- Follow others' maps by trading, passing, or holding them up, one at a time, for all to see and follow. The song is always sung while maps are followed.

A PROCEDURE FOR MAPPING 3

Song/Movement	After a song is well known to the children and they have had the chance to coordinate starting and stopping their movement with the song, each child puts an arm in the air and "sings" the song with that arm. Give a starting pitch and gesture so all students begin their movement with the song.
Inner hearing	"Feel the movement of the song with your arm as you sing in your inner hearing. Be sure to start and stop your arm with the song. Let the music carry your arm. Notice which movements seem to fit the music."
Paper	"Now fit your map onto the paper. Choose a starting place and make an 'X,' then put your finger there and wait for the song. If certain movements felt good with the song, try to keep them. If other movements seemed not to fit the song, you may want to try some different paths. Wait for the song."
Marker	Pass out markers, but instruct students to leave the caps on. "Practice your map with the cap on your marker."
Write	"Take the cap off your marker, make an 'X,' put your marker on the 'X,' and wait for the song. Be sure your markers and your voices are ready for the song."
Read	"Look around at all these different maps. Let's see if your finger can read your map as you sing the song. Does reading your map feel the same as making your map?"

■ Read their maps as portions of the song are sung. "See if you can find this part of the song in your map." The teacher (or a student) sings the song up to a certain point and then stops. Students follow their maps and stop as the leader stops singing.

■ Find a specific place in the maps: the end, an anacrusis, a word, a phrase, rests, a rhythm pattern, a pitch pattern, and so on.

■ Examine maps for places that seem to fit the song especially well. "Find places in your map that feel especially good. Let your partner decide which places in your map feel especially good, and compare your ideas. What is it about the movement that feels good in those places—the loops, the speed, the repetitions? What happens in the music at those places?"

To combine and connect maps with other symbols, this sequence could be helpful:

1. Find a place in the map where a specific word or phrase occurs.

2. Highlight that portion of the map by making the line thicker or by tracing it with a different color.

3. Write an alternative symbol near the highlighted part of the map so that students see it when singing the song and following the map. It rarely works to draw the symbols right on the line of the map, since maps make too many turns and twists. Alternative symbols could include words, pictures, song dots, rhythm notation, pictures of hand signs, solfa (letters), notes on the staff.

Song Dotting

Song dots are simple notations for the sounds of all or a portion of a song. Song dotting (or simply dotting) requires no previous notational knowledge or skill and can be an effective introduction to the individual units of conventional notation. Song dotting is a means of writing down what one hears that combines auditory, kinesthetic, and visual modes. Each dot represents a single, unitary sound (Richards and Langness 1984). The coordination of movement with the dots and with the song demands concentrated listening.

Song dotting builds on students' abilities to hear and move to the individual sounds of a pattern, and it lets students notate the individual sounds of a pattern simultaneously with performance of the pattern. Movement to a pattern is translated into notation in the song-dotting process, but dotting involves more than moving accurately to a pattern or a song. It also involves recognizing that a pattern is composed of individual sounds in a series. Students who are not accurately dotting a pattern may not be abstracting the individual sounds from the pattern as a whole.

Dotting can be effectively combined with antiphonning by alternating dotting and singing between the leader and the responders. For example, the leader can sing while the responders dot, or the leader can dot while the responders sing. (Detailed discussions and sample lessons for teaching song dotting can be found in *Song-Works 2*.)

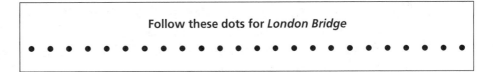

▶ As you read the song dots for London Bridge, did you touch a dot each time you sang a syllable?

▶ Did your finger move more quickly on some dots than on others?

▶ Are the dots in the following score easier to follow? They were spaced according to the rhythm of the words.

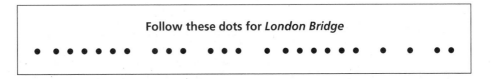

Some Procedures for Song Dotting

Song dots are made by tapping the rhythm of a pattern or a song with chalk or a marker, leaving a visual record of this movement. Students' initial experiences with dotting can come in the form of reading a set of dots that the teacher has made on the board, and students can lead the class in following the dots. In this process, they will begin to see how dots function as symbols for sound. They will learn

- how to follow dots—that each dot represents a particular sound;

- how dots will be used—that they will be studied and respected as representations of sound;

- that dots are made from left to right so that they will be more easily read.

A PROCEDURE FOR SONG DOTTING

Song/Movement	When a song is well known to the students and they have had opportunities to coordinate moving with the rhythm of the song or pattern, they tap the pattern or song on their hands with their fingers. "Listen to your finger sing the song (or pattern)."
Inner hearing	"While your finger sings the song (or pattern), listen to the words in your inner hearing."
Paper	"Now tap the words (rhythm) across the paper just as you would read, going from left to right."
Marker	"Let's practice having your marker sing the song (or pattern), but leave the cap on."
Write	"Take the cap off your marker and be ready for the song. Have your marker and your voice sing the song."
Read	"Can you sing (or hear) the song as you read the dots?"

These additional song-dotting experiences can be planned for students:

- Make dots of other songs and patterns.
- Read others' dot scores.
- Find the dots for particular places, words, or phrases in the song.
- Read dot scores as portions of the song are sung. Sing the beginning of the song to a certain point, then stop. Students sing back that portion of the song while they follow their dots and mark the place where the teacher stopped. Have students give each other similar challenges.
- Circle the dots for certain words or patterns. (See Figure 5-3.)
- Write conventional notation for patterns that have been circled. (See Figure 5-4.)

FIGURE 5-3

Three Blind Mice:
Dots and instructions

1. Circle "mice" — add ears.
2. Circle "wife" — add a hat.
3. Circle "knife" — add a blade.
4. Substitute a different sound for each dot circled. Sing the song, read the dots, and perform the sounds when they occur.
5. If the song begins and ends with "Three blind mice," why are there four dots in the final group?

FIGURE 5-4

Uncle Joe:

Dots and notation

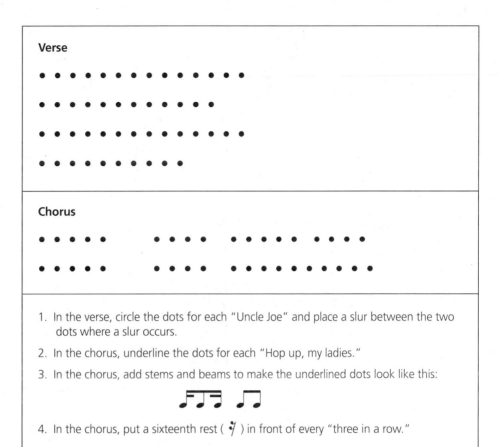

1. In the verse, circle the dots for each "Uncle Joe" and place a slur between the two dots where a slur occurs.
2. In the chorus, underline the dots for each "Hop up, my ladies."
3. In the chorus, add stems and beams to make the underlined dots look like this:
4. In the chorus, put a sixteenth rest ( ) in front of every "three in a row."

Ideographs

An *ideograph* is a pictograph of a song or an instrumental work (Richards 1980, 40–41). In ideographs, symbols or pictures are used in place of conventional notation to represent patterns of sound rather than individual notes. Patterns of sound represented in ideographs could be as long as phrases or as short as song chunks (the smaller units within phrases). Identical phrases or chunks of a song are represented with identical symbols in an ideograph, and phrases that are similar have symbols that look similar but are slightly different.

In the ideograph of *Daddy Loves the Bear* (Figure 5-5), there are four symbols. The bear symbol is repeated, matching the repetitions in the music. A different symbol, a plane in this case, stands for the concluding, different phrase. Sing the song as you read the ideograph.

FIGURE 5-5 Daddy Loves the Bear: *Ideograph, score, and words*

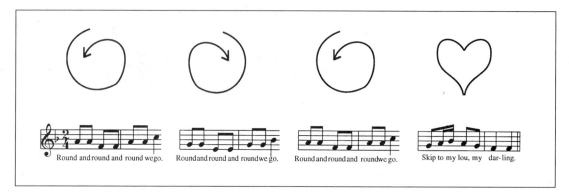

FIGURE 5-6   Skip to My Lou: *Ideograph, score, and words*

In *Skip to My Lou,* the second phrase of the song is a melodic variation of the first. In the ideograph (Figure 5-6), therefore, the symbol for the second phrase is slightly varied from the one representing the first phrase. Sing *Skip to My Lou* as you read the ideograph.

Ideograph symbols often represent units of a song that are four beats in length, but some symbols may represent units as short as two beats. The four-beat units are usually the equivalent of the song's phrase structure and tend to be easier for students to read and sing. In the ideograph for *Circle Left,* shown in Figure 5-7 (the score is in Figure 5-8), the first symbols represent units of two beats and the last one represents a unit of four beats. In the next section, Figure 5-8 shows a *Circle Left* ideograph that uses only four symbols, each representing patterns four beats long. Smaller units can provide for musical interest and surprise but can also make some of the follow-up activities for reading and singing more difficult. Hearing that students can sing the units independently and with reasonable accuracy tells you that a particular division of the song is well suited for use with the class for ideographing.

The word phrases of a song (the figural groupings), rather than the beat or measure divisions (the metric groupings), should determine the units that the symbols depict. As you examine the examples presented here, notice how the song is divided less on the basis of bar lines and more on the basis of language phrases. Ideographs represent the way we hear songs rather than the way we see songs conventionally notated. Because this figural rather than metric organization closely matches our mental structuring of a song, students are helped "to hear what they see and see what they hear" when using ideographs. Because they use student-constructed symbols and figural organizations of song material, ideographs give students the opportunity to write, read, compose, and arrange music with confidence and accuracy.

For the purposes of analysis, the previous examples of ideographs are presented with music score and words to show exactly how a song can be divided. Under normal classroom conditions, the score and the words would be omitted. Music notation

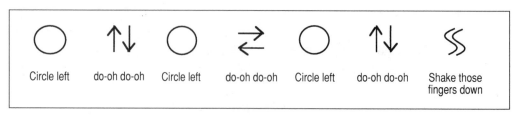

FIGURE 5-7   Circle Left: *Ideograph, words, smaller divisions*

PRINCIPLE 4

A PROCEDURE FOR INTRODUCING IDEOGRAPHS

Divide the song	Divide a song that is familiar to students into appropriate units according to phrases or language chunks.
Select symbols	Choose a symbol for each unit of the song. The symbols can be pictures, shapes, or some other kind of notation.
Notate	Notate the song on the board (overhead or chart) using the selected symbols.
Study	Lead students to study the ideograph score by challenging them to figure it out: "I've written a song on the board. Do you have an idea what it is? Study it a moment; then I'll ask for your ideas."
Read	When students offer an idea for solving the ideograph puzzle, they come to the board. As the class sings, the student shows how the symbols fit the song. As each student points to the symbols, challenge the class to sing only what is indicated and to sing only when it is indicated—they follow the leader, not the flow of the song as they know it.

---

and words, as will be described later, can themselves be used as symbols for portions of an ideograph.

Introducing Ideographs

The following sequence may be helpful in introducing ideographs to your classes. For younger grades, simple ideographs are most appropriate, but children in Grade 1 through Grade 6 have successfully experienced studying ideographs.

To introduce a new song or to reintroduce a familiar one, draw the symbols and then ask students to describe what they see and to predict what the song might sound like. In the ideograph example for *Circle Left* in Figure 5-8, students might notice that there are four symbols, the first and third are the same, the second is similar to the first and third, and the fourth is very different. Among other observations, students may make some predictions about the text: that it is about circles, that it indicates directions, that it shows motions or game actions, or that the last phrase involves a tree. When they compare these predictions with songs they know, students might be able to guess that this ideograph represents *Circle Left*. Singing the song while pointing to the symbols is one way to check how well the song fits the ideograph. If this technique of studying and predicting is used to introduce a new song, students will be able only to predict what the song might sound like given the relationships they see. When you do sing the new song, however, the prior study of the ideograph often elicits active listening as students check which predictions fit the song and which do not.

Changing Ideograph Symbols

By asking "What other symbol could we use for this part of the song?" you can encourage students to make their own symbols for the song units. As each new suggestion is offered by a student, the previous symbol is erased and the new one drawn. Students can participate in creating new symbols for a song by working in small groups, with partners, or individually. After ideograph scores are completed, the

In reading and performing ideographs, providing accurate responses immediately is less important than thinking, problem solving, and studying the symbols and sounds.

PRINCIPLE 4

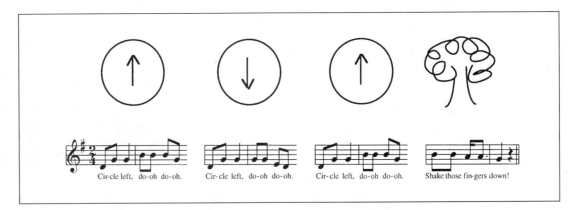

FIGURE 5-8   Circle Left: *Ideograph, score, and words*

entire class reads them by singing the ideograph symbols. By singing, reading, and substituting symbols, students gain understanding of the structure of a song.

Drawing intricate symbols takes time that you may not have in class. When students are making their own ideographs, inform them of the time requirements so that they can choose their symbols accordingly. Students can also prepare ideographs outside class and bring them to class for reading and studying.

Conventional music notation can add to the intrigue of making and reading ideographs. Challenge students to use symbols that they know (rhythm or pitch notation, solfa, song dots) for certain units of the song. (See Figures 5-9 and 5-10.) Using conventional music notation in ideographs further associates the sound of the song phrases with written notation. A word of caution is in order here, however. If students use too much conventional notation, they may become less fluent in reading ideographs and their perfomance may become less musical.

Movements and Ideographing

Another way to introduce ideographing is to create movements for each unit of the song to be symbolized.

1. To begin, choose a unit that repeats, and challenge students (individuals or partners) to make up a movement that they will perform each time they hear that part. For example, using the divisions of *Circle Left* described in Figure 5-7 students could select and demonstrate a movement each time they sing "circle left" in the song.

2. Students choose a movement for "shake those fingers down" and perform the selected movements each time they sing "circle left" and "shake those fingers down."

3. "Do-oh, do-oh" would require one movement that is repeated (for the first and third repetitions) and one that is slightly different (to indicate the melody change for the second repetition of "do-oh, do-oh").

4. Students coordinate performance of all the movements with the singing of the song. They can be challenged to identify which portions of the song are repetitions requiring the same actions, which are variations requiring similar actions, and which are contrasts requiring different actions. From this process, little dances result and movement occurs throughout the song.

5. Groups or partners can perform their actions with the song as the class first observes, then attempts to imitate the actions.

FIGURE 5-9

Old House: *Ideograph using some solfa notation*

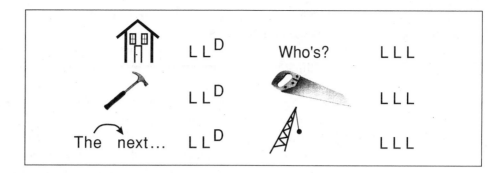

FIGURE 5-10

Circle Left: *Ideograph using some conventional notation*

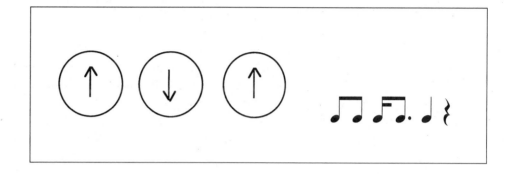

When students are working with ideographs, the song is always sung to guide the symbolizing process—when making up movements and when writing and reading ideographs.

PRINCIPLE 4

6. Students symbolize the accompanying actions with pictures or other signs. The symbols can show repetition and contrast and can be adjusted to show similarities between units of song. Decide which procedure is best for your class: Have each set of students create their own movements and ideographs, or have all students choose one set of movements that the entire class will use to create an ideograph as a class effort.

7. Students suggest symbols for their movements, write them on the board or on a large piece of paper, then read and study them.

Arranging with Ideographs

By rearranging the patterns that are present in a song, students can use ideographs to manipulate sound, then read and write what they see and hear. An important aspect of this process is that the students, not the teacher, are creating what they will read and study. With parallels to composition and creative writing, working with ideographs by rearranging symbols motivates students to gain confidence and competence in singing and reading.

First Arrangements   Lead the class in reading an ideograph by pointing to each symbol. To challenge students' observing and reading, however, point to the final symbol several times in a row. Once students get the idea that they are to sing each time you point to a symbol, follow the ideograph score again and lead students in repeating other parts of the song by repeatedly pointing to the appropriate symbol. "Sing what my finger points to. Watch out for surprises."

Students can be involved in giving the class challenges as they read and sing. "Follow Amy's finger and sing her arrangement of the song." Remind student leaders to point to the upcoming symbol slightly before students are required to sing it. This is especially important when anacruses are involved. Keeping an even tempo also helps readers to be successful.

At some point, ask students how many times a particular symbol was repeated and challenge them to use the given symbols to notate what was performed. This form of transcribing sound or song dictation can be done as a class effort, with partners, or individually.

With partners or in small groups, students can write their own arrangements of the song, repeating any unit as many times as they want. Initially, it is best to use a common set of easily drawn symbols for this activity. Encourage students to create and perform several versions of the arrangement, then write down on chart paper the one they like best. Remind students that they should be able to sing whatever they write. This activity can be a good time for students to think about what makes a good beginning and what makes a good ending. The first ideograph in Figure 5-11 uses the *Circle Left* score shown in Figure 5-7 as a key for reading the score that follows it. The second ideograph is an example of an arrangement with repetitions. Can you read it? Why are some symbols smaller than others?

Performance Indications   Dynamic variations (loud, soft, getting louder, getting softer) can be effectively introduced and applied at this stage of ideographing. Students can indicate changes in loudness by adjusting their ideograph symbols—making the symbols larger or smaller for louder or softer—or they can use conventional music notations and abbreviations (*p, mp, f, ff*). The symbols shown below for getting louder and softer, *crescendo* and *decrescendo* respectively, can also be used. Tempo variations are also possible and will need appropriate indications, either by adjusting the ideograph symbols or by using musical terms (*adagio, allegro, presto, moderato*). When reading arrangements with dynamic and tempo changes, a student conductor is most helpful for giving preparatory gestures to begin, timing the move to a new symbol, and guiding the dynamic and tempo suggestions. Once an arrangement has been performed, students should be encouraged to reflect on and assess how well the tempo and dynamic changes were performed.

Crescendo (getting louder)   Decrescendo (getting softer)

Inner hearing can be introduced as an additional way to read and perform ideographs. Students sing some of the units in their inner hearing as they read and sing arrangements, and they can be challenged to think of appropriate indications for

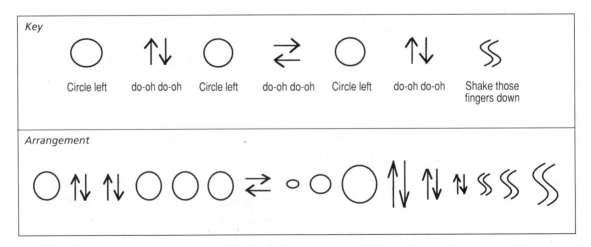

FIGURE 5-11   Circle Left: *Key and arrangement with repeating symbols*

inner hearing sections. "Let's think of a way to indicate which units are to be sung in our inner hearing."

Before the class performs a new arrangement, let students have time to study the score silently before reading it as a group. "Are there any places where you are unsure what the arrangers wanted? Are there any symbols you don't recognize?" As the class reads students' arrangements, notice what choices the arrangers made so that you can offer comments and feedback. "Arrangers, did the performance sound the way you expected it to?" "Which part do you think we need to practice?"

Reordering Symbols   In addition to repeating symbols, students can reorder symbols to create new arrangements. Introduce this activity by presenting an ideograph and following the symbols from start to finish, with students reading the symbols as you point. "You followed my direction that time, but watch what happens this time." On the second turn, start with the first symbol, then proceed to the second and back to the first. Once students understand that you are going to change the order of the symbols and phrases of the song, you can jump around, pointing at symbols in different orders. If students have difficulty singing the melody or remembering the words, reinforce their knowledge of the song by returning to following the symbols in order. You may repeatedly point to some symbols for extra practice when needed. For more practice and for additional challenges, students can be chosen to guide this activity, though they need to be reminded to point to the symbols slightly before the class is expected to sing them.

After introducing the reading activity of reordering symbols, write the symbols on the board, some out of order and some repeated. Students study the new ideograph arrangement and comment on what they notice; then they read the arrangement, singing it together. Encourage students to make their own arrangements as they did with symbol repetition, working with partners or in small groups and using dynamic indications and other musical symbols as appropriate.

For this more elaborate procedure of reordering symbols, even simple, well-known songs can be surprisingly difficult. A song with most phrases starting on the same tone is especially appropriate for this activity. Examples of songs that can be used are *Circle Left, Come and Follow Me, Daddy Loves the Bear, I'm Going Downtown, Johnny, Get Your Hair Cut, Old House,* and *Tideo.* Singing a phrase out of its original order can be a challenge even when the starting tones are the same. Songs with words that repeat while the melodies change can pose problems because it may be difficult to keep track of which melody goes with which symbol and because it may be easier to remember one melody over the other. Students need to know the differences between the phrases, and they need to have that difference indicated in the symbols they use. With these precautions in mind, you can elicit exciting arrangements from your students. Interesting reading challenges often develop in student arrangements, and students have many opportunities to comment on and discuss structure, compositional techniques, and overall feeling of the arrangements. With the regular ideograph given first as a reference, an arrangement of *Old House* that reorders and repeats some symbols is presented in Figure 5-12.

Two-Part Singing and Reading   Part singing can occur when half the class sings the original song and half the class sings an arrangement.

- Use one of the symbols as an ostinato to accompany an arrangement.
- Sing the arrangements in canon, experimenting with different entries.
- Experiment with starting the original song at different places in the arrangement.

FIGURE 5-12   Old House: *Key and arrangement with reordered symbols and dynamic markings*

Two arrangements can be sung at the same time. Surprising as that may be, the effects are often pleasantly intriguing. Guide students to appreciate and delight in the interaction between the two parts: "Was there a time when both groups sang the same words at the same time?" "Did you ever hear the other group echoing you?" "How would you describe the ending of our performance?" "Were there any places that were especially difficult for you?" Encourage students to discuss the various sounds and feelings that result from listening to and reading these combinations of arrangements.

Form Books

A *form book* is a series of song scores for a single song, each capturing different aspects of the form of that song (Richards 1980, 70–71). A form book often consists of six to ten pages, and each page reflects a slight change from the previous one. Pages that are chosen for use should reflect the background and study of a particular class. A page can show rhythmic or melodic notation, phrases, melodic contour, beat organization, solfa syllables, and so on.

The form book begins with symbols that require less prerequisite knowledge and progresses to those that use more conventional symbols. The first page is often a map, but it could be an ideograph or some other symbolization that lets students examine the structure of the song. The last page is often a full music score of the song that makes use of symbols, relationships, notation, or other information presented in previous pages of the form book. Because there is a logical sequence, in which earlier pages prepare for succeeding pages, the final page signals accomplishment by arriving at the full score of conventional notation with all the meanings gained from previous pages.

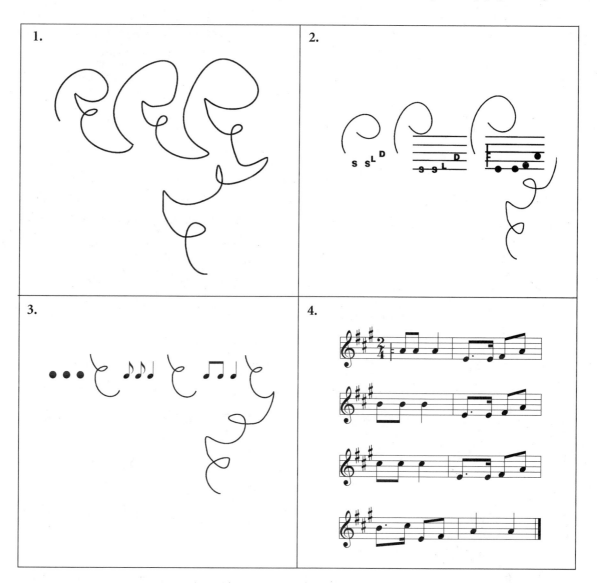

FIGURE 5-13 Sing with Me: *Map and notation, four pages*

Figure 5-13 shows four pages that can be used in a form book based on *Sing with Me.* The first three pages are based on a map. The first page gives the map in full, and the second and third pages replace sections of the map with solfa and rhythm notation to highlight certain features of the song. The fourth page presents a score that is divided according to the phrases of the song.

Most often, form books are read by guiding students to examine each page for the meaning of the symbols presented and then encouraging students to sing the song as they follow the symbols on the page. A primary purpose for reading a form book with a group of students is to have them read and understand the symbols and scores revealed on each page. If you are not careful, however, students can easily fail to track and connect the symbols on the page with the song they are singing. As you find ways to involve students in leading the reading experience as they study a form book, pages that require students to solve problems or manipulate symbols can be most effective.

Here are some sample statements and questions that can prompt students to read and study form book pages.

- "What do you see on this page that is familiar? Unfamiliar?"
- "Can you tell us the names of any symbols you see?"
- "If you were to title this page, what title would you give it?"
- "How do you think we will read this page?"
- "Who could show us how they would follow this page?"
- "Are there any other ways to read this page?"
- "How is this page connected to the previous one?"
- "There is a puzzle here to solve. Study it and raise your hand when you have a possible solution."
- "What will we sing when we get to that part of the page?"

The following sample form book page, based on *Scotland's Burning*, provides an example of how challenges can be incorporated into a form book. Notice that the word "fire" *sounds* as if it has two syllables, but is actually a one-syllable word and therefore receives only one dot. Other form book pages that pose a puzzle can be found in Figures 5-3, 5-4, and page 3 of Figure 5-15.

FIGURE 5-14

Scotland's Burning: *Sample form book page*

Follow these dots for *Scotland's Burning*

● ●

1. Read the dots by touching each one as you sing *Scotland's Burning*.
2. Find the dots where the melody is highest. How many dots are sung on this highest pitch? What words are sung?
3. Find the dots for "pour on water." How many dots from the song are used for singing "pour on water"?
4. Find the dots that have the same melody as "pour on water." Chinning the melody may help you solve this puzzle.

Form books can be used to expose students to conventional notation, to reinforce what they already know about conventional notation, to examine relationships within a song, to place patterns, relationships, and notations in context, and to explore a song from a variety of perspectives. Students need not understand or have previous exposure to all or any of the symbols on the pages. The form book experience serves less to teach about notations and relationships and more to recognize information previously studied and to come in contact with new kinds of symbolization.

Reading a form book is a little like reading a story to a preschooler. The point of reading the story with the child on your lap is less to teach letters and more to associate meaningful sound—a story—with a printed medium, and to do this in a way that lets the child feel comfortable with and interested in the medium. Reading should be a way to have new and exciting experiences, not just to get to the end of the book, and this passion for reading is one of the things the preschooler can gain when sitting on your lap and listening to you read. So it is with the form book: It should be a way for students to have new and exciting experiences of a song, not just to sing the song ten times and see eighth notes and quarter notes pass by.

Making a Form Book

For class study, a large format (18"×24") is best for a form book. Individual student copies can be made smaller, of course, and these can be projected on an overhead for presentation to the whole class. Guiding the study experience is easier when large, single pages are presented to the whole group, but there can be high student interest in having and following their own books, taking them home to read to others, and filling in their own answers on the pages.

PRINCIPLE 3

PRINCIPLE 4

Form books are especially engaging when students take turns guiding their classmates through certain pages. Student turns may include leading maps, pointing to the symbols of an ideograph, tapping dots, leading hand signs, and tracking conventional music notation. Having students guide students in reading form books gives them important experiences in leadership, requires them to demonstrate an understanding independent of the teacher and other students, and provides the teacher with opportunities to assess individuals' skills and comprehension.

Each page of a form book should show the song's structure and phrase lengths. If a song has three phrases, two short phrases followed by one long phrase, the notation is arranged to show that. With shorter songs, such as *Sing with Me* and *Daddy Loves the Bear,* some pages of the form book may not divide the song at all but present it as a single unit. One of the reasons to call this collection of symbolizations a form book is that the notation on each page (a map, an ideograph, or conventional symbols) highlights the form and structure of the song. By preserving the structure in this way for each page, students can more easily determine where they are in the song and which symbols go with what sounds. The format of a form book page should make it easier for students to follow, track, and understand the symbols they are seeing. In the final pages, this rule can be violated if for no other reason than to show that the conventional notation of music does not always show the structure of music. On pages that do not show the structure of a song, students can be challenged to see if they can find where the phrases start and stop even when these places are obscured by the way the song is notated.

PRINCIPLE 4

Common types of symbols for form books include maps, dots, ideographs, rhythm notations, pictures of hand signs, solfa initials (M R D, for example), solfa initials on a five-line staff, and conventional music notation. Combining types of symbols is effective in highlighting relationships in a song. By combining pieces of a map with solfa syllables (as in the *Sing with Me* form book in Figure 5-13), students can focus on certain melodic relationships in the song. Using combinations of song dots and rhythm notation lets students read and perform the rhythm for a whole song and still focus on certain rhythm relationships and notation for only portions of the song. Combining symbols lets certain relationships stand out and keeps students from being overwhelmed by too much new information.

Interactive pages that are puzzles or that pose problems can be especially intriguing. For example, see page 2 in the *Old House* form book shown in Figure 5-15. Students are asked to choose when to point to the unison "tear it down" and when to point to the other "tear it down" that rises in pitch.

The last page of a form book should tie together the materials and relationships presented in the previous pages. In music class, the last page can be the music score. For further study of the music score, add a page that challenges reading skills by making small changes in the song: repeating one phrase, putting the phrases in different orders, omitting the words, or arranging a two-part singing experience. In the *Come and Follow Me* form book (Figure 5-16), the last page repeats chunks of the song. In a language arts form book, the last page might contain a series of verses in which the words are changed, or it might include blanks so that students may fill in their own words. A form book can make a particularly effective introduction to a reading experience.

Form books can be used with songs students already know, and they can be used to introduce unfamiliar songs, including instrumental and concert music. The

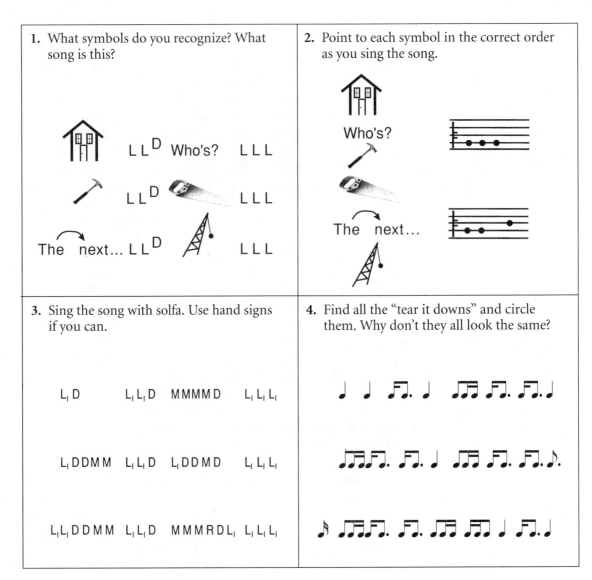

FIGURE 5-15 Old House *form book: Ideograph and notation, four pages*

purpose, and therefore the pages and their sequence, will be different, depending on whether the song is known beforehand. Using a form book to introduce a song or new musical materials demands that students rely on previous studies to solve the puzzles and see relationships on the pages and therefore requires students who have more experiences on which to draw. For obvious reasons, students learning a new song from a form book will not be able to sing with the teacher while following the early pages of the book. Even when students do not sing, having them follow a form book can be an effective way to introduce them to musical sound, notation, and symbolic relationships.

Chapter Epilogue

Listening skills are an essential facet of making music and musical development. The performance modes of chinning, antiphonning, inner hearing, and moving use listening skills to coordinate actions and responses to a song. The notation modes of

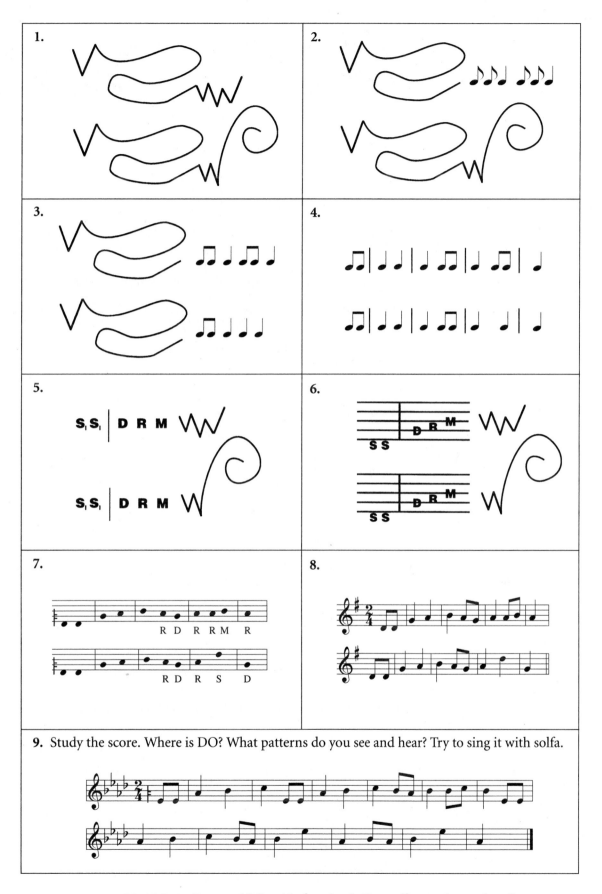

FIGURE 5-16 Come and Follow Me *form book: Map, solfa, notation, and reading challenge, 9 pages*

PRINCIPLE 3

PRINCIPLE 4

PROCEDURES FOR STUDYING A FORM BOOK

Study time	Give students independent study time on each page before reading it. Let them look for repetition and structure. Direct them to the symbols: "Are there any symbols you have seen before? Are there any symbols that are new to you?"
Connecting sound with symbol	Lead students to consider what the relationship might be between the symbols they see and the sounds of the song. Sing the song and follow the symbols. Encourage students to make observations about the relationships between the symbols and the sounds.
Turning the page	The pace is usually fairly quick from page to page. Avoid belaboring individual pages. You will usually know and see more on the page than the students will. They need not see everything on every page to make reading the book a valuable experience!
Sight singing	On most pages, students will sing the words of the song. Some pages, however, may suggest that they sing solfa or rhythm syllables. When the students are singing some parts of the song either aloud or with syllables and other parts normally, chinning can alleviate potential confusion in remembering what words to sing for portions of the song.
Student leaders	When students lead a page for their classmates to follow, the page may be repeated as many times as student interest is maintained.
Skipping pages	Pages can be skipped when appropriate, and other pages can be added. A complete form book could have as many as fifty pages. You may use only five or six at a time and may rarely use more than ten pages for a given lesson. Form books should be custom-designed and the appropriate pages selected by you for each particular class.

mapping, dotting, ideographing, and form books provide visual analogs of the auditory experience. Listening skills like these require considerable thinking, focusing, discriminating, analyzing, and synthesizing skills. Music classes and singing activities are natural and logical places in the elementary school for honing and challenging listening skills.

The Elements of Music in Song

6

Foundations for Music Study

SCENARIO

SINGING A CHILD'S SONG

You are sitting with a four-year-old child, Timothy. Timothy delights you by looking up and asking, "Will you sing *Eensy Weensy Spider* to me?" Not having sung or thought about this song for many years, you are quite surprised to hear yourself beginning to sing to Timothy.

"The eensy weensy spider went up the water spout." Without thinking about it, your fingers begin showing motions for the spider climbing and the rain coming down to wash away the spider ("Down came the rain and washed the spider out"). You make a circle with your arms as you sing "Out came the sun and dried up all the rain." By the time your fingers return to reclimbing the spout ("and the eensy weensy spider climbed up the spout again"), you and Timothy are giggling, singing, and moving in a play that includes just the two of you.

Do you know that you demonstrated musical knowledge when you showed Timothy the actions to *Eensy Weensy Spider*? (The score is in Chapter 9.) Are you surprised that such a simple activity could show what you know about music? Most people do the actions to this song with little attention or conscious effort. The actions seem matched to the music. Just because we pay little attention does not mean that there *is* no attention. We talk, run, ride bicycles, whistle, chew gum, and do a host of other things without conscious awareness of the background knowledge we are using to accomplish those tasks so easily. Being aware that the actions are matched to the song and coordinating the change in actions with the musical phrases indicate that we have this background knowledge. Two purposes of this chapter are to uncover the subtle yet powerful ways that simple responses to song can be used to study the music, and to become aware of and develop the musical knowledge that is already in us.

Why Study Music?

Are you asking yourself either of these questions?

- "After we sing the song until we know it, what else is there to do?"
- "If I'm not a music teacher, why should I study music or teach it to my students?"

PRINCIPLE 5

The effectiveness with which we are able to use song in the classroom is related to what we know about the song: its language, story, movement potential, and music (melody, rhythm, and structure). Making people aware of some fundamental but sometimes overlooked musical material implicit in singing activities can increase the power of singing for teachers and their students.

Why should teachers study the music in song?

- Knowing musical alternatives can help us make quick adjustments and improvements in the way we present songs.
- Knowing study techniques that engage students gives us opportunities to challenge students and develop their listening and attending skills.
- Knowing basic music facts helps create ways for students and teachers to develop vocal and musical confidence and, consequently, musical skills.
- Knowing about musical structure, melody patterns, and rhythm patterns makes setting up language and movement challenges more predictable and gives us more control and flexibility in teaching a lesson.
- Exploring basic musical resources offers students opportunities to interact with each other, manipulate language, develop listening skills, prepare for learning more about music, and participate more freely in musical situations.

What Are the Elements of Music?

Would you agree that everyone knows the elements of a house? A house may have a living room, a dining room, a kitchen, bedrooms, perhaps a study or a library, bathrooms, and other assorted rooms. Those elements seem obvious, but someone else's list might be different: a roof, windows, doors, siding, walls, floors, ceilings, rugs, electrical fixtures, furnace, plumbing, and so on. Yet another list of the elements of a house is possible: joists, studs, trusses, beams, nails, paint, glass, tile, glue, tar, and shingles. And what about warmth, a view, a garden, a family?

When we start to analyze something, to divide it into its parts or elements, things seldom stay simple. The level of detail we want to work with can change. Saying that a house is made up of the boards, nails, and tile is not wrong; it is just working at a different level of detail than seeing a house as walls, floors, and windows. Seeing the parts of the house in the context of rooms, as in the first list, introduces the human and the functional elements. Before leaving this analogy, consider these additional questions:

▶ Which level of analysis would you use if you were trying to sell the house?

▶ Which would you use if you were showing the house to a contractor from another country, unfamiliar with our building techniques?

▶ Which level would be appropriate to begin with if you were teaching fifth graders about house construction?

▶ If you wanted to explain what a house is to a caveman and a Martian, would you begin by showing them nails, glass, and framing lumber?

The level of analysis, how we divide a thing into parts and how much detail we go into, depends on what we are trying to demonstrate or learn.

There are also many ways of looking at music. Even the term "music" has vastly different meanings to different people. Notice these common expressions and the diversity of meaning for the term "music":

- "That's music to my ears." [words]
- "I can't play *Happy Birthday* because I don't have the music." [printed score]
- "Will you turn the music off?" [radio]
- "I'm going to go buy that music." [recording]
- "That was beautiful music!" [concert]
- "Listen to the music of nature." [animals, insects]
- "I'm not good at music." [singing, reading]
- "Do we have music today?" [class]

One common way of thinking about music uses the elements of *pitch, duration, timbre,* and *dynamics;* this is analogous to the nail-tile-lumber-glass analysis of the house. On a larger scale, we can see *melody, rhythm,* and *structure* as the important elements. Besides being more global, this division involves function as well; it is akin to the room analysis of a house.

To fully grasp how this analogy relates to music instruction, look closely at the definitions of the words in bold type in the preceding paragraph. Pitch, duration, timbre, and dynamics are qualities of individual sounds. If you sing a tone, that sound has a particular pitch (its "highness" or "lowness"), a particular duration (the length of time that it lasts), a particular timbre (the unique quality of your voice as opposed to that of an instrument or someone else's voice), and a level of loudness or softness. These four dimensions apply to individual sounds.

Melody, rhythm, and structure, on the other hand, refer to relationships among groups of sounds. When you sing the melody (or tune) of a song, you sing a particular series of pitches. It is the relationships of pitches within that series that makes them a melody. The melody you sing also has a distinct rhythm that results from the relationships among the durations of the sounds you sing. Because you will likely emphasize some words or tones in the melody, either on purpose or because of a pattern of durations and pitches, you will also get a feeling of a beat.

Rhythm has a general and a specific meaning. In its specific sense, it denotes the pattern of durations in a series of sounds. In its general sense, rhythm includes the feeling of beat and meter. In *SongWorks 1,* the terms "rhythm" and "rhythm pattern" will almost always refer to the specific meaning. When reading about rhythm or when using the term with students, be aware of the two meanings and the possible confusion. Be prepared, if the confusion becomes an impediment to clear understanding, to adjust the way you think about the term and to try the other meaning.

Structure, like melody and rhythm, results from the relationships among sounds. In particular, structure refers to a pattern or an organization formed by repetitions and contrasts of phrases and other musical units.

Our sense of musical flow and divisions within a song depends not only on the music but also on our listening experience and sophistication. The more familiar we are with a musical style (classical, jazz, country), the easier it is for us to move from one level of analysis to another. The less familiar we are with a musical style, the less detailed our understanding will be. Because *SongWorks 1* addresses how to use music and singing with children, it is based on a holistic view. Accordingly, the following sections will look at melody, rhythm, and structure, for they are the elements of music most obvious to untrained listeners. What you will find are discussions of elementary musical concepts at a level of analysis appropriate for beginning and inexperienced musicians.

Our discussions of musical elements have three aims. The first aim is to help people understand the parts of music: how they fit together and how they are related to one another. Those who have studied music have already learned much of this information, but we often learn it at a level of analysis so detailed that it is difficult to make the transition to teaching it to elementary-age students. Many people, for example, know the standard definitions of meter signatures and musical forms. Because their experience is limited and because the level of analysis that these definitions assume is so minute, however, they find that these definitions do not help them listen to music or participate in music. Knowing that a quarter note gets one count does not increase one's sensitivity to or appreciation of music, and it can get in the way of trying to read music when the quarter note is not the beat value. Knowing how to drive a nail is fine, but it does not go very far in helping someone appreciate the warmth of a living room or the handiness of a kitchen. A different level of analysis for both house and music is warranted in the beginning. Our discussion of musical elements will begin at the level of whole songs.

PRINCIPLE 4

The second aim is to develop a logical, consistent model for teaching music. This model is based on a "whole-song approach" that maintains a level of analysis appropriate to beginners and encompasses musical effects such as warmth, beauty, and liveliness. Listening permeates the approach. Definitions, explanations, and extensions are all examined and explored. These definitions and explanations can be readily verified in song material, yet they lose nothing when applied to more sophisticated music. Clear, simple, and accurate treatment of the sometimes complex and sophisticated interactions of musical elements is the goal.

PRINCIPLE 5

But why begin music study at the level of the whole song? Why not begin, as many approaches to music education do, with individual notes? Before we answer that question directly, recall the discussion of musical elements. When we separate music into parts, units, concepts, and elements, we do so on the basis of principles of learning, music, and thinking. Using a holistic approach honors the musical vitality, gestures, and purposes that come with larger musical contexts. It is as difficult to see how a single joist will make a homey living room as it is to find musical beauty in a single note. To construct our understanding of music, as opposed to having someone try to give us this understanding, we need to see the whole picture.

The third aim is to illustrate how you can introduce these concepts to students through song, movement, and language experiences. Principles stated at the beginning of the book will find expression in the way music elements are described, in the way they are studied, and in the way they can be presented to students. (For detailed discussion and teaching samples of these topics, see *SongWorks 2*.)

Framing Music Study: Points of Closure

The approach of this book encourages students to focus on the beginning and the ending of a song from their earliest musical experiences. The beginning and the ending of a song are called *points of closure* because they close off what is included in a song and what is excluded from it. Points of closure are something like a picture frame, except that they are really in the picture and not just the thing that separates the picture from the wall.

When students are able to control their movements as they listen to a song and start and stop actions in synchrony with a song, they show that they are paying attention to the song. Being able to start and stop with a song is the beginning of *musical thought*. Focusing on points of closure highlights the musical experience, setting it off from other events and letting the song emerge from background sounds and from the background thoughts of the listeners. Coordinating movement within a song's points of closure practices a fundamental listening skill, a skill of attention and auditory awareness.

To explore the idea of points of closure on your own, sing *Eensy Weensy Spider* and perform the actions while you sing. Did you start the actions right with the song? Did you end the actions on the word "again"? To do this exercise, you must listen for expected things to occur. You cannot start on time with the song if you do not anticipate its beginning, and you cannot stop with the song if you are not predicting the moment that the song will end. Coordinating movement with points of closure is one of the first steps in the study of music.

Our sense of *closure* is closely connected to our natural tendency to group individual elements into larger units. Consider these two illustrations:

- A teacher asks students on what word the "box" falls in the song activity *A-Hunting We Will Go*. The teacher expects to hear the students say, "Catch." Instead, the students respond, "We'll catch a little fox."
- A researcher asks students how *Mulberry Bush* ends. Students do not respond with the last word, tone, or syllable. Instead, they respond, "so early in the morning."

If a whole song is comparable to a whole house, the individual words are comparable to nails and lumber. Students in the preceding examples, however, are not working at that level of detail—they are dividing the song into parts, but those parts are at the level of phrases, or in the house metaphor, at the level of rooms.

Teaching music and learning about music benefit from the use of *context*. Context makes a sense of closure possible. Closure establishes meaning and definition; it puts things into perspective. Removing closure causes instability and incompleteness. When we ask a student to sing two or three different tones—MI RE DO for example—that student may not be able to do so, even when those tones form the same melody that he or she sings readily in a song such as *Hot Cross Buns*. The song context establishes a sense of closure that makes it easier for students to sing rhythms and melodies accurately. Removing the rhythms and melodies from the context, and therefore removing the sense of closure, takes away their stability and definition.

Musical thinking involves thinking ahead of yourself, anticipating what has not yet happened. Without this special kind of thinking, trying to coordinate actions with a song will always be difficult—the moment at which an action is to occur will have passed by the time the action is accomplished. Thinking ahead in time, anticipating moments like the beginning or the end, permits us to time our actions appropriately.

The first step in learning about music, then, is to make sure that we are able to separate the music from what comes before it and what comes after it. Once this *musical context* is established, other musical divisions become noticeable. Smaller divisions of the song become apparent. We begin to hear repetitions of melodies and rhythms. Each of these smaller units has its own sense of closure, derived from the contextual aspects of the whole song.

Thinking ahead in time, along with keeping track of what has just happened, is a fundamental aspect of musical thought, and we practice it every time we try to coordinate actions with music.

PRINCIPLE 4

The point of this discussion about the whole song is not to establish a dogmatic, unbreakable rule that each song must always be sung in its complete form. Instead, the intent is to draw attention to how context, in this case a whole song, structures and affects our listening. It is not that teachers should spend twenty minutes teaching the whole song and then go on to other things. We need to organize our teaching techniques and strategies in ways that recognize the importance of context to listening and attention.

Notice that coordinating actions with points of closure requires very little prerequisite musical knowledge and no specialized vocabulary. Walking along with a song, being careful to start with the song and to stop at the end of the song, may seem simple, but it is similar to listening to a *symphony,* only on a smaller scale. One must concentrate from the opening sounds to the music's conclusion whether ten minutes or ten seconds later.

Within the Framework: Phrases

Phrases: Exploring with Actions

Students demonstrate focused attention when they perform different actions in sequence throughout a song, as in *Eensy Weensy Spider.* Again, just by listening, students coordinate their actions with divisions of the song and change actions as the song changes phrases. The most obvious clues that students have about when to change actions come from listening to the language. More often than not, the repetitions in language and the places where the words change indicate both language and musical divisions. By attending to the language, you and your students can coordinate actions with the structure of the song. (Song scores are in Chapter 9.)

▶ Walk as you sing the song *Come and Follow Me.* Whenever you sing the word "come," change direction.

▶ Walk as you sing *The Farmer in the Dell,* but change direction whenever you sense that the song tells you to do so.

In how many directions did you move during each exercise? In the case of *Come and Follow Me,* you went in two directions, starting in one direction and changing in the middle of the song. There are several possibilities in *The Farmer in the Dell,* but by far the most common would be three or four directions. These challenges illustrate how we can explore musical structure through movement by focusing on the language of a song. In each case, language phrases guide our choices in movement. And in each case, the movement also highlights a musical dimension, most often musical phrases.

Phrases in music are like clauses or sentences in language. They are musical thoughts that have a sense of closure or a satisfying conclusion. Musical phrases somehow seem complete. When students do actions that change with phrases, they are developing their awareness of this structural dimension of music. Accomplishing these changes accurately demands the same kind of musical thinking as attending to points of closure, only to a greater degree.

When coordinating movements with phrases, students sense when one phrase is about to end and another is about to begin. *Cadence* is the musical term used to denote the end of a phrase. The cadence that comes at the end of a song is the *final cadence.* Cadences mark phrases off from one another and give a sense of closure or

Phrases, cadences, and closure are different ways of naming what we feel when we sense that the flow of music has beginnings and endings and can be divided into parts.

PRINCIPLE 4

completion to the phrase. The sense of closure can be strong or weak. This sense helps us predict that an ending of some sort is about to occur. Longer rhythmic values, certain tones in the scale, certain common melodic patterns, successive pauses or rests, and sentence structure all play a part in giving us a sense of closure.

The awareness that musical flow has logical and observable subdivisions is another fundamental step in musical development. Musical understanding and literacy are grounded in this awareness.

Doing actions that match the repetitions of words develops students' awareness of musical phrases. Acting out the meaning of the words of a song sometimes places more emphasis on the literal meanings of the words than on the musical structure, but when actions match repetitions, whether of words, melodies, or rhythms, musical divisions are almost always highlighted.

Actions that correspond to the natural divisions of the song, its phrases, are generally easier to accomplish than those that do not. Doing actions on the cadence phrase can be accomplished fairly easily. A number of song activities have actions that match the structure of the song or that occur in coordination with the cadence phrase. Such activities develop students' awareness and understanding of musical structure. Examples of these activities found in Chapter 9 are *Circle Left, Come and Follow Me, Did You Ever See a Lassie? I'm Going Downtown, Johnny, Get Your Hair Cut, London Bridge, Old Grumbler, Scotland's Burning, Skip to My Lou,* and *Tideo.*

Students can accomplish the relatively simple actions involved in such activities as *Looby Loo* and *Skip to My Lou* without a great deal of music background or previous experience. More intricate actions increase the level of difficulty, and if students are given the opportunity to develop actions themselves, the challenges of the actions can vary widely.

SECNARIO

STUDYING PHRASES IN *SING WITH ME*

"We are waving when the song says 'won't you be my honey?,' and we are now going to make up new actions for the rest of the song. If we did an action each time we sang the 'sing with me' words, how many times would we do the action? Let's check." After the teacher sets up the problem, students sing the song and notice that they would be doing the actions three times.

"We already have our action for 'won't you be my honey?' so what action shall we do on 'sing with me'?" Students decide they will cup hands around their mouths each time "sing with me" occurs in the song. Then they sing and perform all actions to the song.

After soliciting new actions for "sing with me" for three more turns, the teacher gives students an additional challenge. "We've been repeating the same action for 'sing with me' in all three places. Each of these places signals a new phrase. Who will give us a new action for the first phrase? The second phrase? The third phrase?" Students demonstrate and suggest words to describe the three actions, then the class sings and moves to the new song: "Spin and touch the floor, all together. Close your eyes, all together. Stretch up on your toes, all together. Won't you be my honey?" Students continue to suggest actions and words for each phrase of the song.

"Now that we've had several experiences feeling and seeing the phrases of this song, how would you answer this question? How many phrases are in the song *Sing with Me*?" Relying on the experiential base of movement and singing, students are confident when they respond that the song has four phrases.

Coordinating actions with a song, either from beginning to end or phrase by phrase, develops and practices listening skills. Being aware of the phrases, knowing where repetitions occur in a song, and practicing the actions that you want to use will help you lead songs more effectively in the classroom—even if you intend to do nothing more than sing them with your students.

Phrases and Song Chunks: Preserving Context in Smaller Units

Whole songs divide into phrases, and phrases often subdivide into smaller units. Listen to yourself sing the last line of *Mulberry Bush:* "Here we go 'round the mulberry bush, so early in the morning." Many people consider this a single phrase but can also hear that it divides nicely between "bush" and "so." In *Sing with Me,* it is easy to divide each of the first three lines into two: "Sing with me" and "all together." These smaller divisions will be called **song chunks.**

In psychology, the term **chunk** refers to a coherent group of items that can be remembered as a single unit (Hunt 1982). A song chunk is a group of sounds that form a single unit. Song chunks can be performed accurately without a model and can also be repeated easily without distorting their melodic and rhythmic relationships.

Which of these word groupings from *The Farmer in the Dell* could be considered a song chunk?

1. "in the dell"
2. "-mer in the"
3. "Hi-ho the derry-o"
4. "in the dell the farmer"

Because they accurately capture a thought and a cohesive unit of sound and language, examples 1 and 3 are song chunks. Song chunks, like phrases, result from the interaction of melodic, rhythmic, and language relationships. Like phrases, chunks preserve context and musical flow even when separated from the whole and, for that reason, can maintain their musical shape, making their performance musical, even when we are paying close attention to a single element.

Phrases and chunks are organizers within songs that are determined by our perceptions and not by our notation system.

Working with phrases and song chunks divides a song into parts in a way that reflects perceptual tendencies (Bamberger 1991; Bennett 1991a, 1990a). Phrases and song chunks seem to be a fundamental mode of organizing musical material. On the cognitive side, they are parallel to the mind's tendency to organize information into meaningful groupings (Sloboda 1985). On the musical side, they are defined by our experience of musical flow and our sense of closure, not by notations and symbols (Bamberger 1978; Thurmond 1982; Upitis, 1987). Our perception of song chunks, therefore, arises naturally out of singing and listening to songs, and our teaching strategies and behaviors should respect the perceptual organization that people use in listening to music. (For further discussion and specific applications of this topic, see *SongWorks 2.*)

Stress Patterns: Listening for Important Syllables

The sound of language is fully present in song. Like song, language is sound before it is print, and children learn the sound of language before they learn its printed form. Among the examples of language content in song are vowels, consonants, rhymes, alliteration, and poetic meter. Word accents are especially important connections between song and language because they give shape, expression, and meaning to both. In the English language, words have regularly accented patterns, and one syllable of each word is typically louder than the others, shaping the sound. An accent shift can change the meaning of a word and, therefore, the intended expression—"PRES-ent" is a noun, referring to a gift, whereas "pre-SENT" is a verb, meaning to give or offer.

Another feature of the sound of language is the grouping of syllables and words to form larger units. Examples of some common groups are "happy birthday," "open the cabinet," "in a minute," and "whenever possible." In "HAPpy" and "BIRTHday," the accent is on the first syllable, but when combined into the word grouping "happy birthday," "happy" loses its accent, and the grouping then has a single accent on "birth-"—happy BIRTHday.

In larger groupings, one syllable tends to predominate. We call this predominant syllable a *stress*, to distinguish it from the accent that each word has. A ***stress pattern***, then, is a naturally occurring group of syllables that has a predominant or stressed, syllable. Stress results largely from a change of loudness, but it is also affected strongly by rhythm, melody, language, and other structural elements.

The stressed syllable in a group of words can change according to context and speaker intention. "Whenever you want," for example, has a natural feeling of stress on the "want"—"Whenever you WANT." If the speaker wants to emphasize the fact that it is up to the hearer to decide when, the "you" might get the stress—"Whenever YOU want." To emphasize that the timing is open, the "-ev-" may get the stress— "WhenEVer you want." Notice that not all syllables are normally candidates for a stress. The "-er," for example, will not be stressed under normal conditions.

Stress patterns are an important feature of our spoken language.

- The meaning of our speech can depend on stress patterns.
- Stress patterns provide for the efficient structuring of speech.
- Stress patterns give a lilt or shape to our speech, contrasting with early examples of computer-generated speech, which had little or no pitch, little or no stress, and few or no accents.

As in listening to speech, listening for stressed syllables in song phrases involves listening for changes in dynamics. Becoming aware of and sensitive to subtle differences in dynamics prepares us for an understanding of musical shaping and phrasing. The beat of a song, the feeling of a steady pulse, is the result, at least in part, of regularly recurring accents. It is common for the stress to occur on the beat of a song, but it almost never occurs on *every* beat. Consider the power of stress for distinguishing between a musical and a mechanical performance.

- Emphasizing *no* syllable in a phrase yields a mechanical interpretation, lacking direction and personality.
- Emphasizing *every* syllable that comes on a beat, or every accented syllable, results in a performance that is ponderous, punchy, and lacking in subtlety.
- Emphasizing a *single* syllable in a phrase gives a clarity to the interpretation, a focus to the phrase, and a nice shape to a musical gesture.

Students' listening skills and sense of musical shape can benefit from exploring and examining the stress patterns in songs. To assist students who have difficulty telling which syllables stand out, try the following study sequence (Richards and Langness 1984). Students can imitate the teacher doing this action, or they can try it without a model.

1. Speak "the mulberry bush" four times in a row.
2. Tapping one finger on the opposite palm, tap only once during each repetition of the phrase: the mulberry bush, the mulberry bush, the mulberry bush, the mulberry bush.

Attention to stress patterns is basic to the study of rhythm and structure, whether of language or of music.

3. Notice which syllable received the taps. Listening, movement, and repetition combine to reveal the syllable most natural and comfortable to tap, the stressed syllable. Did you hear the MULberry bush, the MULberry bush . . . ?

Being sensitive to stress patterns, observing which tone in a group seems most important, and letting the other tones be somewhat less prominent gives musical shape to phrases and stimulates musical singing.

The stress-pattern chart lists ten common patterns used with great frequency in spoken English, gives several examples of each, identifies a song in which each can be found, and illustrates them with a dot-dash notation system: The stress is symbolized by a dash, and the unstressed sounds are symbolized by a dot.

EXAMPLES OF STRESS-PATTERN SYMBOLS AND WORDS

Dot/Dashes	Examples	Song	Words in Song
• —	July, respect, Marie, Vermont	*Daddy Loves the Bear*	the bear
— •	seven, early, David, Utah	*Circle Left*	fingers, circle
• • —	twenty-one, hit the door, Antoinette	*Come and Follow Me*	in a line
— • •	seventy, playfully, Kennedy, Delaware	*Row, Row, Row Your Boat*	merrily
• — •	eleven, banana, Maria, Montana	*Here We Are Together*	together
• • — •	twenty-seven, in a minute, Alabama	*Punchinella*	Punchinella
• • • —	seventy-one, not on your life	*Old Grumbler*	under the ground
• — • •	"eleventy," geometry, Elizabeth, an elephant	*The Farmer in the Dell*	the derry-o
• — • • —	it's not what I want, whenever you please, bananas and cream	*Mulberry Bush*	the mulberry bush
— • • •	January, February	*Hot Cross Buns*	one a penny, two a penny

Studying Stress Patterns with Language Substitution

Not all activities that ask for language substitution require students to match the stress patterns set up by the original words. Songs such as *Drunken Sailor*, *Circle Left*, *Sing with Me*, and *Daddy Loves the Bear* allow a certain amount of freedom in fitting new words to the original rhythm of the songs. To highlight and explore stress patterns of language and song, however, activities can be structured to focus on the matching process—"How many sounds are in the pattern?" "Where does the stress occur?"

SCENARIO   LANGUAGE SUBSTITUTION IN *COME AND FOLLOW ME*

Come and follow me in a line, in a line. Come and follow me, we will stop this way.

"Every time we sing the words 'in a line,' have your finger tap them." The students looked at each other. "This is going to be easy," they thought. The song started, and almost all the students tapped the words in synchrony with the song, but almost three-fourths of them went on to tap "we will stop" as well.

The teacher looked at them with delight and curiosity. "What happened? Did you think the song was going to say 'in a line' again? I was surprised by what happened, but did you notice how 'we will stop' sounded? Let's do it again, and tap 'in a line' and 'we will stop.'" Students responded, easily able to hear and tap the three examples.

"Did 'in a line' and 'we will stop' feel the same?" ["Yes!"] "How many taps does 'in a line' get?" ["Three!"] "How many taps are in 'we will stop'?" ["Three!"] "Put those rhythms in your feet this time.

"Let's try to put the 'in a line' words in the 'we will stop' place. It takes concentration to avoid singing the wrong words! . . . 'Come and follow me in a line, in a line. Come and follow me in a line this way!'

"What other words would fit in the song and feel just like 'in a line'? Remember how many taps they should get. Raise your hand if you think of some words that we could sing in place of 'in a line' and 'we will stop.'" Students suggested several replacements: "in a room, to the door, down the stairs, into the hallway, to the circle."

Each time a student suggested a set of words, time was taken to try the new words with the song. "Do the words fit in the song?" "How many syllables or taps do they have? Tap the words as you sing this time."

Finding new words that precisely match the rhythm and accents of words in a song involves noting the rhythm and the accent pattern of words and word groupings. Such precision can be a real challenge to listening skills, but it gives a solid foundation for more advanced music study. Being able to match word phrases demonstrates strong language and rhythm skills. Matching new words to a given stress pattern is a rhythmic study, but it focuses more on the number of sounds in a group and the placement of the stress within that group than it does on the length of sounds.

SCENARIO

LANGUAGE SUBSTITUTION IN *OLD GRUMBLER*

Old Grumbler was dead and lay under the ground, under the ground, under the ground. Old Grumbler was dead and lay under the ground, way high up.

"Where else could old Grumbler lie besides 'under the ground'?" Students make suggestions quickly: "in his bed, on the sofa, out in the yard, in the garden, many miles away." Each suggestion is sung in the song; it takes effort to fit some suggestions in comfortably. "What do we have to do to make 'in the bed' fit? That's right, we make the 'in' a little longer, and then it fits fine." "Did you notice how we sped up 'many miles away' to get all the syllables in?

"Here is a tougher challenge. Listen to how 'under the ground' sounds." The teacher then taps these words, placing a slight but noticeable stress on 'ground' as she sings the song. "How many taps did these words get? Four? Three? You check this time." "Four is right, but which syllable is a little different? Listen again. What is different about 'ground'?" Students comment that it sounds higher and longer and that the teacher tapped it a bit louder. "Yes, 'ground' gets a special stress in this song. Now, which of our new sets of words will fit in the song and feel just like 'under the ground' does, with four taps and a stress on the last syllable?" "What are some other phrases that would fit? They don't have to make sense, you know." Students can work in partners to figure out phrases that fit the song pattern.

As students suggest words and phrases, the teacher models the stress pattern, emphasizing the stress when she taps it. Students are directed to listen for the stress and identify both the number of taps and the placement of the stress. Each pattern is evaluated in the same fashion, whether students finally decide that it fits or doesn't fit.

When the pattern fits, as in "sad and dismayed," it is sung in the song. When the suggested words don't fit, as in "on top of the car," a reason is given: "That set of words would be fun to sing, but it has five syllables. After we stop looking for patterns with four, we might have time to sing some favorite words that don't have to fit exactly."

Elements of Music

PRINCIPLE 2

PRINCIPLE 4

This section presents conventional music terminology and concepts and puts them into the experiential context of a song. The purpose of providing this context is twofold: to offer the reader bases for exploring and understanding the information, and to serve as a model for introducing the information to children. Once children and adults have an experiential base of songs, they are better prepared to construct their understandings of the terms and concepts introduced. Within the song context, elements of music are presented with a playful attitude that seeks to engage students, to respect their ideas and perceptions, and to create a safe environment in which they can learn.

What Is Structure?

Structure, our sense of a song's organization, is most obvious in song at the level of phrases. How phrases are put together, how their lengths compare, and the extent to which they repeat and contrast contribute to the structure of a song. A basic principle of structure is that there is interplay between constancy and change, so our ability to recognize similarities directly affects our understanding of structure.

Some use the word *form* as a substitute for structure. The two words have similar meanings, but they are not strictly synonymous, because the form of a song is a larger dimension than its structure. Structure refers specifically to the organization of phrases with repetitions and contrasts, but form refers to the unique way in which a song fills out a certain structure. Returning to our house analogy, structure refers to the blueprints and the floor plan; form is how the house looks and how it feels to live in it. Two songs may have the same structure, but because they have different words, melodies, and rhythms, they have different forms.

Elements of Song Structure

Repetition and contrast in a song result from the interactions of the words, melodies, and rhythms. We expect to hear repetitions in a song, but we also expect to hear contrasts. In most songs, the repetitions are not identical and the contrasts are not complete.

Sing the song *Sing with Me.*

▶ What repetition did you hear?

▶ Was there any contrast?

▶ How would you describe the sequence of repetition and contrast in the phrases of this song?

In *Sing with Me,* the first line of text is repeated in the second and third phrases, and the fourth phrase provides a contrasting text. As you sang this song, you may have noticed that although the first three lines of text are the same, the melodies that go with them are all a bit different. Notice how the tones for the song chunk "sing with me" shift on each repetition.

Now sing *Muffin Man.*

▶ Listen for repetition and contrast.

▶ Did you notice that the first phrase has three repetitions of the words "the muffin man" but each time the melody is different?

▶ Did you notice that the second phrase begins exactly the same as the first but ends with a completely new part?

Sing with Me and *Muffin Man* illustrate another feature of song structure: Some elements of the song can repeat while, at the same time, other elements change.

A common way to categorize song structure is to compare phrase length. The technical way to measure phrase length is to count beats, but we can get a close approximation of comparative phrase lengths through movement. To experience phrase lengths of *Sing with Me,* follow this sequence of movement:

▶ Sing *Sing with Me* and move your hand at a steady rate through the air in front of you, making an arc like a rainbow.

▶ Sing the song again and move your hand, starting a new rainbow each time you hear a new phrase. This should give you a sense of the length of each phrase.

▶ Now try making rainbows to the phrases with paper and pencil. What do you see?

▶ Does your drawing show you what you heard?

As you can see in Figure 6-1, rainbow sketches facilitate making rough estimates and comparisons of phrase length (Richards and Langness 1982).

Common Structures in Folk Songs

If we use text repetition and phrase length as criteria, we find that three common structures emerge in English-language folk songs for children: **short-short-long, balanced,** and **echo.** The analysis here does not represent an exhaustive study of folk songs, and these three structures do not account for all the structural features found in this repertoire. The following are common structures, however, and each structure has several variations.

FIGURE 6-1

Rainbow phrases for Sing with Me

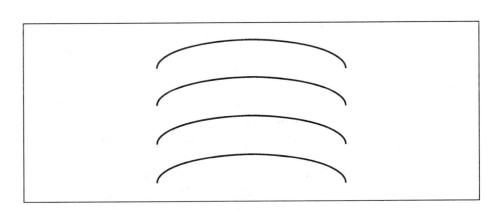

THREE COMMON SONG STRUCTURES

SHORT-SHORT-LONG STRUCTURE

Description	Three phrases: two short phrases and one concluding longer phrase. The last phrase is usually equal in length to the first two combined.
Examples	*Hot Cross Buns* *Drunken Sailor* *Daddy Loves the Bear* *The Farmer in the Dell*
Comments	Deciding whether a song is balanced or short-short-long in structure is often a matter of interpretation. Key to the decision is the strength of connection we feel between the first and last halves of the longer phrase. Is it a sentence? Does it have a connecting word such as "and," "who," or "so"? A longer last phrase provides contrast to the two shorter first phrases.

BALANCED STRUCTURE

Description	Phrases of equal length, often four beats. Most commonly, there are two or four phrases.
Examples	*Twinkle, Twinkle, Little Star* *Scotland's Burning* *Sing with Me* *Come and Follow Me*
Comments	The widespread use of this structure may reflect a desire for symmetry and equilibrium. A distinct break between the last two phrases distinguishes this structure from the short-short-long. There are many variations in the way melodies and words are repeated in these phrases.

ECHO STRUCTURE

Description	The second chunk of the first phrase is immediately repeated twice, like echoes. The second phrase begins like the first phrase, omits the echoes, and concludes with new material for the cadence chunk. The arrangement of words looks like this: **X Y Y Y** **X Y Z**
Examples	*London Bridge* *Mary Had a Little Lamb* *Mulberry Bush* *Did You Ever See a Lassie?* *Rig-a-Jig-Jig* *Johnny, Get Your Hair Cut*
Comments	Melodic variations are common on the echoes. The echo structure can resemble short-short-long when the second and third echoes seem to form a single, linked phrase. The cadence unit can feel like an extension of the last repeat or like a separate phrase.

Other Structures

Songs can be made into longer structures through the use of **verses** and **chorus.** Many songs that tell stories use multiple verses, each verse having different words but utilizing the same melody and structure. *Old Grumbler* is a good example of a song with multiple verses. In some songs a chorus, sometimes called a **refrain,** is inserted between the verses. The chorus is a section of music, often about the same length as a single verse, that has the same melody and words each time it is sung. *Drunken Sailor* has the form of verses ("What shall we do . . . ?") and chorus ("Weigh, hey, and up she rises . . .").

In music notation, the end of a verse is often indicated by a **double bar.** In general, a double bar indicates the end of a section in a piece of music. A *final double bar,* found after the final cadence, has a second bar thicker than the first. **Repeat signs** look like final double bars, but they have two dots positioned near the thinner line and on either side of the middle line of the staff. The repeat sign that has dots to the left indicates a return either to the beginning or to a previous repeat sign, for a second performance of the music. See Figure 6-2.

FIGURE 6-2
Double bars

Another common musical structure, ***binary structure,*** has two sections that contrast with each other and are often symbolized with the letters *AB.* ***Ternary structure*** has three sections; the third is a repeat of the first but need not be an exact repetition. The common symbol used to represent ternary structure is *ABA.* The symbols AB and ABA are commonly used to identify the organization of these larger structures, but they do not appear in the printed musical score.

In contrast to the common folk-song structures listed earlier, binary and ternary structures are often much longer and have more elaborate variations. They can have beginning sections, called *introductions,* extra endings, and surprising twists and turns, sometimes making it difficult to tell the second part from the third part. As musical structures get longer, they often have special sections that help the listener recognize that the music is coming to a close. These ending sections are called ***codas,*** from the Italian word for "tail." The designation *D. C. al Fine* at the end of a B section tells the performer to return to the A section and perform it again. *D.C.* is an abbreviation for the Italian term *da capo,* meaning "to the beginning," and *fine* means "the end." *D. C. al Fine,* then, means "Go back to the beginning and play to the end." Can you find an example of *D.C. al Fine* in the song scores of Chapter 9 and read the score as the markings suggest?

What Is Melody?

If you were to sing the first phrase of *Hot Cross Buns,* and then sing the first phrase of *Mary Had a Little Lamb,* you might notice that each phrase is made up of the same tones but that the tunes are different. The series of tones and changes in duration that give a song its "tune" is the ***melody,*** and melody is one of the primary means of distinguishing one song from another.

Although it seems like a simple term, melody may be the most difficult element of music to describe and explain because it may be the most intangible. Movement externalizes rhythm, making it possible for us to see it and to feel it kinesthetically without the interference of a learned vocabulary. We cannot see a melody, and we can only feel the melody in our voices as they change between one tone and the next. For most of us, this feeling is obvious only at the extremes of our vocal registers, very high and very low. Our challenge with melody, pitch, and tone is to find ways to make the relationships between them visual and kinesthetic, to make this dimension of sound concrete so that we can see, feel, compare, and describe melody, pitches, and tones.

Pitch Relationships

Melody is made up of individual pitches in a series. ***Pitch*** refers to the dimension of sound that we describe as relative *highness* or *lowness.* Related to the frequency of vibrations, the pitch of a sound identifies a specific place on a high-to-low continuum. When asked, "What pitch is that?" we might answer with one of the seven letter names we use to identify specific pitches (A, B, C, D, E, F, G).

Sometimes the terms "pitch," "tone," and "note" are used interchangeably, but they have distinct shades of meaning. *Pitch* refers to the dimension of sound we

**Making the distinction
between the term
"tone," indicating a
sound, and the term
"note," indicating a
symbol, maintains an
important difference
between the sound of
music and the notation
of music.**

PRINCIPLE 5

describe as high or low. Sounds can have indefinite or definite pitch. An indefinite pitch cannot be sung or replicated on a pitched musical instrument. A hiss can be higher or lower, but it cannot be played on a piano key. A cymbal crash, the roar of the surf, and the thud of a book are other examples of sound with indefinite pitch. A *tone* is a sound with a definite pitch. A tone can be sung or replicated on a musical instrument. To complicate matters, the term "tone" sometimes refers to the timbre, or individual quality, of a sound, as in the expression "She sings with a full tone quality." When referring to pitch, however, tone identifies a sound that has definite pitch. Both pitch and tone refer to sound. A *note,* on the other hand, is a written representation of a pitch, though sometimes "note" is used to refer to a particular sound on an instrument, as when we say, "He played a really low note." Pitch, tone, and note can have strict definitions in scholarly writing, but they are so close in meaning, and they overlap in enough cases, that they are used loosely in everyday language, even by musicians. Recognizing how these three terms are used and how close they are in meaning, and becoming aware of how easily they can be confused, can lead us to sort out our own thinking and avoid confusing our students.

Seeing pitches notated on a staff conditions us to think of them as moving up and down, being higher and lower than each other. The terms we use to describe pitch and melody—higher and lower, up and down—are learned terms. The concept of vertical distance and movement is the conventional way of thinking about pitch. Using that vertical association, we can show what a melody looks like by drawing a line that represents the vertical relationships. Such a line is called a *melody graph,* and it is a visual representation of the changing directions of and the relative distances between the pitches of a melody.

The figure that is formed by a melody graph shows *melodic contour,* the shape of a melody resulting from changes in pitch height. In a melody graph, individual pitches can be shown by heavy dots arranged in correct vertical relationships and connected by a line to make the contour more obvious. Follow these steps in making a melody graph for *Mary Had a Little Lamb:*

▶ As you sing or chin the song, listen to the rise and fall of the pitches and draw a dot for each pitch.

▶ Place your dots higher or lower as you feel the changes in your voice and as the melody moves higher or lower.

▶ Connect the dots and look at the shape of the line, the melodic contour.

▶ Do you see, hear, and feel the highest pitches? Do you see, hear, and feel the direction of the melody at the cadence?

▶ Does your melody graph for *Mary Had a Little Lamb* look like Figure 6-3?

For further practice, sing the song *Happy Birthday* and make a melody graph for it. Chinning the song may help you listen for the melody. Does your graph look similar to Figure 6-4?

FIGURE 6-3
Melody graph for
Mary Had a Little Lamb

FIGURE 6-4

Melody graph for Happy Birthday

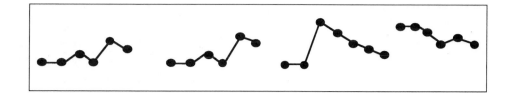

As you look at the contour of *Happy Birthday,* you can spot the highest and the lowest dots, representing the highest and the lowest tones of the song. The aural distance between these two most extreme tones, the distance between the lowest and the highest pitches, is considered the ***range*** of a song. Songs have range, and so do voices. You may have heard people say, "That's out of my range," when they are referring to singing a song that goes too high or too low for their voices. The distance between two adjacent tones is called an ***interval.*** Do you see intervals that are larger than others in the melody graph for *Happy Birthday*?

▶ Notice where the biggest jump occurs between tones in the song and in the melody graph. Sing the song, follow the graph, and listen for this jump. What words or syllables are being sung during that jump?

▶ Did you come up with the third "hapPY BIRTHday?" The jump from the -PY to the BIRTH- is the largest interval in *Happy Birthday.*

▶ Sing the song again and follow the graph. Listen to the intervals. Notice which are larger and which smaller, and feel the changes in your vocal production as you sing them.

Scales

The word ***scale*** is related to the Italian word for "ladder," *scala,* and when we sing a scale we climb up and down a musical ladder. A scale is a sequence of tones arranged in a specific pattern of intervals, an abstract frame that gives us underlying information about a song.

In Western European music, we commonly use a seven-tone, or ***diatonic,*** scale, which comes in two basic forms, ***major*** and ***minor.*** One of the ways a scale is identified as major or minor is by the pattern of ***whole steps*** and ***half steps*** between the intervals. Here we find another visually descriptive term, "step," applied to something that is purely aural—the relationship of tones.

An easy way to understand whole steps and half steps may be to envision a piano keyboard (Figure 6-5). Each key on the keyboard produces a specific pitch when depressed. Notice the pattern of alternating white and black keys. A half step is the interval between any key and the immediately adjacent key, to the left or the right, white or black. No other key falls between them.

FIGURE 6-5

Segment of a piano keyboard

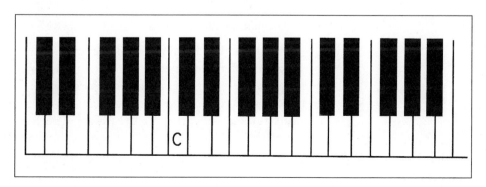

A whole step spans two half steps. There will always be one key between any two keys that form a whole step. The keys that form a whole step can both be black, or both be white, or one can be black and one white. Study the keyboard illustration and find whole steps in all three configurations of black and white keys.

When we sing a major scale with the syllables DO RE MI FA SO LA TI DO, we are singing the whole steps and half steps of a major scale. (These syllables, called solfa, will be discussed in the next section.) Notice that there are eight syllables, counting the DO at either end of the sequence. The interval spanning the eight steps of a diatonic scale is called an *octave.* Going up or down an octave always brings us back to the same pitch letter name, even though the pitch is an octave higher or lower.

Find the white key directly to the left of one of the groupings of two black keys. This key is C, and each key in this position on the keyboard is also a C. *Middle C* is in the middle of the **grand staff** and also happens to be in the middle of the piano. The other Cs are octaves apart from each other. Find the C one octave higher and the C one octave lower than the C indicated in Figure 6-5.

Not all tones of a scale are equally important. More often than not, the tone on which a song cadences tends to be the most important tone. The most important tone in a melody or a scale is called the *tonic.* In Western European culture, songs very often end on *DO.* DO is the tonic and the most important tone in nearly all the songs to which we refer in this book. Knowing the range of a song and its tonic will help you find appropriate starting pitches for the songs you sing with your students.

Solfa Syllables

Musical tones can most easily be identified and described when we label them. Several labeling systems exist for musical tones, and the one you may remember best from childhood is the one that names tones with letters of the pitches (A B C D E F G). In *SongWorks 1* and in many music classrooms, especially those for young students, *solfa* syllables are used to teach the relationships between tones. *Solfeggio* and *solfège* are synonymous with solfa.

There are two main varieties of solfa: *fixed DO* and *movable DO.* In fixed DO, DO is always the pitch C. In the fixed-DO system, the pitch and the piano key C is always DO, the next white key to the right is RE or D, and so on, matching the solfa sequence with the pitch sequence.

In the movable-DO system (sometimes called tonic solfa), which is commonly used in North American elementary music classrooms, the syllables do not represent pitch names but pitch relationships. DO or any other syllable can be any pitch. Once one tone is labeled with a specific syllable, the remaining syllables become matched to specific tones as well. A number line provides a visual example: When a line is drawn with points that identify regularly spaced intervals on the line, zero can be anywhere. As soon as you decide where zero is, however, all the other numbers become matched to their respective places on the line.

| The major scale in solfa is | DO RE MI FA SO LA TI DO[1] |
| The minor scale in solfa is | LA$_1$ TI$_1$ DO RE MI FA SO LA |

Notice the markings in the scales above that are additions to the solfa syllables. Notice the difference between the marking in the major scale and the two in the minor scale. These markings are called *superscripts* and *subscripts* and are used in writing solfa syllables. Superscripts and subscripts designate which octave is intended, a superscript indicates an upper DO (or any tone above it), and a subscript indicates any tone below DO.

Another common scale is the *pentatonic scale,* made up of five tones, as its name suggests. Many children's songs are based on this tonal structure. A pentatonic scale, common in English-language folk songs, has the form DO RE MI SO LA, skipping the fourth and seventh tones of the diatonic scale. This results in a scale without half steps between adjacent tones. The black keys of the keyboard naturally arrange themselves into a pentatonic scale.

You may have learned to use numbers to identify pitch relationships. For example, the tonic would be "1" rather than DO, and the second tone would be "2" rather than RE. This numbering system for the scale degrees is more concrete for some people because it taps into our background in number relationships. Solfa syllables, however, are preferable for three primary reasons:

1. Solfa syllables are logically supported with hand signs. (See the next section.)
2. The vowel sounds of the solfa syllables are more compatible with good vocal production than those of the number system.
3. Numbers are used for many other purposes. In musical situations, for example, they are used in designating meter, identifying measures, counting rhythms, and naming chords. Solfa syllables are used only to study pitch relationships.

Hand signs are physical gestures that represent solfa. They systematize movement up and down following the melody line (contour) of a song or phrase. Sometimes referred to as arm signs when both arms and bigger motions are used (Richards 1980), these gestures help us see and feel the *relationships* of tones we are singing and hearing. Hand signs connect the auditory with the visual and kinesthetic senses.

Hand signs originated in the late nineteenth century with John Curwen. Curwen, a British minister and respected teacher, created the hand signs as a way of showing the tones of the tonic solfa (movable-DO) system. Composer Zoltán Kodály (pronounced KOE-die) borrowed the idea for hand signs and employed them in the system of music education he began in Hungary. As Kodály's method became better known in the United States, beginning in the 1960s, the hand signs became more popular among music teachers.

Study the Curwen hand signs illustrated in Figure 6-6. Mirror the child in the drawing as you sing the solfa syllables and make the hand signs. Even though the illustration begins with low SO, you may begin with DO if that is easier for you.

▶ Did you notice how your hand changed shape and vertical position each time you sang a higher pitch?

▶ Sing back down the scale, using the appropriate hand signs.

Here are the solfa syllables for *Hot Cross Buns.* Sing the solfa to *Hot Cross Buns* as you make the hand signs.

MI RE DO   MI RE DO   DO DO DO DO RE RE RE RE MI RE DO

Hand signs and solfa are useful with children and novice music students for several reasons:

1. The movements of the hands when doing hand signs outline the melodic contour.

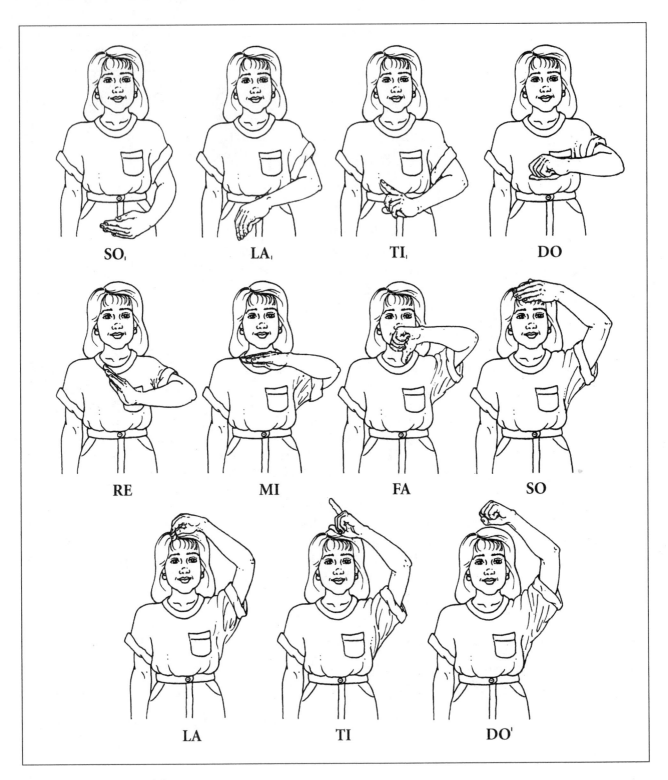

FIGURE 6-6   *Curwen Hand Signs*

2. The shapes of the hand indicate information about pitch relationships and provide kinesthetic and visual representation of the pitches. For example, when the index finger of the TI hand sign points up to DO, it shows the tone's tendency to resolve to DO.

3.   Hand signs and solfa can be performed while singing. Teachers can monitor students' achievements easily by observing students using hand signs. Students can also demonstrate their hand signs and listening skills by leading hand-signing activities.

4.   Students can study pitch relationships without knowing about either note names or key signatures. For example, the pitches for the opening phrase of *Happy Birthday* can be spelled in twelve combinations of notes and can be shown in many ways on the staff. We need learn only one set of solfa syllables, however, to sing the first phrase of *Happy Birthday:* SO₁ SO₁ LA₁ SO₁ DO TI₁.

Staff Notation

A written record of music is called a *score.* Solfa scores, rhythm scores, and beat scores are some of the ways we can write what we hear. Song maps, song dots, and ideographs are also scores of musical sound. In a solfa score, syllables can be abbreviated by using just the consonants. The solfa score for *Mary Had a Little Lamb* would look like this:

M R D R M M M   R R R   M S S   M R D R M M M M R R M R D

The five-line grid on which music scores are traditionally written is called a ***staff.*** Transitions of melodic patterns from solfa to the staff can evolve from the solfa score to solfa letters on a staff, then to noteheads on a staff. To write the solfa score of *Hot Cross Buns* on a staff, place letters in appropriate positions on the grid (Figure 6-7).

Noteheads, small oval shapes designating pitch or tone, can then replace solfa letters and are positioned on the staff grid to either fill up a *space* or form around a *line,* showing how high or low each pitch is in relation to the others. Figure 6-8 shows a score of *Hot Cross Buns* using noteheads only. A DO sign is included to indicate which place on the staff is DO.

Clef Signs

A *clef* is the sign at the left edge of a staff that determines the pitches of the lines and spaces for that staff. A ***bass clef*** has two dots that indicate the pitch F, and the middle swirl of the ***treble clef*** indicates the pitch G. Because they indicate specific pitches, these signs are sometimes called F and G clefs, respectively. When a bass clef staff and a treble clef staff are linked, a ***grand staff*** is formed. Almost all piano music is written on a grand staff. Look at Figure 6-9. Do you see how middle C got its name? Notice the small horizontal line on which C is placed—this is a ***leger line.*** Leger lines are used to extend the staff either up or down.

DO Sign

Because DO is often the most important tone in a song, it has its own symbol to indicate its position on a staff: the ***DO sign*** (Figure 6-10).When melodic patterns are

FIGURE 6-7
Hot Cross Buns: *Solfa letters on staff*

FIGURE 6-8
Hot Cross Buns: *Noteheads with DO sign on 2*

FIGURE 6-9

Pitch names on a grand staff

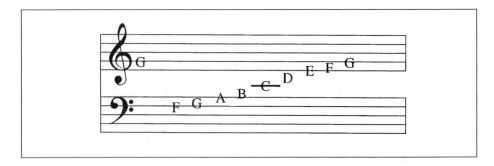

FIGURE 6-10

The DO sign

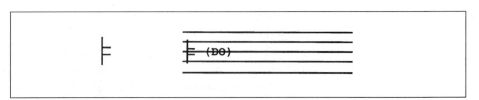

notated on a staff with noteheads, a DO sign can be used to indicate where DO is. With a DO sign, notes can be written on a staff without the initial complications of using pitch names and bass and treble clefs. DO signs are used to assist beginners in studying music, but they rarely appear in traditional music-staff scores. Look at the song scores in Chapter 9 to see if you can identify the solfa syllable of the first note by looking at the DO sign. Can you also identify the cadence tone by its solfa syllable?

The Hand Staff

A convenient way to prepare for the line staff is to use the **hand staff** (Figure 6-11). The hand staff permits students to experience pitch relationships aurally while seeing and feeling them on a five-line–four-space grid. Fingers and thumb provide the lines, and the spaces are found between the fingers and thumb. Pointing to their own or to a partner's hand staff is a way for students to perform pitch relationships on a staff instead of only reading them from a staff. The kinesthetic sense of a melody, both its rhythm and its contour, can be maintained in a very physical way with a hand staff. Once students are able to perform melodic patterns accurately on a hand staff, they will be able easily to transfer this to the notation of those patterns on a conventional music staff.

Hold your hand in front of you, palm facing you, thumb on top, and fingers spread slightly apart. The five fingers and the four spaces between your fingers correspond to the five lines and four spaces of the music staff. Your hand forms a grid, a frame, on which we can write music and from which we can read music. A number-

FIGURE 6-11

The hand staff

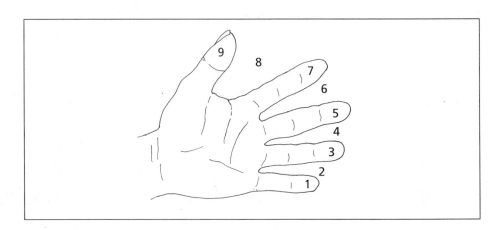

ing system identifies each placement on this grid. To number your hand, name your little finger (on the bottom) 1 and your thumb 9, then count consecutively, pointing to fingers and spaces. Notice how each finger gets an odd number, 1, 3, 5, 7, and 9, and the spaces between them are even numbers, 2, 4, 6, and 8 (Richards 1980, 42–45).

Melodic patterns can be performed on the hand staff by pointing to the appropriate places, and they can be read from the hand staff by singing the tones to which a leader is pointing. Once performed on the hand staff, melody patterns can easily be transferred to a staff on a chalkboard by pointing to the placement of the tones in the same way. The same numbering system applies to both the hand staff and the music staff. (See Figure 6-12.)

▶ Look at the *Hot Cross Buns* solfa score that appears in Figure 6-7.

▶ Sing the first three notes of *Hot Cross Buns* with solfa: MI RE DO (M R D).

▶ On your hand staff, locate 4 (between your ring and middle fingers), 3 (your ring finger), and 2 (between your little and ring fingers). For M, point to 4, for R point to 3, and for D point to 2. Point to these places as you sing M R D.

▶ Now sing the whole song, pointing to the appropriate places on your hand staff.

▶ Did you end on 2? Were you able to coordinate singing different pitches with pointing to different places on the staff? Could you see, hear, and feel the melodic contour of *Hot Cross Buns*?

The hand staff is an effective tool that can be used in a number of ways to study and notate melodic patterns:

▪ Students can watch someone write a pattern on the chalkboard staff and "write" it on their hand staffs by pointing to the appropriate line or space simultaneously with producing each tone.

▪ Students can figure out a problem on their hand staffs before writing it on the music staff.

▪ Melodic patterns can be presented as exercises to sing and write on both hand staff and music staff by referring to the numbers of the lines and spaces: "If DO is on 5, write the pattern MI MI RE RE DO."

▪ The staff grid with numbers makes interval relationships constant even when they are moved to different positions on the staff. For example, if low SO is on 1, DO is on 4, but if SO is on 5, DO is on 8, and if SO is on 3, DO is on 6. Or, if DO is on 1, MI is on 3 and SO is on 5; or, if DO is on 4, MI is on 6 and SO is on 8. The number system illuminates the mathematical relationships between pitches on the staff.

FIGURE 6-12

Staff numbers

Key Signatures

Key signatures, which appear directly to the right of the treble and bass clefs on a staff score, perform essentially the same function as solfa: They set up an arrangement of whole steps and half steps to form a diatonic scale. The **sharps** and **flats** found in key signatures adjust notes either up or down to create half steps in the appropriate places for the scale. A sharp raises a note by a half step, and a flat lowers a note by a half step. A **natural sign** cancels the effects of sharp and flat signs. See Figure 6-13.

Generally, the music scores we find in books do not help us by including a DO sign. To find DO from a key signature, count up or down from the sharp or flat farthest to the right in the key signature. To be accurate in counting, you must designate the sharp or flat as "1" and count the requisite number of positions (lines and spaces) either up or down, not skipping any lines or spaces. The following three rules cover all possible cases:

1. When sharps are in the key signature, the sharp farthest to the right is always TI. The next note up, or seven notes down, will be DO.

2. When flats are in the key signature, the flat farthest to the right is always FA. Find DO by going four notes down or five notes up.

3. If there are no flats or sharps in the key signature, C is DO.

Figure 6-14 shows several key signatures with DO signs added. Find the last sharp or flat and count the appropriate number of positions to the DO signs to check your counting method. Remember to begin counting with the sharp or flat as "1."

Figure 6-15 is a score of *Hot Cross Buns* in the key of F in conventional music notation with a treble clef. Look at the song scores in Chapter 9 and examine the relationships between the DO signs and the key signatures.

FIGURE 6-13

Sharp, flat, and natural signs

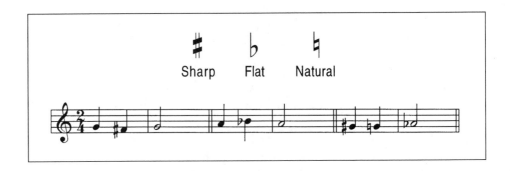

FIGURE 6-14

Key signatures and DO signs

FIGURE 6-15

Hot Cross Buns: *Treble clef with F major key signature*

What Are Rhythm, Beat, and Meter?

Rhythm and Beat

▶ Sing the song *Looby Loo.*

▶ Tap the song as you sing, putting the sound of each word and each syllable in your tapping.

▶ Did you notice that nearly every movement of your lips as you sang coordinated with a tap?

▶ Trying not to exaggerate your lip movements, tap the song again, until you sense that you are hearing and tapping all the sounds in the song. What you are tapping is the rhythm.

▶ Now sing *Looby Loo* again, but tap your foot, keeping time to the song. Do you feel that the pulse of your tapping does not get faster or slower, it just stays the same throughout the song? Your foot is tapping the steady beat to the song. Repeat this exercise until you can confidently tap the beat.

▶ What differences did you notice between the rhythm and the beat?

▶ Did your hands tap more times for the beat or the rhythm of the song?

Rhythm results from the long-and-short, fast-and-slow relationships of sounds. The sounds themselves have length, and so does the time between the sounds. The measured silences between sounds are called **rests.** The rhythm of music is the arrangement that results from the durations of sounds and silences. In other words, rhythm is a pattern of durations.

In a song, our experience of rhythm is closely connected with the words. In fact, if we tap the syllables of a song while singing, we are almost always tapping the rhythm of the song. The one exception is when one syllable is set on more than one tone. This is called a **slur.**

Slurs are indicated in notation with a curved line bridging the notes to be sung on a single syllable. You can see a slur in Figure 6-16, and you can also see slurs in the following songs in Chapter 9: *Mary's Wearing Her Red Dress, Rig-a-Jig-Jig, Uncle Joe,* and *Wild Birds.* When this curved line bridges two notes of the same pitch, it is called a **tie.** A tie adds the duration of the second note to that of the first.

The rhythm of music is notated with a variety of stems and other shapes. **Stems** are the vertical lines extending up or down from the noteheads. **Flags,** attached to the stems, show differences between note lengths—the more flags a note has, the shorter its duration will be and the quicker you will move to the next note. Notes have rhythmic names that refer to their approximate durational relationships: whole note, half note, quarter note, eighth note. Rests have equivalent names: whole rest, half rest, quarter rest, eighth rest. A *dot,* when placed directly to the right of a notehead or a rest, extends the note's or the rest's duration by one half its original value.

Flags can be linked to form **beams,** thick horizontal lines connecting stems. Notes with single flags or beams are *eighth notes,* and those with double flags or beams are *sixteenth notes.*

FIGURE 6-16

Slur and tie

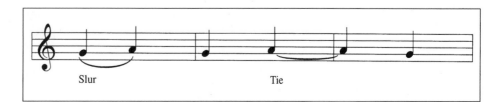

NOTES AND RESTS

Name	Note	Rest
Whole	𝅝	▬
Half	𝅗𝅥	▬
Quarter	♩	𝄽
Eighth	♪	𝄾
Dotted quarter	♩.	𝄽.
Dotted eighth	♪.	𝄾.

FLAGGED AND BEAMED NOTES

Name	Flagged	Beamed
Eighths	♪ ♪ ♪ ♪	♫♫
Sixteenths	♬ ♬ ♬ ♬	♬♬

Rhythm Syllables

As solfa is used for pitch relationships, so certain syllables are used to symbolize rhythmic relationships. In fact, several different systems of syllables can be used for this purpose. There is not, however, any general agreement about which system is most effective in all situations. One common system, developed in nineteenth-century France but popularized by Kodály, uses syllables as a substitute for the fractional names whole, half, quarter, eighth, and so on.

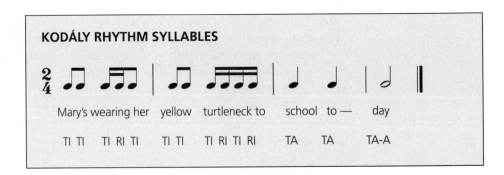

The Education Through Music (ETM) approach, pioneered by Mary Helen Richards in the United States in the 1970s, adapted the rhythm syllables used in the Kodály approach.

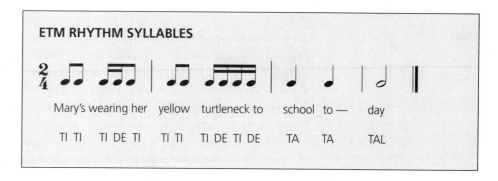

Another system that is popular with music teachers, sometimes called the metric system, identifies the beat with a number, indicating which beat in the measure it is. Sounds that occur halfway between beats are identified with the syllable "and" (often written "&").

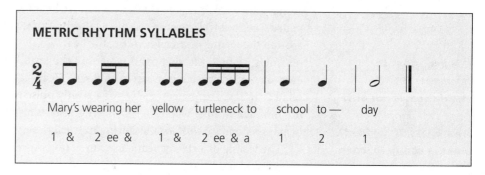

A fourth system was developed by Edwin Gordon and identifies each beat with the syllable DU (pronounced "doo"). Intervening syllables are identified either as DE (pronounced "day") or as TA (pronounced "tuh"), depending on where the intervening sound occurs (Gordon 1984).

Rhythm syllables provide a way to sing rhythm patterns. The Kodály and Education Through Music syllables focus on note names and values. The metric approach emphasizes meter, and the Gordon syllables focus on where sounds occur in relation to the beat. *What seems most important, for those who are learning to hear, read, and write rhythms, is that rhythms that sound the same be sung with the same syllables.* The Gordon syllables meet this criterion most completely of the syllable systems described. A primary purpose of rhythm syllables is to help us aurally identify sound relationships. If we are required or expected to use different syllables when two patterns sound the same but are notated differently (musical homonyms), the syllable system may be more cumbersome than helpful. (A full discussion and comparison of rhythm-syllable systems can be found in *SongWorks 2*.)

Beat

An important aspect of how rhythm sounds is the feeling of a *beat.* Our experience of beat is a feeling of a steady pulse. This feeling results from regular emphasis by accent, duration, or pitch. Factors of movement, expectation, and language can be involved as well. We describe the beat as a feeling because it is not always clear what physical factors are involved in our perceptions of it. In fact, we can experience the feeling of beat even when there is no physical cause (Kramer 1988).

Notice the difference between feeling the beat and moving to the beat. Moving to the beat (doing the beat) requires a motor coordination not necessary to feeling the beat. For example, you can feel the beat of the music at a dance, but when you try to make your feet *do* the beat, you may not always be successful.

When we clap our hands with the music at a concert, when we march to music, when we tap our feet to the sounds on the radio, we are almost always moving to the beat. Natural movements like these may not stay exactly with the beat all the time. We may have to switch our feet as we march to get in step, our fingers may start tapping along with the words (the rhythm) when we listen to music on the radio, or we may pause when we feel a rest in the music. Each of these motions, however, is organized around the feeling of a steady pulse, the beat.

You may be somewhat confused about the term "beat" because it is used both in everyday speech and in music terminology. "Beat" can mean at least two different but related things. The general feeling of a steady pulse is called the beat, but each pulse, the moment in time when we feel an emphasis, is also referred to as a beat. Counting beats is a standard tool for measuring musical time.

The feeling of a steady beat comes in various speeds and characters. The beat that is typical of a walking or a marching speed to music is often called the *walking beat.* Here is an exercise to illustrate the walking beat with *London Bridge.*

> **It is important to remember that the steady beat is not obvious to all people. Awareness of the beat and the ability to move to it require coordination of listening and motor skills, and a basic sensitivity to musical flow and its divisions.**

▶ Sing *London Bridge* as you walk around the room. Notice that some walking speeds fit the song better than others.

▶ If you are very nonchalant and casual in your movement, you might not find the beat in your walking. When you do find a walking speed that fits with the song, tap your hands each time you step. Your hands are now tapping a walking beat.

Tempo is the rate or speed of the beat. There are different beat speeds even when the tempo of a song does not change. When you tap a beat at a rate slower than the walking beat by half (or, in some cases, slower by a third), you are tapping the slow beat. When you tap a beat at a rate twice (or three times) as fast as the walking beat, you are tapping the fast beat. Experiment with slow and fast beats.

▶ Tap the walking beat while you sing *London Bridge.* Sing the song at the same speed, but tap a slow beat. You should be tapping on the syllables "Lon-," "fall-," "my," and "la-." Try it again.

▶ Sing the song again and tap the fast beat. For the fast beat, you'll be tapping on nearly every syllable. Did you pause on the word "down"? Try to feel the fast beat continuing even between some words.

▶ Experiment with tapping beats at two speeds. Tap a beat with your foot and tap twice as fast with your hand. Some people feel that doing this is like rubbing their stomachs and patting their heads at the same time! For others it is effortless.

▶ For an additional challenge, reverse the actions. Tap on the slower beat with your hand and the faster beat with your foot. Or tap the slower beat with one hand and the faster beat with the other.

▶ How did you do? Not all of us are immediately skillful at these tasks, so do not worry too much if you are feeling rather uncoordinated.

Just from this brief discussion and exercise, we can conclude that when someone asks or tells us to put "the beat" in our feet, a legitimate response could be, "*Which* beat? Even if I assume you mean the steady beat, there are several speeds of beat I could perform." In knowing and learning about music, it is important to recognize that we can sense different speeds of beats as we listen to any given song or musical work. *An overemphasis on moving to the beat can distract students from other important ways of responding to musical flow.* The beat is but one aspect of this musical flow.

The beat plays a part in writing rhythm. When beams are used, they almost always begin on a beat and almost never link sounds across bar lines. Therefore, beams organize rhythm visually so that we can often see how many beats there are and how many sounds occur on each beat or between beats.

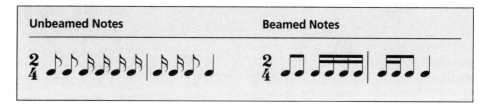

Meter

Meter describes the way in which beats are grouped and divided. Meter is the organization of beats into groups, usually according to an accent (or the *feeling* of an accent) that marks the first beat of a group. We tend to feel beats grouped by twos, threes, or fours, and we sense them as *duple* or *triple* meter. As its name implies, meter, like beat, is a way of measuring musical time.

Meter is indicated by means of ***meter signatures,*** which are found at the beginning of music scores (Figure 6-17). The top number of this sign refers to the grouping of beats. If the top number is a four, beats are arranged in groups of four, the first and every fourth beat after it having the feeling of an accent. If the top number is a two, beats are arranged in groups of two, and every other beat is accented.

Usually, the bottom number of the meter signature indicates what note value represents the beat. If the bottom number is a 4, this usually, but not always, indicates that a quarter note is the beat value. A 2 on the bottom usually indicates that the beat value is a half note, as a 2 in the denominator of a fraction indicates a half. An 8, however, does not accomplish its purpose so easily. It can indicate that the beat value is an eighth note, but more commonly it indicates that a dotted quarter is the beat value.

EXAMPLE 6-17

Meter signatures

Reasons for the ambiguity have to do with the history of our music notation system, and it can be misleading to think about meter only in terms of how it is notated in the meter signature.

Despite the ambiguity in how meter is notated, heard, and felt, meter signatures function in very predictable ways in notation. Each group of beats is separated from other groups by *bar lines.* Between each bar line and the next is a *measure.* A meter signature organizes written music into measures. In notation, the top number of a meter signature works with the bottom number to specify the number of notes that can fit into a measure. If the top number is 2 and the bottom number is 4, only the equivalent of two quarter notes can fit into the measure. Combinations of four eighths, of one quarter and two eighths, and of one half by itself are each equivalent to two quarters' worth of time. If the top number is 6 and the bottom number is 8, only the equivalent of six eighth notes can be represented in a measure. Some equivalents of six eighth notes are two dotted quarters, two quarters and two eighths, and a dotted half.

Consider Figure 6-18. Notice how the measures are separated by bar lines, how each measure can contain different quantities of notes and rests, and how those quantities are determined by the meter signature.

FIGURE 6-18
Measures

The Anacrusis

An *anacrusis,* also called a pickup, is an unaccented sound that precedes an accent at the beginning of a music unit or phrase. Anacruses are common in the English language and in songs because grammar dictates that important words (nouns) be preceded by words of lesser importance (articles, adjectives, prepositions). Here is one way you can tell if a song or a phrase begins with an anacrusis.

▶ Sing the song *Mulberry Bush* and begin tapping the beat when you begin the song. Did you begin tapping at precisely the same time you began singing? Did you clap on "here"? Because the first word begins on the beat, *Mulberry Bush* does not begin with an anacrusis.

▶ When you sing just the words "the mulberry bush," on what syllable do you tap? Did you clap on "mul-"? Although *Mulberry Bush* does not begin with an anacrusis, the phrase "the mulberry bush" does: "the MULberry bush." In this phrase, "the" is the anacrusis.

▶ Now try the same beat exercise with *The Farmer in the Dell.*

▶ Did it feel more comfortable to clap on "the" or on "farm-"? The "the" is the unaccented sound that precedes the accent on "farm-"; it is an anacrusis.

▶ Check some other songs and phrases to see if they begin with an anacrusis.

When an anacrusis is notated, it is often separated from the accent that follows it by a bar line; it falls outside the measure to which it is related. That means that an anacrusis *looks* as if it is related to the group of sounds within the same measure rather than to the sounds in the following measure. In Figure 6-19, the anacruses are indicated by curved arrows leading from the unaccented sound to the accent. In conventional music notation, no special symbol indicates an anacrusis. Notice how the

EXAMPLE 6-19
Anacruses

The far - mer in the dell.   The far - mer in   the dell.

Ma - ry had a   lit - tle lamb, its   fleece was white as   snow.

We need to let how we feel music guide how we interpret our notations for it.

arrows cross bar lines and connect notes that are beamed to other notes. Look for anacruses in the song scores of Chapter 9.

The notation of anacruses highlights the fact that meter, like beat, reflects only one aspect of our experience of music. It also helps put into perspective the importance of a knowledge of beat and meter. More immediately, and perhaps more fundamentally, musical flow is structured according to patterns or groups of sounds. Word phrases are important ingredients of song structure, but the relationships among tones and durations also plays an important role. It is from these patterns, their characteristics, and their interactions that beat and meter arise.

If we let our understanding of meter be guided by how we notate meter, we are putting the cart before the horse. Forcing music into rigid metrical frameworks often overemphasizes the normally subtle effect meter has on our experience of song (Thurmond 1982). Meter reflects how we *feel* music. It reflects the interaction of musical elements, an interaction that is normally complex and fluid.

Chapter Epilogue

Music can be divided into many parts, in many ways—just as a house can. Knowing the elements of a house helps us understand and use our houses more fully. Building a house takes imagination to keep in mind how all the parts will fit together to make a place that gives warmth, shelter, and focus for family life. Our students, when studying music and learning musical terms, may become so challenged by the technical aspects of music that they are not able to keep the vitality, grace, and purpose of music in mind. By grounding our teaching of structure, melody, and rhythm in the *sound* and *flow* of music, we can make better use of all that music can offer in the education of children. Then, our knowledge of the elements of music can make our musical experiences more full.

EXERCISES FOR SKILL DEVELOPMENT

These activities are means for helping you and your students recognize and practice what you know and are learning in the beginning phases of your study of music. Be creative in offering students intriguing ways to notate and study the sounds of music. Writing and studying what we know about songs gives us varied opportunities to

- recognize our progress in learning;
- demonstrate our understandings and misunderstandings;
- document our "work" in studying music.

(continued)

EXERCISES FOR SKILL DEVELOPMENT (continued)

Notation Skills

These skills can be practiced alone or with partners. Students' papers can be collected for checking or simply used for private practice. You may select (or have students select) which and how many songs will be written.

1. Write the words for songs.
2. Write song dots for songs.
3. Map songs.
4. Map songs and find select words or phrases.
5. Write song dots and circle cadence chunks.
6. Write song dots and circle slurs.
7. Map songs and show anacruses at the beginnings.
8. Write solfa scores for songs.
9. Write a song (*Hot Cross Buns,* for example) on the staff, choosing three different DO placements.
10. Write the rhythm score to a song.
11. Write the beat score to a song and circle the rests.
12. Write song dots for cadence chunks and underline the primary stress in each chunk.
13. Compose a melody on the staff using the tones M R D (or some other pattern).
14. Make a map showing echo (short-short-long or balanced) structure and find songs that fit.
15. Make a form book showing what you know about a song.
16. Find songs that have **unisons** (and other specified tonal patterns).
17. Find songs that have certain rhythm patterns.

Performance Skills

These skills can be demonstrated individually, in large groups, or in small groups of two or three, or used as opportunities for private practice.

1. Clap/tap the rhythm of songs.
2. Clap/tap the beat of songs.
3. Sing songs, putting select words or phrases in inner hearing.
4. Hand-sign songs.
5. Chin songs.
6. Sing a song in a low, a medium, and a high range.
7. Start songs with a "ready" pitch and a gesture.
8. Start songs that begin with an anacrusis.
9. Lead antiphonning—singing, speaking, tapping.
10. Alternate tapping beat and rhythm while singing a song.
11. Sing partner songs, ostinati, and rounds with another person.
12. Perform songs on the hand staff.
13. Sing songs with solfa syllables.
14. Sing songs with rhythm syllables.

Becoming the Teachers We Want to Be

7

Reflections on Good Teaching

Why do you want to be a teacher? Some in the teaching profession liken their commitment to a calling or a mission to make the world a better place.

> Deciding what to instruct and nurture and how to instruct and nurture are decisions made by each of us in our classrooms. These humble decisions, each affecting only a few students, operate to shape the reality of humanity, for all of us are created in some part by our teachers and by the [teaching] models they use. (Joyce and Weil 1986, 496)

Some say their love of children and young people drew them to teaching. Some cite their fascination with a subject and their enthusiasm for sharing their knowledge as incentives to become teachers. Whatever their reasons, many who have made the decision to teach can recall at least one teacher from their past who serves as a model and an inspiration for their career choice.

▶ Can you recall a teacher who made a subject come alive for you?

▶ Can you recall a time when, in the presence of a good teacher, you made the decision to become a teacher yourself?

▶ What prompted you to become a teacher?

▶ Can you recall when you began to believe that you have the potential to be a good teacher?

What does it mean to be a teacher? Most of us can offer opinions about what makes a good teacher and why a particular teacher had a positive impact on us. Our opinions, though, often differ, and sometimes students in the same class can disagree about whether their instructor is a good teacher. Is one person's opinion more valid than another? Why or why not?

Various profiles are available, but a magic formula for making a good teacher does not exist. Although we can argue passionately about the required qualities, our varying opinions may be more indicative of our own preferences and beliefs than of a universal model for good teaching.

Commitment to good teaching and reflection on how to become a better teacher are part of a continuing, career-long quest. How committed are you to becoming the best teacher you can be?

▶ Who were your best teachers? What made them good teachers?

▶ Did you like the subjects they taught before they were your teachers and after they were your teachers? Did the appeal of the subject affect your view of each teacher's ability to teach?

▶ Did the way in which they treated you affect your opinions of your teachers' teaching?

▶ How important was it for you to feel that the teacher liked you?

▶ Why are you being asked to distinguish between liking and learning as you reflect on teachers from your past? What do you think the connection is between liking a teacher and learning a subject?

Characteristics to Cultivate

As you recall and reflect upon good teachers from your past, you may find it helpful to envision specific teacher qualities to emulate. Seeing others' behaviors as models for our own is different from patterning ourselves after someone else. Rather, we become observers of the qualities of action, reaction, and interaction that we see in others. When we detect a quality that we would like to cultivate, we use that observed behavior as a model, an example, or a standard to develop. Modeling someone else's behaviors can be an extremely valuable means of changing our own behavior. Many times, the positive image of another's behavior can guide us through our own tough moments, especially when the impression we want to give is not the one our behavior or feelings are giving at the moment.

When prospective, new, or experienced teachers debate the characteristics of a good teacher, they often mention qualities that reflect a teacher's classroom demeanor.

- *Fairness* in dealing with students and issues
- *Enthusiasm* for the subject
- *Willingness* to listen
- *Compassion* toward students
- *Interest* in students' progress

Do you agree with those five characteristics? What characteristics would you add to the list?

▶ Ponder your list of characteristics that define a good teacher. How many describe you?

▶ Which characteristics do you think your friends, family, classmates, teachers, supervisors, and acquaintances would ascribe to you?

▶ Are there some qualities that are not currently your habit but are worth cultivating?

VALUING OPENNESS IN LEADERSHIP

Openness to participation	Gives each person in a group the right to be heard "without interruption, in an environment of trust and open communication."
Openness to diversity	Challenges the position that "If you and I disagree, I need to convince you to come around to my way of thinking" and instead values disagreement as the opportunity to listen intently in order to gain a better perspective from which to make a decision.
Openness to conflict	Moves toward, not away from, points of tension, values conflict resolution over the appearance of harmony, and separates issues from personalities so that a strong collective decision can be made.
Openness to reflection	Acknowledges the time involved and needed to talk things out and to find reflective time for resolving important points.
Openness to mistakes	Encourages participants to think aloud during creative problem-solving, celebrating rather than criticizing radical or unusual ideas, and encourages leaders and groups to accept that their decision ultimately might not be the best solution.

(Patterson 1993, 57–59)

PRINCIPLE 5

Becoming a Leader

Teachers are leaders. Fortunately, we belong to a profession that allows us to develop and monitor our values and our behaviors so that we can continually pursue the goal of becoming the finest people and leaders possible. The qualities of a good teacher are also the qualities of a vital and supportive human being, citizen, and life-long learner.

Emerging concepts and definitions emphasize openness as a cornerstone of effective leadership. Reflections on our tendencies toward openness can offer insights for interactions in classrooms, schools, and communities. Patterson's five types of openness provide thoughtful parallels for the qualities of good teaching and good leading.

It is never too soon or too late to cultivate qualities that will help us become the teachers we want to be. Both undergraduates who have never worked with children and veteran teachers with many years of experience will profit from being aware of how we treat and react to others. Certainly, having the skills and knowledge of our chosen discipline is important, yet it is often the day-to-day, minute-to-minute ways in which we respond to people that make teaching such a satisfying and rewarding profession. Looking back to your list of characteristics of a good teacher, notice how many deal directly with how we treat others.

Developing Empathy

Only when we have the capacity for compassion and empathy are we able to meet the needs of our students by being firm and being patient, being tolerant and being demanding.

PRINCIPLE 5

There are diverse models of teaching that shape teachers' roles and priorities for students' learning. Inquiry training, inductive thinking, attaining concepts, mastery learning, cognitive learning, cooperative learning, nondirective teaching, shared responsibility, role playing, and constructivist classrooms are just a few of the numerous models that can help us become good teachers (Joyce and Weil 1986). At a fundamental level, however, becoming good teachers requires that we become aware of our thoughts, feelings, and understandings both toward ourselves and toward others.

Teacher empathy is the ability to step emotionally or cognitively into the shoes of a student. Imagining the feelings or understandings that students experience in classroom settings gives us important clues for how to teach them. Understanding students and their learning requires compassion and empathy, but these traits do not release us from our responsibility to teach them. *Compassion and empathy help us know how to teach, they do not excuse us from teaching.*

Verbal and nonverbal teacher behaviors are a part of every teaching model and will be points for focus and reflection in the following discussions. Reflect on these sensitivities that contribute to your classroom and school behaviors.

► How sensitive are you to how others around you are feeling? What steps do you take to make those around you feel comfortable?

► Do you know what effect you usually have on people? Would people describe you as cheerful, sullen, distant? Do you normally appear energetic, depressed, or calm?

► Do you initiate greetings or conversations with people who are not necessarily friends or acquaintances?

► Do you monitor how much complaining, gossiping, or criticizing you do?

Being Honest

Be natural. Be yourself. Be honest. Although those recommendations for teaching sound simple and clear, they may not be as wise or as true as they seem. Unless we have spent time thinking about it, being honest often means saying or doing what we *feel*, not necessarily what we *want* to feel. Maturity gives us the power and perspective to choose how we want to behave rather than behaving as we feel or according to our habits.

► What problems do you foresee if a prospective teacher has a long history of being negative, sarcastic, or critical?

► If it feels natural for this person to see and treat others in this way, what would you recommend he or she do in the classroom?

► Why should this future teacher change, if this behavior feels natural and honest?

"Children can tell when we are being genuine with them!" Is this adage about children true? Is it true about adults? According to Madsen and Kuhn, following our natural behaviors and attitudes is not always the path to take in a classroom (1978, 57–59). Some teachers have used the cliché that "children can tell when we're being honest" as an excuse to continue a behavior pattern, rather than making the behavior changes that may be best for children. Because we do not always *feel* the way we want to *behave*, teachers are sometimes called upon to act, to pretend. Behaving the way we choose, rather than the way that feels most natural, is foundational to our own leadership, maturity, and ability to help our students grow and develop.

With theatrical flair, superior teachers usually possess the ability to act or pretend during their lessons as they interject activities that intrigue and engage students (Rubin 1983). Few would dispute that one characteristic of a master teacher is to convincingly show excitement, curiosity, intrigue, compassion, energy, and patience (Brand 1990). These moments of acting may or may not reflect a teacher's natural or honest feelings, but they do make the best of the situation and provide alternatives to unproductive and habitual reactions.

No recommendation is being made here for the practice of teacher deception in the classroom. Instead, we recommend that the teaching process be allowed to pull the best from us, to foster our own growth and development.

Perhaps we are closer to being honest with ourselves and others when we act the way we know is best for the situation and act the way we want to be rather than acting according to habit and what feels natural.

Being Respectful

"Demand their respect!" is advice often given to teachers, but it rarely works. Respect cannot be demanded, it must be earned. To how many people have you willingly

Personal dignity is something to which everyone has a right. As teachers, it is important that we believe this about others and that we model this belief for our students and colleagues.

PRINCIPLE 1

PRINCIPLE 5

given respect when it was demanded of you? It can work more to our advantage to treat students and colleagues with respect, to acknowledge their right to dignity, and to model the behavior we wish to see from them. An important distinction is made here between respecting someone and demonstrating respectful behaviors toward that person. Our students may need to be taught what respectful behaviors are.

Although our behaviors differ depending on the context, consistency in our attitudes and behaviors toward others contributes to our classroom demeanor. Do you treat your family and friends with the same empathy, compassion, and respect that you want to convey to your students?

▶ Are you able to patiently listen to the opinions and views of others, showing respect but not necessarily agreement?

▶ Can you disagree without being disrespectful?

▶ Describe the behavior you would see if you were being treated with respect. Collect and list these ideas. Collect and list ideas that describe disrespectful treatment.

▶ How many of these respectful and disrespectful behaviors do you currently practice in or out of a classroom?

▶ How much of a challenge would it be for you to exhibit respect on a consistent basis?

Being Constructive

"Be positive." "She's so positive with the students!" Few would argue about the desirability of being positive. For many, however, the connotation of positive is "nice," and many exchanges between teachers and students could not be described as, nor should they attempt to be, nice. Rather than trying to be positive and nice, teachers may be better served by trying to be constructive.

If we think of "constructive" as synonymous with building and progressive and "positive" as synonymous with nice and upbeat, we can see that the terms are not equally useful in describing teacher behaviors and classroom interactions. Situations that call for firmness, direct confrontation, commands, or accurate but not necessarily complimentary feedback can be handled in constructive rather than destructive ways. Being constructive means that we are striving for choices that may not seem nice but that contribute to learning or discipline.

PRINCIPLE 6

Being Animated

Degrees of animation are the variable intensities with which we act and speak. Using our faces, eyes, gestures, body positions, and vocal inflections as means of communication, we develop a vocabulary of behaviors that can serve us well in the classroom (Cassidy 1990; Madsen and Cassidy 1989; Yoder-White 1993). When our vocabulary of behaviors is small and our degrees of animation are fairly limited, we risk *not* having adequate communication skills for use in the classroom. Additionally, when the limited avenues we use for communicating are ineffective, we risk being misunderstood and our messages may be misinterpreted.

PRINCIPLE 3

▶ Have you experienced a teacher's using the same tone of voice throughout a lesson? What effect did it have on your listening?

▶ Have you experienced a person's using extreme variations in vocal pitch and inflection? What effect did it have on your listening?

▶ What effects can a teacher's speaking too loudly or too softly have on students?

► Have you known a teacher who stood in one area of the room and did not move among the students? Perhaps you have known a teacher whose proximity to students was too close or too varied, too static or too frantic. What effects did that have?

► Have you known a teacher whose eyes looked everywhere but at students' eyes, who looked above students' heads, or who only looked down at his or her notes? What message could that give?

► Have you noticed yourself or others using filler comments or phrases (for example, "OK," "Basically," "You know," "Let's get quiet," "Who's talking?") when other words do not immediately come to mind? What impressions do these repetitive speech patterns give to listeners?

Certain behaviors can be distracting to listeners. In classrooms, more is not necessarily better when it comes to degrees of animation. There is a tendency to think that teachers need *more* rather than *less* animation in their teaching behaviors. Some teachers and some situations, however, call for a subdued, calm, or matter-of-fact manner. Teachers working with students who have mental handicaps, severe behavior problems, or learning difficulties such as Attention Deficit Disorder (ADD) and dyslexia may meet with more success when they decrease rather than increase their levels of animation.

SCENARIO   LESS CAN BE BETTER

Kristin, a student teacher, was about to teach a music lesson to a fifth-grade class for her student-teaching evaluation by her university supervisor, Dr. Barros. As Dr. Barros stood in the hall waiting to enter the classroom, she saw the fifth-grade class talk back to their classroom teacher, flip water on each other from the drinking fountain, knock classmates' music notebooks to the floor, and ignore their teacher's attempts to halt the disruptive behavior.

"Whew! Kristin is in for a workout with these students!" Dr. Barros thought as she followed the class into the room where Kristin was waiting. For the next forty minutes, Dr. Barros watched in surprise as Kristin taught a relatively uninteresting lesson, spoke quietly and slowly, and appeared fatigued. At no time, however, did Kristin need to reprimand these previously rowdy fifth graders. In spite of the lesson and the low energy level in the room, students were quiet and politely attentive. Had the students been threatened to behave by another teacher? What made their behavior change so drastically between the hallway and Kristin's lesson?

Before meeting with Kristin about her lesson, Dr. Barros asked Mrs. Cotton, the cooperating music teacher, to spend a few moments discussing Kristin's progress. After initial summaries of what Kristin had been working on, Dr. Barros asked, "Is Kristin always that sedate as she teaches?" "Yes," replied Mrs. Cotton. "Isn't it amazing?!" Before Dr. Barros could respond, Mrs. Cotton went on, "I go in to class raring to go, and my excitement and energy soon have the students bouncing off the walls! When Kristin teaches, the kids stay calm, and it seems to be working fine for her. Watching her has taught me a lot!"

Consider a continuum for degrees of animation in *facial expression, posture, eye contact, tone of voice,* and *vocal assertiveness.* At the right is a high level and at the left is a low level of animation. The extremes of the continuum indicate too much or too little animation for the given situation.

▶ Where would you place your usual behaviors on the continuum in each of the categories listed above?

▶ Where would you place your classroom behaviors in comparison with your home behaviors?

▶ Consider situations that call for behavior changes in one direction or the other on this continuum.

Degrees of Animation

Low   **High**

SCENARIO   A LOOK IN THE MIRROR

It was her least favorite class. Betty could not pretend anymore that she was happy to see these students. After nearly a year of watching this rowdy bunch enter her classroom, Betty could not muster her usual pleasant smile and greeting. Each class was a battle, and she noticed that by the time class was over, her forehead had a deep crease, her eyes were squinting, and her mouth was tight.

One day, a teacher passed Betty in the hall and, with good-natured humor, called attention to Betty's scowl saying, "Well, you either just had, or are going to have, those third graders for class. Which is it?" Until this time, Betty had no idea that her feelings toward this class were so transparent.

That night, Betty went home, looked in the mirror, and practiced a pleasant expression to use with those third graders. She practiced how she would look as she greeted them at the door, and she practiced looking interested in and accepting of their responses. She memorized what the looks *felt* like and what she looked like as she made them.

The next day, Betty's relationship with the third-grade class turned around. She credited practicing her facial expressions with changing her attitude about these students and, consequently, changing theirs about her.

Facial Expression   Have you known someone who always seemed to look grumpy? Some of us have found, after getting acquainted with a grumpy-looking person, that we have misread that person's expression. How common is it that we confuse aloofness with shyness, grumpiness with fear, or boisterousness with social discomfort? Perhaps someone has misinterpreted *your* facial expression. If that has happened more than a couple of times, your habitual facial expression may be sending a message that you do not intend.

PRINCIPLE 1

PRINCIPLE 2

SCENARIO   DEVELOPING A FACIAL VOCABULARY

"The children don't take her seriously. She's working hard, and she is a sweet person, but when she has to deal with discipline, she's not very convincing." Those were the cooperating teacher's words that greeted the university supervisor as he observed and evaluated a student teacher, Sasha.

Watching Sasha, Dr. McGuire could see the problem. Sasha had a very kind, almost meek, demeanor in the classroom. When she needed to get students' attention or

issue a command, the words were appropriate, but the facial expression and the voice were not. Sasha did not look firm, confident, or demanding.

In the discussion that followed the observation, Dr. McGuire learned from Sasha that she had always felt uncomfortable and embarrassed showing anger, determination, or firmness in her face. Sasha lacked a range of facial vocabulary that would be helpful to her in the classroom. Even though she became convinced of the need to develop more facial expressions, Sasha felt uncomfortable with these new displays of emotion.

After practicing before a mirror, Sasha saw that she indeed was not making the changes in her facial expression that she thought she was. Because she was accustomed to keeping the same expression on her face most of the time, even a slight change felt like a drastic one to Sasha. With the help of the mirror and the determination to become a good teacher, Sasha developed facial expressions that convincingly portrayed a wide range of appropriate teacher reactions.

Students' discipline improved, Sasha's confidence improved, and her new air of command in the classroom transferred to new-found levels of assertiveness in her personal life.

▶ What is your habitual or most common facial expression? Become aware of the look that is on your face—in classes or meetings, walking through hallways, listening to someone's explanation, or roaming the aisles of a grocery store. Some people, without knowing it, have developed a habit of scowling, squinting, or looking melancholy. Are you one of them?

▶ Consider the impact of a teacher's facial expression on his or her teaching. What effect has a teacher's facial expression (pleasant or unpleasant) had on you?

Posture   As you are reading this book, notice how you are sitting. Sitting leisurely or slouching in a chair is synonymous with feeling relaxed to some. To others, however, this posture may communicate defiance or a lack of interest. Like other kinds of communication, posture messages can be misinterpreted. Tall, erect sitting or standing posture generally communicates confidence and competence; yet, if our posture is rigid rather than relaxed, we may send a message of aloofness or fear.

▶ Have you considered what your posture reveals about your mood, your attitude, or your mental or physical health?

▶ Are there times when it is best not to let your posture reveal how you are feeling? When are those times?

Imagine a string pulling up from the top of your head as jaw, neck, shoulders, and back are loose and relaxed. This image can place your torso in a tall, extended, lifted position of confidence and lightness. Those who have investigated healthy practices for backs also agree that thinking "up" rather than "down" and "light" rather than "heavy" can save us from years of compressing weight on our spines.

Knowing how we usually walk and stand can help us become aware of our posture habits. In studying "kinesthetic lightness," F. Matthias Alexander (1869–1955) developed ways of moving and ways of thinking about moving that have become known as the Alexander Technique. According to Jones (1976), the Alexander Technique helps us inhibit habitual motor responses, thereby freeing ourselves of *physical* patterns that have hampered our movements and *mental* patterns that have interfered with our thinking. For teachers, then, being aware of the ways we sit, stand, breathe, speak, and move can contribute to our own health as well as our students' impressions of us.

▶ Begin noticing the posture habits of those around you. What are your impressions?

▶ During a class, faculty meeting, or workshop, notice what your posture may be communicating to the presenter. Notice what it may be communicating to the listeners or the students. Is that what you wish to communicate?

PRINCIPLE 5

Eye Contact   Eye contact and eye expression can be potent communicators. Notice the ease or difficulty with which you and others establish and maintain eye contact with teachers, students, and peers. As you read this, practice showing alertness through your eyes. Now try anger. Notice the difference in your eye expression as you portrayed these feelings. You may need to look in a mirror to check your abilities to convey these expressions deliberately.

As we teach, we scan our classes so that each student knows we acknowledge and convey our interest as we linger briefly on his or her eyes. Scanning that moves too quickly can seem to be darting and fearful, and moving too slowly can seem staring and intimidating. Students notice when teachers look above their heads, fixate on one place in the room, or make no eye contact during lessons. Although the message may be completely inaccurate, the communication is often interpreted as aloofness, a lack of interest, or lack of confidence on the part of the teacher.

The concept of "soft eyes" can be helpful in shaping a look to use as we interact with others (Pater 1988; Swift 1985). With eyes relaxed and wide open, take in as much peripheral vision as possible. As you take in this expanse of your vision, have a sense of going within yourself. These combined actions create soft eyes. Soft eyes can be especially helpful in maintaining a desired demeanor in stressful or confrontive situations. How would your eyes look and feel if you had soft eyes right now? For contrast, change your expression to hard eyes.

▶ Feel and see the difference in your eyes as they communicate vitality, compassion, dullness, and firmness.

▶ How could awareness of eye contact and eye expression increase your effectiveness as a teacher?

PRINCIPLE 1

Tone of Voice   As we discussed in Chapter 4, we hear voices all the time, but rarely do we listen to and think about the sounds that voices are making. When you hear an extremely soft voice that projects little energy, uses a small range of pitches, and sounds raspy instead of clear, what impressions do you get about the person's state of mind, mood, or attitude? Reactions such as "She doesn't want to be here," "She isn't interested in us," "He isn't feeling well," and "He seems depressed" are common. If you were a student of this person, would your classroom attitude change according to your interpretation of the meaning behind the voice? The person may not be feeling well and may not be aware of how her or his voice is sounding. Students, however, may display obvious reactions to the misinterpreted message "She doesn't care about us."

> Your voice is your personal trademark. It serves as a calling card, presenting you and your ideas and your personality to a judgmental world, a world that will remember your voice image as vividly as your physical image, and perhaps more vividly. (Cooper 1984, 51)

Our voices are one of our most powerful and revealing tools, in and out of the classroom. In the classroom, our voices will be called upon to excite, calm, demand, comfort, encourage, focus, welcome, and intrigue. Do you currently have a range of vocal production that convincingly communicates those messages?

PRINCIPLE 5

▶ Notice how, like facial expression and posture, your voice can communicate *or* miscommunicate your mood, attitude, and general health.

▶ Are you easily able to increase the volume of your voice without making it sound harsh or angry?

▶ In what ways can your awareness of your speaking voice contribute to your effectiveness as a teacher?

Vocal Assertiveness   "Sit down."

▶ How would you say that command if you were speaking to a quiet group of fifth-grade students who had just finished saying the Pledge of Allegiance?

▶ How would you say it if that group had become noisy and distracted immediately following the pledge?

▶ How would your command sound if students had used inappropriate words as they spoke their version of the pledge, taking pleasure from eye contact and encouragement from each other?

In classrooms, our voices must be able to show various levels of assertiveness to effectively communicate our meaning. Consider in what situations you may need to use a different level of vocal assertiveness. What conditions affect the level of vocal assertiveness needed? If you were to err in your judgment, would you prefer to err toward less or toward more assertiveness than the situation called for?

Practice saying some classroom commands using the Levels of Vocal Assertiveness scale that follows. Because we sometimes miscalculate how assertive we sound, it can help to tape-record our voices or to have a friend or colleague give us feedback about what level of assertiveness he or she heard. Practice varying your assertiveness as you say these phrases: "Everyone get quiet." "No talking." "Listen."

LEVELS OF VOCAL ASSERTIVENESS

	1	2	3	4
Type	Nonassertive	Assertive	Aggressive	Harsh
Characteristic	Polite	Matter-of-fact	Demanding	Authoritarian
Message	"It's okay if you sit down."	"Let's sit down."	"Sit *down!*"	"Sit down now, and don't you *dare* disobey me!"

What specific qualities of your speech change as you increase assertiveness? Notice the degrees to which the pitch, pace, enunciation, and volume of your voice change as you increase the level of assertiveness. In the commands, did you note the absence of courtesy words that imply a request? A worthwhile exercise is to practice vocal assertiveness without adding "Please" or "Thank you" because those terms can indicate nonassertiveness—that the phrase is a request rather than a command. Certainly there are many times in classroom settings when adding courtesy words is appropriate, acceptable, and effective.

▶ Under what conditions is a nonassertive request appropriate?

▶ What would cause you to shift from an assertive response to an aggressive one?

▶ What concerns do you have about underestimating and overestimating the need for assertiveness?

Become aware of tendencies to end a command with "OK?" The habitual "OK?" after instructions or commands not only diminishes the assertiveness of your message; it also can turn into a full-fledged speech mannerism that is distracting and undesirable. For purposes of developing a range of vocal assertiveness skills, it is best to omit words that may contradict your intended message.

Becoming Aware of Sarcasm

PRINCIPLE 1

In American society, it is becoming increasingly common to build one's interaction with another person on a kind of critical humor that demeans, defaces, and devalues. Characters in television sitcoms and professional comedians are especially adept at making fun of others. Inserting this type of so-called humor into a conversation or discussion is so prevalent that it can go unnoticed much of the time.

▶ How prevalent is sarcasm and put-down humor in your relationships with other people?

▶ How could the habitual practice of put-down humor affect your behavior toward students in your classroom?

Notice how frequently your communications with people are sprinkled with zings about their appearance, their intelligence, or their behavior. Consider what effect those words may have on their self-respect—and on their respect for you. If sarcasm is standard in your interactions with friends, more than likely sarcasm is a part of your classroom practices.

PRINCIPLE 5

You can increase your awareness of the frequency and effect of sarcasm in your own life by devoting a few days to monitoring your sarcastic comments and those of others. If you accept this challenge of self-monitoring, note the lingering messages from the subtly disrespectful practice of sarcasm.

PRINCIPLE 3

> Many adults use sarcasm as a form of wit. Teachers often do so with students intending only to be clever and witty. More often than not, however, their sarcasm sounds clever only to themselves and not to the students receiving the comments. Too often sarcasm produces hurt feelings and damages self-esteem. Students seldom understand sarcasm and feel that they are being made fun of or belittled. It is better to avoid sarcasm altogether than to risk hurting feelings. (Charles 1985, 54)

Even if students understand a teacher's sarcasm because it is a staple of *their* interactions, teachers are advised to avoid setting this example. Differences do exist between light-hearted cajoling of students, which could be considered constructive teasing, and mean-spirited sarcasm, which may have a destructive effect on self-esteem, classroom attitudes, and classroom climates. Observing and monitoring the reactions of students when we tease, cajole, or joke is critical to knowing how our humor is being taken.

★   **SCENARIO**   **CLASSROOM HUMOR**

"What pattern of tones do you hear at the cadence of *Muffin Man*?" Ms. Snodgrass asked her third-grade class. For several class meetings, they had been finding patterns of RE SO₁ DO in various songs. Because the students had just sung *Muffin Man,* their attention was directed to the melody of the cadence phrase. "I know what!" shouted Mia excitedly. "The street is very ugly with lots of trash and no trees and everything is gray and old. That's why it's called Dreary Lane!"

Reaction 1

A bit astounded by this off-the-wall response, Ms. Snodgrass sensed this was one more example of the lack of focus she often found in these students' responses. "Where is your brain today, Mia? Come on, girl, get with the program. If I had wanted you to step into the Twilight Zone, I would have made that clear. If you would listen for a change, maybe, just maybe you'd get some idea of what we're trying to study here!" Impatiently looking at Mia, Ms. Snodgrass emphasized, "I'll repeat the question for those of you who think you can listen this time. What *pattern of tones* do you hear at the cadence of *Muffin Man*?"

Reaction 2

A bit astounded by this off-the-wall response, Ms. Snodgrass light-heartedly observed, "Oh my, Mia! Your mind sure took a trip with that question! I must admit that the connections you make fascinate me sometimes—Drury Lane and Dreary Lane! Right now, though, let me ask the question again." Ms. Snodgrass grinned encouragingly at Mia as she repeated, "What *pattern of tones* do you hear at the cadence of *Muffin Man*?"

▶ How does the portrayal of sarcasm differ from the portrayal of teasing in the foregoing scenario?

▶ What makes a response sarcastic? Even if Mia had found humor in Ms. Snodgrass's responses in Reaction 1, what message did she and her classmates receive?

▶ The differences between good-natured teasing and mean-spirited sarcasm lie in more than just the words used. Where are the other differences?

PRINCIPLE 1

PRINCIPLE 2

PRINCIPLE 5

When we comprehend that teasing and sarcasm, even if innocently intended, can have negative effects on our students, we will pay more attention to communicating with sensitivity so that our metamessages are not misunderstood.

> Even when the metamessage is received intact, the recipient may still feel offended by clever sarcasm. The interpersonal dynamics of face-to-face talk are sufficiently complex to ensure that we always run a risk in mocking those with whom we are verbally playing. (Norrick 1993, 76–77)

Teachers and Stress

PRINCIPLE 2

PRINCIPLE 5

Reflecting on good teaching will not only help us maximize the well-being and growth of children as citizens of the world; it will also help us preserve and promote our own mental and physical well-being. One of the greatest threats to our ability to become the teachers we want to be is job-related stress. Concern about the levels of stress that teachers often endure is the focal point of this section. Let us consider some perspectives on stress in the lives of teachers.

▶ How often do you believe that stress is affecting your mental health?

▶ How often do you believe that stress is affecting your physical health?

▶ Do you consider yourself relatively stress-free?

▶ When you are feeling stressed, what do you do to relieve the tension?

▶ How do you know when you are feeling stressed?

Stress is a high-profile affliction in this society and is often identified as the cause of the various maladies we may contract. The popularization of stress, however, has taken its toll on us. Many of us identify what we are feeling as stress simply because that is the easiest and most vogue terminology for our condition.

The term "stress" has been used to describe bad moods, fatigue, excitement, anxiety, and tensions. Do all those feelings equate with stress? No. They may not be pleasant feelings, but labeling them as stressful can actually make them seem worse. Why could mislabeling our feelings as stress work against our constructive acceptance or resolution of those feelings?

If we make a distinction between pressure and stress, perhaps the destructive impacts of stress will become clearer. Stress involves threat. Under stress, we may feel that our health, our jobs, our reputations, or our relationships may not survive the ordeal that we are going through or the solution we are about to encounter. Stress, then, is destructive and unhealthy because it eats away at our armor of self-protection and self-determination.

Pressure can propel us into action. Looming deadlines and lofty aspirations can be motivating and stimulating. Unlike stress, therefore, pressure can be a constructive, propelling force in our reactions to life situations.

▶ To what extent is it our choice to interpret something as pressure rather than stress?

▶ What could be the benefits of reframing our reactions so that we treat situations as "pressureful" rather than stressful?

▶ What could be the harmful effects of mislabeling situations and feelings as stressful rather than "pressureful"?

DIFFERENCES BETWEEN PRESSURE AND STRESS

Pressure

We see a time line as an incentive to complete a project.	"I need to get my grades calculated so that they are ready to send home in two days."
Our desire to do well is a motivation to study or practice.	"I want my principal to see how well I can meet those appraisal criteria, so I will carefully prepare my lesson for that evaluation."

Stress

We feel a threat to our well-being when a time line closes in on us.	"If I don't get my grades calculated so that they are ready to send home in two days, my students' parents will think I am incompetent and may complain to my principal."
We feel threatened with reprisal if we don't do well on a given task.	"If I don't do a good job during my appraisal lesson, my principal will think I'm a poor teacher and won't support my program."

Often, the difference between pressure and stress is the level of "catastrophizing" we do about a specific expectation (Williams 1993, 236): "If I don't do a good job, everyone will think I'm incompetent. If people think I'm incompetent, they won't support me. If I have no support, I'll get terminated. If I'm terminated, I won't be able to support myself or get another job. If I can't get another job to support myself, I'll be at a loss for what to do. If I'm at a loss and have no options, I will collapse. If I collapse, I will die." Of course, the ultimate catastrophizing ends in death.

Differentiating between pressure and stress is important to the way in which we interpret what we are feeling and the potential resolution of those feelings.

▶ How prone are you to catastrophizing your daily situations?

▶ What adjustments may help you stop this pattern of thinking?

▶ Does it seem reasonable to you that the level of pressure or stress in an expectation lies more in us than in the expectation?

"A Tribute to Teachers" (Bennett 1992b, 37, 39) lists the many paradoxes of being a teacher—the subtle yet significant forces that may keep teachers off balance in their personal and professional lives.

1. We spend long hours of exhilarating and exhausting intensity, yet do not stop thinking about our work when we leave school.
2. We love our jobs and subject matter, yet must cultivate hobbies and time away from school-related thoughts and activities.
3. We achieve success, yet are continually drawn to become better teachers.
4. We must be compassionate, fair, and accepting of students, yet acknowledge that few other professionals are required to maintain such uniformly loving, compassionate attitudes toward all clients, patients, or customers with whom they come in contact.
5. We know the tremendous importance of our profession, yet see the low priority and feel the frequent devaluing of our work, based on teachers' salaries and public opinion.
6. We feel buoyed by 30 students' engagement, yet can feel devastated by one troubled student among them.
7. We sometimes must use mandated materials or systems, yet may never be asked what we think, what we know, or what we believe about the values of those requirements.
8. We must test students' achievements, yet know that the most important and most lasting learning cannot be measured or identified on a test.
9. We see "great teachers" spotlighted as those who go to extraordinary lengths to entertain or capture students' attention, yet recognize that quiet, nonassuming demeanors can be equally effective and sometimes more substantive.
10. We know that sometimes what students need most at a given moment is *not* more academic knowledge and skills, yet we are often unequipped to accommodate the complex emotional and physical needs of today's students.

The daily push and pull that teachers experience can result in stress and self-doubt. When these destructive forces enter our lives, few of us can be the teachers we want to be at any given moment. Feeling threatened, either momentarily or over a period of time, can cause what is known as the *fight-or-flight* response. This response is the body's reaction to perceived threat, and our systems are mobilized to either hit or run. Physical reactions include quickened breathing, clenched teeth, widened eyes, and tense muscles.

Just as crises come and go, so does the fight-flight reflex. . . . After teachers have been on their toes for seven hours a day for several years, the physical mobilization of the fight-flight reflex becomes a chronic condition. It is no longer under our control, and in a perverse twist of nature, every aspect of the fight-flight reflex originally designed to save our lives becomes a symptom of chronic hypertension. (Jones 1987a, 28)

Potential medical and psychological conditions resulting from teaching-related stress are high blood pressure, gastrointestinal problems, dental problems (teeth grinding), muscular tension (back, neck, and headache), substance abuse, chronic tiredness, depression, short temper, and anxiety. Jones cited National Education Association (NEA) statistics showing that teachers are second only to air traffic controllers in the levels of job-related stress they experience. This stress is due in part to the approximately 500 management decisions teachers make per day (Jones 1987a, 29). When stress is too intense and too constant, people suffer burnout. Five telltale signs of burnout in a teacher, even when he or she denies or represses it, are identified in Jones's section on "How You Can Tell When You're Dead" (p. 35).

1. *Exhaustion.* You are constantly dealing with discipline.
2. *Futility.* It doesn't get any better.
3. *Resentment.* It finally becomes them against me.
4. *Cynicism.* You can't do anything about it anyway.
5. *Rationalization.*
   - "It's just the way kids are at this age."
   - "I can't teach them if they don't want to learn."
   - "The noise doesn't bother me that much."
   - "I wouldn't want them to be just little robots."
   - "You can't be expected to deal with all the little stuff. You'd never get anything else done."
   - "The kids from these neighborhoods have home lives you wouldn't believe. What can you expect?"
   - "It's all the TV. Their attention span is as long as the time between commercials."
   - "Kids learn from talking to each other, don't they?"
   - "I don't have any 'major' problems."
   - "It's my job to present the material. It's their job to learn it."

According to Curwin and Mendler (1988, 118–119), teachers who are prone to burnout form four categories. The "Please Like Me" teacher depends on student approval and is willing to ignore misbehavior in order to continue feeling liked. The "Muscle Flexer" resorts to power-based methods that invite resistance, retaliation, and rebellion. The "Guilt Giver" uses whining and complaining to appeal to the guilt of students and to beg for behavior. The "Marine Sergeant" relies upon rigid rules but is unable to make modifications for the tough-to-reach students. Have you known any of these types of teachers? Do you see yourself fitting one of these categories?

In *Stress Without Distress*, Selye (1974) asked why some teachers feel stress as distress and ultimate burnout whereas other teachers use the stress to generate new energy and enthusiasm. He proposed that it is the perception of the behavior that causes a teacher to decide whether to interpret and react to it as a threat or as an opportunity to connect. Chopra (1993) echoed the view that the ways in which we perceive the world have powerful effects on our physical and mental health: "One thing you can own free and clear in this world is your interpretation of it" (p. 25). . . . "If you want to change your body, change your awareness first. Everything that happens to you is a result of how you see yourself" (p. 37).

Is it possible, then, to change our reactions so that stress is minimized in our lives? We believe it is. We may not be able to control what happens to us, but we *can* learn to control how we respond to it.

The way we plan for, think about, and react to our behaviors and our students' behaviors can make a difference in the energy, enjoyment, and satisfaction we feel as we pursue the principles and practices that help us be the teachers we want to be.

A Comparison of Teaching Contexts

Teachers are especially vulnerable when we compare ourselves with other teachers. By observing and listening to other teachers, we try to get a sense of whether or not we are doing all right, especially if we are beginning teachers. Do you find yourself on a self-esteem roller-coaster, depending on what you see and hear as you watch and listen to your colleagues? Consider your reactions to these possibilities:

- You hear that another teacher is doing great things in his or her classroom.
- You hear reports of outstanding achievements of students in another teacher's classes.
- You hear how loved and valued another teacher is at his school or in his community.
- You see happy, relaxed teachers who seem not to be struggling with the same challenges you are.
- You see another teacher's surprised, puzzled, or judgmental expression when you describe a particular problem you are having.
- You see another teacher's concert or program and wonder how she is able to accomplish such excellence.
- Your students remind you that "Ms. Holston [their former teacher] knew how to do that!" "didn't make us do that!" "made this stuff *fun*!" "let us chew gum (watch videos, sit anywhere we want, have a party, sing songs from the radio)."

At such times, remember that differences in context help explain different results. Comparing yourself unfavorably with another teacher is rarely constructive in developing your own teaching skills. When you begin to feel inadequate, ask yourself what is different about the teaching situations.

Acknowledging differences in context is not intended to downplay quests for excellence. To make excuses for why something is more difficult to accomplish in one setting than in another is not the aim. Nor is acknowledging how teaching is affected by context intended to demean or devalue a teacher's work because one context is "better" or "worse" than another. Rather, informed views of context can give perspective and breadth to the struggles and achievements each of us experiences in the teaching profession.

SCENARIO   AN ISSUE OF CONTEXT

At a regional in-service for music teachers, Jane joined three teachers from a nearby school district for coffee and conversation at break time. The topic of discussion was "What do you do with your sixth graders?" One teacher immediately bemoaned the fact that she could not find anything that appealed to her older students and that it was a chore even to see them come into the room. Jane began to feel relieved that she was not alone in her frustrations. Although she was too timid to admit how dispirited she had become, she began to feel somewhat affirmed to learn that other, more experienced teachers could also feel incompetent with certain classes. Just as she was feeling more secure and less uncertain about her abilities as a teacher, another teacher in the group, Sylvia, spoke up.

"I guess I just don't have those problems. My sixth graders *love* to come to music. We have such a good time! They even gave a wonderful madrigal concert this fall, singing in four part-harmony, a cappella! I refuse to resort to fru-fru as I call it. I want them to study *serious* music. We just finished a unit on opera, and they wanted to compose their own opera, complete with homemade costumes and original libretto. So I let them. They even wrote a full score with staff notation, all the parts, and the words. It is on display in the superintendent's office right now. The evening news channel even came out to film and interview them. I could send you my materials if you want. Would that help?"

By this time, Jane just wanted to go home. "What am I doing wrong? I must not be cut out for teaching. I should be able to teach my students so that they are really learning music."

Understanding the context in which we teach helps us to identify its potential and to construct meaningful activities for our students.

Has something similar happened to you? To a lesser degree, perhaps, we have all fallen into the "why can't I accomplish what she does?" mentality. What contextual factors might influence what Jane could accomplish?

There are great differences in what these two teachers can and should expect from themselves and their students. We must remember that different contexts may produce different levels of expectation and achievement. By grounding ourselves firmly in the context within which we teach, we can more confidently and realistically construct our goals and develop expectations. (See Chapter 9 for further discussion on the factors that affect teaching contexts.)

COMPARING TWO CONTEXTS

When Jane returned from the workshop, she called an experienced music teacher in her district to try to sort out some of her feelings of inadequacy. Fortunately, her friend gave her more information about Sylvia's teaching situation. Jane soon learned that Sylvia's context was quite a contrast to her own.

Sylvia's Situation	Jane's Situation
Sylvia had been teaching at the same school for 15 years.	Jane was in her second year and was teaching at three schools.
She taught at a school with very little turnover of administration, teachers, or students.	She taught at a school with a 60 percent turnover rate for students and 10 percent for teachers.
Most of her students came from upper-middle-class economic settings, all were native English-speaking, and all came from similar ethnic backgrounds.	Her students came from a mixture of economic settings; 70 percent were not English-proficient; it was common to have six nationalities represented in one class.
Her classes were no larger than 20 students.	She had double classes (45 to 60 students).
She met her classes every day.	She met her students once a week.
Each music class lasted 45 minutes.	Each music class lasted 25 minutes.
Many students took private lessons in music.	Most students did not have access to music activities or concerts outside school.
She received generous financial support to attend courses and workshops and to buy instruments and materials.	Budget was a major concern throughout schools; no money was provided other than replacement costs.
Many parents volunteered to help in class and with programs.	There was little or no community attendance at school functions.

Most stories about what other teachers do give only part of the picture. Taking a closer look at the contextual differences between your situation and other situations may show that you are being unnecessarily and destructively hard on yourself and your students.

Creating an Environment for Learning

Each time we enter a classroom with our students, we create an environment for learning. Whether we intend to or not, we set the stage for how our students feel about themselves and us, as well as school, learning, and classmates, when they are in our presence. Creating an environment for learning is largely our responsibility, and in assuming that responsibility, we must keep in mind our needs and goals as well as those of the students. Teaching over a period of time can cause us to forget that the *students,* not the demands of performance, curriculum, administration, and subject matter, are the most important factor in our being effective teachers. We must continually consider and reconsider, "Why am I here?" and "What am I trying to do?"

▶ What do we want children to believe about themselves when they are in our classes?

▶ How do we show our students that we value them and their ideas?

▶ What conditions contribute to maximum learning in a classroom?

▶ What conditions tend to impede learning?

Accepting differences and displaying curiosity about students' thoughts, skills, and behaviors play critical roles in building a foundation for learning.

PRINCIPLE 2

Creating an environment for learning means shaping the classroom setting so that students are free and challenged to learn in an atmosphere of group comfort and cooperation. This environment must be re-created each time we enter the room. Although physical setting, equipment, materials, and resources play a part in classroom opportunities, they are not essential to learning. By watching and listening to students, we will see what they need from us to learn. Learning can occur most easily when students feel safe from threats of embarrassment, humiliation, and failure.

Developing Trust

PRINCIPLE 1

PRINCIPLE 2

PRINCIPLE 3

Building trust among students and between students and teachers has both short-term and long-term benefits for learning and general citizenship (Johnson and Johnson 1989/90). Teachers' behaviors toward students and colleagues can be the model for trustful and respectful interactions. Trustworthy settings can be established by using principles and practices that vitalize group acceptance and cooperation, affirm individuals, offer students choices, view mistakes as learning opportunities, set limits for behaviors, and elicit and accept student responses within lessons.

To some extent, our ability to function in any social system is built on trust. To reveal thoughts and attempt tasks, we expect certain levels of acceptance that minimize our vulnerability to each other. Though commonly acknowledged as means of motivating students, praise, rewards, and competition "set up a breeding ground for distrust" because we lose our connections with each other. Instead of connections that foster group cooperation, effort, and encouragement, chasms develop that isolate and detach us from those around us (Kohn 1993, 142). In building trustful relationships, we should rethink the extent to which we make use of praise, rewards, and competition. (See Chapter 8 for detailed discussions on these issues.)

▶ How can students learn to become trustworthy and trusting in classroom settings?

▶ What role does the teacher play in establishing the guidelines for acceptance and trust among students?

Affirming Individuals

An environment for learning is a setting wherein the worth and contributions of each student are acknowledged and affirmed. Our challenge as teachers is to finds ways to encourage students' participation from a variety of levels and perspectives. Song activities provide opportunities for such affirmations by acknowledging and incorporating students' *names, ideas,* and *voices.*

Names

PRINCIPLE 1

Knowing and using a student's name in considerate and respectful ways gives the impression that the teacher values that student. Our names often function as a kind of symbol for who we are. Family names have represented employment, status, honor, tradition, and history. Ridiculing people's names is no small matter. Name-calling can hurt. As much as we might want to make a distinction between our names and who we are, many students do not. Our names are not simply labels; they are also important aspects of who we are. The use of names in accepting, welcoming ways can be one of the simplest initial strategies in establishing an environment for learning.

Do you recall a time when your name was mispronounced or you were called by a name other than the one you preferred? Part of respecting a person is calling him or her by the name requested. When learning a student's name, ask him or her to say the name for you. Then try to follow the student's pronunciation as closely as possible. Within reason, nicknames and abbreviated names deserve acceptance in the classroom. "Junior," "Chip," and "Missy" can be names closely connected with a child's identity, especially within his or her family. Insisting upon use of students' proper names (Frederick, Leonard, and Melissa) may be an impediment to acceptance and rapport between teachers and students and among students. Constantly mispronouncing a name or making little effort to pronounce a name correctly implies a lack of respect for the person and for languages, regions, or cultures different from our own.

Song activities such as *Here We Are Together* and *I'm Going Downtown* focus specifically on learning names and singing names within the activity context. Other song and study activities, however, can be personalized by including students' names to acknowledge whose idea has been offered (*Circle Left*), whose turn it is (*The Farmer in the Dell*), or whose voice is starting the song. Refer to the folk-song games in Chapter 9 as you consider the following questions.

▶ When names are used within a song context, what messages are given to the students?

▶ What values for your classroom environment are being established by the use of song activities that highlight or include students' names?

Use caution in selecting discipline management strategies that use students' names as punishment rather than affirmation.

When disciplining a student, it is important that we avoid using his or her name in a scolding or derogatory manner. Use the name to gain the student's attention; then deliver the warning or the reprimand. Consider what issues might arise in using students' names as part of a punishment process.

▶ If a teacher's comments move into the aggressive or harsh levels of vocal assertiveness, are there any reasons to exclude the student's name from these commands or scolding?

▶ Does it matter that names are used to scold? Is it possible to use the name to gain a students' attention, but to avoid saying or using the name with anger, harshness, impatience, or chastisement?

▶ Why might it be worth a teacher's efforts to protect a student's name from being used in a derogatory or demeaning way?

A curious change has occurred in American education in the way names are used in the punishment process. In many American classrooms before the 1980s, having one's name written on the board was generally a complimentary recognition. In recent years, however, writing a student's name on the board has been used to chart his or her misbehavior.

> The 1980s might someday be remembered as the decade when admiration was reserved for principals, cast as folk heroes, walking around schools with baseball bats, and for teachers and whole schools that systematically embarrassed students by writing their names on the chalkboard. (Curwin and Mendler 1988, 24)

Ideas

Creating activities, questions, and challenges that do not require correct answers can help achieve a climate for welcoming students' ideas and responding to them with an attitude of acceptance and interest. Within this context, when students are asked for their ideas and opinions in class, they are given the message that they have value and that their ideas have value.

PRINCIPLE 2

Questions such as "What do you think?" "What do you see?" "How can we move?" and "What do you hear?" have no wrong answers. Instead, they elicit responses that show how a student is perceiving the task, the question, or the instructions. In short, the teacher is interested in how a student *thinks,* rather than whether or not he or she has a right answer.

▶ What song activities in Chapter 9 elicit and incorporate students' ideas? What forms can these ideas take?

▶ How do these activities limit and structure students' contributions?

▶ What are some categories for the types of student ideas used in song and study activities?

Voices

Speaking and singing are ways for a student to contribute to the lesson. For some students, speaking in class can be terrifying, and singing in class may be even more risky. By behaving in a way that supports vocal participation, that accepts voices at varying phases of development, and that offers gentle, supportive feedback about vocal production, a teacher is laying the groundwork for healthy, tuneful, confident, life-long singing. Speaking voices are valued means of vocal participation, and even when a

PRINCIPLE 1

PRINCIPLE 2

singing response is requested from a student, a speaking response can be an acceptable way of reducing risk or embarrassment.

▶ What song activities in Chapter 9 incorporate individual vocal responses from students?

▶ How can your responses to students' vocal participation be encouraging and descriptive rather than demanding and evaluating?

Offering Students Choices

PRINCIPLE 2

Students can be empowered by opportunities to make choices during lessons. Instead of relinquishing responsibility for the class and the lesson, the teacher maintains leadership by selecting the choices that students can make within activities—structuring the freedom. When students are offered choices, several important results can occur.

- Activities become more immediately meaningful to students.

PRINCIPLE 3

- Students feel as if the activity and the class is theirs—they gain a sense of ownership.

- Students become engaged and invested in the process and the end result of the activity.

Ways for Students to Make Choices

- "Whose name shall we sing first in our song?"
- "Who will choose our first farmer (or person in the center)?"
- "How many more turns shall we have: three, four, or five?"
- "Choose a partner by the count of five."
- "Think of a way to move for this turn of the song."
- "Who will start the song for us?"
- "Choose an idea to tell us about."
- "Where shall we put the beat this time?"
- "Which direction will our circle move?"
- "For this turn of the song, choose someone to go to the board."

Ways for the Song to Make Choices

- "Look where the song stopped your feet. Who is closest? That's who the song chose." [*The Farmer in the Dell, I'm Going Downtown*]
- "Look where the song stopped your finger. Follow your finger to see whose turn it will be." [*Punchinella, Circle Left*]
- "I wonder where the song will take us this time. Can your feet stop when the song does? The closest person to you will be your new partner." [*Come and Follow Me*]

What If a Student Has Difficulty Making a Choice?

Some students are overly conscious of making a mistake. Others are overwhelmed by being the center of attention, and some have difficulty choosing an idea within the song's time frame. Fear of embarrassment or of ridicule from peers or the teacher can interfere with development of choice-making skills. Therefore, we must build trust by modeling the principle that ideas are received with curiosity and acceptance.

Sometimes students can make a choice, but it is not an appropriate choice for the activity or the school setting. A movement or a word choice that is inappropriate for the classroom is best handled swiftly and without undue chastisement. "That movement is too dangerous for our classroom space. Think of another quickly." "We are not all comfortable saying those words. How else could you describe your idea?" "Those gestures are inappropriate for schools. Do you have another idea, or shall we have the song move to the next verse?"

SCENARIO   MAKING CHOICES 1

Punchinella is one of the group's favorite song activities. With each new turn, students in the second-grade class seem increasingly eager to show their ideas for a motion. As she hears the second verse ("Oh, what can you do, Punchinella, Punchinella?), Becca smiles and demonstrates a somersault.

SCENARIO   MAKING CHOICES 2

As Barbara enters the circle to be the new Punchinella, she looks tentative during the first verse as she watches the children circle her. When the group sings and watches for her movement idea on "Oh, what can you do, Punchinella" Barbara stands stiffly, not indicating a motion at all. The song and activity come to a screeching halt as the children stop and stare at Barbara, impatiently waiting for her idea.

If you were the teacher in these situations, what would you do? Becca's idea clearly shows that she wanted to demonstrate a skill she had learned. As a teacher, however, you have several options for redirecting Becca's suggestion:

- "Becca, you were so limber for that somersault! Not all of us can do one, though, and even if we could, it is not safe in this space for us all to do one. We'll sing that verse again so you can show us another idea—one that we can all do."
- "Becca, we'll take a watching turn as you show us your somersault skills."
- "If you can find a safe place to do it, you may join Becca in her idea. If you would rather have a watching turn, you may watch and sing for that verse."

Barbara's temporary inability to offer an idea is not an uncommon occurrence in classrooms. Our challenge is to offer students support for learning choice-making skills while at the same time minimizing their discomfort. It can be helpful to respond to the idea from a hesitant child's delayed contribution or to his or her use of an idea donated by a classmate with the same affirmation and acceptance that you would if the child had offered it promptly and without help. In building Barbara's confidence, here are some responses you might offer.

- "Raise your hand if you have an idea to share with Barbara."
- "Barbara, you could clap your hands, stomp your feet, or wave your arms."
- "Barbara, can you think of something to do with your fingers?"
- "Barbara, can you think of something to wiggle?"

- "Let's imitate the way Barbara is standing and the expression on her face."
- "Let's sing that verse again to give Barbara a little more thinking time."

You could make suggestions to Barbara quietly, whispering in her ear to give her support and privacy as she makes her decision; or you could make them to Barbara so that the whole group could hear.

Students who do not possess choice-making skills need to develop them. Punishing or embarrassing students for not having those skills does little to aid in their development of them.

▶ Why would you choose one suggestion over another for Becca or Barbara?

▶ For Barbara, what benefits are inherent in the "private conversation"? What benefits may be gained from revealing the suggestions to the group?

▶ When, if ever, might you take a punitive approach to Barbara or Becca? "Barbara, if you can't have your idea ready when the game calls for it, you lose your turn. Go back to the circle, and let's have someone else take a turn." "Becca, that is not something that's allowed in our class. Let's have Tanner take your turn to see what he will do."

What If a Student "Copies" Another Student's Idea?

PRINCIPLE 1

PRINCIPLE 2

Copying is not inherently a bad thing to do. In education settings across the continent, however, children are reprimanded for copying a classmate's idea. Quickly, children adopt a critical viewpoint and cry accusingly, "She *copied*!" "He took *my* idea!" Why is it acceptable for children to copy the teacher but not other classmates? Imagine the potential confusion and mixed messages that come from trying to figure out from *whom* it is all right to copy and *when* it is all right to copy. Are the applications of this subtle classroom rule easy for children to differentiate? Are we overly concerned about the issue of copying during normal classroom activities? Read the scenario for *Daddy Loves the Bear* in Chapter 9; then consider the following questions.

It is wise for us to help children learn to value using others' ideas, to take delight from discovering the use of the same ideas, to compare sameness and difference of similar ideas, and to recognize the author when we knowingly use his or her ideas.

▶ What would you do if students continued to offer the same idea over and over?

▶ Would it be a problem for you if each student wanted to rock the bear?

▶ Why might students use the same idea for their turn that students preceding them used?

▶ Do these students lack choice-making skills? Is the answer to this question easy to determine?

▶ When is the "no copying" rule necessary and when is it unnecessary in classrooms of children?

▶ Is it ever appropriate to copy or to encourage copying?

We all choose to use standards and models that other people knowingly or unknowingly set for us. That two people come up with the same idea, however, does *not* clearly indicate that one copied from the other. Copying is not necessarily taking the easy way out; and it may clearly not be cheating.

▶ Did you ever think of an idea as you listened to a group discussion, and when you verbalized your "ah-ha!" the others tauntingly exclaimed, "We just *said* that!" What would you have preferred their response to be?

▶ What are some reasons that a student would repeat someone else's idea?

▶ What are some ways to encourage ideas, even when they are repeated ideas?

Would a student voluntarily offer an idea that would meet with scorn from the teacher and other students? Sometimes, perhaps, but not normally. Focusing more on why a student repeated someone else's idea than on scolding him or her for doing it gives us clues as to how to help a child develop the confidence to take a risk in contributing an idea.

Avoid the following statements, because they impede students' thinking and participation.

- "We've already used that idea, think of something else!"
- "You obviously weren't listening (watching), Carol. We just heard (saw) that idea!"

The following statements acknowledge students' thinking and participation.

- "Oh, we'll get another turn to clap our hands!"
- "This is sure a popular idea today!"
- "Betsy, you may not have heard Kathy say that, but new words for a similar idea help us get a picture of what you are thinking."

What If a Student Makes a Mistake?

What are mistakes? Many mistakes that are made in classrooms are simply actions or responses that do not match an expected or requested model. A standard of accuracy or acceptability, usually known by the teacher, defines what constitutes a mistake. For a variety of reasons, most of us fear making mistakes. Although mistakes in the classroom rarely have harmful, life-threatening, or long-term consequences, they can feel threatening to some students.

▶ What are some of the reasons that mistakes are feared or avoided?

▶ Has a teacher ever used one of your mistakes to embarrass you?

▶ Has a teacher embraced your mistake to show a different way of seeing an idea?

▶ Describe a worst-case scenario for the treatment of students' mistakes in classrooms.

▶ Describe a best-case scenario for the treatment of students' mistakes in classrooms.

When we develop curiosity about answers, we become intrigued by what is right about wrong answers and what obscure connections a student may be revealing in stating his or her answer.

Brooks (1984) and Elkind (1976) identify the "one-truth" orientation as a teacher's approach to learning that treats knowledge as a given, identifiable body that is learned by right answers. Anything not matching those right answers, therefore, would be a mistake. A casualty of the one-truth orientation is openness—"Little effort is made by teachers to discover and understand other truths that exist in every educational setting: *students' points of view*" (Brooks 1984, 24). When they are expected to deliver right answers, students often try to recall or figure out what the teacher wants to hear rather than thinking independently to solve a problem. In other words, when they know that their answers should match the teacher's view of right, students offer answers that they believe are valued by the teacher instead of pondering other possibilities. In these settings, it is questionable whether learning is taking place.

Saving a student's dignity and incentive to respond are priorities when responding to incorrect or unexpected answers in a classroom. Delivered with sincerity and interest, teacher responses to mistakes can become fruitful, teachable moments.

- "Oh, that's not what I expected you to say. What made you think of that?"
- "Hmm. I see where you got that answer, but listen to the question again."
- "Tell me more about why you think that."
- "That answer is very similar to the one I was looking for."
- "We did study that, and I'm glad you remember that information, but this question asks for a different answer."

SCENARIO   A SURPRISE SECRET SONG

"There's a secret song in my hands," Mr. Martinez began. "What song do you hear?" Using his inner hearing for the song, Mr. Martinez tapped the rhythm to *The Farmer in the Dell.* The first-grade class sat listening, then eagerly raised their hands at various points during the song as they decided that their song matched the one he was tapping.

"Wow, we have lots of ideas! Let's listen to what song you heard in my hands. What do you think, Marsha?" *"The Farmer in the Dell!"* "You did? What did you hear, Ericka?" *"The Farmer in the Dell!"* "How about you, Stanley?" *"The Farmer in the Dell!"*

Seeing all children's hands raised, Mr. Martinez inquired, "Did *all* of you hear *The Farmer in the Dell*?" "Yes!" the children chimed. One voice, sounding confused and hesitant, offered, "I didn't."

"Well, Danny, what song did you hear?" Danny replied, "I thought it was *Hickory Dickory Dock.*" Puzzled, but curious, Mr. Martinez continued, "Well, let's check *The Farmer in the Dell* and see if it fits my hands all the way through the song. Sing and check." Most of the children began nodding as the song ended.

"Now, let's sing *Hickory Dickory Dock.* After the class reviewed the song by singing it, their teacher said, "Listen again, and maybe we'll hear what made Danny think the secret song was *Hickory Dickory Dock.* Use your inner hearing as you listen to my hands."

As the children sang the song in their inner hearing and listened to Mr. Martinez's tapping, their eyes widened and mouths opened as they realized what they were hearing. Smiling, Mr. Martinez asked, "Hmmm, what did you discover?"

Being curious rather than closed and observational rather than judgmental about students' responses can minimize or alleviate fear of mistakes in the classroom.

FARMER IN THE DELL	HICKORY DICKORY DOCK.
The farmer in the dell.	Hickory dickory dock.
The farmer in the dell.	The mouse ran up the clock.
Hi ho the derry-o, the farmer in the dell.	The clock struck one, the mouse ran down.
	Hickory Dickory Dock.

▶ Sing and tap the words to *The Farmer in the Dell,* then *Hickory Dickory Dock.* What did you discover? When are the rhythms of the two songs alike?

▶ What would have happened if Mr. Martinez had *not* encouraged the children to check Danny's "wrong" answer?

▶ By the way in which Mr. Martinez handled the "wrong" answer, what messages and models were being given to the class?

Teaching strategies endorsed here do not include pretending that an answer is accurate when it is not or treating every answer as if it is a good answer. Rather, truthful, curious, and matter-of-fact reactions help guard against overreacting to a response. Overreacting can include being overpositive and overpraising as well as being over-critical and overnarrow in accepting and interpreting students' responses. Exaggerating our reactions to students' responses with extremely positive or extremely negative statements can work against learning. (See the section on "Eliciting and Accepting Students' Responses" later in this chapter.)

PRINCIPLE 6

What If a Student Says No to an Invitation?

In games that include an invitation to "go to town," "join the train," or "be the cheese," children are encouraged to practice their social skills by extending an invitation: "Would you like to go?" "Do you want to join us?" and so on. As is true for adults, children's invitations carry with them the possibility that someone may say no. *If a game is set up to include invitations, a teacher should not treat a turn as if it is mandatory.* A play activity based on invitations is a golden opportunity to help children learn that there are polite, acceptable responses for declining an invitation: "No, thank you" or "Not right now, thank you." Invitation games are also contexts wherein a child may learn what to do when someone does say no to his or her invitation. Read the scenario for *The Farmer in the Dell* in Chapter 9 for specific examples of how to respond to invitations.

PRINCIPLE 1

PRINCIPLE 2

Often, the less attention given to the child saying no, the better. As soon as a child responds, "No," to another child's invitation, one option is to say to the child extending the invitation, "Jesse, Alice doesn't want a turn right now, so who is the next closest person you can ask." Or you might say to the child who declines the invitation, "Alice, ask someone to take your turn for you." Usually it is the child extending the invitation, not the child saying no, who needs the teacher's support.

It is important to recognize that there may be very good reasons for a child to say no to an invited turn. He or she may be tired, may not feel well, may be shy and hesitant to participate, may want to watch the procedure of the game a little longer, or may be intent upon having a specific child ask him or her.

We want to offer children the same respect that we give to adults who decline invitations, whatever the reasons. A refusal does not necessarily mean that the person dislikes us. Of course, if saying no to invitations turns into a classroom epidemic, that is a clear message to change the activity or to change the invitation procedure. Invitations can be temporarily omitted from some games until students feel more comfortable delivering and accepting them. Some students approach invitations rather shyly, quietly whispering the invitation to another student. Some teachers prod students to make their invitations heard by the class, to project their voices so all can hear, and to speak loudly enough that everyone can listen to the exchange: "Can you speak so that we all can hear your invitation?" "Let's all listen for Robert's voice as he asks someone to come along." This strategy merits review. Rather than tampering with the volume of a personal invitation, it seems reasonable and natural to allow a student to speak at a private or conversational level—respecting quiet, private invitations as well as ones that are audible to the class.

Observing Students

Teachers must constantly read students' behaviors to know how to proceed. Although clues we receive from observing students help guide our choices for leading them, we should not presume that we ever truly know what is best for students or for learning at any given time. Staying open to what students need helps keep us attuned to and present in our classroom environments. This openness and curiosity also follows the researcher model that asks us to look continually for evidence that may support or contradict our conclusions about students' needs and motives.

PRINCIPLE 3

The following suggestions can be used to assess the dynamics in your own or someone else's classes.

WAYS TO OBSERVE AND REFLECT ON TEACHING

- Notice the general comfort of the group and of individuals. Does the comfort level change during the lesson? What happened to cause the changes?

- Notice students' level of engagement in the activity, and track any shifting that occurs during the lesson.

- Notice speaking voices used during the lesson (teacher's and students'). Is the teacher's voice easy to hear and easy to listen to? Is there sufficient and appropriate inflection and animation in the voice? What do you hear in students' speaking voices during the lesson? Is there a change in their inflection or projection at any point?

- Notice singing voices used during the lesson (teacher's and students'). Does the teacher's singing voice gently support students' singing voices or overwhelm them during activities? Do students' voices move in and out of being in tune? What happened to cause the changes?

- Notice ways in which students are asked to make contributions to the lesson. To what extent are students allowed to make choices within the lesson? Characterize the types of contributions or decisions that are requested from the students.

- Notice how questions, challenges, and statements are used to engage students, elicit responses, respect ideas, manage behaviors, and so on. What structure is built into the freedom that is given to students as they offer responses?

- Notice the types of verbal and nonverbal feedback given to students during the lesson. Is it in the form of compliments, complaints, criticisms, simple observations, or combinations of all of these? Is a full range or a limited range of proximity and facial expression used to communicate with students? What is the apparent reaction of individuals and the group to the types of feedback used?

Focusing Students' Attention

Teachers must have ways to capture students' attention quickly and efficiently. Do you have a variety of ways to do this that avoid scolding or punishing students for their lack of attention? Do you know some silent attention-getters that rest your voice? The following suggestions may not be equally effective. They are dependent on the context, the age of the students, and students' familiarity with the strategy. Note that one particular attention-getter may work for a time, then become so predictable to students that it becomes ineffective.

PRINCIPLE 5

A common attention-getter in elementary classrooms is the echo-clapping strategy in which the teacher claps a four-beat pattern (often consisting of quarter and eighth notes) and students immediately echo-clap the pattern. The echoing continues until focus is regained. Although this strategy blends musical skill (echoing, performing rhythm patterns) into a focusing device, it is often used without regard for musicality, variety, or arousing students' curiosity.

ATTENTION-GETTERS

1. Begin singing instructions on a simple melody. To the tune of *Muffin Man*, sing "Oh, let's all stand up tall, tall, tall. Let's all stand up tall, and be ready to walk to the door." Songs such as *London Bridge, Mary Had a Little Lamb,* and *Circle Left* are easily adapted to this procedure, which is especially appropriate for primary grades and younger.

2. Use an instrument in the room (piano, xylophone, tambourine) to perform a pattern that means "please be quiet." Whenever the students hear that pattern, no matter what they are doing, they are to become silent.

3. Select a signal that is the "quiet sign." When students see this signal they are to get quiet immediately. Some teachers have students imitate them by raising a hand, with the index finger of the opposite hand over their lips, until all are quiet. Or teachers may raise a hand and students imitate, closing lips when they raise their hands.

4. Some teachers effectively use a counting strategy even though no specific consequence has been identified if students are not quiet by a particular count. Counting can be seen as a tool to track or chart students' skills in getting quiet rather than as a warning or punishment for taking too long to get quiet. A challenge can be set up by asking, "George, how many counts do you think it will take us to get quiet as a class once the counting begins?"
   a. Count aloud.
   b. Give a silent count with your fingers.
   c. Write the number count on the chalkboard.

5. Begin clapping a four-beat pattern for students to echo. Wait four beats after you clap, then clap a different pattern. Continue this until students catch on and begin echo-clapping. Gesturing to students when it is their turn to clap may help initiate this procedure.

6. Quickly turn the lights off and on. This strategy may be most appropriate used in very large groups whose focus is diffracted (square dance, small-group activities).

▶ When you use echo-clapping, how can you make it a musical exercise for students?

▶ What would be the benefits of modeling musical flow and inflection when echo-clapping?

Consider modeling musicality during echo-clapping by using phrases from songs as the patterns to be echoed. Use light tapping rather than heavy clapping, and vary the volume within the pattern so that the tapping sounds like music rather than mechanics. Nuances, dynamics, and phrase shapes can be demonstrated and incorporated into echo-clapping strategies.

Focusing and regaining attention during transitions in the lesson can be especially challenging. Transition times in which students move from one area of the room to another can escalate behavior problems and waste valuable class time. Structuring the freedom with which students move during transition times offers a balance between freedom and structure for both students and teacher.

PRINCIPLE 3

Eliciting and Accepting Students' Responses

Getting Responses versus Getting Right Answers

Teaching is not synonymous with learning. Yet, for many of us, getting correct answers during lessons implies that we have done a good job of teaching because students

---

STRUCTURING FREEDOM DURING TRANSITIONS

Counting

"Willard, how many counts between the numbers 1 and 15 do you think it will take us to move from our places into a standing circle?"

"Let's make a sitting circle by the count of eight. Wait for the count to begin moving. Challenges are no talking, no bumping, and be there by the number 8."

"Because it is good for me to rest my voice, I will give you a silent count of seven to pass your instruments to the helpers. You will see the count in my fingers."

Listening

"As I sing a new song, walk quietly to a sitting circle. When the song is finished and we are in our circle, I will ask you some questions about what you heard."

"As I sing a new song, walk quietly to a standing circle. At the cadence of the song, when we are in our circle, I will ask you what you think the song is about."

"As you walk back to your chairs, I will take a singing turn alone. You will recognize the song, but I may add some new words. Let's see if you can listen as you walk."

Listening and singing

"Spot your chair from where you are standing. Your challenge is to sing the song, walk to your chair, and sit down as you sing the cadence word, not before, not after. This challenge takes auditory-visual-motor coordination and pacing. Good luck!"

"How many times through our song will it take us to move back to our places? Listen as you sing, and notice the number of repetitions."

---

seem to have learned. Right answers, however, do not necessarily indicate that students are thinking or understanding. Would you agree that thinking and understanding are more lastingly important than the momentary satisfaction of a right answer?

PRINCIPLE 2

PRINCIPLE 3

PRINCIPLE 4

Teaching for understanding requires that we continuously investigate whether our students recognize, demonstrate, explain, and apply ideas and information. While they are exploring and constructing these understandings, students learn from their own sorting processes as well as those of other students and the teacher.

Teaching for understanding also means that we are willing to look for new answers, broader visions, and unique perspectives from our students and ourselves. Key to freedom in learning and responding is the absence of the threat of humiliation for making a mistake. In discussing leadership within school settings, Patterson proposes a framework that is open to mistakes and that works from the premise of "I could be wrong, and you could be right" (1993, 32). Perspectives presented here on eliciting and accepting students' responses do not neglect or negate the importance of getting and giving accurate answers in certain learning situations. However, it is important to recognize the richness of experience and the liberation of learning that can result from eliciting and accepting responses that are beyond right answers.

Openness to making and learning from mistakes is connected to the ways in which questions are framed and the ways in which answers are treated.

▶ When you are asked a question by a person who expects you to give a right answer, how does that expectation affect your response and your willingness to respond?

▶ If a correct answer is expected, in what way does your thinking about the question change?

Imagine a classroom setting as you study and compare the teacher and student responses in the following scenarios.

| | **SCENARIO** | SECRET SONG 1 |

[With the fingers of one hand tapping on the opposite palm, the teacher lightly taps the rhythm for *Muffin Man*.]

Teacher 1:	What is the name of the song that my hands were singing?
Student 1:	*Mary Had a Little Lamb?*
Teacher:	No.
Student 2:	*London Bridge?*
Teacher:	No.
Student 3:	*Muffin Man?*
Teacher:	Yes.

| | **SCENARIO** | SECRET SONG 2 |

[With the fingers of one hand tapping on the opposite palm, the teacher lightly taps the rhythm for *Muffin Man*.]

Teacher 2:	Did you hear a song or any words of a song that my hands were singing?
Student 1:	Whose fleece was white as snow!
Teacher:	Is that what you heard? Listen again and see if you hear the same thing.
Student 2:	Mary had a little lamb.
Teacher:	That's what you heard. You'll get another chance to check it
Student 3:	Who lives on Drury Lane!
Teacher:	We have several ideas for what my hands were singing. How many of you think it might be *Mary Had a Little Lamb*? What song is Tina thinking about when she hears "who lives on Drury Lane"? Let's sing those ideas to get the songs in our heads. [Sing *Mary Had a Little Lamb*.] Now, here is my secret song again. Sing *Mary Had a Little Lamb* in your inner hearing and see if it fits my song all the way through. [Tap song again.] Did it fit?
Student 4:	Yes!
Teacher:	Did it fit all the way through or for a little part of the song?
Student 2:	Only the last part fit.
Teacher:	Do you remember what words you were singing that fit what my hands were singing? [Sing and tap again if necessary.]
Student 2:	Whose fleece was white as snow!
Teacher:	Here's what my hands were singing when you sang those words. Do the songs match there? [Tap cadence pattern.]
Student 5:	Yes!
Teacher:	Good listening and checking! But since only the last part of the song matches, my secret must be another song. Let's check Kim's guess. [Sing *Muffin Man*.] Now put that song in your inner hearing and see if it fits my secret song. [Tap *Muffin Man*.] Did any of your song fit what my song was singing?
All:	Yes!
Teacher:	Are you sure? Did it fit all the way through? You'd better check it again, here comes the song.
All:	It IS *Muffin Man*!
Teacher:	You are right. That was my secret song, and you figured it out! Let's sing it!

▶ Describe the differences between scenarios with regard to the teachers' goals and the levels of student engagement.

▶ What are the differences between the teachers' opening questions? How might these differences affect the number and types of responses each may receive?

▶ What messages are given to students through each teacher's responses?

▶ Which scenario gives the sense that more or most students in the class have solved the puzzle, determined the correct answer, and can confidently say why their answer is correct? What was the teacher's role in fostering this?

▶ How were mistakes handled and what effect could these choices have on students' learning? Why would the teacher in Scenario 2 delay telling students they had the right answer? What purpose could repetitions of the song serve?

▶ When we accept the first right answer from the first student with his or her hand up, what happens for that student? What happens for the other students with a hand up? What happens for those students who have not yet come up with an answer or have a different answer?

▶ Scenario 2 takes more time than Scenario 1. What could be the advantages of investing the time for the results of Scenario 2? Describe a scenario that will take less time than Scenario 2 yet be more open to responses than Scenario 1.

Questions That Elicit Responses

In the preceding two classroom scenarios, notice the extent to which the teacher-student interaction hinges on the teacher's use of questioning. Questioning is a powerful tool in the classroom to engage students in the activity, to encourage their thinking, and to elicit their responses. Yet, depending on the attitudes of the teacher, questioning can also be intimidating and confusing and can lead to student detachment. By expecting students to give the "right" answer, we may be giving them a clear message that we are more interested in the answer that is in our heads than in the ways in which they are figuring out the solution. It also presumes that our questions are clear and obvious and have only one "right" answer (Bartholomew 1994b).

Why do we ask questions of our students?

■ To get answers

■ To find out what they understand, know, or can do

■ To explore possibilities

■ To have them figure things out

■ To motivate them

■ To engage them in the activity

■ To stimulate thinking

■ To gather information

■ To encourage them to verbalize or demonstrate their thoughts and ideas

■ To collect a variety of observations and information

■ To stimulate problem-solving and investigative skills

■ To nurture collaborative expression and acceptance of others' ideas

To get the most out of questioning strategies, we must become more interested in students' thinking, learning, and understanding than in getting right answers.

Since the 1970s, research on the use of teachers' questions has provided clues about the interactive effects of different types of questions on students' learning. Several systems are available for classifying types of questions, but two categories clearly distinguish most questions: *fact* and *thought*. Fact questions challenge the recall abilities of the responders. Thought questions trigger higher levels of thinking that may engage cognitive, affective, or psychomotor skills for solutions. When thought and fact questions are combined, students are stimulated to apply information they recall to new and different circumstances.

Polling teachers about their preferences for clarity and time efficiency would likely give us a wide range of the ways in which to handle student responses. Some would agree with the findings of Rosenshine. In 1976, Rosenshine took the position that learning can best be achieved when teacher questions "tend to be narrow [fact questions]. Pupils are expected to know rather than guess [the] answer, and the teacher immediately reinforces an answer as right or wrong" (p. 365). The "yes-no-right-wrong" possibilities in this sequence are comforting to some students and teachers because they are clear-cut, definitive, and teacher-directed.

TYPES OF QUESTIONS

Thought questions
Questions that have no wrong answers. They ask the student to tell or show something from his or her own perspective. Students have great latitude in answering these questions and it is their own experience that is the source of their answers.

> "What do you think?"
> "What do you remember?"
> "What do you hear?"
> "What do you see?"
> "What do you know?"
> "What do you imagine?"
> "How would you solve. . . ?"

Fact questions
Questions that ask for recall. They funnel students' thinking to correct, specific answers.

> "How many beats are in this song?"
> "What is the first word of this song?"
> "What kind of clef is this?"
> "Does this song begin with an anacrusis?"
> "Where should the next bar line go?"

Combination questions
Questioning strategies that combine thought with fact. They show our curiosity about students' thinking as well as about their recall abilities and require students to synthesize experience and information.

> "What do you remember about how to play this game?"
> "What conclusions can you draw about the hand signs for that section of the song?"
> "Tell us what you know about the song score that is written on the board."

PRINCIPLE 1

Although experiments by Winne in 1979 led to the conclusion that the types of questions used by the teacher make little difference for student achievement, Redfield and Rousseau's 1983 analysis of teachers' questioning behaviors concluded that "predominant use of higher level questions during instruction has a positive effect on student achievement" (p. 241). Andre (1979) reached the same conclusion with regard to written text and concluded that textbook learning is facilitated more by higher cognitive questions (thought questions) than by fact questions.

Broadening the research base on the use of questioning, Dillon found that use of questions is more effective than no questions but that nonquestioning alternatives such as "declaration of perplexity" and "deliberate silence" may be equally effective (Dillon 1981b, 1978). Gall makes the salient point that "improving the quality of teachers' questions, then, is not sufficient. Students also need to learn the response requirements of different types of questions" (1984, 46).

If we accept Gall's recommendation to teach students how to respond to various questions, then it would seem imperative that our classroom practices include this aspect of the learning process.

The benefits of accepting many and varied answers from students are clear. There are times, however, when, given the constraints of time or the directions of the lesson, asking for a response from a student who you think has the right answer is the most efficient choice.

Planning Questions

Unless you are already skillful at asking probing, investigative questions, you may need to spend time planning the wording of questions for a lesson. Preparing questions helps to convey your attitude and curiosity more clearly so that you elicit the responses you want. Sometimes puzzled looks, incorrect answers, unexpected responses, and off-the-wall reactions indicate a lack of clarity in your questions. Knowing what type of question you are asking, what your goals are for asking it, and what reaction you will give to students' answers provides you and your students with the power to create a nonthreatening environment for learning and studying.

PRINCIPLE 3

PRINCIPLE 4

"Teachers' questions that require students to think independently and those that require recall of information are both useful but serve different purposes. The

---

HOW WE HELP STUDENTS RESPOND TO QUESTIONS

THINK about the purposes of the questions we are asking.	Am I interested in stimulating students' thinking about the topics I am presenting, or am I interested in finding out whether they can recall the terms and symbols we have studied?
PLAN for a variety of questions, challenges, and statements for instruction.	Am I finding out whether students recall the terms we studied; am I finding out whether students can explain the terms we studied; and am I finding out if students can demonstrate the terms we studied?
INFORM students about the kinds of responses that we expect.	"I am interested in hearing your own understanding. You don't need to use the words or phrases I used to explain it." "A specific term is what I am asking for. Can you recall it?"
RESPOND to students' answers with informative, constructive feedback.	"I haven't thought of it that way before. The term you used is related to my question, but it is opposite from the term that would answer it." "Tell us a little more about your explanation."

PRINCIPLE 1

PRINCIPLE 2

challenge for teachers is to use each type to its best advantage" (Gall 1984, 41). There is definitely a place for asking questions that have right and wrong answers. Most important to our students is that our expectations for their responses are clear and that our attitudes toward both right and wrong answers do not compromise their sense of dignity and trust.

As we are learning to teach, it is not uncommon for us to ask questions that elicit responses we do not intend. Asking a question that is too ambiguous ("What's another idea?") may result in a response that does not reflect what we were asking ("Let's sing a new song!"), causing us to become annoyed with students for misinterpreting our question ("We are working on *this* song. If you can't give a serious answer to my question, put your hand down!").

When planning questions, consider how vaguely or how specifically they might be interpreted. Also consider when vagueness or specificity can serve your purpose for the lesson and the students. What degrees of specificity are apparent in the following questions?

DEGREES OF SPECIFICITY IN QUESTIONS

Sample 1

1. "How much longer should we play this game?"

2. "How many more turns shall we have for this game?"

3. "Between the numbers of 2 and 5, how many more turns shall we have for this game?"

Sample 2

1. "What do you see on this page?"

2. "What notes do you see on this page?"

3. "How many different kinds of rhythms do you see on this page?"

4. "How many quarter notes do you see on this page?"

Sample 3

1. "What did you hear?"

2. "What did you hear in this song?"

3. "What word or words did you hear in this song?"

PRINCIPLE 3

When we solicit many and varied ideas and accept answers as indicators of what is being heard, seen, and thought, we learn more about our students' understandings. This attitude and process provide a rich environment for expression, investigation, and integration. Giving the right answer or fact may be the last step in this process rather than the first. Getting to the right answer may be more important than having the right answer.

Responding to Answers

The questions we ask and the way we react to student responses have an effect on what goals we accomplish. When calling on students to answer a question, some teachers continue only until a student offers a correct answer. Although this may be a time-efficient method of review, how sure can we be that other children understand the answer? How freely do all students participate in this process? Why do we stop calling on students after a correct answer is given? What can we do to encourage further efforts? If our responses indicate that a correct answer has been given, do students get the message that this round of the question-and-answer game is over and that further attempts to participate are futile? If we want to maximize the effect of our questions, we need to review how we respond to student answers.

PRINCIPLE 3

We evaluate the correctness of each answer as it is offered, but our responses need not indicate our evaluation. It is critical that we be aware of the effects our verbal and nonverbal behaviors can have on how students are engaged in the process of answering questions. Our words and facial expressions indicate that we are curious or critical, open or closed, and whether students should continue or have been successful. When teachers signal the rejection of students' answers too abruptly or too harshly, they do little to help students learn. When teachers show interest only in the right answer, they show little interest in their students.

PRINCIPLE 1

Few of us are comfortable answering questions when we believe our answers may be ridiculed, either by our teacher or by our classmates. When a teacher's attitude about using questions communicates "Will you measure up?" rather than "I'm curious what you think about this," the pedagogical benefits either for students or for the teacher are questionable. When delivered in an intimidating way, a question can result in mental "downshifting." Downshifting slows our ability to access the information we *do* know. When downshifting occurs, we may not be able to respond, to respond appropriately, or to respond accurately (Hart 1983, 108).

One thing teachers can do to mitigate the effects of mental downshifting is to plan what to say or do following a student's response to a question. Planning informative, constructive feedback *while* observing and listening to students' answers trains us to be thoughtful, reflective, and progressive in building cooperative and constructive classroom interactions. One way of giving informative feedback is to describe the students' behavior.

PRINCIPLE 6

> Comments that describe student behavior point the students in a particular direction. They direct the students' attention to those behaviors that the teacher wants to see continued or discontinued. Specific descriptions provide "expert witness." Comments such as "Your voice matched mine that time," "The intonation was faulty in the third measure," and "You talked during Allison's turn" let the students see their own actions through the expert eyes and ears of the teacher. (Bartholomew 1993, 41)

EXAMPLES OF INFORMATIVE FEEDBACK

To show interest or recognition

"Joanne has an answer she is eager to share. Keep it a secret a little longer."

"Brett, as I watch you read, you seem to be understanding how to figure this out."

To encourage

"You're on the right track!"

"Megan, your practicing is paying off, especially in your lower register. I can hear the difference, can you?"

(continued)

> **EXAMPLES OF INFORMATIVE FEEDBACK** (continued)
>
> **To describe**
>
> "You kept a steady tempo all through the song."
>
> "Your dotting is clear, easy to read, and accurate. You even added a double bar at the cadence!"
>
> "Such in-tune singing!"
>
> **To evaluate**
>
> "You didn't get the rhythm in the third measure, but you sang the right notes."
>
> "Did you forget to listen for the cadence? Your feet didn't stop with the song."

Teachers can encourage independent thinking, provide for fuller and more detailed answers, encourage divergent thinking, gather more information, and be more sure that students understand if they are careful about the way they respond to their students' answers.

PRINCIPLE 6

Evaluation and assessment of students' responses is necessary in the learning process. Assessment that points out inaccuracies in students' work may not be positive, but it need not be destructive. When you assess a student's performance by saying, "You are still missing that rhythm pattern in the cadence phrase because you're performing the sixteenth notes too fast. Try relaxing as you tap those notes," the feedback may not necessarily feel positive to the student. The information, however, is not negative, and the tone of voice is not destructive (assuming it is not delivered with sarcasm or scolding). The evaluation, then, is informative and constructive because it encourages the student to keep trying, tells the student what is missing, and gives a hint for remediation. With regard to assessment and feedback, constructive and destructive may be more meaningful categories than positive and negative. For more examples of feedback categories and statements, see "Types of Feedback" in Chapter 4.

In summary, questions are valuable tools for engaging students in learning and eliciting answers. What questions we ask, how we ask them, what answers we expect, and how we respond to answers can either enhance or detract from the value of our questions. Consider your own classroom habits in framing questions and responding to answers.

▶ How often do you tell students the purpose of a question?

▶ What proportion of your questions are fact questions? What proportion are thought questions?

▶ Do you try to find out why a student answered the way he or she did? How do you pursue wrong or right answers?

▶ How frequently do you repeat (echo) students' answers rather than challenging students to listen to each other?

▶ How frequently do you reword students' answers to make them correct or accurate? Why do you do this?

▶ Do you interpret or overinterpret a student's answer without checking the interpretation with the student?

PRINCIPLE 1

PRINCIPLE 2

PRINCIPLE 3

PRINCIPLE 4

PRINCIPLE 5

PRINCIPLE 6

HOW TO GET MORE THAN A RIGHT ANSWER

1. Provide for thinking time. Challenge children who know the answer to keep it a secret. Utilize wait time and study time with encouraging expressions.

2. Remain neutral (verbally and nonverbally) in fielding answers.

3. Provide opportunities to check answers before committing to the right answer. Let students know you want them to check their answers.

4. Provide clues. Clues may be auditory (speaking, humming, chinning, or singing a word or phrase, playing a pattern on an instrument) or visual (showing a gesture or motion, or reading a portion of a score, presenting a map or song-dot score).

5. Recognize that, when students rephrase responses, the different words can provide more information and additional perspectives ("Tell us what you were thinking").

Checking answers is an important skill for students to learn.

How we respond to answers our students give is as important as the kind of questions we ask. How we respond tells students how much we value their presence and their contributions. While it is easy to see that we should avoid belittling and demeaning students because of their answers, we need to be aware of the effect that echoing and re-wording student answers might have on further responses. (Bartholomew 1994b, 19)

Chapter Epilogue

Throughout this chapter, teaching has been treated as a co-responding activity that challenges us to observe ourselves and our students. This observational approach to teaching and learning offers rich opportunities to see, hear, modify, and acknowledge expectations for our teaching context. When we cultivate attitudes and behaviors that bring out the best in ourselves as well as our students, teaching matures us into the leadership roles and skills that befit our profession and benefit our personal lives.

Rethinking Rewards, Praise, Competition, and Misbehavior

8

PRINCIPLE 3

PRINCIPLE 4

An important theme throughout this book is that the responsibility for learning in a classroom is best shared by teacher and students. Students need opportunities to make contributions to classroom activities, and they deserve chances to say what they think, to support their ideas, to change their minds, and to come to their own conclusions based on evidence, reason, and communication with others. Yet, many students need help in knowing how to act responsibly with others.

Chapter 7 explored some of the issues involved in establishing a classroom environment that promotes greater student involvement in lessons through moving, singing, and contributing ideas. When students make use of the opportunities we give them to respond, we must be prepared to respond to them in turn. This model of student response followed by teacher response gives rise to the idea that teaching is a co-responding activity, a responding to and with our students, who also respond to and with us.

However good that may sound in print, the practice can be quite different. Although we may want students to contribute to classroom activities with their ideas, voices, and movements, they may make inappropriate choices in doing so—at least from the teacher's perspective. Some students all too frequently speak their minds without pausing to think about what they are saying or when they are saying it. As Johnson and Johnson (1989/90) point out, students frequently have not learned how to get along or talk with each other.

This chapter addresses in detail some of the ways we co-respond with our students, and how our responses to students affect their continuing co-respondence. No matter what their ages, students and teachers affect one another. At times the causes and effects of these influences are apparent and at times they are not. Specifically, the ways we use rewards, praise, and competition in the classroom have both obvious and hidden results. When, how much, and in what way we use each of these strategies needs to be rethought. When we take seriously the idea that students need to participate actively in classroom activities, we need to rethink what behaviors we consider to be misbehaviors. Finally, we need to look at ourselves as teachers, to review our roles as leaders, to begin to think of ourselves as experts in our own classrooms, and to monitor the stress that expectations and pressures bring to our job situations.

PRINCIPLE 5

The following sections are devoted to rethinking the ways in which we structure the powerful forces of rewards, praise, competition, and behavior management for our students. Perhaps more than any others, these strategies can sabotage the principles for teaching and learning identified at the beginning of this book.

Warning: Watch That Pendulum!

What you are about to read may be the most easily misunderstood chapter of this book. In rethinking the concept of misbehavior and the use and effects of praise, rewards, and competition, you may be inclined to have a "pendulum swing" reaction, moving to an extremely different position in your thinking. We are not advocating getting rid of rewards altogether, and we are not saying that you should no longer praise students. Our intention is that you reexamine these strategies to check if they are working most constructively for you and your students.

PRINCIPLE 4

As we learned in the previous chapter, context is critically important in understanding the choices we make about our own behaviors and practices and how we respond to our students. That is why each teacher must become the expert in his or her classroom. Being an expert suggests that one is highly skilled, thoroughly trained, and extensively knowledgeable about his or her discipline and teaching context. How do we become experts in our classrooms?

- Responsiveness: by watching, listening, and responding to students
- Scholarship: by pursuing, studying, and investigating possibilities of how and what to teach
- Openness: by presuming that we may not have the answer or the best answer

Self-determination implies that we have choice-making skills that allow us to consider similar and disparate points of view and that we assume responsibility for the choices we are making.

Accepting the challenge to become experts in our classrooms brings with it the responsibility of *self-determination* for ourselves and our students. Valuing and building self-determination is as important for children as it is for adults.

The choices we make for our students are decisions we must live with, and often our choices, whether major or minor in scope, are not easy ones. For precisely that reason, we must become experts. With the same expectations we have for our students, we must take responsibility for the behaviors we choose. Likely none of the authorities on whom we typically rely for answers (authors, administrators, specialists) have been in *our* classrooms, seen *our* students, or worked within *our* context to develop their ideas. By seeking continual growth and development for ourselves and for our students, we filter suggestions, advice, and recommendations through our own knowledge and intuitions. Our challenge as teachers is to stay open to new (and sometimes opposing) perceptions as we acknowledge our commitment and responsibility to make the wisest possible choices for our students.

PRINCIPLE 4

In considering the following provocative issues, moderate your responses and avoid rejecting or feeling guilty about past behaviors that you may now be rethinking.

We must give ourselves credit for doing or saying what we thought was best at the time. One of the benefits of rethinking is finding additional options. Remember, *the approach here is to offer options, not answers.* Emotionally flogging ourselves for what we did not know or understand does little for our growth and development now. It is you, the reader, who will decide whether any options presented here are momentary or long-term answers for you and your students.

Rethinking Rewards

A reward is something given in recognition of merit or superior achievement, yet often rewards are used to get people to do something. We reward a person for getting good grades or for giving information that leads to the solving of a crime. Rewarding good behavior in the classroom is now a common practice. Especially in the context of school, rewards are items or privileges earned as the result of an accomplishment. Rewards at school may range from stickers to party days.

As you begin to rethink your position on rewards, consider what behaviors merit a reward. Reflect on the implications of this barter model—you do this for me and I'll give this to you—not only for teaching and learning but also for human interaction generally. Think about the relationship between the value of the task or achievement and the reward given. Finally, examine the impact that a reward system has on student responsibility.

SCENARIO   REWARDS BACKFIRING 1

"I don't think I've ever talked about this as an adult." That's how the young woman, a participant in a summer course for teachers, began. Her response to the instructor's question, "Can you think of an example of a reward that has backfired?" took Sarah back to her own experiences as a fourth-grade student.

The new teacher spoke quietly as she recalled, "When I was in fourth grade, our teacher gave out blue chips to those individuals who behaved the way she wanted us to. Whoever had the most blue chips at the end of the week would get a present." As she paused, many of the teachers seated around her nodded in recognition of this common way to get cooperation in the classroom.

"This is embarrassing to tell," Sarah continued, "but what happened was not what the teacher had planned. The desire for those presents was so strong that even the 'good kids' started sabotaging the ones who were getting the blue chips. We would do something to make it look like it was their fault, and they would get their blue chip taken away. Isn't that awful? I still feel sorry for what we did."

The room was silent as the reality of what had happened among those children disheartened the teachers. "What a testimony to how rewards can pit students against one another," one teacher said. Another empathized with Sarah's recounting of the story, "What a testimony to the impact of that experience—that it brings back strong emotions for her so many years after it happened!"

SCENARIO   REWARDS BACKFIRING 2

"I have a very disturbing story to tell about my son," Norma said quietly. Teachers in the summer course had been sharing their experiences with rewards backfiring in their schools and classrooms. Norma had not spoken very frequently in the group, but from her facial expression, it was obvious that this discussion struck a nerve for her.

"My son's high school was giving tickets for good behavior. Nearly anything a student did that we would normally expect as standard school behavior or good manners was rewarded with a ticket. Students could save their tickets and, depending on how many they had, they could exchange them for all sorts of items. My son's group of friends decided that they would pool their tickets so that they could exchange more of them for the bigger, more desirable items. Handling their plan almost like a banking system, they elected officers, planned to barter with other students for tickets, and agreed that the president could exclude any member from the group at any time."

"You can probably guess the end of the story," Norma paused. "My son, who incidentally had gathered the most tickets, was ejected from the group. The mercenary natures of these boys took over and my son continues to have great difficulty dealing with this experience. A major irony of this story," Norma concluded, "is that the school's intent for initiating this reward system was to foster self-esteem in students. That is hardly what was accomplished with my son and his friends."

▶ Do you, or would you, give rewards in your classroom? Make a list of the kinds of rewards you have used or have seen used by teachers.

▶ Do you consider some rewards unacceptable? Which ones and why?

▶ Have you ever known rewards to backfire?

A chapter in the book *Building Classroom Discipline: From Models to Practice* by Charles is devoted to behavior modification. In that chapter, "Neo-Skinnerian Models: Shaping Desired Behavior," Charles addresses the benefits of rewards in classrooms and homes, especially when contrasted with punishment.

> Students, like rats and pigeons, responded better to positive rewards than they did to punishment. . . . It [rewarding students] gives teachers the power to work in positive ways. It lets them get away from harshness and punishment, which neither students nor teachers like. It allows them to maintain control within classroom environments that are warm, supportive, and positive, instead of cold, harsh, and punitive. (1985, 37–38)

Reinforcers or rewards can be anything that a student wants badly enough to do something to earn them: from getting a drink to being a line leader, from receiving a commendation to winning a game. Reinforcers may fall into one of four categories (Canter and Canter 1976; Charles 1985):

- Social (words, gestures, facial expression, compliments)
- Graphic (marks and symbols, positive notes to parents, certificates)
- Activity (being a monitor, working on a project, party, television)
- Tangible (real objects earned, stickers, candy, pencils)

As you look over the rewards in the above list, imagine yourself as a child. Would your reactions to these reinforcers as a child be different from those as an adult?

▶ Would some rewards appeal to you more than others? Why?

▶ In what ways might the desirability of a reward depend on your age?

▶ Consider the list in Chapter 9 of "Contextual Differences for Teaching and Learning." How might your particular context influence the effectiveness of various rewards?

▶ How does being a teacher instead of a child change your view of rewards?

The Risks of Rewards

Using rewards presents risks. The following are among the risks posed by any system of rewards.

▪ Rewards may be demanded and expected for any minor activity or behavior.

▪ Students may feel punished when they are not rewarded.

▪ Students may first check to see what the reward is before they undertake a task.

Incentive programs abound in schools and communities. Even if we believe that rewards are effective in changing how people act, we should ask critical questions before undertaking any incentive program.

▶ What are the short-term results of rewards?

▶ What is the long-term conditioning that a reward system can cause?

▶ What do we get and what do we give up when we institute an incentive program?

▶ What messages do incentive programs give to our children?

Rewards and Learning

Two of the first studies investigating the effects of rewards on learning were conducted independently in the 1970s but came to similar conclusions. Deci (1971) found that college students who were offered money to work on a puzzle spent less time working on it than those who had not been paid. As Deci put it, "Money may work to 'buy off' one's intrinsic motivation for an activity" (p. 114). In 1983, Lepper studied the effects of rewards on children in Head Start classrooms. The rewards were successfully used to induce the children to play learning games. Many years later, however, Lepper reflected on the success of these practices: "You didn't have to be a psychologist to see that the rewards worked—they really controlled kids' behavior. But the negative effects were harder to see. I'm not sure I would have noticed them myself if I hadn't gone to these other schools [that didn't use rewards] where kids were loving the activities" (308–309).

> The point, of course, is that reinforcement can also kill a taste for creative writing or financial analysis or generous behavior or anything else we value. In fact, this effect is so predictable that rewarding people might even be regarded as a clever strategy for deliberately undermining interest in something. (Kohn 1993, 72–73)

Asking some questions about reward-giving can be a valuable exercise in reviewing the purpose and the effects of offering rewards to students.

▶ What does the offer of a reward say about the inherent enjoyment, stimulation, or fun (self-reward) of the activity or process?

▶ Are we conditioning students to ask "What's in it for me?" at a young age when we use rewards to modify behaviors?

▶ Are we conditioning students to expect a reward for even minor tasks that would normally be standard school expectations or acts of courtesy or manners?

▶ Are we painting ourselves into a corner with the reward system we use with our students to the extent that the reward system restricts our freedom and flexibility to respond to students?

▶ Are we rewarding students by allowing them not to have our class on a given day? Some of us have rewarded good behavior by giving students a free day, substituting activities of their choice for our regular lessons. What does this say about our view and their view of our lessons?

▶ To what extent is there a correlation between self-esteem and receiving a reward? What could be the constructive and destructive effects of rewards on a person's self-esteem?

Another worthwhile exercise is thinking about intangible rewards and their role in learning and development. What are examples of intangible rewards? What makes something a reward if it is intangible? The following are some intangible rewards.

- The satisfaction we experience in completing a difficult task (repairing an appliance, reaching consensus with a group of colleagues, losing weight, reading a song score)

- The pride we feel at seeing a project completed (writing a paper, painting a picture, planting a garden, dramatizing a song)

- The pleasure we receive when we view the efforts of our labors (preparing a meal, seeing students learn, designing a piece of furniture, making a map)

- The delight we take in becoming inspired (watching a movie, reading a book, having a conversation, enjoying play with others)

Consider examples of intangible rewards you have felt or received.

▶ What are the differences between the feelings you get from an accomplishment and those you get from a reward?

▶ What is the source of intangible rewards? Who gives them out?

▶ What can you do to help your students recognize the self-satisfaction connected with intangible rewards?

▶ What happens to your sense of personal satisfaction when you also receive a tangible reward after accomplishing something important to you? Does it matter what the reward is? Does it matter how important the accomplishment is to you?

▶ What are the difficulties with intangible rewards?

▶ How can the study of a subject yield intangible rewards?

Beyond Rewards

According to Kohn (1993, 92–94), the detrimental effects of "Do this and you'll get that" may be minimized by implementing six suggestions for controlling damage done by the use of rewards.

1. *Get rewards out of people's faces.* Our challenge is to offer fewer of them, make each one smaller, give them out privately, and avoid making a big fuss over the whole process.

2. *Offer rewards after the fact, as a surprise.*

3. *Never turn the quest for rewards into a contest.*

4. *Make rewards as similar as possible to the task.* If you feel compelled to give a child something for having read a book, give her another book.

5. *Give people as much choice as possible about how rewards are used.* Although rewards are basically mechanisms for controlling people, you can minimize the destructive consequences by including the potential recipients in the process of deciding what will be given out and how and to whom.

6. *Try to immunize individuals against the motivation-killing effects of rewards.* [When minimizing rewards is not an option] we might as well do what we can to help people shrug off the implicit message offered by extrinsic motivators.

Many of us have seen the results of overrewarding students. Changing our practices with regard to rewards may be well worth the effort it takes, and preparing for the weaning process may be an important school effort that warrants informing parents. Cooperating as a school unit may stem the tide of the what's-in-it-for-me epidemic we have created for our children and our society. As Kohn says, "One is never too young or too old to have one's interest in a task reduced when that task is presented as a way of getting a reward" (1993, 75).

SCENARIO

REWARDS BACKFIRING 3

As a mature woman who was also a wife and a mother of three, Lezlie was determined to avoid getting trapped into a reward system as a teacher. In her undergraduate classes, she was articulate and convincing about the detrimental effects of rewarding children too often for trivial tasks.

But as she began her seven weeks of student teaching in an elementary school, Lezlie soon realized that the reward issue was bigger than she thought. Her supervising teacher spent a considerable amount of money on huge bags of candy and trinkets and gave rewards during each class period to recognize a variety of behaviors. Meanwhile, Lezlie did her best to help students value compliments and good feelings as rewards for jobs well done or for excellent participation.

Soon, however, the children began resenting Lezlie. They groaned and complained when they entered the room and saw that Lezlie was their teacher for the day. They knew that if Mrs. Ellis taught them, she would give them rewards. Not only did this attitude spread quickly among the children, but Lezlie lost more and more of her confidence. In desperation, Lezlie gave in.

Lezlie realized what other teachers have also discovered: Reward systems can become addictive to children, and the absence of a reward can be equated with punishment. For Lezlie, as for many of us, reshaping students' needs for rewards can feel like swimming upstream, especially when there is little support for our perspectives among our school staff.

Rethinking rewards is less about *whether* we should give rewards, and more about *when* and *why* we give rewards. We need to build independence, self-determination, and confidence in our students by helping them recognize the personal satisfaction that can come from engaging in challenging, effortful, or courteous tasks. Our ability to create tasks that are interesting and appealing and our resolve to minimize rewards for participating in such tasks help students become more interested in the task than in the rewards.

PRINCIPLE 1

PRINCIPLE 2

Rethinking Praise

Praise for achievement is considered a gift by some. Why would such a gift, given with the best of intentions and for the good of the receiver, warrant serious scrutiny by teachers? That praise is used in the classroom to shape students' behaviors is reason enough to examine its effects. Let's consider some information about, guidelines for, and side effects of praise in classroom settings.

SCENARIO   PRAISE IN THE CLASSROOM

It had been a struggle to find activities that would capture the attention of these students. The third-grade class had been a challenge for Mrs. Olsen, and she always felt that she was on the verge of losing control when she worked with them. Three boys in the class, Noel, Sean, and Timothy, seemed to be the instigators of problems. Nearly every activity planned tended to dissolve into Mrs. Olsen's punishing the students for their rowdy and unruly behaviors. Mrs. Olsen felt her resentment toward these boys growing as they seemed to be in control of her class.

One day, unpredictably, the lesson seemed to flow easily and students appeared genuinely cooperative and interested for the entire class. "What a relief!" Mrs. Olsen thought to herself, hoping for a breakthrough in the pattern of disruptiveness in this group.

As students lined up at the door, ready to leave the room, Mrs. Olsen mentally pondered how she wanted to address Noel, Sean, and Timothy to let them know how pleased she was with their behaviors today. As Mrs. Olsen took a breath to commend them in front of the class, Sean surprised her by speaking up, "Well, Mrs. Olsen, that was much better today. We are seeing some improvements. Good for you!"

SCENARIO   PRAISE IN A NEW SETTING

Dr. Cain had been through a stressful day, and she was hoping that the scheduled faculty meeting would begin on time. As the school principal, Dr. Cain was known for her promptness and "down-to-business" faculty meetings. Her attitude was that faculty time after school was valuable—to their school planning, to their families, and to their personal interests. Dr. Cain wanted meetings to be organized and efficient, yet friendly.

Teachers were gathering and most were talking among themselves two minutes after the scheduled meeting time. Dr. Cain began by saying, "Our first item for discussion today is, . . . " but most teachers did not stop talking. "Excuse me, . . ." she continued, but there was little change in the volume of the teachers' talking.

Faculty members finally came to attention as they realized Dr. Cain was acknowledging them: "I *like* the way Marsha is listening." "I *like* the way Bert was ready for the meeting on time." "I sure like what I see in LaVerna's behavior!"

▶ Did Sean's comments to Mrs. Olsen surprise you? Why?

▶ How would you have reacted to Sean's praise if you had been Mrs. Olsen?

▶ If you were leading a meeting of adults, would you use Dr. Cain's strategies for getting them quiet? Why or why not?

▶ What value is there in deciding whether you would say the same things to adults that you say to children? Do you think that children deserve the same respectful treatment that you would give another adult?

▶ Could words or behaviors be disrespectful to adults but not to children or vice versa? Why or why not? What, if anything, would you consider to be disrespectful in the two scenarios presented here?

What Is Praise?

We all need praise. We all need approval. Or do we? What is praise? *Praise is a judgment statement that expresses the approval, esteem, or commendation of one person for another.* As you read this section of the book, you may want to refer to this definition frequently. The term "praise" is not used here to mean *any* overtly or covertly complimentary comment. Key to the definition is the judgment and approval that are inherent in the praise statement. "You did a wonderful job on that project," "I like how you handled that," and "You are brilliant!" are examples of praise statements.

PRINCIPLE 1

Complimenting students is one of the ways we affirm their participation, achievements, behaviors, and attitudes. Use of praise in a classroom may be intended to set a tone of kindness, courtesy, compassion, support, and enthusiasm, as well as many other positive, constructive emotions and gestures. Teachers may use praise as a way to reward students' accomplishments, to support their responses, and to motivate them to continue their efforts.

Some educators have made lists of positive words and phrases to use in classrooms. A list of "99 Ways to Say 'Very Good'" (1974 University of Kansas Project MORE handout) and a list of "Approval Responses" (Madsen and Madsen 1983, 182–183) offer a variety of common classroom feedback statements. What follows is a sampling of statements from those sources. Note the various degrees of praise and the various levels of specific information for the recipient of the praise.

A SAMPLER OF COMMON APPROVAL AND PRAISE STATEMENTS

You're on the right track now!
You've just about mastered that!
Good remembering!
That's *right*!
That's good.
You're really working hard today.
You've just about got it.
I'm happy to see you working like that.
That's coming along nicely.
That's the best you have ever done.
That's quite an improvement.
I knew you could do it.
You're getting better every day.
That was first-class work.
That's not half bad!
That's the best ever.
You've got your brain in gear today.
That's great.

You're doing a good job!
Right on!
You've got it made.
Keep it up!
You did a lot of work today!
That's a good boy (girl).
I'm very proud of you.
Now you've figured it out.
That's the right way to do it.
Nice going.
Congratulations!
That's the way to do it!
Keep up the good work.
That's better than ever.
You must have been practicing.
You're doing beautifully.
Good thinking!
Keep on trying!

(continued)

A SAMPLER OF COMMON APPROVAL AND PRAISE STATEMENTS (continued)

You are really learning a lot.

You do so well.

Now that's what I call a fine job.

Good job, (name of student).

You figured that out fast.

You remembered!

That kind of work makes me very happy.

Good going!

Good for you!

That's better.

I'm pleased.

You make us happy.

We think a lot of you.

Remarkably well done.

I like the way (name) explained it.

Well thought out.

You are improving.

You perform very well, (name).

I'm so proud of you.

This is the best yet.

It's a pleasure to teach when you work like that.

You outdid yourself today.

One more time and you'll have it.

Keep working on it, you're getting better.

Not bad.

That's really nice.

Now you have it!

You are learning fast!

Couldn't have done it better myself.

Nothing can stop you now!

That's clever.

Thank you.

That shows thought.

That's good work.

A good way of putting it.

That's interesting.

You're doing better.

You're doing fine.

That's very good, (name).

I like that.

That's the correct way.

It is a pleasure having you as a student.

Yes.	Good.	Nice.	OK.
Fascinating.	Commendable.	Delightful!	Brilliant!
Fine answer.	Uh-huh.	Positively!	Yeah!
All right.	Exactly.	Wonderful!	Outstanding work!
Of course!	Correct.	Excellent.	Superb!
Perfect.	Satisfactory.	How true.	Absolutely right.
Keep going.	Good responses.	Wonderful job!	Fantastic!
Terrific!	Beautiful work!	Marvelous!	Exciting!

▶ Are there comments on the list that you are not likely to use?

▶ Are there comments on the list that you might consider using? Are some of those comments already in your repertoire? If not, are there some you are likely to add?

▶ As you place the praise statements into categories of "no," "maybe," and "yes," consider your reasons for ranking or valuing them differently.

▶ For the examples that you would likely not use, what might you say instead?

▶ Reflect on what your reactions to these statements would be if they were directed at you.

▶ What would you consider to be a statement (on or off the list) of extreme, lavish praise? List the descriptors (adjectives and adverbs) used in this type of praise.

▶ What statement might reflect just a small dose of praise? List those descriptors.

▶ What influence does the relative dosage of praise have on the student receiving it? How might it affect the students who are witnessing the praise?

▶ How do you know what dosage or what kind of praise to use?

What could be wrong with the use of verbal approval that has so many potential benefits? Some would argue that *nothing* is wrong with praise. Others would argue that, though the intent of praise is noble and the immediate effect may be desirable, careless or inappropriate use of praise can have destructive rather than constructive effects in our classrooms. Praise has the potential to produce effects opposite from the ones we intend.

Not all compliments are equal, and not all positive feedback statements can be considered praise.

> When we tell students that they have done well in class, we may be intending to show interest in them as people, to encourage them in their music participation, to evaluate their work, and to support and reinforce certain behaviors exhibited in class or point them toward other behaviors by giving descriptive feedback. The problems begin when we realize that the statement, "You did well," does not accomplish all of these purposes equally well. (Bartholomew 1993, 40)

The Perils of Praise

Many teachers and administrators are surprised to learn that praise can have a negative effect on students' learning and on classroom environments—even when teachers have the best of intentions. Habitual praise, by its very use, is ineffective. Expressions such as "very good," "great," or "good" become meaningless if they automatically rather than thoughtfully follow students' responses. In an attempt to appear enthusiastic and positive, some teachers develop a habit of puffery; they gush in their praise of students, thus devaluing both language and honest relationships (Harmin 1994, 63). Praise can have other, more serious drawbacks, however. Feelings of superiority, inferiority, embarrassment, or resentment may result from overuse or inappropriate use of praise (Bennett 1989).

PRINCIPLE 6

How can praise produce feelings of superiority? Reread the first scenario in this section. Is Sean showing disrespect toward his teacher by praising her for doing a better job of teaching? Some of us might feel indignant that a student or another adult would praise us—that he or she presumes to be in any position to judge our competence. Would the reverse be true—would students feel offended by our implied superiority when we judge their work? Praise can cause competition among students for teacher approval. Young students, in particular, seem never to be satisfied with the amount of praise they get: "But teacher, what about *me*?" Students who win praise may feel superior because of that praise: "Josh, you were the best student today!" Nonspecific praise may intentionally or unintentionally focus on the personal qualities of the student rather than on the skills or behaviors he or she exhibits: "Good girl, Lisa!" "What a smart guy you are, Tommy!" As Charles (1985, 55) points out, "Knowledge does not make one good. The lack of it does not make one bad." What message is given to students when our words imply that achievement equals goodness?

PRINCIPLE 1

Ironically, feelings of inferiority also result from some uses of praise. Just as there are different types of praise, there are different gradations of praise—OK, not bad, good, great, wonderful, spectacular! Students can become savvy about the degree of praise used on them even though a teacher may not be giving it any thought. When a teacher lavishes high praise on some students, those who receive fairly neutral praise may feel rejected. "Sarah, that was excellent. Good job, Janet. You're trying, Anita! OK, Brian. Wonderful work, David!" What message might you get if you are Anita or Brian? In this sequence, the teacher became trapped in the pattern of praising but felt some obligation to be honest and to respond to many students. When praise causes feelings of inferiority, resentment toward the teacher and the student being praised can form to interrupt cooperative efforts in the classroom. In *T.E.T.: Teacher Effectiveness Training*, Gordon (1974, 53–54) notes that praise bestowed on one student (or a few) often will be felt as negative evaluation of the rest. Gordon also notes that when a student is unhappy or dissatisfied with himself, praise from a teacher can actually aggravate that condition. Praise may communicate that the teacher does not understand a student's feelings, and it can provoke a student to defend his or her low self-esteem by exhibiting negative, albeit affirming, behaviors.

Occasionally, giving or receiving praise results in embarrassment. Have you noticed that many adults tend to cancel a compliment by contradicting it: "Oh, it's really nothing. I was just lucky that time"? If adults are uncomfortable receiving a compliment (whether they feel worthy of it or not), might not children have similar feelings of embarrassment? From where does this rejection of attention come? When praise is too exuberant ("Wow! You *did* do it!"), it may imply that the teacher is quite surprised that the students exceeded his or her expectations of them. The message that the teacher believes they can perform only at a lower level may embarrass those students. The behavior of older students' may actually deteriorate when we praise them because they would rather not have that kind of teacher approval in front of their peers.

Not wanting to appear to be a "teacher's pet" may cause some students to disobey or misbehave to counteract the risk of being embarrassed by praise in front of their classmates.

Manipulation is getting others to do what we want them to do by unfair means; it assumes that our interests supersede theirs. Praise that focuses on teacher approval ("I like the way. . ." or "I like it when you. . .") or that is based on denigrating assumptions ("I know you are too smart for *that*!") manipulates students. Using praise to control behavior, Harmin (1994) claims, sends the message that "it's okay to manipulate people." Manipulative praise, as Gordon (1974) observes, is intended primarily to meet the needs of the teacher, not to support a student's sense of well-being or achievement. Farson (1968, 109) suggests that praise is psychological candy that gets students to comply with behavior expectations and raises the possibility that praise may serve the person giving it more than the one receiving it.

PRINCIPLE 2

One of the harmful effects of praise cited by Curwin and Mendler (1988, 84–85) is the message that "you can have my approval only by doing what I decide is right for you." They also warn that to praise, we must make and consequently impose judgments that reflect our value systems and beliefs about right and wrong. Inherently, "praise is in the form of *judgments*, not *facts*." The authors propose that "the other side of the coin [from the image of a teacher as punitive, critical, and negative] is that praise, like punishment, is still controlling and potentially dangerous. It is like a coin, one side (praise) is heads, the other (punishment) is tails. Regardless of which side is up, it is still the same coin."

Addiction is one of the most destructive side effects of praise—the need and hunger for approval rather than reliance upon self-determination and self-acceptance. When we become addicted to praise, we devalue our own judgments and self-satisfaction in the pursuit of sometimes superficial acknowledgment by others. "[Praise and rewards] provide immediate, easy, and superficial self-satisfaction while smothering our self-motivation and initiative. Like candy, they give us an instant lift, then quickly push our energy level even lower than before while dulling our taste for more nutritious fare" (Harmin 1994, 62). Receiving someone's acknowledgment can help us feel accepted, noticed, and worthy. To what extent, however, do we want our worth and sense of self to be dependent on someone else's recognition of us?

▶ How dependent are you on receiving praise for your work or your efforts?

▶ What happens to you when you do not receive the approval to which you are accustomed or the approval you seek?

CHARACTERISTICS OF PEOPLE WHO DO NOT NEED PRAISE

1. They stop asking, "What does he want?" and ask instead, "What do I want?"

2. They begin to consider a wider array of choices, some of them different from the choices of those who are sources of praise.

3. They stop manipulating others for praise and no longer play praise-getting games such as downgrading themselves, bragging in a way that encourages agreement, and living by the values of others.

4. They begin to discover their own unique, creative, and individual abilities, behaviors, and attitudes. They still try to please others, but their reasons change. They do it to feel good about themselves and for more altruistic reasons, rather than to have others tell them how good they were to do it.

5. They like themselves better. In the long run, their self-concept is improved. They are better able to appreciate themselves without dependence on the approval from others.

(Curwin and Mendler 1988, 85)

PRINCIPLE 3

▶ Are there any parallels between praise and criticism? Reflect on the possibility that praise and approval can be impediments to learning in much the same ways as criticism can.

When we consider the long-term effects that reliance upon praise can have for us as adults, we can more clearly focus on the prospects for our children. Minimizing the use of praise yet maximizing the use of encouragement in our classrooms can help students become less dependent on the approval of others for their sense of self-worth.

One would think that the purpose of praise is to help build students' confidence so that they can achieve. Does it work? Recent research suggests that praise does not work to enhance achievement and, in fact, may inhibit learning. Studies by Butler (1987) and Baumeister, Hutton, and Cairns (1990) raised serious doubts about any uniformly positive effects that praising students may have on their learning. Brophy (1981) concluded that "praise does not correlate with student achievement gains." Based on findings from a broad range of research, Kohn (1993, 98–99) offered four perspectives from which to consider the problems inherent in praising students.

1. When someone is praised for succeeding at tasks that aren't terribly difficult, he may take this to mean he isn't very smart: that must be why someone has to praise him.

2. Telling someone how good she is can increase the pressure she feels to live up to the compliment.

3. Perhaps praise sets up unrealistic expectations of continued success, which lead people to avoid difficult tasks in order not to risk the possibility of failure. . . . Praise encourages some children to become dependent on the evaluations offered by their teachers.

4. Praise often undermines the intrinsic motivation that leads people to do their best.

We may not notice the corner we paint ourselves into when we use more and more praise to try to shape students' behaviors, to get their attention, to motivate them, and to inspire them to greater achivement. Although our intentions may be honorable, the results are not always constructive. What kinds of responses can we give that avoid the perils of praise?

Beyond Praise

Numerous studies, articles, and books have explored the contrasting, perilous effects of praise on some students, but many teachers seem not to have heard or implemented the pleas to soften the use of praise. Why? Perhaps it is because we do not know when we are praising students, or perhaps it is because we do not know what to do instead of praising.

An article in the *Dallas Times Herald* (November 3, 1991) cautioned that we can laud kids too much. Clinical psychologist Robert Brooks offered suggestions to parents that have important applications for classrooms.

1. Don't praise indiscriminately. Children need and deserve realistic feedback about their accomplishments to understand their strengths and weaknesses better. If adults gush over everything, they will never recognize what areas really do need improvement.
2. Focus on the child's special talent. Every child has some small island of competence, one that can serve as a source of pride and accomplishment.
3. Take a helicopter view of the child's progress. Too often, parents reward the results and forget it's more helpful to reward the effort.
4. Never compare a child with siblings or friends. When you exclaim "You're the smartest little girl!" your child may think "What if I goof up the next time? Will I still be the smartest?" Also, children should be encouraged to participate and do well because they enjoy something, not because they want to beat out someone else.
5. Teach children that making mistakes is a natural part of the learning process. While adults will never take away all the disappointment the child will face, they can make sure he doesn't feel defeated by it.
6. Be careful not to give backhanded praise. "I can't believe you finally cleared your dishes" is not helpful. Try instead: "Thanks for putting your dishes away. Now we can read."

In exploring the problems of praise, Kohn (1993, 96–116) says that self-determination is key to the distinction between various forms of positive feedback. Kohn favors straightforward information or "encouragement that leaves the recipient feeling a sense of self-determination" rather than "verbal rewards that feel controlling, make one dependent on someone else's approval, and in general prove to be no less destructive than other extrinsic motivators."

PRINCIPLE 6

All the sources cited encourage teachers to use constructive information rather than praise to promote learning. Without constructive information, students may not know what they did well. And when specific information is lacking in praise, or when praise focuses on the teacher's approval, some students assume that the message is that we like them if we praise them or do not like them if we criticize or do not praise. Liking and being liked by students can make teaching pleasant, but classroom interactions that depend on liking rather than learning are on shaky ground.

Ways of changing the words and messages of praise into remarks that give information, encouragement, or statements of appreciation are offered in the following models.

CHANGING PRAISE TO INFORMATIVE FEEDBACK

Perilous Praise	Problems	Constructive Information
"I like the way Tina is sitting." "I like what I hear from the front row."	Focuses on the teacher's approval to manipulate students' behaviors.	"Tina is sitting tall, ready to sing." "The front row is singing with breath energy today!"
"What a smart boy you are!" "You are such a good girl!"	Focuses on students' knowledge, ability, or character.	"You sure were thinking when you gave that idea!" "Your behavior helped us study today."
"Very good!" "Much better!" "What a good idea!"	Unfocused, automatic responses carry little meaning or information.	"Your voices sounded so clear and light that time!" "We could hear every sound of every ord when you tapped the rhythm. Good job!"

(Bennett 1988a, 24)

Curwin and Mendler (1988) and Harmin (1994) suggest using "I" statements and "I appreciate" messages for praising students. Harmin (63–75) offers nine strategies for responding constructively to students. Notice the difference between the "I" statements suggested here and those mentioned previously that tend to manipulate students.

STRATEGIES FOR RESPONDING TO STUDENTS

"I appreciate" messages	"Thank you." "I appreciate that." "Thanks for giving that a try." "That brings a smile to my face."
"I'm with you" message	"I might make that same mistake." "Lots of us feel that way." "I can see how you would do that." "I'd be proud to be in your shoes."
Attention without praise	Physical touch. Eye contact. Stimulating questions. Time for the student.
Plain corrects	"Yes, that's right." "Yes, that's just what I wanted." "Correct."
Plain incorrects	"No, that's not what I was wanting. The correct answer is Jefferson." "That's an answer for the kidney. Bile is the answer for the stomach."
Silent response	Make a mental note. Keep your observation of errors a secret until later.

(continued)

STRATEGIES FOR RESPONDING TO STUDENTS (continued)

Praise and rewards for all	"This group is making great progress. It's a pleasure for me to work with you." "Let's give ourselves a hand for the way we handled today's lesson."
Honest delight	"Good risk taking, Stu." "I was delighted to see how you stuck with your friend, Terry."
DESCA inspirations	Messages that inspire Dignity, Energy, Self-Management, Community, Awareness.

Nelson (1987, 103–104) proposes emphasizing encouragement rather than praise. As in the Harmin model, Nelson suggests "I" statements but makes the distinction between self-disclosing "I" messages that identify a feeling or an observation and judgmental "I" messages that indicate the teacher's approval.

ENCOURAGEMENT AND PRAISE

Self-evaluation	Encouragement	"Tell me about it." "What do you think?"
Evaluation by others	Praise	"I like it."
Addresses deed appreciation: respectful	Encouragement	"Thank you for helping." "Good job." "Who can show me the proper way to sit?"
Addresses doer expectation: patronizing	Praise	"You are such a good boy." "Good girl." "I like the way Suzy is sitting."
Empathy	Encouragement	"What do you think and feel?" "I can see you enjoyed that."
Conformity	Praise	"You did it right." "I'm so proud of you."
Self-disclosing "I" messages	Encouragement	"I appreciate your help."
Judgmental "I" messages	Praise	"I like the way you are sitting."

PRINCIPLE 6

Seeing the purposes of praising guides us in knowing what to say to students and why we are saying it. Offering purposeful, constructive information and recognizing what we hope to accomplish by giving our students such feedback can help us avoid the pitfalls of and the roadblocks to classroom praising. Substituting or supplementing praise statements with feedback that gives students information about their responses can contribute to their self-determination in learning. Developing the habit of offering observations rather than compliments or criticisms may be worthwhile in our personal lives as well as our professional lives.

In place of flattery, we can provide information. In place of insincerity, we can give encouragement. In place of manipulation, we can nurture the seeds of independence and initiative.

We can show interest in students without an evaluation or judgment. We can describe behavior and performance with a neutral tone. We can encourage without causing self-consciousness and without statements whose veracity may be in question. We can evaluate without causing undue embarrassment or disappointment, and evaluate in such a way that students become more aware of our expectations and their own achievement. We can avoid overuse and misuse of praise by expanding our repertory of verbal responses. The point is not just to have more ways to say "well done," but to have more ways to address specific issues and accomplish different purposes. (Bartholomew 1993, 43)

Rethinking Competition

Some Pros and Cons of Competition in the Classroom

It is critically important that teachers make informed choices so that they do not unintentionally give up what is, in the long term, more important and desirable than what they get in the short term.

Nearly every teacher can recount an incident in which the power of a competitive activity converted dullness to energy, intensity, and engagement in the classroom. To pique interest in a task, all we need to do is add "who will get the treat?" "boys against girls," or "five points to the row that does it most quickly." These incentives turn many students from passive observers into eager participants. But what are we really getting when we add competition to a task, and what are we giving up? Are we getting attention but giving up focused learning? Are we getting eager participation but giving up substantive studying? Are we getting students to like our classes but giving up accomplishment of curricular goals?

The following scenarios, based on the song activity *Three Blind Mice* (see Chapter 9), illustrate how the teacher's treatment of a competitive situation can affect the way students view and react to that situation.

SCENARIO | *THREE BLIND MICE* 1

"Now that you know how to play the game, Ms. Conrad said, "let's be sure to enjoy the spirit of the chase. A lot of strategy and tricky movements can be involved in grabbing the mouse tails and in not losing your own. Let's enjoy the sport as we watch all the various ways people take their turns." Ms. Conrad gave verbal and nonverbal acknowledgments of delight and support for the good tries both to students who grabbed tails and to those who lost them.

SCENARIO | *THREE BLIND MICE* 2

"Now that you know how to play the game, Ms. Conrad said, "let's see who will get the most mouse tails during his or her turn. Whoever wins the most tails in one turn will get a little prize at the end of class. If you misbehave, you can't win the prize, and if you cheat, you lose your tail as well as the chance to win the game."

▶ Compare the way play is treated in Scenarios 1 and 2. How might this affect your feelings about playing the activity if you were one of the students?

▶ Would the reward offered in Scenario 2 help motivate you to push for your best, or would it cause you to lose incentive because you had little chance of winning?

▶ Might the we're-all-in-this-together attitude in Scenario 1 cause you to relax and have fun watching or not care about playing because even the students who were not good at it were getting encouragement and acknowledgment for their turn?

▶ As you reflect on the differences between 1 and 2, consider to what extent other dimensions of the class might change: cooperation among students? possibility of physical injury? need for a "judge" for the activity? satisfaction of a good chase?

Groups of future teachers, when asked to identify some pros and cons of competition based on their own experiences, are often eager and well equipped to do so. What surprises them, however, is the correlation between each pro and each con. Can you add some observations of your own?

PROS AND CONS OF COMPETITION

Pros	Cons
• Fosters motivation	• Fosters frustration
• Increases sense of achievement	• Increases sense of failure
• Offers reward for hard work	• Neglects hard work
• Sets standards of excellence	• Sets standards of excellence that may be narrow or unrealistic
• Builds self-confidence	• Erodes self-confidence
• Creates sense of pride	• Creates senses of superiority and inferiority
• Establishes "expert" opinion	• Establishes "experts" rather than valuing self-assessment

---

▶ As you read these lists, did you presume that the pros list described the effects competition has on winners and the cons list described the effects on losers?

▶ Read the list of cons again. In what ways could this list describe the effects of competition on the winners?

The nature of competition establishes two categories of competitors: winners and losers. Of necessity, for competition to exist, there must be many more losers than winners, and often only one person or one group can be the winner. Parallels between the paradoxes of competition, praise, and rewards are obvious. What began with the intent to improve conditions for someone or some group can function in quite the opposite way.

It is ironic that praise, rewards, and competition are often used in homes and schools as tools for improving students' self-esteem. The irony is that although the tool may be momentarily effective, the quick fix can lead to a lifetime of dependency on and addiction to extrinsic affirmations for self-esteem.

In his 1992 book *No Contest: The Case Against Competition (Why We Lose in Our Race to Win)*, Kohn distinguishes between structural competition and intentional competition. In *structural competition,* the framework of winning and losing is external and the object is "mutually exclusive goal attainment (MEGA)." In other words, the success of one requires the failure of another. The range of structurally competitive situations in the classroom can include the formalized "Who will get the award for best _____?" and challenges like "Who will be the fastest to get the right answer?" (pp. 4–5).

In *intentional competition,* a person constantly compares himself or herself with others even though there may be no extrinsic motivation to do so. "I am a very competitive person" is a statement that we may make to others or to ourselves to justify our drive to excel. Many highly competitive people are oriented toward outdoing nearly everyone they encounter. Inherent in intentional competition is dependency: We become dependent on others with whom to compete. We also become vulnerable, weighing our self-esteem by constant comparison with others, juggling to balance the superiority-inferiority conclusions we draw. With little difficulty, we can see that the ways in which schools and classrooms treat structural competition may result in an orientation that stays with us for life—a habit of intentional competition.

▶ What situations can you list in which you have observed or participated in structural competitions in a classroom setting?

Competition can give messages of unworthiness, dependency, intolerance, and devaluation.

► In general, do you have pleasant or unpleasant feelings about competition among students?

► What changes in the process of competition or its effects would convert whatever unpleasant feelings you may have into pleasant ones?

► To what extent do you believe it is possible to mitigate the damaging effects of competition among students?

If competition depends on besting someone, then what is the constructive use of the standards and models by which we aspire to excellence? "Inspiration" and "motivation" are terms that may more accurately describe our internal desire for improvement. Kohn offers this observation:

> We sometimes assume that working toward a goal and setting standards for oneself can take place only if we compete against others. This is simply false. . . . A comparison of performance with one's own previous record or with objective standards is in no way an instance of competition and it should not be confused with it. (1992, 6)

► What value might there be in helping your students substitute words such as "inspiration" and "motivation" for their internal sense of competition?

► What value might there be in helping students reframe their view of the duality that competition engenders and instead see skills, achievements, and qualities of themselves and others on a continuum of development?

► If you were to lead your students to these changes, what modifications would you need to make in your classroom activities?

Beyond Competition: Cooperative Efforts

Dissolving competition into cooperation may seem threatening to some and impossible to others. "What about maintaining the competitive edge?" you might ask. "Our entire society and economy is based on competition, so this is just preparing them for life," you might add. Should competition be banned from classrooms? Probably not. Rather, informing and preparing students with skills to help them place the power of competition in a healthy perspective seems a worthy goal.

A model in which competition is minimized and cooperation is maximized is compatible with the principles and practices identified in *SongWorks 1*. Maximizing cooperation over competition makes it easier for all students to feel respected and for all students to feel comfortable in expressing their ideas and demonstrating their skills. Central to this model is the we're-all-in-this-together attitude that encourages cooperation (operating together) among students as well as between student and teacher. With this approach, each person in a classroom is seen as a learner and a teacher on a continuum of development, and activities and strategies are chosen with long-term as well as short-term effects in mind. Students learn to help others, to listen to others' points of view, to share information and ideas, and to feel a responsibility (ability to respond) to and for those around them.

> There can be little doubt that the low and medium ability students especially benefit from working collaboratively with peers from the full range of ability differences. There is also evidence that high ability students are better off academically when they collaborate with medium and low ability peers than when they work alone; at the worst . . . [they] are not hurt. (Simpson 1949, 222)

PRINCIPLE 1

PRINCIPLE 2

PRINCIPLE 3

PRINCIPLE 1

PRINCIPLE 6

WAYS TO SHIFT COMPETITION TO COOPERATION

Show students words and behaviors that are supportive of others.

"That gives me another way to understand your work, Annette."

"I'm interested in hearing about your observations, not your evaluations, of class-mates' ideas."

Encourage students to consult with one another for short answers as well as group projects.

"Check with your neighbor about his or her idea before you tell me what you think."

"Consult with a classmate if you need help or if you want to see how your ideas compare."

Minimize external rewards for activities and tasks.

"I hope you are feeling the satisfaction of a job well done."

"Our treat for meeting all those challenges is the feeling within us. Can you feel it?"

Give feedback, rather than praise, to students about their helpful and supportive behaviors.

"When you demonstrate patience and curiosity like that, George, it gives us time to think."

"I think we all can benefit from listening as you sort out your thinking, Alisha."

Avoid asking "Who is the best?" in subtle or obvious ways.

"In this lesson you need to consider yourselves as thinkers, not winners."

"I'm looking for a variety of responses, so take some time to think about your ideas."

Rethinking Misbehaviors

Across America, teachers are desperate for help with discipline in their classrooms. Some come to workshops so overwhelmed by the behavior problems in their class-rooms that they cannot concentrate on anything else. More than any other factor, be-havior problems in classrooms cause teachers to become dispirited, disoriented, and disillusioned with teaching. If you need help in handling severe discipline problems with defiant students, you will likely not find the answers you need here. Addressing the issues and options surrounding a variety of discipline plans is beyond the scope of this book. This section will, however, discuss some perspectives in structuring and re-acting to classroom behaviors that may be helpful to you even when you face severe discipline problems.

Many university teacher preparation programs are criticized for inadequately preparing teachers for their roles as behavior managers. Although those accusations may signal the urgent need for such training, difficulties in teaching behavior man-agement abound. Consider the ranges of ages, populations, and contextual factors that enter into appropriate management of behaviors. Responding to students' be-haviors is a skill, and skills are difficult to master from passive reading, listening, or watching, or when they are practiced out of context. Hands-on experience with stu-dents, therefore, is necessary for a teacher's or a future teacher's ability to understand and apply aspects of behavior management.

Reflect for a moment on the students with whom you have worked.

▶ On a scale of 1 to 5 (5 is the highest intensity rating), rate the severity and frequency of behavior problems you typically encounter in a day.

▶ Using the same scale, rate the intensity of your emotional response to those behavior problems.

With few exceptions, when asked to rate their emotional responses to behaviors, teachers rate their responses two to three points higher in intensity than they rate the behaviors themselves. Why do we have such intense emotional reactions? Teachers offer varying explanations:

▪ "When my students misbehave, I'm to blame. I should know what to do to fix it."

▪ "When I cannot make my students behave and cooperate, I feel like a failure."

▪ "I must not be smart enough to teach, when I can't even get my class under control."

▪ "The principal and other teachers must see me as incompetent when they see how my students behave."

▪ "If I could just find the right activity or the right discipline plan, my troubles would be over."

Jones proposed that we need to worry much more about the effects of the small behavior problems in our classrooms than about the major, more memorable ones.

> The most persistent misconception about discipline is that the most important problems in discipline management are the biggest problems, the crises. Certainly they are the most memorable. When teachers look back over the year, they will certainly remember the time the fight broke out or the time a student told them to do an unnatural act. . . . Ironically, . . . the most important discipline problem in the classroom is the small disruption, not the crisis. It is the small disruption by its very frequency that destroys the teacher's patience by degrees and destroys learning by the minute. (1987a, 27–28)

Would you agree or disagree that the problems most costly to your emotional health are the small disruptions that, by their frequency and subtlety, wear out your patience and tolerance? "Goofing off," talking, not paying attention, speaking out of turn, not cooperating, and, in general, displaying a bad attitude may not be near the top of a severe behavior problem scale. But these behaviors may chisel away at our stamina enough that our reactions to them *are* severe. By looking at and rethinking typical classroom behaviors and the options we may have for interpreting and responding to them, this section intends to offer support and guidance for teachers who are dealing with classroom behavior problems.

What Is Misbehavior?

When does behavior cross the line into misbehavior? Who decides when behavior becomes misbehavior? Because classroom and school rules are based upon an accepted standard of behavior, we could assume that all teachers know and can recognize the difference between behavior and misbehavior. Many teachers could tell you, however, that it is fairly easy to be too lenient or too strict where behavior is concerned. Of course, what is too strict or lenient from one teacher's point of view may not correlate with a student's (or a parent's or another teacher's) point of view.

Most of what goes on in schools and classrooms is simply behavior. Behaviors are our actions, and misbehavior involves someone's judgment as to the degree of inappropriateness or "wrongness" of those actions. Teachers, therefore, are constantly in the position of defining and reacting to what they consider misbehavior. It is difficult to form a uniformly acceptable definition of misbehavior because many misbehaviors are normal behaviors outside the classroom or school setting. In addition, ethnic, regional, and cultural groups can differ as to what constitutes acceptable behaviors regarding such customs as eye contact, speaking voluntarily, movement that resembles dancing, and participation in certain holiday activities. If a student's cultural behaviors do not match those of the teacher, should they be treated as misbehaviors?

▶ What behaviors may be considered misbehavior in the classroom but be normal or even encouraged outside the classroom?

▶ Can you think of a behavior that is wrong in all incidents and settings? Are you sure there are no exceptions to its appropriateness?

Just like adults, young people grow in and out of phases of self-discipline. Personal worries, academic achievements and disappointments, physical conditions, and chemical imbalances are just some of the factors that can affect the quality of adult behavior. Those same factors may have an even stronger effect on young children's behaviors. Young children who are "misbehaving" do not necessarily know that they are misbehaving or what to do about it if they do know. Telling them what to do or threatening them does not necessarily remedy the short-term or the long-term problem.

PRINCIPLE 1

SCENARIO   INTERPRETING BEHAVIORS 1

The second-grade students were in a circle, ready to sing and play *Looby Loo*. As they held hands, sang, and skipped around the circle, Ginny began to scream, "Teacher, teacher, he's hurting my hand!" Ginny was in pain. Joshua looked up surprised and then angry, "I am not!" Knowing that such an action would not be completely uncharacteristic of Joshua, the teacher sent him to "time out" until he could be kinder to others.

SCENARIO   INTERPRETING BEHAVIORS 2

The children took their places, ready to practice their program music. As the class began to sing *On Top of Old Smoky*, Jennifer's voice came blaring across the room. Her loud, boisterous shouting offended the students and the teacher. Frustrated with this behavior the afternoon of the program, the teacher scolded Jennifer and told her, "If you can't sing the way you are supposed to, maybe you'd better not plan to sing with us this evening!"

▶ In the preceding scenarios, both Joshua and Jennifer were accused of misbehaving. Were they?

▶ How would you describe what constituted each one's misbehavior?

▶ Would you respond to Joshua and Jennifer in the same way their teachers did? If not, what might you do differently?

Our responses to students' behaviors can be seen as having three parts: describe, interpret, and respond. In *describing* the behavior, we identify what the student did and confine our description to the facts, not the presumed motive. Our *interpretation* of the behavior includes considerations of motive, intention, and past experience. Was the behavior a major or a minor infraction? Was this a new behavior from the student or has the student been a repeat offender? Was there maliciousness or defiance in the behavior or was it an innocent mistake? Our *response* to the behavior depends, in large part, on our interpretation. Our internal and external reactions to behaviors are closely tied to the accuracy of our descriptions and our interpretations of students' intent.

Joshua squeezed a classmate's hand, and Jennifer sang off pitch and louder than the other students. Those are *descriptions* of the behaviors in Scenarios 1 and 2. When asked earlier to describe their behaviors, did you offer an interpretation, a presumed motive, rather than a description? It is not uncommon for us to observe behaviors of students, to assume we know why they were acting that way, and to confuse description with interpretation. Distinguishing between what a student did (description) and why we think a student did it (interpretation) is key to understanding the notion of misbehavior described here.

Now for *interpretation*. What reasons might Joshua have had for his behavior?

- Was he trying to hurt Ginny?
- Was he trying to get attention from the teacher and his classmates?
- Was he holding tight but not aware that he was hurting Ginny's hand?
- Was he holding tight to keep his balance as he skipped?
- Was he holding tight because he was excited about playing his favorite game?

Why was Jennifer singing so loudly?

- Was she showing off?
- Was she trying to get attention?
- Was she letting everyone know that this is her favorite song?
- Was she letting the teacher know that she had practiced and knew all the words?
- Was she singing the way she is encouraged to sing at church?

▶ Would your responses to Joshua and Jennifer differ according to which interpretation you accept for their motives?

▶ Do we know which of these reasons is accurate for either student?

▶ Do we ever know why another person is doing what he or she is doing?

▶ Are there times when others do not know why we are doing what we are doing?

▶ Do you think asking "Why did you do that?" could help you in choosing how to respond? Are there times when we do not know the reasons for our behaviors?

Depending on how we interpret behavior, our responses differ. Our internal and external reactions are calmer, more neutral, and less anxious when we do not presume a person is intentionally being a troublemaker. Consider these modifications to the teacher's response to Joshua in Scenario 1. What is the teacher doing differently in these options? What messages are given to Joshua and Ginny in each option?

PRINCIPLE 1

PRINCIPLE 2

PRINCIPLE 3

PRINCIPLE 6

- "Joshua, did you know you were hurting Ginny's hand?" ["No, I *wasn't* hurting Ginny's hand!"] "Joshua, I'm not saying you did it intentionally, but Ginny's hand was hurt. How could you hold on this time to make sure you gently grasp her hand? Show me. Let's try that again, because some of us do hold on tighter when we are skipping. Ginny, next time it may help Joshua or anyone else if you would kindly tell them they are holding on too tightly and show them how to hold more gently."

- "Ginny, I feel sorry that your hand was hurt. I'm not presuming it was on purpose, are you? Ginny and Joshua, it would be helpful to us all if you would take a moment apart from the group to decide what the problem was and how to fix it. Step a few feet away so you'll have some privacy to talk, and when you figure this out, come back to join our activity. We may ask you to share your conclusions with us, if you're willing."

Think about these options for responding to Jennifer in Scenario 2, and ask yourself the same questions: What is the teacher doing differently in these options? What messages are given to Jennifer and her classmates in each option?

PRINCIPLE 1

PRINCIPLE 3

PRINCIPLE 6

- "Wow, we had some spirited singing! This time, let's see if we can sing and listen for the voices of students seated next to us. Can you meet that challenge?" [Jennifer continues to sing too loudly.]

- "Jennifer, this must be a favorite song of yours; it is easy for me to hear your voice. Sing with me, Frank, Justin, Darla, and Nancy, this time, and let's see, Jennifer, if you can blend your voice with ours."

- "Jennifer, when you sing with that much energy, it affects your ability to sing on pitch. Be sure to listen to your voice and your classmates' voices as you sing this time."

Seeing a behavior as simply behavior rather than misbehavior does not mean that we ignore the behavior. What it does mean is that our response to the behavior, inside ourselves and to the student, is different because we are not presuming guilt or maliciousness on the part of the student.

Charles (1985) presents a perspective on behaviors that has powerful potential for changing the ways in which we see and respond to students' behaviors in our classrooms. What if we take the position that *misbehavior occurs only when a student willingly and knowingly obstructs the activity, the learning, or the lesson* (p. 4)? If a student does not know he or she is misbehaving, then should whatever he or she is doing be considered misbehavior? If a student unintentionally breaks a rule, is that misbehavior? Remembering that all misbehaviors are also behaviors helps us stay open to options for feedback similar to those described for Joshua and Ginny.

At any age or stage, some children have not yet developed the capacity to see alternatives to defiance or "acting out." Therefore, our goals for discipline management should include helping a student know what to do instead of the behavior that is causing problems. Ideally, a process for self-discipline offers students three phases of self-determination.

1. *Awareness* of his or her behavior and its effect on himself or herself and others

2. *Respect* for himself or herself and others

3. *Ability* to monitor and control his or her behavior

The process of self discipline is a process of growth, and it rarely happens instantaneously. Plan to see students' education about their own behavior as a process

Students deserve to be informed, educated, and reminded about the behavior that is expected of them.

necessary to their development. See the "Index of Classroom Situations" in Chapter 9 for examples of how to guide and shape students' behaviors.

Teachers as Managers

A manager is someone whose challenge is to bring out the best in those for whom he or she is responsible. Teachers' managers are often their principals.

▶ List the qualities in your principal or supervisor that help you be your best.

▶ Are there any qualities that work against your ability to be your best?

PRINCIPLE 1

Now that you have considered what you need to help you, consider that you are your students' manager. Interestingly, the same qualities that teachers want from their principals are the ones that students say they want from their teachers. According to Charles (1985, 6), good classroom managing "facilitates learning, fosters socialization, permits democracy, fills a psychological need, and promotes a sense of joy in learning."

Some may resist use of the term "manager" to describe the teacher's role in classrooms. For them, managing implies "bossing" or having power or control over others. Though we use the term "management," Patterson's concept of "leadership" may provide a less controversial term to explain our position. In his 1993 book *Leadership for Tomorrow's Schools*, Patterson defines leadership as "the process of influencing others to achieve mutually agreed upon purposes for the organization" (p. 3).

PRINCIPLE 5

Being a teacher-manager means being organized, knowledgeable, consistent, fair, respectful, decisive, and democratic so that students can function at their best in the classroom. Because students vary from class to class, grade to grade, and school to school, the teacher's strategies for bringing out the best in his or her students must also vary. Classroom management is not something that is achieved and stays achieved. It must be reconstructed, reevaluated, and redefined, sometimes more frequently than we would like. The group context for schooling creates a dynamic that can be challenging for any teacher—the beginner or the veteran. Recognizing that it is in the nature of growing young people to resist authority and to test limits may not help you choose an appropriate response, but it may put the ups and downs of behavior management in perspective.

▶ Do you recall a time in school (or out) when you were more rude or challenging than you would have been had you not been in a group?

▶ Have you ever misbehaved in school in a way that was more a declaration of independence than a reflection of how you really felt?

▶ If you put yourself in the place of your teacher, how would you have handled your misbehavior?

PRINCIPLE 6

There are occasions when the best behavior management is swift and commanding, letting a student know that the limit has been reached, the behavior must stop, and you will not allow the behavior to have power over the lesson, the activity, or you. A matter-of-fact manner from you rather than an emotional one may help immensely at such times. At other times, your responses will be less intense and may be more gentle.

When behavior problems begin to surface during lessons, look first at your own behaviors for clues to the solution and then at the behaviors of your students.

▪ Consider the *energy* level you are demonstrating.

▪ Consider the *clarity* of behavior expectations for the activity.

▪ Consider the level of *fascination* that the activity holds for the students.

▪ Consider the potential for *success* that students see in the activity.

Be certain that you are teaching students to avoid certain behaviors, not to avoid you. . . . Children need to know that they are valued for themselves, not merely for the degree to which they meet our expectations or follow our rules. . . . Create an environment where failure is not fatal. (McGinnis 1985, 119, 113, 71)

A Moment of Grace

A moment of grace is the interval of time we take to reframe someone's behavior so that we can react with curiosity, compassion, or openness rather than judgment, annoyance, or defensiveness. Giving someone the "benefit of the doubt" allows us to delay our reaction to the comment or action with the intent of looking beyond our immediate response. This form of second-guessing can serve several constructive purposes: It can help us avoid responding in ways that we may later regret, it can help us look further into sometimes innocent reasons for the behavior, and it can help us develop a habit of openness to varying levels and dimensions of understanding others.

PRINCIPLE 1

PRINCIPLE 2

▶ What are some consequences of misjudging a situation and reacting as if the person is doing something intentionally to hurt, offend, or annoy us?

▶ What are some consequences of misjudging a situation and reacting as if the person is not intentionally hurting, offending, or annoying us?

★ **SCENARIO**   THE ODD COMMENT

"How many of you have ever heard of Martin Luther King?" Ms. Vellutini asked her first-grade students as she began a lesson on the civil rights leader. "He's *odd*," Jeremy immediately shouted.

Feeling herself bristle at this obvious display of rudeness that sounded like a racist remark, Ms. Vellutini took a moment to consider how to respond to young Jeremy. Purposely choosing to shrug off the negative reaction long enough to investigate its meaning, Ms. Vellutini asked Jeremy with a look of surprised curiosity, "Why do you say that?"

"Well, he is odd because his birthday is on the fifteenth. And I'm odd because mine is on the nineteenth." Letting this perspective settle in a bit, Ms. Vellutini responded, "Then I'm odd, too, because mine is on the seventeenth!"

Talking with Jeremy's mother later that spring, Ms. Vellutini related the story of Jeremy's response in the classroom and how, at first, it had startled her. "Oh, he is very conscious of birthdays as odds and evens." Jeremy's mother replied. "That is how he and his sister decide who gets to ride in the front seat—they match their even and odd birthdays with the current date."

Ms. Vellutini was relieved that she delayed her immediate reaction to Jeremy's "insulting" remark so that she could find out what he was thinking. The time Ms. Vellutini took ended up being a moment of grace for both her and Jeremy.

SCENARIO

THE ROWDY BOYS

"I just can't see this working in a real classroom," Gail responded, revealing her skepticism. "Kids will think they can get away with anything. Where are the rules?" The professor had just introduced the idea of a "moment of grace" to Gail's graduate class, and teachers were encouraged to use the following week's classes to see beyond the obvious interpretation of misbehavior.

"Well, try it. You may find that taking a moment to respond with sensitivity, compassion, empathy, or even humor rather than annoyance or anger will help you feel better—both in the moment and at the end of the day. I'm just asking you to try it and report back to us next week," responded the professor.

At next week's class, Gail was the first to raise the issue of their assignment. Eager to describe her experience, she wanted to tell the class right away what she had discovered. The other teachers listened with a grin as Gail recounted her story.

"The fourth-grade class had just entered my music room. I have them come in and sit in assigned places in rows on the floor. No talking is allowed before we begin class. As I was writing something on the board, I heard all this rowdiness coming from the back of the room. When I turned to look, I saw several boys gathered together, out of their places *and* giggling and talking! 'What do they *think* they're doing? They're not getting away with this in *my class*!' I thought to myself as I marched back there to enforce the rules they had known about all year.

"As I headed back to them with a scowl on my face," she continued, "I thought to myself, 'Well, maybe I should try the moment-of-grace-assignment now.' So I changed the look on my face and asked curiously, 'What are you boys so interested in back here?' One boy looked up at me excitedly and said, 'Josh has a new pair of fluorescent shoelaces and we're trying to see if they work.' As he said this, four boys were cupping their hands around Josh's shoelaces to make a dark cave. 'Well, let me see,' I said as I dropped to my knees and peeked inside their hand cave. I think that surprised them.

"Taking two seconds to look at those shoelaces, I said, 'It's too light in here. Wait till later when you can be in a dark room and look at them then. Right now, we're ready to begin music class.' The two minutes it took me to handle their behavior that way is probably the same amount of time (or less) it would have taken me to scold them, remind them of the rules, or enforce the consequence system I use. And I was still in good emotional and mental shape to teach the lesson!"

Taking a moment to try to understand another's perspective may not always seem reasonable or appropriate. Sometimes we are swept into the encounter before we know it, and, not knowing what else to do, we try to maintain "control" of ourselves and the situation. Giving someone's motives the benefit of the doubt seems unnecessarily kind when he or she is overtly attacking or challenging us. More often than not, perhaps, difficult encounters can push us off center and cause us to participate in exchanges that are beneath our standards of conduct (Rusk 1993).

SCENARIO

VICTOR'S DEFIANCE

Victor was being especially defiant, offending other children, being argumentative with Ms. Hamilton, shoving other children when he had the chance, and looking angry and sullen. After repeated and increasingly firm suggestions about how Victor needed to change his behavior, Ms. Hamilton ran out of alternatives and patience.

"Victor, I have given you warnings and I have tried everything I know to get you to behave. You are not helping us, so you need to go into the hall and wait until we have finished with music class."

Because it was early in Ms. Hamilton's first year at this school, these second-grade students had not yet seen her take such a stand. The room got quiet as all eyes were on Victor.

"I ain't leavin'!" Victor sat down in his chair and refused to look at Ms. Hamilton. "oooOOOooo," came the response from the other children as they took some pleasure from this showdown.

Ms. Hamilton was in her third year of teaching but had not yet experienced such overt defiance. She felt she couldn't back down, although she wanted to. "Yes, Victor, you *will* leave this room right now!"

"I ain't leavin' and you can't make me!" "ooooOOOOoooo." Ms. Hamilton's stomach churned and her mouth became dry. She had never been so blatantly challenged before, and certainly not with a group of such interested bystanders.

She took Victor's arm to lead him from the room, but instead of standing to go with her, he lay on the floor. "ooooooOOOOOooooo."

Ms. Hamilton saw very few options. She was now in the position of letting go of Victor's arm and backing down or dragging Victor out of the room. She was nauseated from the stress of the situation, and she realized that nothing she was about to do was compatible with how she wanted to treat children.

She dragged Victor from the room.

Fortunately, the room had a tile floor.

▶ What you would have done in a similar situation? Would you have backed down?

▶ Would you have thought of an alternative way to respond?

▶ Have you ever been so upset by and angry with a student that you wanted to punish or shame him or her as thoroughly as possible?

▶ Was there an opportunity for a moment of grace to emerge?

SCENARIO   VICTOR'S DEFIANCE (EPILOGUE)

Ms. Hamilton was so upset by the 9:30 A.M. incident with Victor that it affected her state of mind for her other classes—she felt vulnerable and fatigued. At noon in the teacher's lounge, she could barely eat her lunch. Hesitant to bring up the incident, Ms. Hamilton did not want to reveal her vulnerability to her new colleagues. On the other hand, if she did tell someone, maybe he or she could give her some pointers or reassurance.

As lunchtime was ending, Ms. Hamilton decided to relate the morning's incident to the physical education teacher. As she told the story, all the feelings of those moments came back to her: upset stomach, faster breathing, dry mouth. She was not accustomed to confrontations like this.

Mr. Leedy listened rather passively, and when she finished, he responded. "Did you say that was Victor in Mrs. Mayo's class? Oh, yeah, he's having a rough day. Last night when his family came home from church, they found their house completely wiped out, everything stolen."

Based on what you now know about Victor, would your response to him during class have changed? Would you see his "misbehavior" in quite the same way? Giving students the benefit of the doubt about the causes of their behaviors can do two very important things in this moment of grace.

1. The benefit of the doubt can give the student an opportunity to change his or her behavior without being punished, scolded, or shamed.

2. The benefit of the doubt can give the teacher the opportunity to stay calm, inside and outside, in order to respond with clarity, matter-of-factness, and assertiveness by giving a student information about and direction for his or her behavior.

Effects of Rethinking Misbehavior

When we presume that another person's behavior has a benign rather than a malicious motive or is the result of lack of awareness rather than rudeness, our responses (inside and outside) to that behavior are different. People of all ages deserve the benefit of the doubt for their behaviors.

By seeing behaviors and misbehaviors as inevitable parts of teaching and learning, we may be less likely to blame students for not allowing us to be good teachers. Our emotional and mental state in the classroom is more one of compassionate manager than one of harried adversary.

By defining misbehavior as a *knowing* and *willful* disruptive act, we can more easily recognize behaviors that simply indicate lack of focus, lack of development, lack of confidence, lack of perceptual skills, lack of ability to control the behavior, or lack of alternative behaviors. Although these behaviors must still be attended to, the teacher's choices may more often be to support or guide gently, rather than to punish harshly.

Chapter Epilogue

Being a teacher means that you are in a pivotal position for making choices that affect the learning that occurs in your classroom. Substantial evidence exists, both anecdotally and in research, that the ways in which we approach praise, rewards, competition, and misbehavior shape classroom rapport, freedom, and openness to learning for both teachers and students. The goal of this rethinking process is the maximum long-term health, well-being, and self-determination of both students and teachers.

Folk-Song Games

9

Making Activities Context Appropriate

Few of us have not had the experience of a lesson that worked successfully in one setting and fizzled in another. What causes this to happen? Is it our fault? Is it the students' fault? Were students too young or too old? Were they not able to handle the movement, social, or musical expectations?

SCENARIO   A LESSON GONE AWRY 1

Ms. Lamb had developed the "perfect lesson plan." It contained all the ingredients her university professor had told her were needed for an enjoyable, exciting learning experience. Ms. Lamb was so intrigued with the lesson that she was anxious for class to begin so that she could watch the students' reactions. With all the preparations and planning, Ms. Lamb's expectations were high.

     The lesson, however, flopped. It caused neither the excitement nor the learning that Ms. Lamb had expected.

SCENARIO   A LESSON GONE AWRY 2

At a workshop, Mr. Garner learned an activity that completely captured the attention, musical involvement, and enthusiastic responses of the participants. The combined sound of the group's music making was wonderful, and the procedures followed were so simple. Participants scurried to write down the details as the clinician encouraged, "Your fourth graders will love this!" Mr. Garner was eager for school to begin on Monday so that he could introduce this activity to his students. "They will be so impressed with the sounds they make!" he thought as his fourth-grade class entered the room.

     The lesson, however, flopped. It caused neither the excitement nor the learning that Mr. Garner had expected.

No one is necessarily at fault when good intentions go awry. By investigating characteristics of the context (the physical, temporal, teacher, student, and community attributes that are at work in classrooms), we try to understand why some activities are successful and some are not, rather than trying to affix blame when a lesson misses the mark.

Age and Developmental Appropriateness

Lists of age-appropriate and developmentally appropriate sequences for music activities can be helpful for planning, organizing, and experiencing success with various activities. Relying on age and developmental guidelines may, however, blind us to what our students can learn when they are not limited by our preset boundaries. A tremendous degree of developmental diversity exists among Grade 3 classes, for example; and a program that includes daily instruction is hardly comparable to one that offers weekly lessons. The context, therefore, is a more accurate guide than age or development to appropriate learning activities, especially for new teachers.

PRINCIPLE 3

Rather than following prescribed lists of age-appropriate or developmentally appropriate activities, teachers can make selections based on the needs, interests, and abilities of both teacher and students. From there, observation during the lesson and reflection after the lesson inform the teacher of the appropriateness of an activity for a particular group of students. Each of us is responsible, within his or her own unique setting, to be attentive to students' needs in the selection of materials and methods for teaching. No author, no expert, and no clinician can answer these questions or make these choices for us. The teacher is key to determining the context appropriateness of classroom materials and methods for his or her students. By watching and listening to students, we will see what they need from us to learn.

When we stop watching and listening to our students, we stop teaching.

Classifying activities and expectations by the degree to which they are developmentally and age appropriate is something that many of us do automatically. There are many other factors, however, that affect the success, appeal, and effectiveness of activities and strategies.

What Affects Context?

Many factors contribute to the context in which teaching and learning take place. For example, the physical attributes of the classroom can affect teaching. The time of day our class meets is another factor. To offer our students appropriate learning opportunities, we must make informed choices that match their needs as well as ours. Considerations of context help give us accurate perspectives from which to make informed choices.

The table on page 217 gives a sampling of the factors that influence what we can teach and how we can teach at any given time, on any given day, in any given community or school. Any one of these factors can change the level of appropriateness of our curriculum, our lessons, and our expectations. You can probably think of more factors to add to the list.

As you ponder the list and relate the attributes to your own teaching and learning settings, consider these questions:

▶ Which attributes can be adjusted and which cannot?

▶ Of which attributes might your colleagues or students' parents not be aware?

▶ What would you list if you were to add a category titled "School Attributes"?

▶ How could your knowledge of these attributes affect your teaching?

CONTEXTUAL DIFFERENCES FOR TEACHING AND LEARNING

Physical Attributes

Size of class

Size of room

Temperature in room

Equipment in room

Shape of room

Seating arrangement

Who brings students to music room

Temporal Attributes

Time of day for class

Time of year

Frequency of class meeting

Length of class

Time interval between classes

What preceded class

Special events (before or after class)

Teacher Attributes

Familiarity with students

Number of classes/subjects taught per day

Length of time in same school

Length of time in teachng

Access to training

Freedom to explore/create vs. following prescribed curriculum

Student Attributes

Familiarity with classmates

Mix of gender, ethnic, language, economic, cultural backgrounds

Age

Developmental levels

Abilities: physical, mental, social

Disabilities

Background in experiences (music or other subjects)

View of and investment in their schooling

Community Attributes

Administrative support

Support of colleagues

Expectations for public performance

Parental participation

Community activities that shape or support teaching expectations

---

When *Is* an Activity Context Appropriate?

Numerous factors affect the appropriateness and success of activities we plan for our students. However, given the wide range of options for shaping and reshaping activities, there may be, ultimately, only three fundamental factors for determining appropriateness. Answering the following three questions as you plan and observe activities should guide you toward satisfying experiences. These considerations should also help you avoid selecting activities that cause your students to fail in their efforts to participate. As you watch your students, ask yourself these important questions:

1. Can the students participate in the activity without me?

2. To what degree are students engaged in the activity as they participate?

3. How does the activity provide opportunities for students' growth?

Reshaping Song Activities

Many of us are not immediately successful in teaching activities we learn at a workshop or read about in a book. To transfer activities and ideas from one setting to another, we must tailor those activities to our classrooms. We use our best judgment and our knowledge of our students to make activities context appropriate. Our ability to reshape activities so that they fit the situations in which we teach is a sign of our expertise in recognizing the attributes of our teaching context.

The following examples show how one folk-song game can be played in a variety of ways depending on contextual needs. Each of the five versions is presented as if the students are playing the game for the first time. The activity is adapted from Richards (1985, 75).

RIG-A-JIG-JIG

As I was walking down the street,
down the street,
down the street,
A friend of mine I happened to meet.
Hi-ho, hi-ho, hi-ho!

A-rig-a-jig-jig and away we go,
away we go,
away we go.
A-rig-a-jig-jig and away we go.
Hi-ho, hi-ho, hi-ho!

VERSION 1, *RIG-A-JIG-JIG*

Formation: Standing circle

As all sing the song, the game-starter walks on the inside of a standing circle, then stops at a partner and shakes hands at "a friend of mine." At "a-rig-a-jig-jig," the partners cross arms, take hands, and push-pull their arms back and forth to the rhythm. During "away we go," the partners skip around the inside of the circle, still holding hands. At the next "a-rig-a-jig-jig," partners stop skipping, push-pull arms again, and then continue skipping till the end of the song.

Each partner then begins the turn, so that the number of persons in the middle giving turns doubles with each repetition of the song. When everyone has been chosen and partners have finished skipping, the activity is over and can begin again.

Focusing Attention and Investigating Answers

"When does the song tell us to find a partner?"

"When in the song do we do this action?" [Demonstrate the push-pull action.]

"It is a challenge to sing, skip, and stop at the cadence of the song."

"Hurry to find a partner if the one closest to you gets taken."

VERSION 2, *RIG-A-JIG-JIG*

Formation: Standing circle

As all sing the song, the game-starter walks on the inside of a standing circle, then stops at a partner and shakes hands at "a friend of mine." At "a-rig-a-jig-jig," the partners cross arms, hold hands, and push-pull their arms back and forth to the rhythm. During "away we go," the partners skip around the inside of the circle, holding hands. At the next "a-rig-a-jig-jig," the partners stop skipping, push-pull arms again, and then continue skipping till the end of the song.

The newer partner then begins the game as the original game-starter returns to a space in the circle. The activity continues with one person beginning the turn each time, finding a partner, taking a "rig-a-jig" and skipping turn with that partner, then returning to the circle.

Focusing Attention and Investigating Answers

"When does the song tell us to find a partner?"

"How do we know when to 'rig-a-jig'?"

"Can you sing, skip, and stop at the cadence of the song?"

"Can you predict whom the song will choose to get a turn this time?"

VERSION 3, *RIG-A-JIG-JIG*

Formation: Sitting circle or rows, floor or chairs

Seated, the teacher sings and makes motions to the phrases of the song while the students watch. She "walks" her legs on the floor to "as I was walking down the street," shakes an imaginary hand on "a friend of mine I happened to meet hi-ho hi-ho hi-ho," push-pulls her hands back and forth both times she sings "a-rig-a-jig-jig," and swings her arms from side to side each time she sings "away we go."

As students collect their observations of the teacher's motions and of the song's words, they join in singing and moving.

Focusing Attention and Investigating Answers

"As I sing the song, notice what else I do."

"Show us a motion you observed."

"What words of the song went with that motion?"

"Which motion was first (second and so on)?"

"What other motion could we use for the 'a-rig-a-jig-jig'?"

VERSION 4, *RIG-A-JIG-JIG*

Formation: Sitting circle or rows, chairs or floor

The teacher sings the song and walks among the students to shake a student's hand on "a friend of mine I happened to meet." The student can stand or stay seated. During "a-rig-a-jig-jig," the teacher push-pulls the student's hands back and forth and swings them from side to side on "away we go." When the song ends, the teacher sings and takes another walk among the students as the song leads her to her next partner.

Focusing Attention and Investigating Answers

"I wonder whom the song will lead me to this time. Will you sing for my turn?"

"What words were we singing when I did the motion with Jennifer's hands?"

"Eric, the class has had several watching turns now. Could you be the leader this time?"

"Where do you think Eric's song will take him? Let's sing for Eric's turn."

VERSION 5, *RIG-A-JIG-JIG*

Formation: Any arrangement

The teacher sings the song and asks students what game the song might suggest. Students make suggestions, and the group tries their ideas. Together they create a game activity.

Focusing Attention and Investigating Answers

"What ideas do you have for what we should do or how we should move as we sing the song?"

"Can you think of other games you like that could give you some ideas for this one?"

▶ As you read the descriptions of each version of *Rig-a-Jig-Jig,* did you envision a class that could play and enjoy each game?

▶ Can you picture a class with which you would be hesitant to play one of these versions?

▶ Which version seems most appropriate for older and which for younger students?

▶ Which version would work best if you have limited space?

▶ Which version might you choose if you are unfamiliar with a group of students?

▶ Which version might you try first if your students are moderately or severely mentally or physically disabled?

▶ Which version might be most successful if you have a large number of non-English-speaking students in your class?

No one version of any song activity will be appropriate for all students. Surprisingly, age can be a minor factor in deciding which version of an activity will best meet your students' needs and interests. Teachers have had satisfying, successful experiences and unsatisfying, unsuccessful experiences playing each of these versions of *Rig-a-Jig-Jig*. What qualifies as a successful playing of a game or activity? Success is based on students' levels of interest and engagement as they participate. A successful experience matches the range of students' social, movement, language, intellectual, and musical abilities without being overly limiting or overly challenging to them.

Assess the five versions of *Rig-a-Jig-Jig* using the continuum shown below. How would you rank the skills required of students in each version: (1) social skills, (2) movement skills, (3) language skills, (4) intellectual skills, (5) musical skills?

CONTINUUM OF INVOLVEMENT

Minimum   Maximum

Two factors that are easily adjusted in matching an activity to the physical, temporal, and student attributes of your context are the *formation* and the *movement* required for the activity. Changing formation and movement also affects social interaction. The following chart shows some options for reshaping activities to suit your students' needs.

WAYS TO RESHAPE GAMES

Formation Changes	**Movement Changes**
Circle	***Number of Students Moving***
moving	teacher only
stationary	collective
standing	one or two
seated	everyone
	small group
Chairs or Desks	
circle	***Type of Movement***
groupings	*fine motor:* tapping, snapping, clapping, pointing
rows	*axial:* bending, swaying, twisting
Scatter	*locomotor:* skipping, walking, running, jumping
seated on floor	
seated in chairs	***Patterns for Moving***
	in a circle
	in a line
	in a scatter
	inside circle
	outside circle
	in and out of circle (weaving)
	through rows of chairs

AN INTRODUCTION TO FOLK-SONG GAMES

Folk Songs and Folk Games

PRINCIPLE 7

Folk songs. What are they and who sings them? If, as Chase (1971, 11) suggests, folk are "a group of kindred people," then any of us are folk, especially when we are connected to or gathered with others for a common purpose or interest. Folk songs, then, are the songs we sing together, as a group, with joined voices, and "by heart." No one owns folk songs, just as no one owns the games and activities that folk songs often suggest. Folk songs are sung so that others will learn them, enjoy them, and make them their own. In essence, when we teach a folk song to others, we give it away.

When we learn and then teach folk songs, the songs eventually change. That is why there are so many variants of popular folk songs; we make them our own, and when we teach them, we modify them: We change the words to fit an occasion; we sing the words we heard rather than those that were sung; we sing what we remember of a song rather than giving an accurate rendition of the original. Within groups (a neighborhood gathering of playmates, a class of children), there may be a "right" way to perform the song and game according to the players. But across groups, intentional and unintentional modifications of folk songs and games are expected—that is the oral tradition of folk songs and the action tradition of folk games. This process of change is also what has given folk-song games such a rich history—a legacy that we reenact and unfold each time we sing and play them.

You may have noticed the interchangeable use of terms for these activities: song games, singing games, and song activities. These are not recently coined terms. "Song-games" is attributed to Babcock (1887), and Gomme established the term "singing game" in 1891 and 1894 in her books of *Traditional Games*. "Folk song games" is the term used by Fleurette Sweeney in courses for teachers throughout British Columbia. Whatever term is used to identify them, the games reach their maximum value when they are experienced with the joy and spontaneity of singing and playing together.

Though the songs included here may be called children's songs, they are really songs for everyone. A surprising number of the songs and games that we now identify as children's song games began as entertainment and play for adults, often with saltier lyrics and overt displays of affection or courtship. Age should not be a factor in singing or enjoying folk songs and activities. Songs for all ages is our ideal for these gems, some of which are centuries old. As Seeger said, these folk songs are not just children's music—they are family music (1948, 24).

PRINCIPLE 7

The best way to sing folk songs is by heart and from the heart. Our enthusiasm and joy in singing are the most important factors in sharing songs with children and others. Yes, in previous chapters we have included suggestions for starting a song, leading a song, and monitoring your own vocal production, and those hints may be helpful to many of you. The simple beauty and spirit that have preserved these songs through decades and centuries, however, are what you most want to communicate when you sing them. "It [children's folk songs] is not a music to be worshiped from afar and performed only by those with special gifts or intensively acquired technique—yet it partakes of the quality of greatness. To enjoy it, one need not dress up either oneself or one's voice" (Seeger 1948, 24).

You may be a trained vocalist who has spent years studying and practicing to hone your vocal skills. For these songs, however, a less self-conscious voice is in order. Singing with a light, spirited quality, sometimes with less than perfect diction is fine, even preferred, but please do not lead children with raucous singing. When singing folk songs with children and adults, remember that you are inviting them to join you in singing—for a partnership in song—not asking them to listen to you sing—for a recital of song.

> A true folk singer sings "by heart" and not out of books. He never tries to impress an audience, because at his best he is a real artist. Sincerely he shares his love and knowledge of these things *with* you rather than performing them *for* you. He sings "unthoughtedly," without self-consciousness. He makes his points without overdoing. He never shows his tonsils! Folk arts lose all their magic the instant they are exploited sensationally. (Chase 1971, 16)

The Format

What follows is a brief explanation of the format in which the folk-song games are presented. The format is designed to offer specific, detailed views of how to teach the songs, how to play the games, and how to teach the games, as well as what the games have to offer your students and how they can help you reach your classroom goals. In a sense, the format offers a recipe for teaching the activities. Yet, as in a cooking recipe, we expect that you will see the format as a starting point and that you will modify and personalize the flavors and ingredients as you gain confidence and insight in choosing the ways in which the games best fit the needs and interests of your students.

The following pages present song games that are frequently referred to in the text. These songs represent a corpus, neither an exclusive nor an expansive list, of songs and activities for use with children. Numerous sources are readily available that provide additional musical material, and some of those sources are listed in Appendix A. The thirty-seven songs presented here offer models for teaching, learning, and interacting that can be used and further developed with a variety of song material.

What were our criteria for choosing these thirty-seven songs? Our selections amount to just a handful of songs in the elementary music repertoire. Yet, we chose songs and activities that

- represent good, time-tested folk songs;
- we know and have used in our teaching for many years;
- have been used by many other teachers in many parts of North America;
- we consider valuable parts of our North American heritage and culture;
- have accompanying activities that illustrate teaching principles and techniques;
- fit childrens' voices and engage their thinking and imagination;
- we like.

We are very aware of the lack of cultural and stylistic balance in the selection of these songs, and we encourage teachers to use music series texts and the list of song collections in Appendix A to find songs from all over the world that they love, that their students will enjoy, and with which they will be able to teach.

Scenarios

Presented in story fashion, these vignettes portray real-life settings for folk-song games. Many are based on episodes from real classrooms. Intended to give the flavor of the activity and teacher-student interactions, the scenarios sometimes describe a specific version of the folk-song game, sometimes reveal a way to introduce the song, and sometimes offer further detail about how one version may be played. Each scenario intends to capture authentic perspectives for singing in the education of children. The scenarios model student-teacher interactions, describe ways to deal with

A-Hunting We Will Go

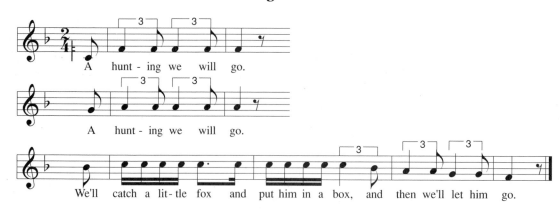

FIGURE 9-1

A-Hunting We Will Go

discipline issues that arise in the activity, and give examples of how teachers might respond to student contributions and comments.

Scores

Song scores are written in conventional music notation. DO signs have been included to help those familiar with solfa. Rather than breaking the scores into phrases—showing a score as it would appear in a form book, for example—we have chosen to present the scores in a conventional format. Figure 9-1 shows how *A-Hunting We Will Go* would look if divided according to phrases. Compare this organization with the score on page 226.

Age Appropriateness

Age-appropriate designations refer more to the way a game is played than to the folk song accompanying the game. As you might imagine, the suggested age appropriateness for each version of a folk-song game is a loose estimate. Ideally, all songs and all game versions would be appropriate for all ages, much like the early American tradition of the play party where everyone, from toddlers to the elderly, would join in the singing games. But, especially for beginning teachers who are unsure how to choose activities that will appeal to their students, the age-appropriate suggestions should be helpful. As you select activities for your students, you may find it useful to review the attributes affecting context appropriateness that are explained earlier in this chapter.

Degrees of Intensity

Selecting activities that will appeal to students and with which they can be successful often depends on the content of that activity. At times, you may want to select games that offer intense experiences in specific areas; at other times, you may want to minimize certain experiences for your students. For example, to correlate with a classroom emphasis, you may want to focus on activities that highlight imaginations, or on a day when students are extremely tired, you may want to choose an activity with low levels of movement. To help you make these context-appropriate choices, the Degrees of Intensity graphs show at a glance the relative content for each of the game versions. The six categories for this content are social interaction, language, movement, decision making, cooperation with others, and imagination. Shaded boxes represent the five relative degrees of intensity for each of these categories.

Learning Opportunities

Learning Opportunities are lists that reveal potential experiences for each game version. By offering specific experiences that students will likely encounter in the folk-song games, the Learning Opportunities offer ways to view student participation in song activities and ways to articulate the skills you are offering your students as you guide their play.

Song and Activity Background

Brief glimpses of the origins of songs and games are provided in the Song and Activity Background sections. Because this information reveals some of the rich history of folk songs, some of it may be worth sharing with your students. By including information available to us about relatively recent versions that were created by contemporary teachers, we hope to give evidence of the continuing history and development of these folk-song games.

Brief Description

The Brief Descriptions offer at-a-glance views of each folk-song game. By scanning, you receive a brief synopsis of the games and their versions.

Script

The detail with which the teaching process is described is intended to offer you guidance and inspiration for leading song activities with your students. The sample instruction statements, questions, feedback statements, and teaching procedures included in each script correlate with the principles and practices endorsed throughout the text. *It is not expected that you read and follow the script in teaching these activities to your students.* Many scripts include ample amounts of teacher-talk to illustrate the teaching process but too much teacher-talk for effective teaching. The specific quotations should be most helpful to you in constructing your plan for leading the activities.

You will note that music terms such as "cadence" and "phrase" are often included in the scripts to be introduced during a folk-song game. You need not give students technical information or elaborate explanations when you introduce these terms. Initially, the students hear the term as they perform or experience the concept. Later, you may want to provide visual reinforcement of the new term by asking a couple of students to consult with each other about possible spellings and write the word on the board while play continues.

Additional Versions

This chapter includes several folk-song games with additional versions, different games for the same song. The versions are included not only to show the vast array of games that have evolved for one song but also to encourage you to develop your own versions with your students based on their interests and needs. Remember the game-like variety that the techniques of chinning, inner hearing, and antiphonning can provide for any of the folk-song games (see Chapter 5).

The drama games, in particular, often feature students sharing their stories of theatrical creations. Performance of folk-song operettas or playlets in the classroom is an opportune time to introduce and encourage audience etiquette. Depending on the activity, some or all of these behaviors may be practiced:

- "A hush falls over the audience as the houselights dim."
- "We encourage the performers by applauding as they take the stage."

- "We don't make distracting noises or move around while the performance is in progress."
- "Let's continue our applause until all performers have left the stage area."
- "While the performance is in progress, watch and listen closely so that you will be able to tell the performers what you liked about their performance."
- "Performers need a good audience. Make sure you have things to say and questions to ask when the performance is over."

Many of the creative drama or creative writing activities described in game versions are opportunities for extended development. Students can share their projects by reading and performing their creations for other (sometimes younger) students.

Index of Classroom Situations

This Index of Classroom Situations is intended to collate specific classroom behaviors that are addressed in the folk-song game formats. Because the song is listed as the location for these situations, the behavior may be described in the scenario, the script, or the additional versions of that song.

Answering out in class	*Paw-Paw Patch; Sing with Me*
Audience etiquette practice	*Old Grumbler; Row, Row, Row Your Boat*
Beginning class with singing	*Circle Left; Here We Are Together; Sing with Me*
Choosing the next turn	*Circle Left; I'm Going Downtown; Punchinella; Ring Around the Rosy*
Concise instructions	*Did You Ever See a Lassie? Hot Cross Buns; Three Blind Mice*
Creating a story	*Did You Ever See a Lassie? Mulberry Bush; Old Grumbler; Row, Row, Row Your Boat; Tideo*
Ending an activity	*I'm Going Downtown; Punchinella*
"Freeze" as a challenge	*Come and Follow Me; Hot Cross Buns; Ring Around the Rosy*
Invitations during games	*Daddy Loves the Bear; The Farmer in the Dell; I'm Going Downtown*
Language substitution	*Circle Left; I'm Going Downtown; Muffin Man; Sing with Me; Skip to My Lou; Whistle, Daughter, Whistle*
Learning names	*The Farmer in the Dell; Here We Are Together; I'm Going Downtown; Muffin Man; Sing with Me; Skip to My Lou*
Listening to other students	*Old Dan Tucker; Row, Row, Row Your Boat; Tideo*
Making observations	*Hot Cross Buns; Skip to My Lou*
Maintaining a circle	*Mulberry Bush; Ring Around the Rosy*

Maintaining a personal space	*Here We Are Together; I'm Going Downtown*
Modifying behavior	*A-Hunting We Will Go; Here We Are Together; I'm Going Downtown; Old Dan Tucker; Old Grumbler; Punchinella*
Musical movement	*Old Dan Tucker; Twinkle, Twinkle*
Music terminology	*Circle Left; Hot Cross Buns; Johnny, Get Your Hair Cut; Old Dan Tucker; Punchinella; Skip to My Lou; Twinkle, Twinkle*
Observation without evaluation	*Ring Around the Rosy; Row, Row, Row Your Boat; Scotland's Burning*
Pacing challenges	*A-Hunting We Will Go; Circle Left*
Practice time	*Hot Cross Buns; I'm Going Downtown; Muffin Man*
Preventing injury	*A-Hunting We Will Go; Ring Around the Rosy; Three Blind Mice*
Running out of time	*I'm Going Downtown; Mary's Wearing Her Red Dress; Paw-Paw Patch; Punchinella*
Signs for getting quiet	*Hot Cross Buns; Row, Row, Row Your Boat*
Silliness in songs	*Sing with Me; Whistle, Daughter, Whistle*
Students' self-assessment	*Skip to My Lou; Three Blind Mice*
Tempo selection	*A-Hunting We Will Go; The Farmer in the Dell (Name Game); Here We Are Together; Row, Row, Row Your Boat; Sing with Me; Twinkle, Twinkle*
Thinking time	*Circle Left; Mulberry Bush; Skip to My Lou*
Using inappropriate language	*Circle Left; Whistle, Daughter, Whistle*

A-Hunting We Will Go

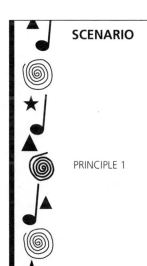

SCENARIO

PRINCIPLE 1

VERSION 2: TRAP GAME

After singing the song, the teacher asked, "What do you think this song is about?" Students suggested various meanings for the words of the song. Further queries from the teacher initiated collaborative discussions about images the song might offer. "Where would we be if we were trying to catch a fox? Have you ever seen a fox? Describe it. Why might we want to catch a fox? The song says we catch him, put him in a box, then let him go; why would we do that?

"Our curiosity about animals and our desire to take care of them can shape our games for this song. Have you ever seen the kind of trap that does not hurt animals? Perhaps you've seen pictures of a boy or a girl hiding behind a tree or a bush holding one end of a string. The other end of the string is attached to a stick that is holding up the box. When the animal wanders into the box, the child pulls the string and catches it. Why would we want to catch an animal just for a short while? What kind of box would we need to be able to see inside and watch the animal? What kinds of things would we be curious about as we watched the fox?"

PRINCIPLE 2

PRINCIPLE 5

As the teacher listened to students and guided them to listen to each other, she knew that although these exchanges took time, they also added to the richness of the experience with the song and the activity. Follow-up questions such as "What do you mean?" "What made you think of that?" "Have you ever had that experience?" offered ways to understand and encourage the ideas students shared.

"As we sing the song, let's pretend that our arms are the box. We'll hold them in the air and let them fall when the song tells us to. Watch, listen, and sing." The teacher modeled a gentle enveloping position for the box by holding arms extended and slightly raised above shoulders. When the word "catch" was sung, the box (arms) quickly descended, dropping to catch the fox. "What word told our arms to drop? Consult with a neighbor and tell us what you think." After ideas were collected from students, the song and the arm gesture were repeated to check out students' perceptions. "Catch" was identified as the word that triggered the box to drop, and the class practiced doing this action in such a way that the fox would not be injured.

After exploring the imagery of the song, the teacher introduced a game in each of her Grade 4, 5, and 6 classes. Two students were chosen to be the box, and they stood in the center, holding hands, with arms raised, making a trap. The class moved through the box as the song was sung, and one student was caught by the box on the word "catch." During the phrase "and then we'll let him go," the student who was caught joined hands with the box, and the box became larger with each turn. "Foxes don't necessarily move in lines. You may wander in and out of the box. Just be careful not to hurt yourself or others."

Seeing the possibilities of the game, several students became very excited. Their attention was focused solely on how to get through the box without getting caught, and they neglected both the song and the safety of themselves and others. The teacher knew she must act quickly before the behavior escalated. "Let's stop for a moment and think about the imagery and purpose of this game. Do you remember that we're being gentle? Remember that the box falls in such a way as not to hurt the foxes as they try to escape. Let's stand still for a turn and practice letting the box fall quickly but gently at just the right moment. Tell us what other safety concerns we have and how we could deal with them so that we can continue."

When all or most of the foxes were caught, the game began again.

A-Hunting We Will Go

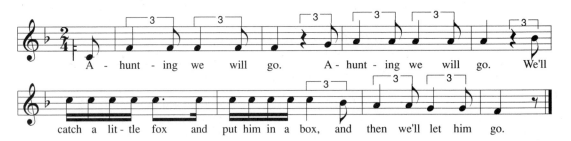

Brief Description

As students sit in a circle for Version 1, the leader walks around the outside and gently "catches" a child on the word "catch." Then the child is framed with encircled arms as the others look at and wave to the chosen child. The leader continues to give turns until students are ready to be the game leader. In Version 2, students move in and out of a "box" constructed of students standing, holding hands, and raising arms. The box (arms) falls on the word "catch." Whoever is caught joins the box, and it continues to expand with nearly every turn. Version 3 adds more imagery to Version 2 by encouraging students to suggest what might be in the box to lure the fox in there and what the foxes must do with that lure before they can scamper out of the box. The game of Version 4 is to make up new verses using rhyming words.

Age Appropriateness

Version 1—Preschool through Grade 1	Greeting Game
Version 2—Grade 4 through Grade 6	Trap Game
Version 3—Grade 2 through Grade 5	Lure Game
Version 4—Grade 3 through Grade 6	Rhyming Game

Degrees of Intensity

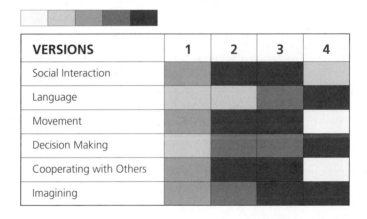

VERSIONS	1	2	3	4
Social Interaction				
Language				
Movement				
Decision Making				
Cooperating with Others				
Imagining				

Learning Opportunities

- *Move* to a specific word in the song: Auditory-visual-motor skills (Versions 1, 2, 3).
- *Eye contact* and *greeting* others: Social skills (Version 1).
- *Pronouns* him and her: Language skills (Version 1).
- *Imagination* to create story lines, scenes, and challenges: Drama skills (Versions 2, 3).
- *Pantomime* language ideas: Auditory-motor skills (Version 3).
- *Word substitution* with rhyming words: Language skills, music skills (Version 4).
- Anacrusis and short-short-long phrase *structure*: Music skills.
- *Melody* patterns of SO$_l$ | DO DO DO DO DO and FA | MI MI RE RE DO: Music skills.
- *Rhythm* patterns of ♪ | ♩♪ ♩♪ ♩ (DI DU DI DU DI DU): Music skills.

Song and Activity Background

A-Hunting We Will Go can be traced to various times and settings. With a melody similar to that of *The Farmer in the Dell,* the tune has been connected to *The Grand Old Duke of York,* which lampoons Frederick Duke of York (1900), Henry Fielding's song *The Dusky Night Rides Down the Sky,* a ballad opera song *A-Begging We Will Go,* and a German student song that made fun of a "fox," or freshman. According to Opie and Opie (1988, 215), this may not have become a children's game until 1909. The traditional game (traced to 1883, 1922, and 1978) involved two long lines of partners. The head couple held hands and skipped down the middle, then back. Then they ran to the end of the lines with the group following them and ran up through the lines. A second verse, from about 1922, says: "We'll ask John Brown to tea . . . If he can't come we'll ask his son, and all his family." From the late 1800s, there is evidence of the song as a rhyming game: "We'll catch a little fish and put him in a dish."

In some regions, the middle section is sung with "Hi-ho the derry-o" or "Hi-ho the merry-o," matching a phrase from *The Farmer in the Dell,* and the cadence phrase is sung "And never let him go." In addition to the line dance described, games to this song may involve a hunter in the middle trying to grab a fox when the singing stops (Opie and Opie 1988, 213). Versions 1 and 2 are from Richards (1985, 38). Version 3, The Lure Game, was developed in Tokyo in 1991 with Peggy Bennett as Japanese teachers were learning English folk-song games to teach their children.

Script. Version 1: Greeting Game

Teacher	Students
Sing the song with a light, gentle tempo and walk around the outside of the circle. When you sing "*catch,*" calmly touch the shoulders of the closest child and bend down beside him or her. As you sing "*and put him in a box,*" make a circle with your arms and place them around the child's face, framing the child for all to see. On "*and then we'll let him go,*" remove your arms and stand to begin the next turn.	Sitting in a circle, children observe as the teacher takes the first turn.
• *On that turn, I caught Cloé and put her in a frame so you could all see her. That's your turn to look in her eyes and wave to her before I let her go. Let's try it.* • *Give Cloé a wave while she's in the box, before we let her go.* [Sing.] "*We'll catch a little fox and put her in a box, and then we'll let her go.*"	While Cloé is framed in the box, students give her a wave "hello and good-bye" before she is "let go" and the song begins again.
• *The song tells me whom to catch as the fox. Listen and watch this time. How does the song tell me whom to choose? Here comes the song . . .*	Students are encouraged to discover that the word "catch" tells the leader to stop and choose the closest child as the fox.
The activity continues until time or children's interest wanes. After several turns of watching the teacher demonstrate, children can take turns "hunting" for the fox.	The quiet and gentle nature of this version is especially appropriate for chronologically and developmentally young students.

Additional Versions of A-Hunting We Will Go

Version 3: Lure Game.   When some foxes become too sly for capture, challenges can be introduced to lure them into the box.

- *What might we place in the box to lure these foxes in there?* ["Pizza!"]
- *Yes! And how many pieces should they have to eat before they can leave?* ["Three! And he has to slice it first!"]

With successive turns, students create scenes in which the foxes are given details about what they must do in the center before they try to escape.

With guidance from the teacher, students' ideas for fox challenges can be exercises ("Do five jumping jacks"), enticing food ("Jump three times to try to reach the piece of meat hanging from the ceiling"), or activities ("Put on makeup and lipstick, then check the mirror"). The game ends whenever there is a sense that it is time to begin again or when no time is left. It can be helpful to students if you inform them, *"Only two more turns for this activity today."*

Version 4: Rhyming Verses Students are challenged to create new verses to the song using rhyming words: "We'll catch a little goat and put him in a boat . . ." "We'll catch a little fly and hope it's not July . . ." Students may work as a class, in pairs, or in small groups to create verses; then the class sings their song creations. On the board or on a page for each child, the words of the song can be written with blanks for the placement of the rhyming words. Once in written form, these new verses can be used for reading experiences. Students may also want to illustrate their verses.

Circle Left

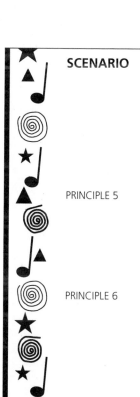

SCENARIO

PRINCIPLE 5

PRINCIPLE 6

VERSION 1: TOUCH YOUR NOSE

With the class seated on the floor in a circle, the teacher began singing, "Touch your knees, do-oh, do-oh. Touch your knees, do-oh, do-oh. Touch your knees, do-oh, do-oh. Shake those fingers down." Each time he sang "knees," he touched his knees, nonverbally inviting the kindergarten children to do the same. Reaching high in the air on "shake those fingers down," he wiggled his fingers down to the floor, lightly touching the floor with his fingertips just as he sang the word "down." From past experience, the teacher knew that small children seem drawn to slapping the floor at the cadence in this activity. To avoid building up too much energy, to maintain musical movement, and to minimize the risk of allergic reactions resulting from pounding the carpet, he purposely modeled lightly touching the floor at the cadence.

"Wow, you listened to the song and did what it told you to do! Let's practice that last part. Hold your fingers high in the air and see if they can be touching the floor right when we sing 'down.' We call that word the cadence word because it ends the song. Let's sing." All sang the last phrase, "shake those fingers down," as children practiced their movements. Their teacher did not hesitate to use proper music terminology, such as "cadence," with these children. He knew that as they practiced the concept in the context of their song activities, they would become familiar with the term and its meaning.

"We touched our knees that time; raise your hand if you have an idea for what we can touch this time." Their teacher sensed that some students were ready almost immediately to take the initiative in offering their own ideas; in other classes, children seemed to need two or three demonstrations before they appeared self-assured in offering ideas.

"Our heads!" replied Jasper. "Are your voices ready? Here comes the song . . . 'Touch your head, do-oh, do-oh'," sang the teacher. To remind students not to answer aloud with "Me!" or "I do!" when he asked for volunteers, the teacher said, "Raise your hand if . . ." before asking the question. In some of his classes, this strategy was neither necessary nor desirable, but when needed, it helped students focus on and listen to one another during their turns to talk.

"Caroline, you look like you have an idea. What do you want us to touch this time when we sing?" the teacher asked encouragingly. Caroline looked hesitant, waited for what seemed like several minutes, then touched her elbow. "I see your idea, Car-

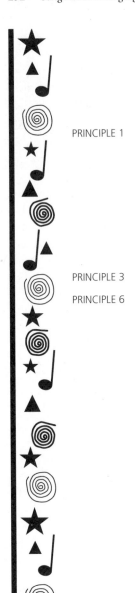

PRINCIPLE 1

PRINCIPLE 3

PRINCIPLE 6

oline. What do we call that?" Caroline responded quietly, "My arm." "That part of our arm is also called our elbow. Which would you like us to sing, 'Touch your arm' or 'Touch your elbow'?" "Arm," Caroline responded. "Let's sing Caroline's idea and put her name in the song. [Singing the starting pitch] Ready . . . 'Touch your arm, just like Caroline . . .'"

For Caroline's turn, the teacher solicited a response not by asking for volunteers but by calling on a specific student to offer an idea. Being called on specifically for an idea can relieve the more shy or hesitant students of the uncomfortable task of volunteering. When Caroline showed her idea rather than saying it, the teacher was tempted to say, "Oh, you want us to touch our elbow." He had learned that filling in students' ideas may be helpful when they cannot or will not speak but does little to aid students in developing confidence, verbal courage, and choice-making skills when all they need is a little more time or support.

"Caroline, look for someone raising a hand. Whom will you give the next turn to?" Looking around the group, Caroline looked at Artie and nodded to him. "Artie, Caroline has decided you get the next turn. What will we touch this time?" "Our penis!" Artie responded enthusiastically with no hint of naughtiness. "Oh, Artie, we don't all have one. Choose something we all can do!" The teacher reacted with swift and neutral attention to Artie. "Our toes!" Artie replied with equal enthusiasm. Knowing naughtiness is relative, the teacher wanted to avoid classroom judgments about what vocabulary is "not nice." Therefore, he was matter-of-fact and neutral whenever he was called upon to respond to inappropriate language in the classroom. In another class, when Sophie had suggested "Shake your butt," the teacher had responded, "That is not a word I'm comfortable using in school, Sophie. Let's say 'bottom' instead."

"Since we've had several turns, can someone tell us how our song is going to sound this time for Artie's turn? Who can sing it?" The simplicity of naming body parts was effective with groups of young children as well as with mentally handicapped students. After several turns or times of playing this activity, students can be asked to predict and figure out how the new words will fit the song as they sing.

One option in choosing students for turns is having students choose students. Although this option gives students more choice-making opportunities during the lesson, it also may offer too many choices for the smooth flow and uninterrupted progress of the activity. Each of the three alternatives for choosing students for turns described here is effective in certain contexts, though all may not be effective when used within the same activity.

Circle Left

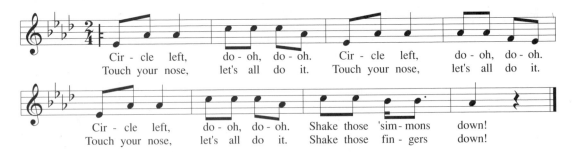

Cir - cle left,   do - oh, do - oh.   Cir - cle left,   do - oh, do - oh.
Touch your nose,   let's all do it.   Touch your nose,   let's all do it.

Cir - cle left,   do - oh, do - oh.   Shake those 'sim - mons   down!
Touch your nose,   let's all do it.   Shake those fin - gers   down!

Brief Description

In a sitting circle or in a scatter formation for Version 1, children choose what part of the body they will name and touch as all imitate. At the cadence, all raise hands above heads and shake fingers to the floor. In Version 2, students stand in a circle with one person in the middle. When the student in the middle suggests a way to move by naming the movement and the body part (such as "Clap your hands"), all imitate and sing. On the cadence phrase, students shake hands from above their heads down to their sides as the person in the center spins with one finger extended, stops at the cadence, and follows his or her finger to the closest person in the circle. That person becomes the new leader in the middle. A moving circle is the format for Version 3 as students create calls for the group by naming the directions the circle should go for each phrase.

Age Appropriateness

Version 1—Preschool through Grade 1	Touch Your Nose
Version 2—Grade 2 through Grade 5	Clap Your Hands
Version 3—Grade 3 through Grade 5	Circle Left

Degrees of Intensity

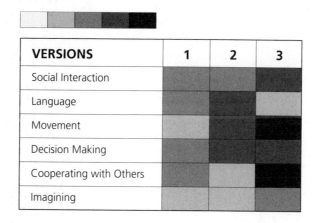

VERSIONS	1	2	3
Social Interaction			
Language			
Movement			
Decision Making			
Cooperating with Others			
Imagining			

Learning Opportunities

- *Coordinate movement* with beginning and ending of sound: Auditory-motor skills.
- *Coordinate movement* changes with word changes: Auditory-motor skills.
- *Pantomime* language ideas: Auditory-motor skills.
- Explore *language* to describe ideas.
- *Word substitution:* Language skills, music skills.
- *Imitate movement:* Visual-motor and figure-ground skills.
- *Name* parts of the body: Language skills (Versions 1, 2).
- *Name* movements using verbs: Language skills (Versions 2, 3).
- Create and demonstrate *movement:* Motor skills (Versions 1, 2).
- *Maintain pace and space* while moving in a circle: Auditory-visual-motor skills, spatial skills (Version 3).
- Balanced phrase *structure:* Music skills.
- *Melody* patterns of SO₁ DO DO and MI MI RE RE DO: Music skills.
- *Rhythm* patterns of ♫ ♩ ♫ ♫ (DU DE DU DU DE DU DE) and ♫ ♫. ♩ (DU DE DUTA DU): Music skills.

Song and Activity Background

Found as both *Circle Left* and *Circle Right,* this song has roots in the American tradition of play parties. The exact melody and words of the version printed here appear as an Alabama play party game called 'Simmons (Rohrbough 1940, 91). Other verses included "Circle right," "Balance all," "'Round your partners," "'Round your corners," and "Prom'nade all." The version presented here changes the cadence phrase "shake them 'simmons down" to "shake those fingers down." Imagining ripe persimmons at the top of the tree helps envision the actions that this phrase suggests. Version 1 is adapted for chronologically and developmentally young children (Richards 1985, 9). In Michiko Nitaira's English classroom, Shimodate City, Japan, students sing "let's all do it" in place of "do-oh, do-oh."

Script. Version 2: Clap Your Hands

Teacher	Students
As all stand in a circle, begin singing and invite students to join the activity. *"Clap your hands. . ."* On *"shake those fingers down,"* wiggle your fingers from above your head down to your sides.	Students sing and imitate the movements of the teacher.
Move to the center of the circle and continue the song with new actions. • *Snap your fingers, do-oh, do-oh . . . down.* • *Twiddle your thumbs, do-oh, do-oh . . .down.* On the last phrase, *"shake those fingers down,"* close your eyes and cover them with one hand. As you point with the other hand, twirl in a circle and stop with the cadence word, *"down."* Then open your eyes, follow your finger to a student in the circle, and invite that student to move to the center. • *José, the song picked you to get the next turn. Would you like a turn?* [José says, "Yes."] *Then go into the center and tell us how you want us to move for your turn.*	Students sing and imitate movements. As José moves to the center, prepare students for their potential turns: • *Class, I clapped my hands, snapped my fingers, and twiddled my thumbs. This is a good moment to take some thinking time to decide on your idea in case the song picks you for a turn.*
Provide feedback and prompts by statements such as these: • *We even know how we're going to stomp our feet, because José showed us.* • *José, did you see what I did when we sang "shake those fingers down"?* • *Remember to spin and stop at the cadence; I'll help you remember by prompting you if you need it.* • *Here comes the song.* [Singing the starting pitch] *Ready . . . Stomp your feet, do-oh, do-oh . . .down.'*	"I want us to stomp our feet," offers José as he shows his idea. José spins, stops at the cadence, and looks a bit bewildered as to whom he should choose. Assist by cueing José: • *If you look all the way down the end of your finger and follow it to the place it is pointing, it will lead you to the next person.* José follows his finger to Mercedes.
As Mercedes moves to the center of the circle, you can give her nonverbal support by your facial expression. See if the students will keep the activity going without your verbal intervention. • *We need some words for the song, Mercedes.* • *What do you want us to call that movement?* The activity continues with students taking turns offering movement and verbal ideas.	Mercedes does a jumping jack. "Do a jumping jack, do-oh, do-oh," Mercedes sings. Foster this independence in starting the song by joining the singing. On another turn, highlight the importance of waiting to start the song until all are ready: • *George, we weren't quite ready yet. Now that we know your idea, begin your song again and we will sing and move like you.*

Additional Versions of Circle Left

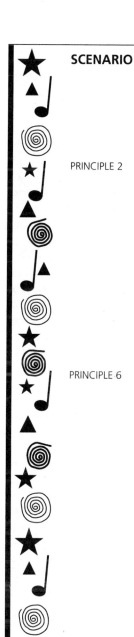

SCENARIO

PRINCIPLE 2

PRINCIPLE 6

VERSION 3: CIRCLE GAME

As soon as the fourth-grade students moved into their circle, Mr. Rosen took the hands of those on each side of him and began moving and singing, "Circle left, do-oh, do-oh . . . down." On the last phrase, the teacher used loose wrists and shook his hands down, as if he were shaking water from them.

Mr. Rosen knew that it was important to set a brisk pace for singing, giving instructions, and leading the activity with his students in Grades 4 through 6 to capture their attention and interest, especially in the initial phases of introducing an activity. Although he knew that a frantic or overwhelming pace would be counterproductive, wise use of energy with older students often set the tone for the activity's appeal. Along this line, he kept explanations to a minimum, capturing students' attention first, then offering needed explanations.

With little pause between verses, Mr. Rosen immediately began singing, "Circle right, do-oh, do-oh . . . down." Again, with no pause, he continued the momentum of the activity by surprising the students during the next song: "Circle left, do-oh, do-oh. Circle right, do-oh, do-oh. Circle left, do-oh, do-oh. Shake those fingers down." The students were momentarily caught off guard, and several bumped into each other when they did not change directions.

"Ah-HA!" teased the teacher. "Some people are catching on that this is a game of skill: listening, sudden change of movement, and coordination within the circle. Good luck, because I have more challenges in store for you!" Mr. Rosen showed a posture of expectancy and sang, "Here we go . . . 'Circle right, do-oh, do-oh. Circle in do-oh, do-oh. Circle down do-oh, do-oh . . . down." With Grades 4–6, Mr. Rosen had found that telling the students what challenges and skills were required for an activity communicated that there was a purpose beyond the play. Naming the perceptual or social tasks that they were practicing in an activity also gave students the terminology to describe what they were learning in school.

"I've had several turns being the 'caller' for this activity. We have time for a few of you to be callers for a turn. Think about the variety of directions you can give the circle, and decide which three you will use if you get a turn. Use a moment right now for your thinking time." Giving thinking time at the beginning of an activity resulted in a productive, constructive, and effective use of time later on and allowed the activity to flow smoothly.

Students soon learned that part of the fun in this game was the reminder to "stay where the song leaves us" at the cadence. Some students forgot to call "circle up" as the initial direction when the previous turn had left the circle "down"—and some left this direction out on purpose. Trying to "circle in" while students were crouched on the floor and "circle in" when they were already squeezed into a tight space appealed to these students' senses of humor.

Cockles and Mussels

SCENARIO

VERSION 1: STORY AND TABLEAUS

"The song we're going to sing today tells a story, but it leaves a lot to our imagination. I'm going to sing it one verse at a time, and I want you to tell me about the people in the story. Who are they, what are they doing, and where do they live? These are some questions the song will help you answer." Ms. Springer sang the first verse. Students identified Molly Malone as the main character, and someone noticed that the

PRINCIPLE 2

PRINCIPLE 4

PRINCIPLE 7

PRINCIPLE 1

person singing the song is also a part of the story. "Who do you think this might be?" Ms. Springer asked. "What is this person's relationship to Molly? I'll sing the song again." More comments came this time as students began to see the song as a puzzle to solve.

"What is a fishmonger?" Juliette asked. "What are cockles and mussels and alimeos?" another student chimed in. Ms. Springer helped them with vocabulary, explaining the nature of street-selling and the kinds of shellfish that you can buy near the sea. "Street vendors, before TV and radio, would wander through the streets with their wares, and they would call out or sing about what they were selling. You can see street vendors in the movies *Oliver, My Fair Lady,* and *Porgy and Bess.* She isn't singing "alimeo," though I know why you didn't understand the word. She's singing "alive-oh," letting people know how fresh her shellfish are. Listen to that part of the song. It's called a refrain, and it comes after every verse. You'll learn it quickly."

Ms. Springer challenged the students to think about what Molly might have looked like, what her clothes were like, what the streets were like, where she got her fish, what time of day it was, when she went to work, what her home was like, where it was situated, and so on. The students filled in details about the sights, sounds, and smells, the weather, the people Molly bought fish from, the sailors on the streets, other street vendors, the people who were buying from the vendors, the buildings Molly would pass, where the boats were, and what the sea was like. Ms. Springer would regularly return to the song, inviting students to join in on the refrain and to sing the verse when they felt comfortable. She collected students' observations, not to get the correct responses, but to see how all these observations might fit together— how some built on other responses and how certain responses put the scene in a new perspective.

As she added other verses, Ms. Springer's line of questioning stayed the same, encouraging students to wonder about the place, people, business, relationships, experiences, history, and thoughts that might be a part of the story of this song.

After they had explored all three verses, Ms. Springer divided the class into groups of six or seven students. Each group was to make a tableau. A tableau, she explained, was what drama companies would use to advertise their plays. Each character would strike a pose, like a statue, that expressed something important about that role—the character's personality, an event, or a relationship with another character. A tableau was a little like a photograph, a moment in time, that would illustrate the important characters, themes, and relationships of the play. Within their groups, students would be designated for the various parts, and some might even be a boat or a lighthouse. They would choose poses that showed the personalities, feelings, and relationships of the characters and objects in the song.

The groups were then given a specific amount of time to create their tableaus, and Ms. Springer alerted them when there was only a minute or two left. "It's time to finish. Your tableau may not be perfect yet, but it's time to share it." Before sharing the tableaus, Ms. Springer reminded students to observe closely and comment constructively on the creations they were going to see. Observers would be free to walk around (and sometimes into) the scene, if they were careful not to disrupt it. During this observation time, Ms. Springer encouraged students to notice details of facial expressions, the shapes of hands, posture, and so on. "While you are a part of the tableau, you may really need to concentrate so that your expressions are frozen and stay in character with your role. If you laugh or giggle, that might spoil the scene you've created."

As students shared their tableaus, they looked at others' ideas closely and had much to say about the different characters and how they were portrayed. After all the tableaus had been shared, Ms. Springer came back to the song. "Let's sing the whole song once more and keep in mind all that we have just explored about the song. [Singing a starting pitch] Ready . . . 'In Dublin's fair city. . .' "

Cockles and Mussels

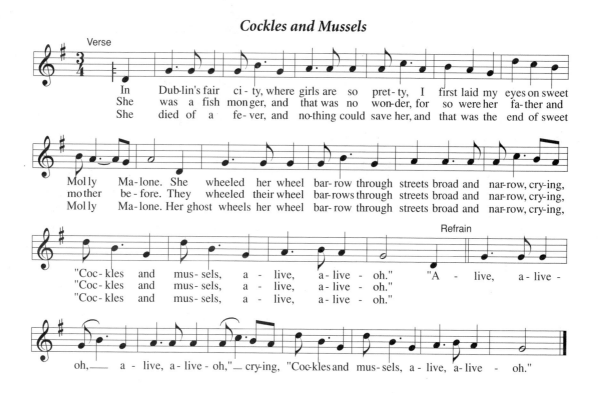

Brief Description

As they sing the first verse in Version 1, students are encouraged to imagine what the song is about, where it is taking place, and who the characters are. Successive verses elicit more imagery and details, providing a fuller picture of what the song might be about. After freely discussing the possibilities of meaning, students are organized into small groups to create a scene or tableau that depicts a portion of the story. Version 2 builds on the discussions of Version 1 by asking students to write four sentences that reflect some of the imagery they experienced while thinking about the story. Students then are instructed to select another student's sentences, choose a favorite sentence from that list, and be prepared to read that sentence at the appropriate time. After singing the song again, students listen as sentences are read, and they read theirs when they think it fits the particular story line or imagery being unfolded.

Age Appropriateness

Version 1—Grade 3 through Grade 6   Story and Tableaus

Version 2—Grade 4 through Grade 6   Creative Writing

Degrees of Intensity

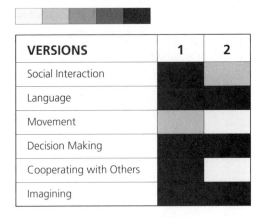

VERSIONS	1	2
Social Interaction		
Language		
Movement		
Decision Making		
Cooperating with Others		
Imagining		

Learning Opportunities

- *Explore* the meaning, context, and language of a song: Language skills, social studies skills.

- *Pantomime* social and cultural features: Social studies skills, drama skills.

- Develop *vocabulary* and discuss *history*: Language skills.

- *Cooperate* with others to produce a dramatic tableau: Social skills, drama skills.

- Anacrusis and AB (binary) song *structure*: Music skills.

- *Melody patterns* of SO₁ | DO DO DO DO MI and DO | RE MI RE DO: Music skills.

- *Triple* meter: Music skills.

Song and Activity Background

Cockles and Mussels is a folk song of the British Isles commonly found in folk-song collections and music series texts. The song offers a brief portrayal of the life of a street vendor, leading the listener to wonder about and imagine the details and images of her workplace, living conditions, lifestyle, and relationship with the admirer who is singing the song.

The activity that prepares and introduces tableaus for this song was developed in the 1990s by drama and music teacher Mary Opland Springer, from Seattle, who also developed the writing lesson in Version 2.

Additional Versions of Cockles and Mussels

Version 2: Creative Writing.   After students have explored the personalities, settings, feelings, and relationships suggested by *Cockles and Mussels,* they can write those images for a collective storytelling.

Students reflect on what they might have seen, felt, smelled, tasted, heard, or thought as a character in the song or as an observer of the imagery that the song suggests. They put those feelings, reflections, and sensations into words, choosing four images to write in sentence form on a piece of paper. When students have finished writing their sentences, they put their papers into a pile. As six to eight sheets are turned in, instruct students to come back and select a piece of paper that is not their own, silently read the four sentences on the page, and choose one that they would like to share. When all have finished writing and each student has the paper of another student, students form one large group while they sing *Cockles and Mussels*. At the conclusion of the song, tell the students that they are now going to read the sentences they chose.

> ■ *You will know when it's your turn by listening to the sentences being spoken. When you hear a sentence that fits with the one you chose, you should read it. Listen closely to know when you can speak, be patient, and avoid reading at the same time as another student. You may also read other sentences on your list if you want.*

Collective reading of students' writings can be a very powerful experience, rich in images, feelings, and personal expression. It builds on the story outlined in the song, it depends on the feelings the song stimulates or suggests, it expands and explores the imagery developed in the discussion of the song, and it captures the immediate and often intimate reactions of the participants.

Come and Follow Me

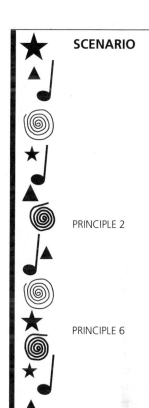

SCENARIO

PRINCIPLE 2

PRINCIPLE 6

VERSION 2: PARTNER GAME

"Virgil, whom will you choose to be your shadow today?" Ms. Jamison asked. "Michael," Virgil responded as Michael smiled and moved to stand directly behind Virgil for this follow-the-leader game. "The partners are ready. Let's sing for them and watch to see what statue Virgil makes for Michael to copy."

"Wait for the song," Ms. Jamison said, and it was easy to see that the kindergarten children had to exercise a good deal of concentration to do that. "Ready," she sang, and all began the song. Virgil knew to freeze when he heard the cadence word, "way," and his clue to get ready to freeze was the phrase "we will stop this way," which, he knew, ended the song. The teacher and the children smiled at the vision of Virgil bending over, touching the floor with one hand and one foot, and stretching the other hand and foot high in the air, and of Michael quickly adjusting his body to match Virgil's statue.

"Wow, they are nearly identical! I can hardly tell them apart!" exclaimed Ms. Jamison. "If you turn around, who will be the leader this time? It's Michael's turn to be the leader. Let's see what he has Virgil do." The group sang and watched Michael and his shadow move around the room, stop at the cadence, and make a new statue. "Your coordination of listening and moving was very precise, boys. Way to go! Each of you invite someone to take your place as we get ready to watch another couple."

When children were familiar with the process, Ms. Jamison structured the activity so new couples joined the shadow activity each time, making it a collective game. At each cadence of the song, time was taken to notice briefly the couples' statues and shadows, noting their unique ideas and their skills in mirroring.

Come and Follow Me

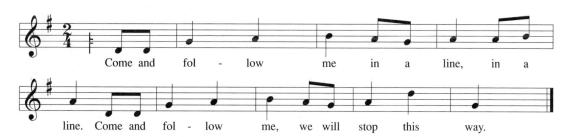

Brief Description

As the group sits in a circle for the Invitation Game of Version 1, one student asks another to follow him or her. At the cadence, the student leader freezes into a statue and the follower imitates the statue. For each successive turn, the leader asks the student closest to his or her feet to join the line as the new leader, and at the cadence, the leader displays a new statue for the followers to imitate. In Version 2, the Partner Game, a leader and a follower move around the outside of the circle, and both freeze into a statue of the leader's choice at the cadence. Then the partners switch roles, and the follower becomes the leader for a turn. Play can continue with one pair at a time playing follow-the-leader, or additional pairs can join with each new turn. In the Line Game (Version 3), all students move in a line following the leader, and the leader demonstrates a way to move during the song (skip, tiptoe) and makes a statue at the cadence. In Version 4 (Read a Statue), all students move in a line as statue ideas are presented, consisting of various drawings of body positions that students read and match.

Age Appropriateness

Version 1—Preschool through Grade 2	Invitation Game
Version 2—Preschool through Grade 2	Partner Game
Version 3—Grade 1 through Grade 2	Line Game
Version 4—Grade 1 through Grade 2	Read a Statue

Degrees of Intensity

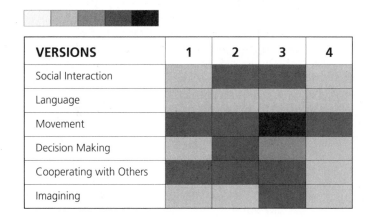

VERSIONS	1	2	3	4
Social Interaction				
Language				
Movement				
Decision Making				
Cooperating with Others				
Imagining				

Learning Opportunities

- *Coordinate movement* with beginning and ending of sound: Auditory-motor skills.
- *Imitate* body positions: Visual-motor skills, figure-ground skills.
- *Cooperate with a partner:* Social skills (Version 2).
- Turns in *leading and following:* Social skills.
- *Locomotor movement* in a line: Spatial skills, auditory-visual-motor skills (Version 3).
- *Maintain pace and space* while moving in a circle: Auditory-visual-motor skills, spatial skills (Version 3).
- *Read and match body position* to a graphic: Visual-motor skills (Version 4).

- *Isolate* one part of the body designated by a graphic: Motor figure-ground skills (Version 4).

- Balanced phrase *structure*: Music skills.

- *Melody* patterns of SO₁ SO₁ | DO RE MI and RE DO | RE SO DO: Music skills.

- *Rhythm* patterns of ♫ | ♩ ♩ ♩ (DU DE DU DU DU) and ♫ | ♩ (DU DE DU): Music skills.

Song and Activity Background

Come and Follow Me apparently originated in Ontario, Canada, in the 1970s as an adaptation of the French nursery rhyme *A Queue Leu Leu* (Richards 1985, 11). Version 2 developed about 1990 in the classroom of Marilyn Winter, a music educator from Butte, Montana.

Script. Version 1: Invitation Game

Teacher	Students
As students are seated on the floor, stand and ask one student to come and follow you: • *Robbie, will you follow me? I'll make a statue when the song ends, and your challenge is to match my statue as closely as you can. So, as you walk behind me, be ready to freeze into my statue at the cadence. Are you ready?* [Singing] *"Come and follow me. . .way."*	Robbie follows the teacher and, at the cadence, freezes into a statue that matches the teacher's statue.
At the cadence, notice that Robbie matched you, then ask Robbie to be the leader. As you follow Robbie around the circle, freeze into the statue that Robbie demonstrates. Call the group's attention to various details of the statues by singing the RE SO DO melody of the cadence. • [Singing] *Look at his feet.* • [Singing] *Notice his hands.* • [Singing] *Just like Robbie.*	The group sings and watches as the pair plays follow-the-leader.
• *Robbie, your feet stopped at the cadence. Notice who is seated closest to your feet. Invite that person to be our new line leader.*	Robbie invites Janet to be the new leader. You could suggest invitations if Robbie is not sure what to say: • *Would you like to come with us?* • *Could we follow you?* • *Would you make a statue for us?"*
• *Janet, we'll try to make our statues look like yours as soon as the song ends! Here comes the song . . .* Turns continue as a new leader is added for each repetition of the song. Playfulness is modeled by the speed and the detail with which the followers imitate the leader.	Students are led to study the statues, noticing details, similarities, and patterns: • *I wonder what Janet will do for her statue. Let's watch.* • *Do you think Mark will do something unusual with his arms or feet for his statue? Let's sing and watch.* • *Do they look alike as they stand like that?* • *Notice how precise Julia was at making her shoulder look just like Veronica's.*

Additional Versions of Come and Follow Me

Version 3: Line Game.   When students are able to follow the leader in a line, the whole group can follow one leader. As the group follows the leader, they imitate how the leader moves during the song (skip, twirl, jog) and freeze into the leader's statue at the cadence. The line leader can move to the end of the line after his or her turn to provide a new leader for the next turn.

Version 4: Read a Statue.   The teacher prepares statue drawings on sheets of paper. The group moves in a line, and at the cadence, the teacher holds up a drawing (or places it on an overhead) that illustrates the statue students are to imitate. For more advanced experiences with reading statues, the teacher can use a different color on the drawing for a hand, a foot, or an elbow to designate which part of the statue the students should wiggle.

Daddy Loves the Bear

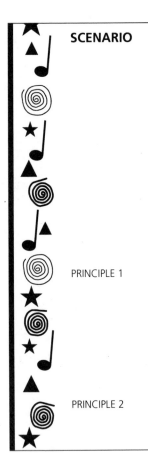

SCENARIO

PRINCIPLE 1

PRINCIPLE 2

VERSION 2: KINDNESS GAME

The four-year-olds watched inquisitively as their teacher, Mrs. Hurley, brought a stuffed toy bear with her to their circle on the floor. "Bear is a *very* special friend of mine," Mrs. Hurley began. "He loves to visit classes of children and get acquainted with them. Bear especially likes it when children are gentle with him and when they think of things to do with him that make him happy."

Looking at the bear, Mrs. Hurley thought for a moment and said, "I think that for my turn with the bear, I will rock him. I think that will make him happy and make him feel good. We have a song to sing for Bear and me." Singing and rocking the bear gently, the teacher sings, "Mrs. Hurley rocks the bear, Mrs. Hurley rocks the bear, Mrs. Hurley rocks the bear because she loves him so."

Passing the bear to the child next to her, Mrs. Hurley said, "Bradley, it's your turn. What will you do to make the bear happy? It could be something that you might do with a friend." After a moment's thought, Bradley replied, "I'd like to rock the bear!" "Okay, let's sing for Bradley and the bear," Mrs. Hurley encouraged. "Bradley rocks the bear . . ."

"Bradley, pass the bear to Leticia, it's her turn next. Let's listen to what Leticia would like to do for her turn with the bear." Without hesitation, Leticia enthusiastically shouted, "I want to rock the bear!" "Let's sing," Mrs. Hurley prompted. "Leticia rocks the bear . . ."

As Leticia passed the bear to April, Mrs. Hurley reminded students, "Boys and girls, remember that there are many ways you can make the bear happy. We could hug the bear, give him a nap, take him for a walk, or give him a bath. Leticia, Bradley, and I rocked the bear. What do you want to do, April?"

"I want to rock the bear!" April responded with glee! "April rocks the bear . . ."

Daddy Loves the Bear

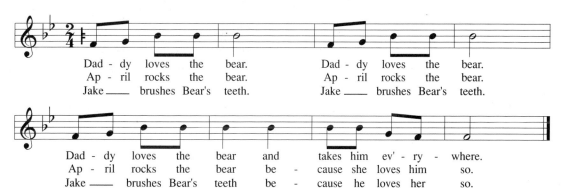

Dad - dy loves the bear.
Ap - ril rocks the bear.
Jake _____ brushes Bear's teeth.

Dad - dy loves the bear.
Ap - ril rocks the bear.
Jake _____ brushes Bear's teeth.

Dad - dy loves the bear and takes him ev' - ry - where.
Ap - ril rocks the bear be - cause she loves him so.
Jake _____ brushes Bear's teeth be - cause he loves her so.

Brief Description

Children are seated in a circle for the Invitation Game of Version 1, and individuals take turns carrying the bear around the circle. At the cadence, the child stops and invites another child to carry the bear. In the Kindness Game (Version 2), children are seated in a circle as they take turns suggesting, singing, and pantomiming ways they can show kindness to the bear. Version 3, the Helping Game, challenges students to recall and demonstrate examples of hygiene and safety practices as they take a turn with the bear.

Age Appropriateness

Version 1—Preschool through Grade 1   Invitation Game

Version 2—Preschool through Grade 2   Kindness Game

Version 3—Preschool through Grade 2   Helping Game

Degrees of Intensity

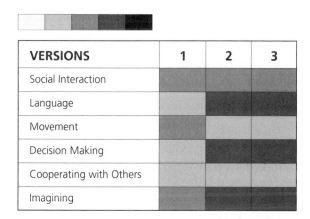

VERSIONS	1	2	3
Social Interaction			
Language			
Movement			
Decision Making			
Cooperating with Others			
Imagining			

Learning Opportunities

- *Coordinate movement* with the beginning and ending of sound: Auditory-motor skills (Version 1).
- *Pantomime* movement to language: Auditory-motor skills.

- *Explore language* by labeling ideas: Language skills (Versions 2, 3).
- *Word substitution:* Language skills, music skills.
- Extend and accept *invitations:* Social skills (Version 1).
- Share ideas for performing *good deeds:* Social skills (Version 2).
- Offer and demonstrate ideas for *hygiene* and *safety* (Version 3).
- Short-short-long phrase *structure:* Music skills.
- *Melody* patterns of SO₁ LA₁ DO DO DO: Music skills.
- *Rhythm* patterns of ♩ | ♫ ♫ ♩ (DU DU DE DU DE DU) and ♫ ♫ ♩ (DU DE DU DE DU): Music skills.

Song and Activity Background

With origins in the southern United States, this gentle song began as *Daddy Shot a Bear* (from *Folksongs of Peggy Seeger).* Locke refers to *Daddy Shot a Bear* as a traditional African American patting activity in which the song was accompanied by hand slaps on thighs (1988, 41). Although the song may have been sung in Alabama as an innocent riddle, the words troubled many contemporary children and their teachers: "Daddy shot a bear. Daddy shot a bear. Shot him through the keyhole and never touched a hair." The punch line is that Daddy shot the bear with a camera. In the 1970s, Margaret Wharram in Ontario, Canada, developed new words after a young girl found the song very disturbing: "Daddy loves the bear . . . and takes him everywhere." The game for Version 1 developed about 1987 in the classroom of Betsy Suvak while she was teaching on the Crow reservation in Wyola, Montana.

Script. Version 1: Invitation Game

Teacher	Students
With students seated in a circle, hold the bear as you would an infant, gently and firmly, with plenty of support for its head.	
• *Do you see whom I brought to class today? This is my bear, Toby.*	
• *Notice how I'm holding Toby. Describe what you see.*	Students answer with various observations.
• *Some of you may have a baby brother or sister at home. You know how important it is to be gentle but to hold a baby firmly. Why is it important to place our hand or arm under a baby's head?*	Students offer several answers, often using the same words as a classmate.
• *We're going to carry Toby as if he is a very small child. Watch and listen as I take a turn. Notice how I am holding and carrying the bear.*	
Walk and sing as you carry the bear around the outside of the circle. Stop at the cadence. *"Daddy loves the bear . . ."*	

Teacher	Students
• *The song brought me to Malcolm. Let me move around in front so he can see me.* [Bend down to eye level with Malcolm.] *Malcolm, would you like a turn to carry the bear?* [Malcolm says, "Yes."]	Students watch and join the singing. The song is sung in a calming, quiet way so that Toby can go to sleep. Prompts to remind children about their turns can include:
• *Let's be very careful as I hand him to you. I'll sit in your space while you have a turn. Remember how to support the bear's head as you walk.*	• *I wonder whom the song will lead Vivian and Toby to.*
• *Let's sing and watch as Malcolm takes a turn.* [Sing the starting pitch.] *Ready, sing . . . "Daddy loves . . . everywhere."*	• *Move around in front of the person you'll invite so that person can see your eyes.*
The play continues as individuals take turns carrying the bear, stopping at the cadence, inviting a new person to take a turn, carefully passing the bear, and sitting in the new person's space.	• *Let's watch Tyrone as he carries the bear.*
	• *What a nice invitation that was!*
Although eye contact is encouraged here, be sensitive to those children whose traditions do not include comfortable eye contact with others.	• *Your acceptance of the invitation sounded especially kind, Aika.*

Additional Versions of Daddy Loves the Bear

Version 2: Kindness Game. (See Scenario.)   In the interest of gender balance, it can be helpful to identify the bear as a male or a female in the beginning of the activity. Changing or identifying the bear's gender for each student's turn can become cumbersome and distracting. Students take turns offering and pantomiming ideas for how to be kind to the bear. As the group sings for individuals' turns, they can join the pantomiming with an imaginary bear.

▪ *David combs the bear's hair.*

▪ *Brittany buys the bear some ice cream.*

Version 3: Helping Game.   This play activity may be adapted for lessons on personal hygiene, ways to help at home, or safety practices. After students have collected various ways to keep themselves clean, be a helper, or be safe, they can practice their ideas on the bear, either teaching the bear or having the bear "act out" the idea:

▪ *Jake brushes Bear's teeth.*

▪ *Bear folds his clothes.*

▪ *Sienna fastens Bear's seatbelt.*

Did You Ever See a Lassie?

SCENARIO   VERSION 1: IMITATION GAME

The teacher began speaking the song's words with upturned palms and shrugged shoulders that expressed the question "Did you ever see a lassie, a lassie, a lassie? Did you ever see a lassie go this way and that?" When she said "this," she crossed her

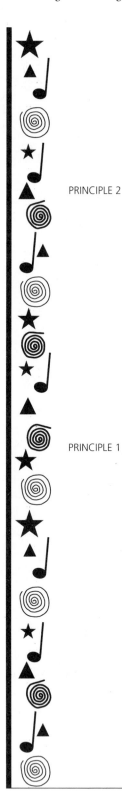

PRINCIPLE 2

PRINCIPLE 1

arms, and when she said "that," she uncrossed them and extended them from her sides. As she continued speaking the song, she crossed and uncrossed her arms each time she said "this" and "that": "Go this way and that way, and this way and that way. Did you ever see a lassie go this way and that?"

The mentally handicapped students watched, and some joined in for the gestures, mirroring their teacher's motions. This day, the plan was to increase gradually the level of initiative and independence in these students' responses. Although the chronological ages of some in the group may have seemed too old for this activity, their teacher knew that they enjoyed such simple, achievable games.

"I saw some of you joining me in the movement. Show what you remember that I did each time I said 'this.' " When students responded, many of them looked at and mimicked the ones who recalled the motion. "Yes," the teacher responded as she modeled the gesture for all to imitate, "and what was the motion for 'that'?" As teacher and students reviewed the motion, she had them say the words "this" and "that" with each change of position.

Without prelude, the teacher began singing the song and using the same motions for the activity as students joined in. Taking the lead in three more turns of the song, the teacher varied her movements, offering large, energetic as well as small, subtle gestures to the song. She knew that these were opportunities to stimulate ideas and choices in preparing students to make decisions for the activity.

"Katie, if I show you a 'this,' will you show me a 'that'? Here is our motion for 'this' [wiggling fingers]; what do you want us to do for 'that'?" Thinking for a moment, Katie slapped her hands on her thighs. "We have our 'this' and 'that'; here comes the song," the teacher said, to focus students' attention on the song and the actions. For the next turn, she offered a motion for "this" and asked Ted to show the group a "that."

Beginning at such a simple level gave the teacher chances to watch her students' responses carefully so that she could decide when to make changes in the activity. She had planned for additional choice-making opportunities and knew that making moderate changes in the activity would renew her students' interest.

One student in the class, Archie, did not have the use of his arms. Sensitive to his inability to participate in certain motions, the teacher made a special effort to smile encouragingly at Archie while the others were participating in actions he could not do. "Archie, I know you couldn't join us on that motion, but you are closely observing others' motions, and that is an important way of participating, too." At various intervals during the play, the teacher inquired of Archie, "What motion would you give us for a 'that'?" knowing that Archie's ideas might involve moving only his eyes. In an effort to help the other students become aware of and sensitive to others' physical limitations, the teacher occasionally challenged, "Please give us a motion this time that Archie can do."

When they were ready, the teacher planned to ask one student to give both the "this" and the "that" motions and to add challenges such as "Give us a 'this' and 'that' moving only your arms (feet, legs, fingers, head, face, toes, and so on)." Though the students seemed to enjoy playing the game, the teacher knew that the challenges were important steps in the development of their auditory-visual-motor coordination: thinking of and demonstrating a gesture or a movement, observing a gesture or a movement, and coordinating movement precisely with the words of the song.

Did You Ever See a Lassie?

Did you ev-er see a las-sie, a las-sie, a las-sie? Did you
ev-er see a las-sie go this way and that? Go this way and that way, and
this way and that way. Did you ev-er see a las-sie go this way and that?

Brief Description

With students in a circle or in a scatter formation for the Invitation Game (Version 1) and the Surprise Game (Version 2), the teacher sings and models a movement simultaneously on "this" and a different movement on "that." Students participate by imitating and initiating movements as they sing, observe, and listen for the specific words on which movements occur. The Partner Game of Version 3 challenges students to create movements as partners or small groups, and the Cumulative Game of Version 4 challenges students to recall, sequence, and perform all previous movement ideas shared. The Story Game of Version 5 asks students to imagine the life and context of the lassie and create motions for some activity that she may be doing.

Age Appropriateness

Version 1—Preschool through Grade 2		Imitation Game
Version 2—Grade 2 through Grade 4		Surprise Game
Version 3—Preschool through Grade 2		Partner Game
Version 4—Grade 2 through Grade 4		Cumulative Game
Version 5—Grade 4 through Grade 5		Story Game

Degrees of Intensity

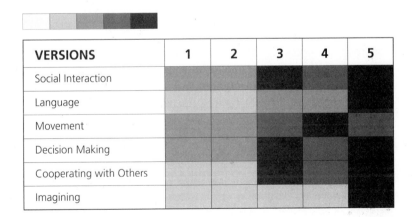

VERSIONS	1	2	3	4	5
Social Interaction					
Language					
Movement					
Decision Making					
Cooperating with Others					
Imagining					

Learning Opportunities

▪ *Coordinate movement* with beginning and ending of sound: Auditory-motor skills.

▪ *Coordinate movement* with specific words: Auditory-motor skills.

▪ *Create and demonstrate* an action: Motor skills, body awareness.

▪ *Imitate* movements: Visual-motor skills.

▪ Work with a *partner*: Social skills (Version 3).

▪ *Cooperate* within small groups: Social skills (Version 4).

▪ *Imagine* a story: Thinking skills (Version 5).

▪ *Create* and *role-play* a story: Drama skills, thinking skills (Version 5).

▪ Echo phrase *structure*: Music skills.

▪ *Melody* pattern of DO | RE SO₁ SO₁ DO: Music skills.

▪ Triple *meter*: Music skills.

Song and Activity Background

The melody of *Did You Ever See a Lassie?* comes from a German tune, *O du lieber Augustin,* which has been in print since 1788 (Opie and Opie 1985, 297–298). As a modification of *When I Was a Lady,* the "this way and that" gestures invite a playful mimicking of others (teachers, ladies, gentlemen, and so on). In the early 1900s, this game, whose lassie implies an obvious connection to Scotland, was played with one person in the center of the circle as all sang "Did you ever see a lassie, a lassie, a lassie? Did you ever see a lassie who acted like this?" During the second section of the song— "This way and that way, this way and that way. Did you ever see a lassie who acted like this?"—all would imitate the motion made by the person in the center.

Script. Version 2: Surprise Game

Teacher	Students
After students have learned the song and practiced several gestures in coordinating movement with "this" and "that," the pace of the activity can change considerably for those students who would benefit from greater degrees of interest and surprise.	Students are prepared for the sequence of the activity with as few words and instructions as possible. Brief, concise instructions can sound less like giving orders when your inflection and facial expression indicate enthusiasm and interest.
• *Now that you have lots of ideas for "this" and "that" motions, you are ready for faster challenges.* • *You will know by my gesture to you that it is your turn to give us an idea. I will gesture to two people for each turn. If you are the first one I gesture to, will your motion be on "this" or on "that"?* [The first person gestures on "this," the second on "that."]	
• *Have your idea ready for "this" and "that" because when I gesture to you, it's your turn.* • *As soon as the rest of us see your motions, we'll join in during the remainder of the song.* • *You'll notice that the song doesn't stop in this activity, it keeps going continuously. Here we go . . . let's sing, observe, and copy!*	Part of the allure of this activity is that students are caught a bit off guard and the "that" motions can be comically different from the "this" motions. The two students offering ideas for each turn may be chosen from different sections of the room, or turns can proceed in order around a circle or in rows.

Additional Versions of Did You Ever See a Lassie?

Version 1: Imitation Game. (See Scenario.)   This activity is described in its simplest form first, a form that requires little initiative or movement of the students. Because it requires so little initiative, this version may be most context appropriate for chronologically or developmentally young children.

Version 3: Partner Game.   Partners can create a motion for "this" and a motion for "that." After having some time to develop and practice their ideas with the song, classmates can share observations of partner ideas. Small groups can also collaborate to create a group "this" and "that" with similar expectations and follow-up class observations. Additional challenges for individuals, partners, and groups may include creating motions for "this" and "that" that are similar to and opposite from each other. Encourage students to observe others' movement ideas.

- *Tell us what you observed about the ways they moved their legs.*
- *Describe how they moved.*
- *Compare and contrast the movements of this set of partners with those of that set of partners.*
- *What surprised you about their movement ideas?*

Version 4: Cumulative Game.   This activity is a challenge for upper elementary students, and students can participate as individuals or as partners. Each time a new movement is shared, the entire song is sung; at the cadence of the song, all continue to repeat "go this way and that" as they review the previous actions in sequence. The most recent movement is performed first, and the activity ends with the first movement that was introduced. When the number of movements in the sequence approaches six or seven, it becomes difficult to remember them all. Some classes enjoy seeing how many movements they can remember. Others prefer to start a new sequence when remembering the current sequence correctly becomes too difficult.

Version 5: Story Game.   In small groups, students create motions that illustrate what a lassie may do for "this" and "that." In preparation for the small-group creations, students think about the person central to the song.

- *What is a lassie?*
- *Where would you expect her to live?*
- *What kinds of things do you think she is expected to do during a day?*
- *What kinds of things do you think she enjoys doing?*

The following questions can be asked of the group or of individuals at intervals before or after a group sings and demonstrates their ideas. Sometimes more imagery is created when one student is asked to enter into the story or to take the role of storyteller.

- *Jeanie, how old is this lassie?*
- *Scott, where is her house?*
- *Manny, how many rooms does it have?*
- *Mabel, if you're the lassie, what are you wearing? Where did you get it?*

After watching a group's idea, the teacher and other students can ask questions that create more imagery for the activity.

- *Why is she sweeping the floor? Did someone make a mess?*
- *Milking the goat? Why is she doing that? What is the goat's name? How long has she had her? Describe the goat.*

The teacher guides the group in building a scenario that is all their own, weaving students' ideas into a scene about the lassie, tying ideas together from one group to the next. *"Well, we know that Lassie likes to gather flowers [from a previous group's idea]. When does she have time to do all that laundry?"* This activity could easily evolve into an art project and a creative writing project.

Drunken Sailor

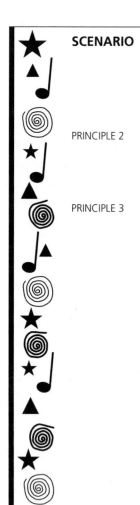

SCENARIO

PRINCIPLE 2

PRINCIPLE 3

VERSION 1: CREATING VERSES

"Remember the sea chantey we sang the other day? Here is a verse from that song." The teacher then sang, "'What shall we do with a seasick sailor?. . . morning.' Here is a sailor, sick in bed in the middle of the ocean. The sea is rolling, the boat rises and falls, all of which just make the poor guy sicker. The other sailors have to work harder when one of them is sick, so they do everything they can think of to make him better. They sing about what they can do to help the sailor feel better. What would make him feel better?"

As students pondered the question, the teacher realized they needed a little help to get started. "Well, when you haven't felt well, what did your mother or father do to help you feel better?" Students began suggesting, "Give him an aspirin," "Feed him chicken soup," and "Let him sleep."

"On the ship, as in many songs of this type, people would add their ideas to the song—they would sing the new words as a new verse for the song. How would we put your ideas in the song? What would we sing?" The teacher then sang "Feed him chicken soup" to the beginning few pitches of the melody and hummed the remaining pitches of the phrase. The students realized more words were needed to complete the melodic phrase.

"Feed him chicken soup in the morning," shouted Frankie. "Let's sing it!" responded the teacher enthusiastically. Soon the students were offering complete phrases: "Give him an aspirin and let him sleep," "Never let him get a whiff of dinner," "Keep it quiet till he's better."

Each line offered by the students was sung, repeated three times, and completed with "earlye in the morning" at the cadence ("earlye" was pronounced with a long *i* sound, as in "eye"). "Can we draw pictures of some of these ideas?" asked Brandy. "Sure, that would be a great idea," responded their teacher. "We don't have time to do it during music class, but if you want to make some pictures at home, I'll be happy to help out. At the next class, I'll furnish the paper so that we're all working with the same size. Then you take it home and make colorful drawings of the verses, and when you bring them back to me, we can make them into a book for our class. Perhaps some of you would like to share your books with the primary students; I could probably arrange for you to read to them. You may want to think of new verses for our next class. See you then!"

Drunken Sailor

Brief Description

Through questions and song repetitions, students explore and learn about the context of a sea chantey, the work on a sailing ship, and the terminology associated with a sailing ship. Students dramatize the work of swabbing decks, hoisting sails, weighing anchors, manning the crow's nest, and other tasks. This movement can be done in a circle formation, in a scatter formation, or beside desks.

Age Appropriateness

Version 1—Grade 4 through Grade 6   Creating Verses

Version 2—Grade 4 through Grade 6   Drama Activity

Degrees of Intensity

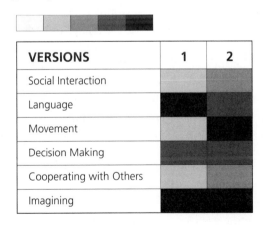

Learning Opportunities

- Create *movement* to dramatize ideas: Motor skills.

- *Imagine* and *pantomime* the work, world, and life of a sailor: Drama skills.

- *Create verses* that match the *rhythm* and *structure* of a song: Language skills, music skills.

- Explore the *meaning* and *cultural context* of a song: Social studies skills.
- Consider ways to *assist* a sick person.
- AB (binary) song *structure*: Music skills.
- *Melody* patterns of unisons (LA₁ LA₁ LA₁ LA₁): Music skills.
- *Rhythm* patterns of ♫♫ ♫♫ ♫ ♫ (DU DETA DU DETA DU DE DU DE) and ♩ ♩. ♫ ♫ (DU DU TA DU DE DU DE): Music skills.

Song and Activity Background

Drunken Sailor is a sea chantey, sung by sailors to accompany their work. Sung with all the color and rhythmic vitality one might expect from a song of this origin, *Drunken Sailor* could be used for capstan or halyard work, both of which would require a long, steady song. The capstan is a large spool-like drum used to wind up the cable that raises and lowers the anchor. Removable arms extend from the top of the capstan and are used to push the capstan around. The work that a song like this would accompany was walking around, pushing on the capstan arms, slowly winding a cable. A halyard is the rope used to hoist a sail. To hoist a sail, several men would take hold of the halyard and, depending on the size of the sail, would either walk or run down the deck of the ship, hauling the sail aloft. The rhythm of the capstan and halyard chanteys was even, the tempo was steady, and many verses might be needed.

Each chantey has a specific purpose, and some might be fit for one job only. The timing needed for hoisting one sail might not be the same as that needed for a smaller or a larger sail. We can imagine that the chanteyman, the sailor responsible for the songs, would make up verses about the particular sailors on the boat and their personal experiences. His fellow sailors would sing the chorus, and the chanteyman, with a good memory and a ready wit, would sing both traditional and improvised verses. The sea chantey coordinated the work of groups of sailors, providing a timing mechanism to increase their efficiency, and an open forum to voice the hardships of a life at sea and maybe with an uncompromising captain. The chanteys were a way to speed up or slow down the work as needed and a form of entertainment that might spark a smile or a laugh, however grim, from the sailors at their work.

A 1984 article about sea chanteys in *Folksong in the Classroom* cites British poet John Masefield's observation about sea chanteys: "It often seemed as though new life entered the singers as they sang. Perhaps nobody ever heard one of these songs being sung at the rope or capstan without feeling that song was indeed a divine thing and a gift of the gods to men." And that is in reference to a work song!

A melodic variant of *Drunken Sailor* was found in Seeger (1948) as *Rose, Rose, and Up She Rises*. Verses included "What shall we do with sleepy Jackie? . . . Hoo'ray and up he rises . . . so early in the morning."

The alternative title of *Seasick Sailor* came from a group of undergraduate education students at Montana State University who were concerned about the reference to excessive use of alcohol. This small change does not seem to alter the rhythm, vitality, or story of the song, and it was an easy adjustment for those students to make. Other students and teachers, however, have been split on whether to sing "drunken" or "seasick." Some feel that the meaning and context of the song is fundamentally changed by this substitution and that it is important not to change cultural artifacts, which reflect the mores and beliefs of other generations and societal groups, to fit present-day opinions. Considering that "sleepy Jackie" is a historical version of the song, it is difficult to hold a firm view that the words of a song should not be changed. Songs such as this are meant to serve the needs of the people who sing them. We can learn about other people by thinking about the songs they sang and can also change songs to learn more about ourselves.

Dr. Anna Langness (Colorado) developed the idea of making the seasick sailor feel better, which helps students to focus on supportive and helpful actions and treatments. Traditional verses of the song—"Shave his belly with a rusty razor," for example—reflect the roughness of a sailor's life. Even if a comparable roughness is a part of students' lives, it may make sense to provide them with models of kinder behavior.

Script. Version 1: Creating Verses

Teacher	Students
Sing the chorus of the song: *"Weigh, hey, and up she rises."* • *Can you figure out who might be singing this song?* • *I'm not asking if you know, I'm asking you to speculate.* • *Who is the "she" and why is she rising?*	Often, students think the song suggests an ocean or a sailing feeling. Students try to decide what is rising. Common suggestions are "The moon over the bay," "The sun as the ship is getting ready to set sail," "A whale sounding," "A sailor trying to get out of bed," "The anchor," "The sails." As students suggest ideas, repeat the chorus and encourage the class to sing along.
• *This is a song about the sea. In fact, it is a sea chantey, a song that sailors sang to accompany their lives on the sea.* • *This song is a work song, and sailors sang it as they worked on the ship. What kind of work would sailors have to do?*	Students discuss possible chores that sailors had to do: swabbing the decks, hoisting the sails, cooking the grub, and weighing (lifting) the anchor.
As ideas are presented, ask students to imagine and demonstrate how that type of work would look. Then sing and act out the chore, capturing the spirit and the context of the song. • *How would we look if we were doing that work? Show us.* • *Can you imagine why sailors would sing as they worked?* • *Let's sing as we act out that idea.*	Use comments or questions to add details to the dramatizations: • *You're swabbing the deck? How big is the mop?* • *We see you cooking the grub. What's for dinner? Do you like your job as cook?* • *How many men does it take to lift that anchor? What does the anchor look like?*

Eensy Weensy Spider

Eensy Weensy Spider
(Itsy Bitsy Spider)

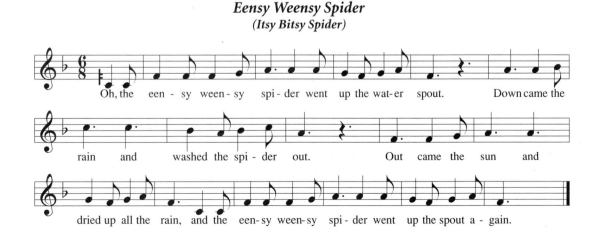

Oh, the een-sy ween-sy spi-der went up the wat-er spout. Down came the rain and washed the spi-der out. Out came the sun and dried up all the rain, and the een-sy ween-sy spi-der went up the spout a-gain.

Brief Description

As the first phrase is sung, illustrate a climbing motion by touching thumbs to index fingers and continually reaching up with the lower fingers as "the eensy weensy spider went up the water spout." With younger children, you may want to climb by using thumbs together and index fingers together, continually reaching the lower fingers up to climb. Fingers are spread, and they wiggle downward for "down came the rain"; then they make a sweeping motion outward for "and washed the spider out." Make a large circle with your arms for "out came the sun and dried up all the rain." For the final phrase, "and the eensy weensy spider climbs up the spout again," repeat the climbing motion of the first phrase. (See Chapter 6 for descriptions of motions and the musical skills they represent.)

Age Appropriateness

Version 1—Preschool through Grade 1

Degrees of Intensity

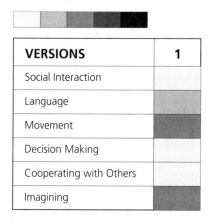

VERSIONS	1
Social Interaction	
Language	
Movement	
Decision Making	
Cooperating with Others	
Imagining	

Learning Opportunities

- *Coordinate movement* with beginning and ending of sound: Auditory-motor skills.
- *Coordinate movement* with specific words: Auditory-motor skills.
- Experience musical *phrases* through movement changes: Music skills.
- Short-short-long phrase *structure* and anacruses: Music skills.
- *Melody* patterns of SO₁ | DO DO DO RE MI MI and MI | RE DO RE MI DO: Music skills.
- *Rhythm* patterns of ♪ | ♩ ♪♩ ♪♩. (DI DU DI DU DI DU) and ♩♪ | ♩ ♪♩ ♪♩. ♩ (DU DI DU DI DU DI DU DU): Music skills.

Song and Activity Background

The well-known song *Eensy Weensy Spider* is a finger play enjoyed by many children from toddlers through primary grades. Seeger noted that it originated in North Carolina (1948, 126). The song is known also as *Itsy Bitsy Spider,* and the title may be spelled in various ways: *Eency Weency Spider* (Seeger) or *Incey Wincey Spider* (Baring-Gould and Baring-Gould 1967, 235).

The Farmer in the Dell

SCENARIO

PRINCIPLE 2

PRINCIPLE 1

VERSION 2: INVITATION GAME

The second-grade class was playing *The Farmer in the Dell.* As the sitting circle of children watched, the teacher focused their attention by saying, "I wonder where the song will take me?" Then, she sang, "The farmer in the dell, . . . dell." As she sang, Ms. Tyson walked around the outside of the circle and stopped at the cadence. "Look at this. The song had me stop behind Felicia."

"Can you point to where I was when the song began?" Ms. Tyson asked, prompting the children to recall and point to her starting space. "In the next part of the song, we sing, 'The farmer takes the wife,' so let's see where the song will cadence this time. Any guesses?" The children predicted where the song would stop the teacher. "Well, let's find out. [Singing] Start here . . . The farmer takes the wife . . . wife."

When the song cadenced, Ms. Tyson stopped behind Mahmoud, moved around in front of him and asked, "Mahmoud, would you be the wife?" "Yes," he quietly replied and stood, took Ms. Tyson's hand, and followed her in a line around the circle. Ms. Tyson had learned that it seemed more comfortable for students to ask "Do you want to be *the wife*" than to ask "Do you want to be *my wife*." Therefore, she chose the wording of her invitation carefully and knew that the way she introduced this portion of the activity would likely affect the way her students approached and responded to the invitations. "We're role playing in this game, and that means Mahmoud and I are actors, portraying characters that we may not be like in real life. It can be fun to pretend you are something or someone different."

"Let's see whom the song picks to be the child," Ms. Tyson prompted as she began the song. "'The wife takes the child, . . . child.'" When Mahmoud's feet stopped moving at the cadence, Ms. Tyson suggested, "Mahmoud, your feet stopped right at the cadence. Who is sitting closest to your feet?" After some consideration, Mahmoud answered, "Trent." "Why don't you move around in front of him so he knows you're speaking to him. Then, look in his eyes and ask him if he wants to be the child." Quietly, shyly, Mahmoud and Trent exchanged words, and Trent got up to join the farmer and the wife. As the song progressed, children were reminded to sing, to stop with the cadence, and to invite a classmate to become one of the family of characters. Although Ms. Tyson encouraged eye contact, she did not enforce this portion of the invitations. She knew that just by mentioning it, she was giving students options for practicing their communication skills.

When the farmer, wife, child, nurse, dog, cat, rat, and cheese were collected, Ms. Tyson focused the children's attention: "Watch and listen to what happens now that the family is all collected." Singing "The farmer says 'good-bye,' [waving and speaking 'good-bye' on the rest], the farmer says 'good-bye' [good-bye!]. Hi-ho the derry-o, the farmer says 'good-bye' [good-bye!]." Ms. Tyson circled with the students and left the group to move into a space in the sitting circle. Characters continued to walk, sing, and say good-bye during their verse. "How would a cat say 'good-bye'?" prompted Ms. Tyson as she encouraged students to role-play their characters during their short speaking solos.

Characters continued to say good-bye and leave the group until only the cheese was left. "The cheese stands alone, the cheese stands alone. Hi-ho the derry-o, the cheese stands alone" was sung as the cheese moved into the center of the circle and the students sang and clapped.

The Farmer in the Dell

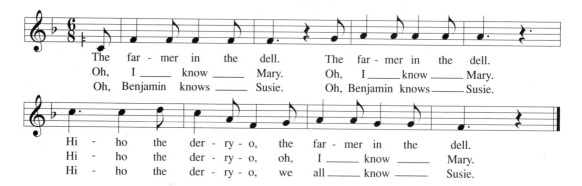

The far - mer in the dell. The far - mer in the dell.
Oh, I ____ know ____ Mary. Oh, I ____ know ____ Mary.
Oh, Benjamin knows ____ Susie. Oh, Benjamin knows ____ Susie.

Hi - ho the der - ry - o, the far - mer in the dell.
Hi - ho the der - ry - o, oh, I ____ know ____ Mary.
Hi - ho the der - ry - o, we all ____ know ____ Susie.

Verse 2—*The farmer takes the wife.*   Verse 9—*The farmer says "good-bye."*

Verse 3—*The wife takes the child.*   Verse 10—*The wife says "good-bye."*

Verse 4—*The child takes the nurse.*   Verse 11—*The child says "good-bye."*

Verse 5—*The nurse takes the dog.*   Verse 12—*The nurse says "good-bye."*

Verse 6—*The dog takes the cat.*   Verse 13—*The dog says "good-bye."*

Verse 7—*The cat takes the rat.*   Verse 14—*The cat says "good-bye."*

Verse 8—*The rat takes the cheese.*   Verse 15—*The rat says "good-bye."*

                                             Verse 16—*The cheese stands alone.*

Brief Description

In Version 1 (the Knowing Game), students are seated in a circle, and the teacher takes several turns saying whom he or she knows: "Oh, I know Mary, Oh, I know Mary. Hi-ho the derry-o, oh, I know Mary." Students are then asked to tell whom they know, and the song is sung about both students ("Oh, Benjamin knows Susie . . ."). In the Invitation Game of Version 2, students are seated in a circle and one student (the farmer) walks around the outside as all sing the first verse. The farmer stops at the cadence, then continues to walk as the second verse is sung. Characters are invited to join with each turn as the song's cadence determines who will be invited. When all characters have joined the "family," individuals say "good-bye" one at a time and rejoin the sitting circle as the group sings. The cheese stands alone in the center of the circle for the final verse. Version 3 is a name game in which names are sung, three at a time, around a seated circle. The Interview Activity of Version 4 engages students with a partner and involves finding out what partners like. The ideas are then written as phrases to the song, illustrated, and sung by partners and the class.

Age Appropriateness

Version 1—Preschool through Grade 2   Knowing Game

Version 2—Preschool through Grade 2   Invitation Game

Version 3—Grade 1 through Grade 4   Name Game

Version 4—Grade 1 through Grade 2   Interview Activity

Degrees of Intensity

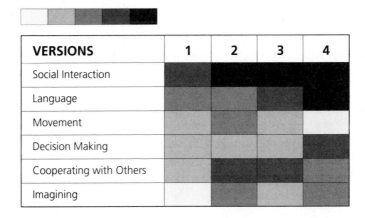

VERSIONS	1	2	3	4
Social Interaction				
Language				
Movement				
Decision Making				
Cooperating with Others				
Imagining				

Learning Opportunities

- *Coordinate movement* with beginning and ending of sound: Auditory-motor skills (Version 2).

- Speak in complete *sentences*: Language skills (Version 1).

- Extend and accept *invitations*: Social skills (Version 2).

- *Role-play* characters of the song: Drama skills (Version 2).

- Recall and sequence *names* and connect them with faces: Social skills, auditory-visual skills, thinking skills (Version 3).

- *Share information* about oneself: Social skills (Version 4).

- *Converse* to focus on and collect information about others: Social skills (Version 4).

- *Write and draw* ideas: Language skills, visual arts skills (Version 4).

- Short-short-long phrase *structure*: Music skills.

- *Melody* patterns of SO₁ | DO DO DO DO DO and RE | MI MI RE RE DO: Music skills.

- *Rhythm* patterns of ♪ | ♩ ♫ ♫. (DI DU DI DU DI DU) and ♩. ♩ ♫ ♫ (DU DU DI DU DI DU): Music skills.

Song and Activity Background

The Farmer in the Dell apparently originated in Germany, and came first to America and then to Britain. The first recorded version of this traditional folk song can be traced to 1826. In that version, the farmer sits on a stool, then chooses a wife, who sits on his lap. Then a child, a maid, and a serving man are chosen in turn and sit on the lap of the person who chose them. Finally, the stool is pulled from beneath them, or they may kiss and leave one by one (Opie and Opie 1985, 187).

The well-known melody resembles *A-Hunting We Will Go* and appears in several sources with varying rhythm patterns. One of the earliest sources for the version appearing here is Newell's *Games of American Children* (1883). This "best known of ring games," as the Opies call it (p. 185), is usually played with the farmer in the center of a circle, picking a wife (sometimes with eyes closed) to join him in the center when the song tells him to do so. In successive verses, new characters are picked and join the group in the middle, who sometimes circle in the opposite direction from the outer circle. Word variations include "The farmer's in his den," "The farmer wants a wife," and "The cat takes a mouse (rather than rat)." By far, the phrase that offers the greatest range of variants is "Hi-ho the derry-o": "E I E I," "Heigh ho! for Rowley O," "Heigh ho the cherry ho," "Hey hi cherry-i," "E O the alley oh," and "B-I-N-G-O" (Opie and Opie 1985, 184–189). In a favorite version of some children in Britain, the dog chooses a bone and the game ends with "We all pat the bone." At this point, children would pat the child who was the bone. Although some children may enjoy this version, the physical roughness has made some adults quite uneasy.

Version 1 of this game was learned from Margaret Wharram as she taught special education students in Ontario, Canada, about 1974. Version 2 and Version 3 are adapted from Richards (1985, 19). Version 4 was found in the Grade 1 classroom of Ray Levi in Oberlin, Ohio, about 1975.

Script. Version 3: Name Game

Teacher	Students
This activity can begin without prelude. Gesture to each student as you would in making an introduction, and sing the names of three students in order around the circle. • *"There's Michael and Todd and Fredricka. There's Michael and Todd and Fredricka. Hi-ho the derry-o, there's Michael and Todd and Fredricka."*	Students sit in a circle as they watch and listen to the teacher.
• *Did you notice how I gestured to each student as I sang his or her name? Let's sing the name again, so you can join me in using gestures and singing names. Be sure you look at their eyes as you sing each name.* The song is repeated, and a palm-up, relaxed hand is used to indicate each student as names are sung. Model looking at each student as his or her name is sung.	Students are prompted to imitate the teacher model for gesturing and are reminded to make eye contact with others. A brief discussion on making introductions could be interjected here.
• *Notice whose names will be sung next. Using your inner hearing, do you hear how their names will sound in the song?* • *Let's sing, gesture, and look at their eyes. [Sing.] Ready . . . "There's Tina and Kim and Angie . . ."*	The song is sung at a tempo gentle enough to allow the children to pronounce the names clearly and to linger momentarily on the individual whose name is being sung.
The activity continues as names are sung around the circle. When students are ready for an extra challenge, the three whose names are being sung may stand. Then on the "hi-ho the derry-o" phrase, they quickly change places so that the group must sing the names on the final phrase in whatever order the students appear, left to right.	Some classes enjoy closing their eyes during "hi-ho the derry-o" so that the order in which they sing the names will be a surprise.
As a brief review of class names or as a personal acknowledgment of all students in a class, the song can be sung with three new names for each phrase, therefore adding nine names for each repetition of the song. • *"There's Steve and Lin and Taylor. There's Meggie and Veronica and Rosemary. Hi-ho the derry-o, there's Keegan and Mack and Natasha."*	As students sing, gesture, and look at students whose names are being sung, they are given the leadership role in singing the song. In this activity, it is important to avoid overleading as you sing the challenges set up for the students.

Additional Versions of The Farmer in the Dell

Version 1: Knowing Game.   As students sit in a circle, the teacher takes the first few turns, saying whom he or she knows, singing and gesturing to that student.

> ◼ *Oh, I know Linton. Oh, I know Linton. Hi-ho the derry-o, we all know Linton.*

Then students take turns acknowledging someone in the circle that they know. As a student is acknowledged, all sing his or her name in the song. The acknowledged student then names someone he or she knows. The simplicity of this version makes it especially appropriate for chronologically or developmentally young students. Some classes enjoy creating a movement or a gesture for the "hi-ho the derry-o" phrase of the song.

> ◼ *Benjamin, whom do you know?* Benjamin answers, "Annie," and is encouraged to use a complete sentence.
>
> ◼ *Would you please use the whole sentence "I know Annie"?* Benjamin speaks, "I know Annie." The group then sings the second phrase, *Oh, Benjamin knows Annie. Oh, Benjamin knows Annie. Hi-ho the derry-o, we all know Annie.*
>
> ◼ *Annie, whom do you know? When you decide, would you please state the sentence?*

Version 4: Interview Activity.   In pairs, students interview a partner to find out what their partner likes. After sharing ideas, they write the words to the new verse of the song: "Oh, I know Tim. Oh, Tim likes me. Hi-ho the derry-o, Tim likes me." Students can be prompted by naming categories: *"Think of something you like to eat or do." "Think of the people you like."* Depending on the age and the reading and writing skills of students, the teacher can print a model on the board for students to copy and fill in the blanks. After writing their verse, students can illustrate it on the same paper. Papers can be shared for the class to read and sing and can be displayed for further practice with reading and singing.

Here We Are Together

SCENARIO

VERSION 1: NAME GAME

"Oh, here we are together, together, together. Oh, here we are together, all sitting on the floor." It was the first week of school, and the teacher, Ms. Coffin, intended to capture the young children's attention as they were seated on the floor in a circle. She sang the song several times without interruption, nonverbally eliciting their attention and participation. "Did you notice what my hands did when we sang 'floor'?" "They touched the floor!" chirped a chorus of eager children. "Yes! Let's see if you can do that this time. Your challenge is to touch the floor when you sing the word. It takes precise listening and moving—good luck!"

As the group sang the song again, many children coordinated their movement with the final cadence of the song, and some touched the floor before or after the song ended. "I saw so many of you listening that time and connecting your movement with your hearing! I wonder if you can still touch the floor at the end of the

PRINCIPLE 2

PRINCIPLE 3

song if you keep your hands on your head as you sing. Will we be able to do it? Let's find out!" The simple suggestion to hold hands on heads and the challenge to touch the floor at the cadence seemed to delight the children. After two more turns, children suggested where to place their hands for the beginning of the song. Both teacher and students received each new idea with interest and eagerness.

Bobby began slapping the floor with his hands as the song ended, and a few children joined him in this variation on the game. Wanting to reframe this behavior before it spread, Ms. Coffin added a challenge: "Let's see if we can tap the floor lightly, just with our fingertips this time." Because not all children responded immediately to the new challenge, Ms. Coffin added a variation and, with a twinkle in her eye, prompted, "How many of you think you can touch the floor with only your fingernails? Let's try it."

Here We Are Together

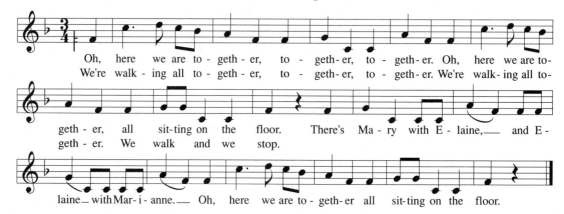

Oh, here we are to - geth - er, to - geth - er, to - geth - er. Oh, here we are to -
We're walk - ing all to - geth - er, to - geth - er, to - geth - er. We're walk - ing all to -

geth - er, all sit - ting on the floor. There's Ma - ry with E - laine,___ and E -
geth - er. We walk and we stop.

laine ___ with Mar - i - anne. ___ Oh, here we are to - geth - er all sit - ting on the floor.

Brief Description

As students sit in a circle for Version 1 (the Name Game), they coordinate movements with the cadence points by starting and stopping movement with the song. Then, the song becomes the context for learning names and focusing on individuals. Guided by the teacher, students learn to gesture invitingly to one another, to treat others' names with respect, and to challenge themselves by making decisions within the play. Version 2, the Pattern Game, challenges students to sing and sequence names according to patterns suggested by classmates. In the Move and Stop Game of Version 3, locomotor movements are used for practicing moving and stopping with points of closure. Version 4 further challenges students to pace their locomotor movements so that they can return to their spaces at the cadence.

Age Appropriateness

Version 1—Preschool through Grade 1	Name Game
Version 2—Grade 2 through Grade 5	Pattern Game
Version 3—Preschool through Grade 2	Move and Stop
Version 4—Grade 2 through Grade 4	Move and Return

Degrees of Intensity

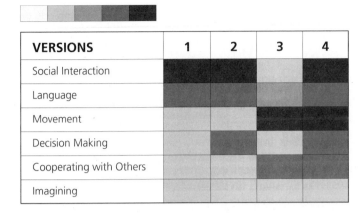

Learning Opportunities

- *Coordinate movement* with beginning and ending of sound: Auditory-motor skills.

- *Learn names*: Visual skills, language skills (Versions 1, 2).

- *Word substitution*: Language skills, music skills (Versions 1, 2).

- Read and perform *patterns* for singing names: Thinking skills (Version 2).

- Demonstrate and name *locomotor movements*: Motor skills (Versions 3, 4).

- *Maintain pace and space* while moving in a scatter formation: Auditory-visual-motor skills, spatial skills (Version 4).

- Echo phrase *structure*: Music skills.

- *Melody* patterns of DO | RE SO₁ SO₁ MI DO and DO | RE RE SO₁ SO₁ DO: Music skills.

- Triple *meter* and *rhythm* pattern of ♩ | ♫ ♩ ♩ ♩ (DU DU DE DU DU DU): Music skills.

Song and Activity Background

An adaptation of the familiar melody *The More We Get Together the Happier We'll Be*, one version of the song continues, "For your friends are my friends and my friends are your friends, the more we get together the happier we'll be." The tune is very similar to *Did You Ever See a Lassie?* and may also be related to the German song *O du lieber Augustin*. The name game and the movement games presented here were developed in the 1970s by Richards to have a name game for working with large groups of people and to incorporate movement into the singing activity (1985, 29). Taking the hand of the person whose name is sung next developed in the classroom of Margaret Wharram, Wheatley, Ontario, in the 1970s.

Script. Version 1: Name Game

Teacher	Students
With facial expression and gestures, elicit focus and participation as you sing the song twice. Each time you sing the cadence word, "floor," lightly touch the floor with fingertips. • *What did you see my hands do when we sang "floor"?*	Students answer with various descriptions of their observations.
• *You try it this time. Your challenge is to touch the floor when you sing the word. It takes precise listening and moving. Let's all sing the song.* Sing a starting pitch and begin the song.	As they sing the song, students may show varying degrees of skill in coordinating their movement with the cadence.
• *Many of you were listening and connecting your movement to your hearing! "Cadence" is the word we'll use to identify the end of the song.* • *You know my name—it's Mr. Moss. Let's find out who's seated beside me. Would you please tell us your name?* [Gesturing to Harley]	After Harley speaks his name, the teacher encourages: • *Would you say your name again so we can all say it after you do?* • *Let's all say his name just like he said it.*
• *Now let's find out who's sitting next to Harley. Let's listen and say her name right after she says it so we can remember it.* • *We know three people's names, and we can sing them in our song!* Begin to sing names in order around the circle to the song melody. • *"There's Mr. Moss with Harley and Harley with Anna. Oh here . . . floor."* As each name is sung, use a gentle, welcoming gesture to indicate each student.	Anna speaks her name and the class repeats it. Students' attention is focused on individuals and their names through the song and the gestures. Gestures are similar to those used in introductions, with palms up and fingers relaxed. Students can be led to discuss whether this gesture feels inviting.
• *Did you hear how those names fit into our song? Let's sing them again and gesture to each person as we sing the name.* [Singing the starting pitch] *Ready, sing. . . "There's Mr. Moss with . . . floor."* • *Let's find three more people whose names we can learn and sing. Let's listen for the person beside Anna to say her name, then we'll repeat it. Would you please say your name for us?* • *Let's say her name just like she said it, everyone . . . 'Diane.' And let's listen as we add two more names.* Special care is taken to listen to how a child says her or his name so that the teacher and the students match the child's pronunciation.	 "Diane," the child replied. As the teacher gestures, Erica and Marylou say their names for the class to repeat. Then names are added to the song, three at a time, using gestures to help focus and acknowledge.

Teacher	Students
At various intervals, challenges can be added: • *Let's go all the way to the beginning and see if we remember all the names we have learned so far. [Singing] "There's Mr. Moss with Harley, and Harley with Anna, and Anna with Diane, and Diane with Erica, and Erica with Marylou. Oh, here . . . floor."* • *Let's start with Luke's name and sing to Maggie's name. Can you find them with your eyes before we sing?* • *Whose name shall we begin with this time, and how far shall we sing?* • *Who can sing each name? Are you ready to read faces and sing names? Here comes our song.*	Children use gestures and sing as they track faces and names around the circle. The repetition of names within this song helps children learn and sing each person's name. The activity is a way of learning names, reviewing names, and acknowledging each person.

Another class time, Mr. Moss began singing and, as he added the name of the child seated next to him, he reached over and took her hand. "There's Mr. Moss with Veronica [taking her hand], and Veronica with Sarah [gesturing for Veronica to take Sarah's hand] and Sarah with Max [Sarah takes Max's hand]. . ." The song was sung at a speed that allowed children a moment to take the hand of the person next to him or her, and all the children's names were sung. The song ended with all holding hands in the air for "Oh, here we are together," then touching the floor lightly for "all sitting on the floor."

Additional Versions of Here We Are Together

Version 2: Pattern Game. When students know others' names, they can be challenged to sing names in various patterns around the circle. Suggestions for patterns come from students as they are seated in a circle or in rows. Here are some sample challenges to prompt student ideas.

- *Let's sing every other name this time, skipping one in between.*
- *Let's sing a pattern of three forward and one back.*
- *Let's sing only names that have two syllables.*
- *Sing only names that begin with consonants.*
- *Someone give us a new pattern for singing names.*

Version 3: Move and Stop Game. Playing with movement and practicing coordination with points of closure are emphasized by suggesting ways to sing and move.

- *Listen to this song and tell us what you predict we will be doing as we sing it. "We're walking all together, together, together. We're walking all together, we walk and we stop." Who can describe what our activity will be?*

Students predict and describe; then they walk and sing, coordinating their movements and pacing themselves with the song. They are encouraged to "freeze" when the song ends, focusing on the cadence. When students are adept at listening, starting, stopping, and singing simultaneously, new ways of moving may be suggested.

- *"We're jogging (swaying, shuffling, hopping) all together . . . stop."*

Version 4: Move and Return Game. Students are challenged to move away from a space and back again, coordinating and pacing movement with the song.

■ *Look at the space on which you are standing. Notice the people and things around you. Could you find that space again if you left it?*

■ *Listen to the song and tell us what you predict we will be doing as we sing it. "We're walking all together, together, together. We're walking all together, right back to our space." Describe what we will be doing.*

Students describe walking and ending back at their space.

■ *Draw an imaginary circle around yourself. You may think of it as a bubble if you like. Your challenge will be to keep a space with you, walk without colliding, and be back on your space just when you sing the word "space." Let's try it!*

Students walk and sing, coordinating their movement and pacing themselves with the song. Students offer suggestions for ways to move. Moving and singing names may be combined into one activity. Choice-making for students increases as they gain confidence and competence in meeting the challenges of the activity.

■ *How else could we move away from our space this time?*

■ *Whose name shall we begin with and which direction shall we go when we get back to our space and are ready to sing names?*

Hot Cross Buns

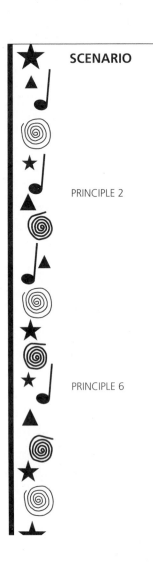

SCENARIO

PRINCIPLE 2

PRINCIPLE 6

VERSION 1: HAND-JIVE GAME

"Find a partner by the count of six, please. One, two . . ." Students scurried to join a partner before their teacher said "Freeze" after counting to six. When students were facing their partners, she challenged, "Lips are closed. Eyes and ears are on me for further instructions." Students responded to these concise directions by quietly focusing on the teacher.

"Some of you may have experience with hand jives. Those are the hand-clapping games that many young people have played since long ago. Can any of you show us some movements that you have done or seen as part of a hand-jive activity? Try out an idea with your partner; then raise your hand if you have something to share." The practice time with a partner allowed students to try out their ideas before they shared them with the class. From past experience, their teacher knew that she could expect more confident participation in the activity if she invested a short amount of time in practice before the activity began.

"I see hands raised for these partners to share. Let's listen and watch their idea." As the teacher called on partners to share, she accepted the ideas—from those who showed one simple movement to those who could demonstrate a sequence of movements.

Demonstrating as she spoke each term, the teacher offered students terminology with which to describe their various movements. "I've seen claps, pats, snaps, and stamps as well as variations of each of those ways of moving. Now that we have seen a variety of ideas, listen to the song that we'll use with our hand-jive movements." As the teacher sang *Hot Cross Buns,* many students joined in singing the familiar melody.

"Your assignment is to create a hand jive to this song with your partner. Your challenge is to sing and coordinate your hand jive with your singing. When you sit down on the floor facing your partner with your lips closed, I'll know you've completed your assignment and are ready to share."

As the whole group sang and practiced their hand jives, they soon discovered that they could not all work at the same tempo. After briefly acknowledging this discovery, the teacher invited partners to demonstrate their ideas as the class sang and ob-

served. To encourage observation, the teacher would occasionally ask questions of the group: "What did you notice about this couple's movements?" "Did anyone notice a similarity between this couple's idea and another pair that we've seen?" "Describe the pattern of this pair's movements."

As closure to the activity, the teacher selected a moderate tempo for singing the song and asked students to match that tempo for their hand jives. Then all sang and performed their hand jives together. "Just before we finish this activity, listen to the rhythmic sounds our hand patterns make. We'll use the same moderate tempo, but let's sing the song in our inner hearing this time. I'll give the starting pitch and signal the beginning, then we'll sing 'inside' as we listen to our hands." Faces showed obvious delight as the students listened to the intricate rhythmic sounds created by their combined hand-jive movements.

Hot Cross Buns

Hot cross buns. Hot cross buns. One a pen-ny, two a pen-ny, hot cross buns.

Brief Description

Version 1 is a hand-jive activity in which partners create hand movements to the song. Version 2 introduces hand signs and solfa syllables for the melody of the song. Version 3 challenges students to explore language and create new verses.

Age Appropriateness

Version 1—Grade 3 through Grade 6	Hand-Jive Game
Version 2—Kindergarten through Grade 3	Hand-Sign Game
Version 3—Grade 1 through Grade 4	New Verses

Degrees of Intensity

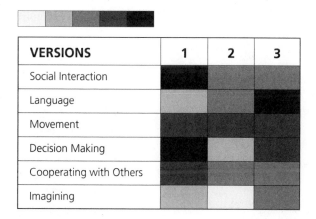

VERSIONS	1	2	3
Social Interaction			
Language			
Movement			
Decision Making			
Cooperating with Others			
Imagining			

Learning Opportunities

- *Coordinate patterns of movement* with patterns of sound: Auditory-motor skills (Versions 1, 2).

- *Work* with a partner: Social skills (Versions 1, 2).

- Make nonevaluative *observations*: Social skills, language skills (Version 1).

- Coordinate *hand signs* with *solfa syllables* and melody: Music skills, auditory-motor skills (Version 2).
- *Word substitution* in creating new verses: Language skills (Version 3).
- *Explore language* by labeling ideas: Language skills (Version 3).
- Short-short-long phrase *structure*: Music skills.
- *Melody* patterns of MI RE DO: Music skills.
- *Rhythm* pattern of ♫ ♫ ♫ ♫ ♩ ♩ ♩ (DU DE DU DE DU DE DU DE DU DU DU): Music skills.

Song and Activity Background

Hot cross buns are often advertised in bakery windows during the Easter season. According to *The Annotated Mother Goose*, this song began as a street chant for Good Friday (Baring-Gould and Baring-Gould 1968, 185). *Hot Cross Buns* is standard repertoire for many classrooms of children, and its simple melody and rhythm patterns make it a staple for beginning instrumentalists as well. The hand-jive version of this song may have developed in the classroom of Peggy Bennett in Arlington, Texas, in the early 1980s. The hand-sign version is from Richards (1984), and the new-verse version developed in Betty Hoffmann's classes in Montana in the early 1980s. The teaching strategies offered in Version 3 are from Marilyn Winter (Montana).

Script. Version 2: Hand-Sign Game

Teacher	Students
As you place your hands at your eyebrows, fingers are together and straight with palms facing down (the hand sign for MI). Capture students' attention with a challenge: • *Can you do this?* As you challenge students to imitate, lower elbows so that both hands slant down (the hand position for RE). • *Now can you do this?*	Students imitate the hand position of the teacher. Students continue to imitate.
• *Now try this!* The third hand sign (DO) is both hands in a fist and the two fists touching as if extending out from the nose. • *Now let's do all three. I'll watch to see that you're getting them.* • *Who can describe our first hand position?* • *Who can describe our second? Our third?*	Students practice the hand positions as they imitate the teacher. Creating and listening to descriptions is an added way to learn and recall the hand signs.

• *Listen to the song as you imitate my hands.*
 	
Sing the regular words to *Hot Cross Buns,* coordinating hand signs with the melodic contour of the song:
 	
  MI RE DO
  MI RE DO
  DO DO DO DO RE RE RE RE MI RE DO
 	
Younger children can be challenged with these simple repetitions of the song and hand signs. Additional challenges for older students can include work with a partner.
	Students imitate the hand positions, and some join the singing of the song. After several repetitions of the song and hand signs, prompt students to notice the connection:
	
	• *Did you notice anything about how our hands changed and how our voices changed during the song?*
	• *Compare what you heard with what you saw in the hand signs.*
	• *Closing your eyes may help you listen to your voice as you perform the hand signs.*

Teacher	Students
• *Sit facing a partner and practice performing the hand signs as you sing. Notice whether your partner's hands are moving when yours are.* • *Also, notice whether your partner's hands are in the same positions as yours.*	Through varied repetition and observation, students gain confidence in hand-signing the song and improve their coordination.
Solfa syllables may be introduced by singing the song using syllables and hand signs. • *Listen to the new words to the song. Join me as soon as you know what to do.* • *MI RE DO MI RE DO* *DO DO DO DO RE RE RE RE MI RE DO*	Students learn solfa syllables of the song through repetition and imitation. Various challenges may be introduced to check their independence in singing syllables and using signs: • *Antiphon me with your hands and voice.* • *What syllable shall we sing in our inner hearing each time we come to it?*
Further developments could include these: (1) Students sing an ostinato on MI RE DO while the class sings the song. (2) Students sing a new melody for the song by reading the teacher's hand signs. (3) Students create a new melody for the song by leading others with hand signs. (4) Students write the solfa score (M R D . . .) for the song. *Note:* It may be easier for students to sing the solfa syllables than to sing the original words of the song during the four developments described.	

Additional Versions of Hot Cross Buns

Version 3: New Verses.   Students can be stimulated to think and sing about different kinds of buns, different kinds of bread, what kinds of things can be eaten on buns, and other things that are baked in ovens. When ideas are offered, they are sung in the song. Hand signs can be continued as actions to the song during these developments.

■ *What are hot cross buns? What different kinds of bread do you know about?*

■ *What other kinds of buns have you seen?* [Someone will mention human buns, no doubt!]

■ *What kinds of things do we put in buns?*

■ *Can bread be cooked somewhere other than in an oven?*

■ *What other things are baked in ovens?*

■ *Let's sing our new verse, "Sesame seed buns . . ."*

I'm Going Downtown

SCENARIO   VERSION 1: INVITATION GAME

The game was not going smoothly. The Grade 2 class included several students who were not cooperative. Although this was the second time they had played *I'm Going Downtown,* there were too many problems today for more time to be devoted to the game.

Mr. Babcock saw several students refuse to hold hands with the person next to them. On other days and in other classes, he had discussed with students the social custom of shaking hands, that being able to take another's hand is a skill that adults develop and that this ability is important in business, social, and political situations. Today, however, he decided to change the pattern of the game to avoid the problem. "We've been walking to town, but let's drive this time. We each have our own steering wheel, but remember to keep a space between you and the person you're following. We'll sing 'We're driving downtown.' Here comes the song . . ." For the next three turns students suggested ways of getting to town: "Let's skip." "We could tiptoe to town."

Shifting to various ways to move as they went to town seemed to temporarily solve this class's problem with holding hands. Soon, however, several other problems seemed to crop up all at once. Fifteen of the twenty-five students were in the line and getting restless. Cyndi asked Bill to come to town, and he said with a grin, "No, thank you." Cyndi then proceeded to ask two more students, who each thought Bill had a pretty good idea and in turn replied, "No, thank you."

With only five minutes left in class, Mr. Babcock moved quickly to Cyndi. As he whispered in her ear, all the other students grew quiet, wondering what he was doing. As Mr. Babcock moved back to his place in the line, Cyndi smiled and, with self assurance said to those who remained seated on the floor, "This is our last trip to town today. If you would like to come, please join our line." Hesitant at first, all but two of the remaining students stood to join the line.

"For our last trip to town," Mr. Babcock began, "the next-to-last person in line—that's you, Darren—will decide how we will get there. And as Darren thinks about that, the last person in line—that's you, LaShonda—will decide what we will buy once we get there. By the way, LaShonda, money is no object! So, Darren, how will we get there?" Darren answered that the group will rollerblade to town. "What will we buy, LaShonda?" Mr. Babcock prompted. "Some ice cream!" LaShonda enthusiastically answered. "Let's practice putting those new words in the song before we move. Here's the practice turn . . . 'We're rollerblading downtown. We're rollerblading downtown. We're rollerblading down to Lincoln to buy some ice cream.'" After the students sang, moved, and stopped at the cadence, they sang all the names around the circle before they were dismissed for their next class. "And Jenny is taking William, and William is taking Patrice, and Patrice is taking Jeremiah . . ."

I'm Going Downtown

I'm go - ing down - town. I'm go - ing down - town. I'm
We're go - ing to the zoo. We're go - ing to the zoo. We're

go - ing down to Cleve - land to show my friends a - round. And
go - ing to the San Di - e - go zoo to see a gi - raffe.

Fine (Optional)

Joe is tak - ing Ma - ry. And Ma - ry is tak - ing A - li - cia.

Brief Description

The class sits in a circle, and one student walks around the outside as the song is sung. At the cadence, the student stops and decides who is closest to his or her feet and invites that person to join the group to go to town. The newest student in the line moves to the end of the line and becomes the next one to decide who is closest when the song stops. After each new person is added, all gesture to each student and sing the names on the cadence melody, starting with the first person in line and continuing to the end of the line: "And Jason is taking Flo, and Flo is taking Maggie, and Maggie is taking Thomas . . ." Version 2 is played the same way as Version 1, but students sing about a real or an imaginary field trip as they create a new verse each time they offer an idea.

Age Appropriateness

Version 1—Preschool through Grade 3   Invitation Game

Version 2—Preschool through Grade 2   Trip Game

Degrees of Intensity

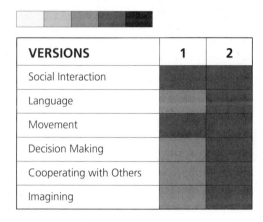

VERSIONS	1	2
Social Interaction		
Language		
Movement		
Decision Making		
Cooperating with Others		
Imagining		

Learning Opportunities

- *Coordinate movement* with beginning and ending of sound: Auditory-motor skills.
- *Maintain pace and space* while moving in a circle: Auditory-visual-motor skills, spatial skills.
- Extend and accept *invitations*: Social skills.
- *Gesture* to indicate recognition of a person: Social skills.
- Sing *names* in sequence: Visual-auditory skills.
- *Word substitution* (names) to a familiar melody: Language skills, music skills.
- Short-short-long phrase *structure* and anacruses: Music skills.
- *Melody* pattern of DO | MI MI RE RE DO: Music skills.
- *Rhythm* pattern of ♪ | ♫ ♫ ♩ (DE DU DE DU DE DU) and ♪ | ♫ ♩ ♩ (DE DU DE DU DU): Music skills.

Song and Activity Background

The rich lessons in geography, transportation, farming, and history that *I'm Going Downtown* suggests come from the context of the rugged life of transporting the tobacco crop from farm to market in Lynchburg, Virginia. Although there are many versions, Sandburg (1927) presented a song, *Goin' Down to Town*, of which the song presented here is a variant: "I'm a-goin' down to town . . . I'm a-goin' down to

Lynchburg town, To carry my tobacco down." Millions of horses and mules were familiar with this song, according to Sandburg, because many drivers sang to themselves as they sat on the wagon seat for long hours. The verses of "comic poetry" tell tall-tale stories of a horse, a gal, and a tomcat. Another version of *Going Down to Town* can be found in Seeger's work (1948, 158). Although the refrain offers yet another melody, the verses fit the tall-tale mode of poking fun at people and animals: Master sold the old gray horse for half a dollar and only a quarter down, Old Eli (the master) was richer than a king but made me beat the old tin pan while Sara Jane would sing, and Old Eli brought a little girl that he had fetched from the south and her hair was wrapped so tight that she couldn't shut her mouth. The dramatic play Seeger suggested encouraged children to take imaginary trips to the store and sing about their travels and purchases (Version 2). Singing the names as part of the activity can be found in Richards (1985).

Script. Version 1: Invitation Game

Teacher	Students
Stand behind the sitting circle, prompt students to listen to the song, then sing the song as you walk around the outer edge, stopping at the cadence. • *Guess where I'm going!*	Students watch and listen.
• *Did you hear where I'm going? And did you hear why I'm going downtown?* • *If you were to show your friends around Arlington, what would you show them?"*	Children respond with "downtown" and "to show your friends around!" Children respond with a variety of favorite places: Six Flags, the mall, Toys R Us, my grandpa's farm.
• *The song is going to take me around the outside of the circle and help me choose a friend to take to town. Let's see whom the song leads me to. [Sing the starting pitch.] Here comes the song . . ."I'm going downtown . . . around."* • [Bending to look into Patty's eyes] *Patty, would you come to town with me?*	By the teacher's thinking aloud, students are instructed as to how they will participate: • *Did you notice that my feet stopped just when we sang 'around,' the cadence word?* • *The song brought me to this space, and as I look down at my feet, I see that Patty is seated closest to where they stopped.* • *Let me go around in front of her and ask if she'd like to come with me.* Nodding, Patty gets up and joins the teacher.
Sing the names and prepare Patty for her turn to invite. • [Sing.] *"And Ms. White is taking Patty."* Can you sing our names as you look at us? • *Are you ready to go, Patty? I wonder whom the song will lead you to.*	Students are encouraged to join in singing the names. Repetition is used as necessary to encourage participation in singing.

Teacher	Students
Lead Patty around the circle, stopping at the cadence. • *Do you remember what to do, Patty? Decide who is closest, move so you can see that person's eyes, and issue your invitation.*	After Patty momentarily studies her feet and decides who is closest, she moves around in front of Richard, bends down to look at him, and asks, "Do you want to go with us to town?" "Yes," replies Richard as he gets up to join the line. Support for courteous invitations can come in the form of teacher feedback: • *It's a nice feeling to get an invitation like that, isn't it, Richard?* • *What a kind message you sent!*
Challenge students to gesture as they add a new name to their singing. • *Everyone get your hands ready to gesture to us as you look at us and sing three names.* [Sing.] *"And Ms. White is taking Patty, and Patty is taking Richard."*	Students look at each individual in line as they gesture with a gentle, open palm and sing the names.
When the activity needs to move a bit faster because of time constraints and students' attention span, present a new way to add students to the activit: • *Until now, Marty, we have had the song choose the next person. The song chose you, but will you now invite someone from anywhere in the circle to come along?* In this way, the game moves a little faster, names are sung each time before the line moves "downtown" again, and children going to town are chosen both by the song and by another student.	Students are involved in more decision making as they choose someone from within the circle to invite. When many are in the line, a student can be asked to decide which names will be sung for a given turn. Continue to sing names in sequence, however. • *Tiffany, instead of singing all the names, tell us whose name we'll begin singing this time.*
When all students are in the line to go downtown, the activity can be ended by having the last student in line decide what we'll buy when we get there (*"Money is no object!"*). • *"We're going downtown . . . to buy a new bike."*	When it seems important to their focus, students can be challenged to suggest ways of going to town, and these words can be added to the song: "We're biking downtown . . ."

Additional Versions of I'm Going Downtown

Version 3: Trip Game. The song and the game naturally lend themselves to variants that focus on a trip the students might take. This game can also evolve into students' drawing or writing a story about their chosen idea.

- "We're going to the store. We're going to the store. We're going to the grocery store to buy some artichokes."

- "We're going to the zoo. We're going to the zoo. We're going to the Fort Worth zoo to see some gorillas."

Johnny, Get Your Hair Cut

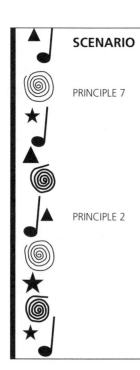

SCENARIO

PRINCIPLE 7

PRINCIPLE 2

VERSION 1: FINGER SCISSORS

"Oh, let's put away our scissors, scissors, scissors. Let's put away our scissors, it's time for us to go." As Ms. Nelson improvised this last verse for the song *Johnny, Get Your Haircut,* she looked at the clock. Only two minutes remained in the school day, and her class of Grade 1 children would need to gather their wraps and personal items quickly. Ending the day with a singing game was one of Ms. Nelson's favorite ways to experience a sense of camaraderie with her students and to give closure to their day.

The class had just spent the last ten minutes creating imaginary finger scissors and exploring ways that their fingers could move to make the scissors operate. The children thought the activity was fun, but Ms. Nelson knew that the manual dexterity practiced with each repetition of the song aided students' development of fine motor coordination as well.

Just as Ms. Nelson was about to move to the doorway, Barbie ran up to her and exclaimed, "Look Ms. Nelson! Look what I did!" All Ms. Nelson could do was gulp as she stared at Barbie's outstretched hand. Apparently, Barbie had been inspired by the game they had just played—in her hand was a sizable clump of Barbie's own hair, which she had cut with her real scissors.

From that day on, Ms. Nelson never taught her students the game *Johnny, Get Your Hair Cut* without also cautioning them not to cut their own or anyone else's hair.

Johnny, Get Your Hair Cut

Oh, John-ny, get your hair cut, hair cut, hair cut. John-ny, get your hair cut just like me.

Brief Description

In Version 1, children create pretend scissors by moving their fingers and hands in ways that suggest a scissors motion. Students create scissors and imitate the scissors of others. In Version 2, students are challenged to explore scissor movements based on vocabulary suggestions.

Age Appropriateness

Version 1—Preschool through Grade 2   Finger Scissors

Version 2—Kindergarten through Grade 2   Silly Scissors

Degrees of Intensity

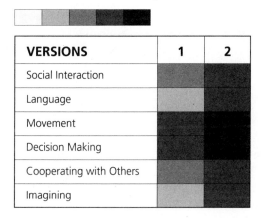

VERSIONS	1	2
Social Interaction		
Language		
Movement		
Decision Making		
Cooperating with Others		
Imagining		

Learning Opportunities

- *Coordinate movement* with beginning and ending of sound: Auditory-motor skills.
- *Pantomime* scissors: Drama skills, motor skills.
- *Pantomime movement* to language: Auditory-motor skills, language skills (Version 2).
- *Move* fingers in a scissors motion: Fine motor coordination.
- *Imitate* the actions of others: Visual-motor skills.
- Cooperate with a *partner:* Social skills, motor skills (Version 2).
- *Vocabulary development:* Language skills (Version 2).
- Echo phrase *structure* and anacrusis: Music skills.
- *Melody* patterns of LA₁ SO₁ and LA₁ TI₁ DO: Music skills.
- *Rhythm* pattern of ♩ | ♫ ♫ ♩ ♩ (DU DU DE DU DE DU DU): Music skills.

Song and Activity Background

The tune of *Johnny, Get Your Haircut* has a historical link to *Hey, Betty Martin,* which may have begun as a drumming tune during the War of 1812: "Hey, Betty Martin, tiptoe, tiptoe. Hey, Betty Martin, tiptoe fine." During the War Between the States in the 1860s, the tune became *Johnny, Get Your Gun:* "Johnny, git your gun and your sword and your pistol. Johnny, git your gun and come with me." During the 1890s, young men teased the few young women who were bold enough to get their hair cut in a bob by singing: "Chippy, get your hair cut, hair cut, hair cut. Chippy, get your hair cut, hair cut short" (Sandburg 1927, 158). The words and melody presented here can be found in Seeger (1948, 142) and Richards (1985, p. 48).

Script. Version 1: Finger Scissors

Teacher	Students
• *What do you think my fingers are doing as I sing this song?* While singing, open and close your first and second fingers, in a scissors-like fashion.	Students answer with various descriptions of their observations. "Your fingers are scissors." "You're cutting Johnny's hair." "Your fingers are going back and forth, like this." "Your fingers are doing the beat." "I was watching the other hand. It wasn't doing anything!"
• *Watch again. Notice what word my fingers begin to move on, and notice when they stop.*	Students listen and observe. "Your fingers stopped on the last word of the song!"
• *On the "Oh," I pick my scissors up and then start cutting.* • *That "Oh" is called a pickup or an anacrusis. Can you say that word? Many songs begin with an anacrusis, but anacruses aren't always an "Oh."* • *Now, you try. Pick up your fingers on the anacrusis and then start them moving. Stop your scissors on the last word of the song.* • *Let's watch to see what kind of listeners your fingers are!*	Students have several opportunities to coordinate their movement with the anacrusis and the cadence. Identifying and feeling these points of closure help students develop a sense of structure for the song.
• *Can you tell what the last word of the song is—the cadence word?* ["Me!"] • *That's when your fingers should stop. Let's listen for the cadence word and stop our fingers just when we sing it.* • *Your fingers are waiting for the song. Let's sing.*	Students have their hands or fingers wait for the song, pick them up on the "Oh," make a scissors action while they sing the song, and stop on "me." When they are secure with the timing, ask them how else they could make scissors with their hands or fingers. After a practice turn, one student demonstrates an idea and the others imitate as they sing.
After students have played this game, they can be encouraged to role-play getting a haircut. One student is chosen to be "Johnny" and another is chosen to be the hair cutter. While Johnny sits still, the hair cutter pretends to give Johnny a haircut using his or her fingers as scissors.	As students observe the haircut, they can practice with their scissors. A discussion on the gentleness and trust required for getting and giving a haircut could accompany this activity.

Additional Versions of Johnny, Get Your Haircut

Version 2: Silly Scissors Game.   For added challenges, students can explore making various kinds and numbers of scissors. Students can participate individually, with a partner, or in small groups. They can be challenged to make

- scissors that use particular parts of the body (legs only, neck up only, fingers only);
- scissors with particular dimensions (large, small, medium);
- scissors that work at particular speeds (fast, slow, medium);
- scissors that use a certain number of people (two, three, or more);
- scissors that employ a combination of these challenges (two scissors—one fast, one slow; two scissors—one large and slow, one small and fast).

London Bridge

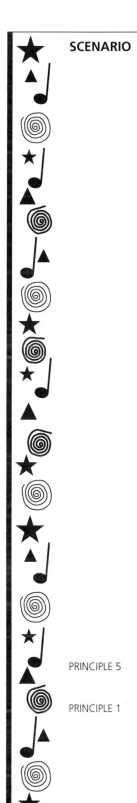

SCENARIO

In a kindergarten class, the teacher decided to teach the children the game *London Bridge.* Choosing two students, Derail and LaTonya, to be the bridge, she explained that they could go over to the corner and decide two secrets, one secret each. Offering them some guidance, the teacher encouraged, "Your secrets should be two things that children like: cats or dogs, cake or pie, rock music or country music, and so on." Staying with the other children, the teacher practiced the song while the "bridge" students were deciding.

"Let's keep your secret from the class, but whisper to me what your decision is." Derail quietly told the teacher they had chosen strawberry ice cream and chocolate ice cream as their secrets.

"Let's all raise our arms in the air and practice what the bridge will do. Our arms stay in the air until the cadence word. What is the last word of the song?" asked the teacher. "My fair lady!" the children shouted. "Those are the last words of the song, but what is the last word of those words?" "Lady!" the children exclaimed. "Let's sing the song and listen for that last word—the cadence word. That's when our arms will come down. Here comes the song; let's practice with our arms," prompted the teacher. The children raised their arms and watched each other and the teacher to co-ordinate letting their arms drop at the cadence.

"Now let's practice what those of us who are not in the bridge will do. We sing, walk through the bridge, and stop at the cadence. Let's practice walking, singing, and stopping. [Singing the starting pitch] Ready . . . 'London Bridge . . . lady.' Were you able to stop when the song did?" When students were confident of their listening and movements, the activity continued.

LaTonya and Derail formed a bridge with their arms extended above their heads and hands clasped. At the cadence, when La Tonya and Derail's arms fell, they caught Cleophus. The children giggled at the sight of Cleophus being "locked up." All sang as the bridge gently swayed back and forth to jostle Cleophus. "Take the key and lock him up, lock him up, lock him up. Take the key and lock him up, my fair lady."

As the class sang "Off to prison you must go . . . my fair lady," the bridge took Cleophus to a private area in the room and asked him to choose between the two secrets. Whispering, LaTonya and Derail asked their prisoner if he wanted strawberry ice cream or chocolate ice cream. When he responded, "Chocolate ice cream!" LaTonya told him, "You're on my side of the bridge now." As Cleophus took his place behind LaTonya, he placed his hands on her shoulders and the class sang, "Build it up with sticks and stones, sticks and stones, sticks and stones. Build it up with sticks and stones, my fair lady." The secret was maintained throughout the activity as the verses were repeated and more children were caught in the bridge. At the end of the game, the teacher chose to avoid declaring the longer side of the bridge the winning side and to forgo the traditional tug-of-war between the two sides. Instead, she displayed curiosity about why children chose one secret over the other.

PRINCIPLE 5

PRINCIPLE 1

One of the reasons Derail was chosen to be a bridge was the teacher's interest in giving him a leadership position. A quiet child, Derail had not shown an interest in music or in initiating ideas during activities. The whole class played the game with much delight.

Each day of music class for the next three weeks, Derail would walk shyly to the music teacher at the beginning of class and quietly ask, "Could we play *London Bridge* today?" The song had a new and lasting meaning for Derail.

London Bridge

Lon - don Bridge is fall - ing down, fall - ing down, fall - ing down.

Lon - don Bridge is fall - ing down, my fair la - dy.

Verse 2—*Take the key and lock her (him) up.*

Verse 3—*Off to prison you must go.*

Verse 4—*Build it up with sticks and stones.*

Brief Description

Two students form a bridge with their arms, and the class sings the first verse and walks under the bridge. At the cadence, the bridge falls, capturing a prisoner. As the second verse is sung, the bridge swings the prisoner. The third verse sees the prisoner being taken off to prison to make a choice between two secrets. Depending on which secret he or she chooses, the prisoner joins one side of the bridge, and the game begins again.

Age Appropriateness

Version 1—Preschool through Grade 1

Degrees of Intensity

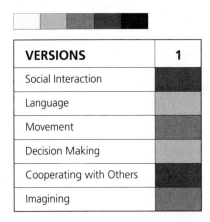

VERSIONS	1
Social Interaction	
Language	
Movement	
Decision Making	
Cooperating with Others	
Imagining	

Learning Opportunities

- *Coordinate movement* with beginning and ending of sound: Auditory-motor skills.

- *Maintain pace and space* while moving in a line: Auditory-visual-motor skills, spatial skills.

- Keep a *secret.*

- Echo phrase *structure:* Music skills.

- *Melody* patterns of SO LA SO and RE SO MI DO: Music skills.

- *Rhythm* pattern of ♫ ♩ (DU DE DU): Music skills.

Song and Activity Background

Although it is one of the best-known songs in the English language, little is known about the origins of *London Bridge*. The game is not always played with a bridge and in many regions of the world is not an arch game; the first bridge-game wording appeared in Newell's work of 1883. There is evidence that about 1790 the song was being danced like a medieval carol, and about 1659 a dairywoman said she danced "the building of London Bridge" in her youth (Opie and Opie 1985, 63). Nearly all versions examined include singing about a bridge broken down, building it up, and a lady (Lady Lea, Lady Lee, a gay lady, and Lady-O).

The song first appeared in print in *Tommy Thumb's Pretty Song Book* (1744) with these verses that show a chain of ideas following the dialogue pattern of "Try this." "No, that won't work!" (similar to the folk song *There's a Hole in My Bucket*): "London Bridge is Broken down, Dance over my Lady Lee. London Bridge is Broken down, With a gay Lady. How shall we build it up again . . . Build it up with Gravel and Stone . . . Gravel and Stone will wash away . . . Build it up with Iron and Steel . . . Iron and Steel will bend and bow . . . Build it up with Silver and Gold . . . Silver and Gold will be stolen away . . . Then we'll set a man to watch." The Opies conjecture that having a man watch the bridge may be connected to the ancient tradition of human and animal sacrifices (some were built into the foundations) to gain the goodwill of the river and the gods. Whatever the original meaning of the song, it remains a favorite with small children over three centuries later.

Looby Loo

Looby Loo

Brief Description

In a standing circle, students sing as they walk or skip. During the second section of the song, an individual suggests what part of the body he or she will "put in," and the group joins the actions and the singing. After the students gesture in, gesture out, shake, and turn, the song and the activity begin again. Version 2 introduces more movement: As they sing and circle, students imitate the way one student is moving during the first section of the song.

Age Appropriateness

Version 1—Kindergarten through Grade 2   Circle Game

Version 2—Grade 3 through Grade 5   Follow-the-Leader

Degrees of Intensity

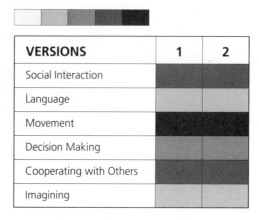

VERSIONS	1	2
Social Interaction		
Language		
Movement		
Decision Making		
Cooperating with Others		
Imagining		

Learning Opportunities

- *Coordinate movement* with beginning and ending of sound: Auditory-motor skills.

- *Maintain pace and space* while moving in a circle: Auditory-visual-motor skills, spatial skills.

- *Locomotor movement* in a circle—skipping, walking: Motor skills.

- *Whole-group cooperation:* Social skills, motor skills.

- Name *parts of the body:* Vocabulary skills.

- *Imitate* actions: Visual-motor skills.

- *Sequence movement* with words—in, out, shake, turn: Auditory-motor skills.

- Short-short-long phrase *structure* and ABA (ternary) song form: Music skills.

- Pentatonic *melody* and pattern of SO LA SO FA MI RE DO: Music skills.

- *Rhythm* patterns of ♫♩ ♩ ♪♩. (DUDADI DU DI DU) and ♪♩ ♪♩ ♪♩. (DI DU DI DU DI DU): Music skills.

Song and Activity Background

"Here we go Lubin Loo. Here we go Lubin Light. Here we go Lubin Loo. All on a Saturday night." That is the version of *Looby Loo* found in Kidson's *Eighty Singing Games* (1907). Additional descriptions of *Looby Loo* can be found in records from 1835, 1840, 1876, and 1880. In *The Young Lady's Book* of 1876, Mrs. Henry Mackarness described "Looby looby looby, All on a Saturday night" by warning that when the children put their heads in the middle of the circle, they "must take care . . . or they may come unpleasantly near their neighbours."

Origins of *Looby Loo* also may be connected to *Sally Go 'Round the Sun;* in some cases, the melody is the same. Several British versions of *Looby Loo* contain nonsense words: "looby loo," "Halligal eagle eagle," "alley galoo galoo," and "Hilli ballu ballai." About 1900, the game was one of perpetual motion, with the circle dancing first in one direction, then in the other, and the participants kicking their legs high in the air at the end and shouting "Oh!" or "Whoops!" In the 1920s, James Kirkup described seeing the game at the age of 2 and feeling uneasy about the abandon with which the game was played when, on the final word, "the girls lifted up their frocks at the back and shoved their bottoms out in a way which I found very distressing" (Opie and Opie 1985, 399). As with many games, the words of *Looby Loo* (many sang it as

"Loopty Loo" as children) suggest the actions. Many have noted the similarity between the games of *Looby Loo* and *Hokey Pokey*, although *Okey Kokey* (*Hokey Pokey*), Jim Kennedy's action song of 1941, has a separate history as the big dance favorite in Britain during World War II (Opie and Opie, 392–393). If the verse section of *Looby Loo* sounds familiar, it is because that section is nearly identical to *The Farmer in the Dell* and *A-Hunting We Will Go.*

Script. Version 1: Circle Game

Teacher	Students
• *Here comes the song, watch and you'll know what to do.* Begin singing and skipping *"Here we go Looby Loo . . ."*	In a standing circle, holding hands, students watch and listen for the teacher's instructions. Students join the activity, circling as they skip.
Continuing to the middle section of the song, sing as you put your hand in toward the center (*"I put my right hand in"*), then outside the circle (*"I take my right hand out"*), then shake it (*"I give my right hand a shake, shake, shake"*), and turn around in place (*"and turn myself about"*). Without a pause, sing *"Oh"* and look expectantly at the students as you take the hands of students on either side of you, begin the song again, and skip: *"Here we go . . ."*	Without explanation or preparation, students begin to sing along as they learn the song and the activity.
After two or three turns, pause after turning around and prompt: • *Who will give us an idea for what to put in this time?* [Nadia raises her hand.] *Nadia has an idea, so when we get to that part of the song, listen for and watch her.*	Just before singing "I put . . ." all pause, and Nadia speaks "I put my shoulder in," and the class imitates the motion and sings the song.
The game continues with students offering ideas for what to "put in" for the next verse of the song. When students need added challenges, introduce an element of surprise by not announcing beforehand who will receive the next turn to offer an idea. • *Think of what you will have us put into the circle this time. Have your idea ready because you may not know when your turn is coming.* As all sing and skip, say *"Jody"* and look at Jody encouragingly during the first section of the song. At the middle section, after Jody says "thumbs," immediately lead the group in singing and moving, *"I put my thumbs in . . ."* The activity continues with students offering ideas when you call their names.	The unpredictability of not knowing when a turn is coming may be more appropriate for Grades 3–5 than for Grades K–2. This unpredictability can engage and challenge the older students, but it can overwhelm and confuse younger students. You may find that younger students are more successful with the activity when you use a gentler pace for singing the song, skipping, listening for ideas, and making changes in the play.

Additional Versions of Looby Loo

Version 2: Follow-the-Leader Game. *Looby Loo* with older students (Grades 3–5) can include varying the ways to move in a circle for the first section. Turns to name the body part can go in order around the circle. The teacher can introduce unpredictability, surprise, and humor by saying, *"Let's move like Curtis is moving this time"* just before returning to *"Oh, here we go Looby Loo. . . ."* Once students know that someone in the group will determine how they move, the teacher can say a name (*"Jeremy"* or *"Watch Jeremy"*) to get the group to focus on that individual.

Mad Man

SCENARIO

PRINCIPLE 7

VERSION 2: RHYMING GAME

A third-grade class entered the room begging, "Can we *please* sing *Mad Man* today?" *Mad Man* was a song most of the students had learned in previous years, and it was a favorite of this class. A whimsical song, it details a sequence of events that have the "mad man" jumping from one thing to another. The students clearly enjoyed the humor and the rhyming that is a basic feature of the song.

This day, Mrs. West had already planned to work with *Mad Man*. So, after singing through the song once, she began, "We're going to make some changes today. What else could this man be besides mad?" She sang the first line, "There was a man and he was _____," leaving the last word out. The students eagerly suggested several possibilities: "crazy, hot, tired, hungry."

Mrs. West drew the students' attention to how changing this word would suggest changes to the rest of the song, changes that asked them to rhyme. They tried several possibilities with the first few verses, rhyme by rhyme and line by line:

> There was a man and he was *smart,* he jumped into a *shopping cart.*
> The shopping cart it was so *hard,* he jumped into his *neighbor's yard.*
> His neighbor's yard it was so *green,* he jumped into a *window screen.*

PRINCIPLE 2

Knowing they were full of ideas and eager to share them, Mrs. West asked the students to find partners and create a new set of lyrics for this song. Soon, the students were deeply engaged in writing a whole new set of verses based on the structure of the initial song. They tried out rhymes, considered different objects and places for the man to jump, checked their efforts by singing them, wrote their verses out, and shared their work with other students. Their delight in the project, the song, and their own creations, as well as those of their classmates, was palpable.

Mad Man

There was a man and he was mad, he jumped in-to a pud-ding bag. (Pudding bag!)

Verse 2—*The pudding bag, it was so fine, he jumped onto a porcupine.* [echo] *Porcupine.*

Verse 3—*The porcupine it did so prick, he jumped onto a walking stick.* [echo] *Walking stick.*

Verse 4—*The walking stick it was so narrow, he jumped onto an old wheelbarrow.* [echo] *Old wheelbarrow.*

Verse 5—*The old wheelbarrow it had a crack, he jumped onto a horse's back.* [echo] *Horse's back.*

Verse 6—*The horse's back it did so sag, he jumped onto a greasy rag.* [echo] *Greasy rag.*

Verse 7—*The greasy rag it was so rotten, he jumped onto a bag of cotton.* [echo] *Bag of cotton.*

Verse 8—*The bag of cotton it caught on fire and so he went to Jeremiah!* [echo] *Jeremiah!*

Poof! Poof! Poof!

Brief Description

Seated, students listen as the teacher sings the song. Students echo the cadence words of each verse as they imitate the teacher's hand signs for the melody, MI DO DO. At the end of the song, the *poof*s can be an opportunity for vocal exploration. Each *poof* is higher and longer than the preceding one, and the third one consists of a long vocal glide, often starting high in the voice and descending in coordination with hand movements. The teacher's hands mime successively larger "explosions," coordinating with the vocal *poof*s. In Version 2, students are challenged to create new verses by suggesting adjectives and rhyming words. All sing the new song created with verses that students compose.

Age Appropriateness

Version 1—Grade 4 through Grade 6 Action Song

Version 2—Grade 4 through Grade 6 Rhyming Game

Degrees of Intensity

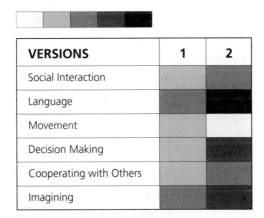

VERSIONS	1	2
Social Interaction		
Language		
Movement		
Decision Making		
Cooperating with Others		
Imagining		

Learning Opportunities

- *Word substitution:* Language skills (Version 2).
- Create *phrases* with *rhyming words:* Language skills, music skills (Version 2).
- *Voice play* for "poof": Voice skills.
- *Anacrusis* to phrases: Music skills.
- *Melody* patterns of SO$_\text{l}$ | DO DO SO$_\text{l}$ and MI DO DO: Music skills (Version 1).

■ *Curwen hand signs* for MI DO DO: Music skills (Version 1).
■ *Rhythm* pattern of ♪ | ♫ ♫ ♫ ♪ (DE DU DE DU DE DU DE DU):
Music skills.

Song and Activity Background

Push the Business On, from about 1897, may have been a precursor in melody and form of *Mad Man:* "I'll hire a horse and steal a pig, and all the world shall have a jig . . ." (Opie and Opie 1985, 382). The SO₁ DO DO SO₁ SO₁ LA₁ LA₁ SO₁ melody also begins the British *Jolly Miller,* "one of the most popular singing games at the end of the nineteenth century" (Opie and Opie, 314), and another comic song of Britain about 1780, *Bobby Bingo. Bobby Bingo* was an adult song that became the children's song *Bingo* (Opie and Opie, 410).

Meant to create a comic image and a flavor of buffoonery, *Mad Man* can be found in Seeger's 1948 book, although the phrase endings are not echoed: "pudding bag . . . bottle of wine . . . bottle of beer . . . walking stick . . . wheelbarrow . . . horse's back . . . taching end . . . bag of cotton . . . blew him up to Jeremiah. Pouf! Pouf! Pouf!" A suggested activity was to improvise couplets with children and use what Seeger called tone play, a strategy comparable to antiphonning (pp. 76–77).

Script. Version 1: Action Song

Teacher	Students
• *Listen to this song about an unusual man who does unusual things.* • *Your challenge is to listen and to echo me at the end of each phrase. You'll see and hear what to echo, so watch and listen.* With this introduction, begin singing the song. As you sing "*pudding bag,*" place one hand to your forehead as if shading your eyes on "*pud-*", and lightly tap one fist twice on the other fist in front of your chest for "*-ding bag.*" Do the same on the other phrase cadences. These hand signs symbolize the MI DO DO tonal pattern of each phrase ending. For the "*poofs,*" use your hands and voice in successively larger motions and higher pitches to simulate an explosion.	Students watch and listen to the story, told in song by the teacher. Though they imitate the hand signs, they do not necessarily know their meaning. The students learn hand motions as part of the play with the song.
• *So, now that you've heard the song, tell us about some of the unusual things that the* Mad Man *did.* Repeat the song as needed for students to recall the words and weave a story.	As a way of learning the song, students collectively recall words and images from the song. Imaginations can be further prompted if you ask, • *Why was he called the mad man?* • *What is a pudding bag?* • *Why was the man doing so much jumping?* • *What do you imagine that looked like?* • *Why do you think that happened?*

Teacher	Students
• *Show us how our hands moved for the cadence of each phrase.* • *Who can hum or chin the melody we sang each time we showed our hand signs?* • *Did you notice that the melody is the same each time we show our hand signs?* The hand gestures are introduced as part of the game and as a way to show the echo. Because the hands approximate the solfa hand signs, they show the melodic contour of the phrase endings. In successive repetitions, you may use antiphonning to help students gain confidence and independence with the song.	Through their responses, children recall and demonstrate the song and the movements. No explanation of the hand signs is necessary, but students may be told about their use and function: • *Many musicians and music students use these hand signs to help them study and perform music.* • *The vertical movement of our hands approximates the contour of the melody.* • *Each time our hands are flat and level, we call that sign MI, and the fist shows us DO. We can substitute these solfa syllables for the song words, because they give us information about the melody.*

Mary Had a Little Lamb

Mary Had a Little Lamb

Verse 2—*Everywhere that Mary went, Mary went . . . the lamb was sure to go.*

Verse 3—*It followed her to school one day, to school one day . . . which was against the rules.*

Verse 4—*It made the children laugh and play, laugh and play . . . to see the lamb at school.*

Verse 5—*And so the teacher turned it out, turned it out . . . but still it lingered near.*

Verse 6—*Patiently it waited there, waited there . . . till Mary did appear.*

Verse 7—*Why does the lamb love Mary so? love Mary so . . . the eager children cry.*

Verse 8—*Why, Mary loves the lamb, you know, the lamb you know . . . the teacher did reply.*

Brief Description

After they know the song, students can act out the story in several ways. Some can volunteer to play the role of the lamb or Mary for the class. Small groups can be assigned to act out one verse. Small groups can be assigned to create a scene (without movement, a still life or a tableau) from one verse that depicts that part of the story. Verses 1 through 4 of *Mary Had a Little Lamb* are commonly known. Verses 5 through 8 (Verse 6 was slightly modified here) can be found in *The Annotated Mother Goose* (Baring-Gould and Baring-Gould 1967, 127).

Age Appropriateness

Version 1—Preschool through Grade 2

Learning Opportunities

- *Cooperate* within small groups: Social skills.
- *Role-play* the meaning of a song with actions or statues: Drama skills.
- Echo phrase *structure:* Music skills.
- *Melody* pattern of MI RE DO RE MI MI MI and MI | RE RE MI RE DO: Music skills.
- *Rhythm* pattern of ♪ | ♫ ♫ ♩ (DE DU DE DU DE DU) and ♫ ♫ ♫ ♩ (DU TA DU DE DU DE DU): Music skills.

Mary's Wearing Her Red Dress

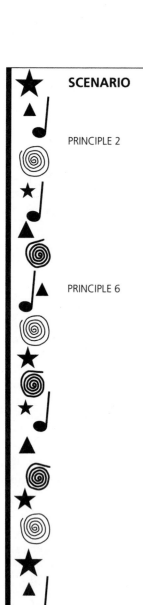

SCENARIO

PRINCIPLE 2

PRINCIPLE 6

VERSION 3: GUESSING GAME

"Someone's wearing something blue, something blue, something blue. Someone's wearing something blue, who do you think it is?" With no introduction, the teacher sang the song. The Grade 5 students had only five minutes until lunch, and their teacher knew it was the perfect opportunity to introduce this game. Hesitantly, students began looking at others. The teacher sang the cadence chunk to prompt students to offer a guess: [Singing] "Who do you think it is?"

"Raise your hand if you have a guess, and we'll see if your guess matches my idea," challenged the teacher. Students began looking at classmates and raised their hands to guess. "I think it's Jenny," guessed Chuck. "What do you see on Jenny that's blue?" asked the teacher as she cued Chuck to respond more completely. "Her blue jeans," Chuck said. "Jenny is wearing blue jeans, and that could be my secret, but it's not," the teacher replied.

As students continued to guess, the teacher guided them to include both "who" and "what" in their guesses. She also modeled constructive feedback by not answering simply "no." Instead, she acknowledged the guesses in a variety of ways: "It could be that, but that's not what I was thinking." "Oh, I hadn't noticed Curt's blue watchband." "That's a good guess, but that's not my secret." "That's a pretty detailed observation, but that's not my idea." From experience, the teacher knew that making the effort to verbalize responses to ideas this way gave students a model of respect after which to pattern their own responses when they had turns as the leader.

"I think it's Vernon's blue belt," guessed Don. "That's what I had in mind! Let's sing the song about Vernon's blue belt while Don looks around for another idea. We do have time for one more turn. Let's sing 'Vernon's wearing his blue belt, his blue belt, his blue belt. Vernon's wearing his blue belt, yes he is.' "

After the class had sung the song, the teacher asked Don for the color of the clothing he had as a secret. Then as all sang the verse, "Someone's wearing something [pause]," Don filled in the color and the class sang the rest of the song. Instantly, they began looking around at classmates' clothing and raised their hands to offer their guesses. "Don, it's your turn to ask for guesses. As you select students to guess, remember your choices in how to respond to their ideas."

Standing by, watching, and participating in guessing the secret, the teacher noticed that in this game, the students spent much more time talking and guessing than singing. This activity did not offer frequent experiences in singing the song. It did, however, fulfill a vital need in this classroom: Students were noticing each other, saying others' names, focusing on details of others, and indiscriminately interacting with classmates in a way that dissolved the overt cliquishness and gender distinctions that sometimes plagued other classroom activities and interactions.

Mary's Wearing Her Red Dress

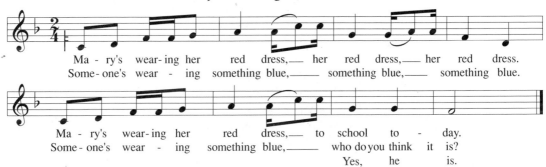

Brief Description

In a sitting circle or in a scatter formation, students sing about articles of clothing they are wearing. Using adjectives that describe color, texture, or pattern, students can choose the words for their turn or for the song, or the teacher can choose the adjectives and the articles of clothing. Version 2 challenges vocabulary, asking students to decide yes or no in regard to a given description of an article. Version 3 changes the activity to a guessing game in which students try to locate the secret person and article of clothing.

Age Appropriateness

Version 1—Preschool through Grade 2	Describing Game
Version 2—Preschool through Grade 1	Yes or No Game
Version 3—Preschool through Grade 6	Guessing Game

Degrees of Intensity

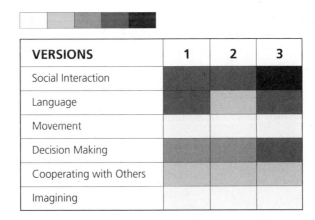

VERSIONS	1	2	3
Social Interaction			
Language			
Movement			
Decision Making			
Cooperating with Others			
Imagining			

Learning Opportunities

- *Coordinate movement* with beginning and ending of sound: Auditory-motor skills.
- *Observe details* of another's clothing: Visual figure-ground skills.

- *Name, compare, and contrast* colors, textures, patterns, and articles of clothing: Language skills, vocabulary skills.
- *Use adjectives* to describe articles of clothing: Language skills.
- *Scan* for specific colors, textures, or patterns: Visual figure-ground skills (Version 3).
- Echo phrase *structure*: Music skills.
- Pentatonic song and *melody* pattern of SO₁ LA₁ DO DO RE MI MI SO and RE RE DO: Music skills.

Song and Activity Background

In 1948, Seeger offered ten verses for *Mary Wore Her Red Dress,* a folk song from Texas: "Mary wore her red hat . . . wore her red shoes . . . wore her red gloves . . . made a red cake. . . . Where'd you get your shoes from? . . . Got them from the dry goods. . . . Where'd you get your butter from? . . . Got it from the grocery. . . . Mary was a red bird . . . all day long" (pp. 130–131). Seeger also presented a guessing game similar to the one described in Version 3: "Who wore a pink dress . . . all day long?" Several teachers have made substitutions for the cadence phrase: "all day long," "to school today," and "yes, she is." Version 2 and the "yes, she is" phrase were developed by Akiko Inagaki and Michiko Nitaira in the 1990s in Michiko's classrooms in Shimodate City, Japan. Both were using English-language folk songs to offer Japanese students experiences with English as a Foreign Language. Version 2 may be particularly appropriate for students who are learning English.

Script. Version 1: Describing Game

Teacher	Students
In this song, students sing about children's clothing. The child for whom the song will be sung can be chosen by the teacher or another child.	Students are focused to observe details of other's clothing. The children are allowed and encouraged to use various descriptions in sharing their observations.
• *I see something Jerry is wearing that you may not have noticed.*	
• *Do you see what design is on his shirt?*	
• *How would you describe the design?*	
• *Jerry, is it all right with you if we sing about your dinosaur shirt?*	
• *Here's how our song will sound: "Jerry's wearing his dinosaur shirt, his dinosaur shirt, his dinosaur shirt. Jerry's wearing his dinosaur shirt, yes, he is."*	
• *Please sing with me this time.* [Sing the starting pitch.] *Ready . . .*	Asking the child's permission to sing about his clothing demonstrates respect for his wishes and personal property.
• *Jerry, do you see something that someone is wearing that you would like us to notice?*	Jerry looks around the room and answers, "Todd."
• *What do you notice about Todd's clothing?*	"His shoes," answers Jerry.
• *Let's see if we can guess what Jerry noticed about Todd's shoes. How would you describe them, class?* Descriptions of clothing can be brief or prolonged, depending on the responses of the group, the goals of the activity, and the time available.	Students offer descriptions of Todd's shoes, and it becomes obvious that Todd is very proud of them as he places his feet so all can see.

Teacher	Students
• *Jerry, after hearing all those descriptions, which was the one you were thinking of when you noticed Todd's shoes?* • *Todd, you may have the final say in which words we use in your song. What shall we sing about your shoes?* • *Here comes Todd's song. Get your voices ready . . .* Not all turns need to include extensive discussion about the article of clothing. Vary the degree of description according to the interest of the students.	Jerry answers that he noticed that Todd's initials were written on the shoes. Todd decides he wants the group to sing about his brand-new shoes.
Children may wish to stay in their spaces while the class sings about their clothing; they may wish to stand near the seated teacher or sit on a special chair so all can see; or they may wish to walk around the circle so all children can see their clothing "up close" and perhaps, with the child's permission, touch the fabric as it goes by. • *Chase, would you mind if the children touch the legs of your corduroy pants as you walk by?* • *Jackie, some students may not have touched patent leather before. Would it be okay with you if they quickly touched your shoe as you walk by?*	Children can be challenged to notice, identify, and compare textures, patterns, and colors. • *Do you see any examples of plaids or checks in our class?* • *Let's sing about someone else who is wearing purple today.* • *Find some stripes with your eyes and raise your hand to tell us what you found.*

Additional Versions of Mary's Wearing Her Red Dress

Version 2: Yes or No Game.   Especially appropriate for children learning English words, this version sets up problems for children to solve by describing an article and asking students to decide yes or no.

- The teacher selects Gary to sing about, because Gary is wearing a green shirt: "*Gary's wearing a green shirt . . . yes or no?*" Students consider the question and respond: "*Gary's wearing a green shirt . . . yes, yes, yes!*"

- To check students' observing, listening, and vocabulary skills, the teacher (or a student) may challenge: "*Tyrone is wearing a yellow shirt . . . yes or no?*" Realizing the teacher's trick, students answer the question in song by reponding: "*Tyrone is wearing a blue shirt . . . yes, yes yes!*"

Muffin Man

SCENARIO   GRAB GAME

The class sang the *Muffin Man* as they moved into a circle with their partners. "Today, think about something that the rest of us may not know about you. What will you tell us about yourself if you get a turn as the muffin man? Since I am the muffin man for the first turn, I would like you to know that I have a new puppy named Bubba." Questions immediately came from the group: "What kind is it?" "How old is it?" "How much did it cost?" "Is it housebroken?" "What color is it?"

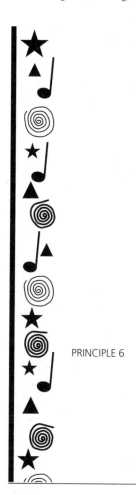

PRINCIPLE 6

"Well, you have reminded me that some things about ourselves cause others to become more curious. So that our activity doesn't get too bogged down, let's say that only two questions can be asked of the muffin man for each turn. Now, I'll answer two questions before we sing our song." Mrs. Murdock briefly responded to two students' questions.

"How will you put my name in the song?" "Oh, DO you know Mrs. MURdock? . . ." sang some students. Others said, "Oh, DO you know MRS. Murdock, MRS. Murdock? . . ." "I hear two different ways of singing it. Let's check the language pattern. Say my name four times in a row and tap a pulse in your palm each time." At this point, the teacher modeled speaking the name and tapping a finger on the opposite palm, reversing hands with each repetition. "Did you hear the accent on my name? Mrs. MURdock? How will we keep that accent for our song? Let's sing it. . . Oh, do you know Mrs. MURdock . . ." As they sang, the class put the first syllable of their teacher's last name in an accented position in the song.

"Now, how will we fit in my idea about my new puppy named Bubba? Let's sing the rest of the song and see how that idea fits at the cadence." After singing, listening, and occasionally checking the accent pattern of the language by speaking the words and tapping the accented syllable, Mrs. Murdock and the students created a new verse for *Muffin Man:* "Oh, DO you know Mrs. MURdock, Mrs. MURdock, Mrs. MURdock? Oh, DO you know Mrs. MURdock, who HAS a new puppy named BUBba?"

Although this exercise took time before the activity began, Mrs. Murdock knew it was time well spent. Not only was she modeling the importance of maintaining the natural pronunciation of language when students worked with word substitutions in songs, but she also was giving them a tool for listening to and checking sound patterns. Students could then monitor their own use of language in future turns and in other songs.

"We've got the song and we're ready to go. Walk, sing, and freeze at the cadence."

Muffin Man

Oh, do you know the muf-fin man, the muf-fin man, the muf-fin man? Oh, do you know the muf-fin man who lives on Dru-ry Lane?

Brief Description

In a standing circle, students walk beside a partner. In the center is the muffin man who tells the group something about himself or herself. The group walks and sings as they fit the person's name and idea into the song. At the cadence, everyone freezes until the muffin man says "Grab." Everyone, including the muffin man, grabs a new partner, and the activity begins again. For additional challenges, students can be asked to find something in common with another before accepting that person as a partner.

Age Appropriateness

Version 1—Grade 3 through Grade 6   Grab Game

Degrees of Intensity

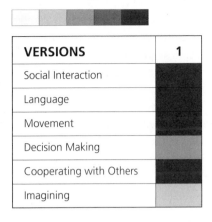

Learning Opportunities

- *Coordinate movement* with beginning and ending of sound: Auditory-motor skills.
- *Maintain pace and space* while moving in a circle: Auditory-visual-motor skills, spatial skills.
- *Word substitution:* Vocabulary skills, listening skills.
- Move to and name the *anacrusis:* Music skills, motor skills.
- Find and change *partners* frequently: Social skills.
- Pantomime *introductions:* Social skills, drama skills.
- *Share information* about oneself: Social skills (Version 4).
- Echo phrase *structure:* Music skills.
- *Melody* patterns of SO₁ | SO₁ DO DO and DO | RE RE SO₁ SO₁ DO: Music skills.
- *Rhythm* patterns of ♪ | ♫ ♫ ♩ (DE DU DE DU DE DU) and ♪ | ♫ ♪ (TA DU DE DU): Music skills.

Song and Activity Background

Muffin Man is of British origin, and the earliest record of it is 1810. According to the Opies, muffins were popular fare from the 1700s to the 1900s. They lost favor to crumpets in the 1930s and were not common again until about 1965. This perspective makes one of the versions of the muffin man a curiosity. As early as 1866, one version of the song had the muffin man living on Crumpet Lane. Though Drury Lane may be the muffin man's best known address in many regions of the United States and Canada, the muffin man has also been known to reside on Dorset and Cherry Lanes.

An anecdote in *The Art of Amusing* (1866) describes a hilarious version of the *Muffin Man* game in which a party of people sat in a circle. The first person sang, "Do you know the muffin man . . . who lives in Crumpet Lane?" Then the next person sang the answer, "Oh, yes, I know the muffin man . . . who lives in Crumpet Lane." When the song had traveled around the circle, all joined in singing "We all know the muffin man . . . who lives in Crumpet Lane." The game was to keep a grave face at all times, and if you laughed, you were out of the game. As Frank Bellow recalled the event, the group ranged in age from 3 to 70, and "we were all in convulsions of laughter . . . there was something so idiotic and absurd in a large party of respectable, rational beings, congratulating themselves in song that they 'knew the muffin man of Crumpet Lane'" (Opie and Opie 1985, 379–382).

In the 1890s, the muffin man game was played with a child in the center who, blindfolded, had to catch someone from the circle and guess who he or she was. By the 1950s, a version of the game had the student in the middle of a circle move to someone in the circle and sing the question verse. Then that person would sing the answer verse, and both would then dance around singing, "Two of us know the muffin man." The version of muffin man that is described here, with the circle of partners, a person in the center, and a scramble for new partners at the end, matches other games that are played this way, especially the early versions of courtship games, such as *The Jolly Miller* and older versions of *Skip to My Lou*.

Script. Grab Game

Teacher	Students
• *Please choose a partner and begin walking beside your partner in a circle until you hear me say "Freeze."* This is usually an efficient way to organize students into partners in a double circle.	Students select partners and join the group in walking around in a circle. When the circle and partners are organized, "freeze" stops them in their places to listen to instructions.
• *Although these aren't the words we'll be singing today, you may remember this song. It's very common, known by many people. At the cadence of the song, freeze in your place.* Hum or chin the melody of *Muffin Man* as students practice walking beside their partners and freezing at the cadence. • *Who can tell us what song you heard?* • *What words do you remember to this song?*	Students are asked to recollect the song *Muffin Man*. After ideas are collected, students sing the song as they walk around in a circle. Students are reminded to freeze on the cadence. • *Did you remember to stop your feet just as you sang the last word of the song?* • *What is the word that we freeze on?*
• *I'll take the first turn as the muffin man. So let's put my name in the song instead of "the muffin man." But I don't live on Drury Lane, I live on Sunflower Drive.* • *If you change the song to fit my name and my street, how will we sing it?*	Students practice singing the song, substituting the new words. "Oh, DO you know Mrs. MURdock . . .who LIVES on SUNflower DRIVE?"
• *Our song is ready. I'll stand in the middle as you walk, sing, and freeze at the cadence.* [Sing the starting pitch.] *Ready. . . ."*	Students take a practice turn of the game, singing the new words.
At the cadence of the song, remind students that they are frozen and only their eyes can move. • *When you hear me say "Grab," get a new partner as quickly as possible and find a place in the circle so we can begin again. . . . Grab!"*	As students find new partners, one person will be left over. He or she is the new muffin man. Students may seem reserved in their grabbing of new partners during the first few turns. After several turns, however, they eagerly enter into the spirit of the game. If there is an even number of players, add a rule that after the muffin man says "Grab," he or she must choose two students to make one group of three for that turn.

Teacher	Students
Encouragingly introduce the new muffin man: • *Brad, it looks like you're our new muffin man. You get the next turn. What will you tell us about yourself?* • *You could tell us someplace you've been, something you like, someone you know, or something you have done.*	 Taking a moment to ponder his response, Brad offers, "I am going to my grandparents house next weekend."
• *Let's practice fitting Brad's words into our song.* Sing the tune to the last line of the song. "Oh, do you know Brad who . . ," and pause so that students fill in the rest of the song with Brad's idea. • *Good thinking and listening! You'll get lots of practice fitting words to the song in this game! Here comes Brad's song. Be ready to freeze and listen for Brad's voice.*	After some effort, students offer "who is GOing to his GRANDparents' house next WEEKend." "Grab," Brad says after the cadence, and all students scurry to get a new partner. Soon, all see that April steps to the center, and the game continues.
• *April, while you're thinking of your idea, we'll practice some motions.* • *That anacrusis "Oh" helps us get ready to sing and walk together. It also gives us a nice feeling for gesturing toward the muffin man. Let's sing and practice that anacrusis gesture.* All begin with one arm extended toward the outside of the circle as they sing "Oh." Then the arm coordinates with the anacrusis to gesture in toward the muffin man as "do" is sung.	 The anacrusis gesture helps the group to focus as they begin the song and coordinates movement with the pickup sound of the song.
• *As we walk, partners on the inside will pretend that we are introducing April to our partner on the outside.* • *What gestures and facial expressions will you use in pantomiming the introduction?* • *Show us some of the expressions and gestures you can use as you introduce April.*	Students explore a bit of drama for the activity as they pantomime with gestures and facial expressions. The game continues as the students share ideas, and words are checked for accuracy of pronunciation in the song.
Intensity (and noise) in grabbing a partner is added when the teacher or the students give ideas for how partners are to match with other partners. The idea is given while students are still frozen, before the "grab." • *I will add a new twist to our game today. Grady, I want to give a challenge before you say "Grab." Let me remind you, class, that you are frozen, but when you hear Grady's voice, find a partner wearing the same type of shoes as you.*	 Several students may start to move right away, then hurriedly return to their places until Grady says "Grab." Creative and humorous interactions can result as students incorporate their own challenges for finding a partner.
These are some possibilities for imagination questions the students may discuss: Why was the muffin man important enough to have a song composed and sung about him? Why do you think the song asks the question "Do you know him?" Why would someone want to know if we each know the muffin man? Why would the muffin man live on Crumpet Lane? Why are there variants that include at least four different "Lanes" as addresses for the muffin man?	

Mulberry Bush

SCENARIO

PRINCIPLE 2

PRINCIPLE 4

VERSION 1: CIRCLE GAME

With the children in a standing circle, the teacher prepared her Grade 2 students for the song by engaging their imaginations. "We're going to skip around a mulberry bush. Does anyone know what this kind of bush looks like? Who is willing to describe what you imagine?" As some students shared their ideas, the teacher offered questions to prompt their thinking: "Does it have leaves? How big is it? Could a rabbit hide under it? Would a bird build a nest in it?" After some discussion of students' imaginings, the teacher gave them an assignment: "Ask someone in your family what a mulberry bush is. Then look up the description in a book. Where will you look? I'll ask you what you've learned about mulberry bushes the next time I see you."

Building imagery for the song activity, the teacher stretched her arms overhead and said, "Oh, it's early in the morning and here we are going around a mulberry bush. Why might we be doing that?" The teacher was more interested in stimulating imaginations than in having the group come to a consensus about the real or original meaning of the song. After listening to possibilities, the teacher continued, "Well, it's difficult to know what this song originally meant, so let's use one of your images for our activity. Let's say that a beautiful mulberry bush is right outside the door of our house and that we must walk around it to get to the sidewalk.

"Sometimes getting up early in the morning and getting ready for school is easier when we enjoy our routines—especially when we know our friends will be here to greet us when we arrive!" Singing, the teacher and the students held hands and skipped in a circle around the mulberry bush. "Here we go 'round the mulberry bush, the mulberry bush, the mulberry bush. Here we go 'round the mulberry bush, so early in the morning."

Continuing with the next section of the song, the teacher sang, "This is the way we brush our teeth, brush our teeth, brush our teeth. This is the way we brush our teeth, so early in the morning." As she sang, she pantomimed the motions of brushing teeth and stretched her arms up and to the side as she sang "so early in the morning." The children imitated her. "What else do we do to get ready for school?" Jackson answered, "Eat our cereal." "How many of you have cereal for breakfast? Jackson, how will we look as we're eating our cereal?" Jackson pantomimed the action for all to imitate. "Let's sing about it. Get ready to go around the mulberry bush. Remember to hold hands gently as you skip so you won't hurt others' hands."

The activity continued as students offered ideas for getting ready in the morning. With her Grade 3 classes later that day, the teacher introduced an element of surprise by instructing the circle to "go the other way," "tiptoe," "march," and so on as they circled the mulberry bush. Although they were familiar with the song and the game, the Grade 3 students enjoyed this new twist to a familiar activity.

Mulberry Bush

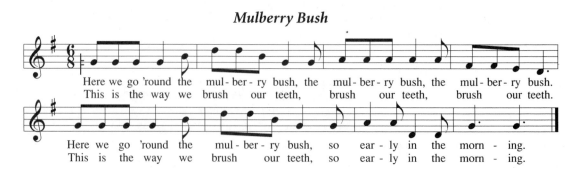

Here we go 'round the mul-ber-ry bush, the mul-ber-ry bush, the mul-ber-ry bush.
This is the way we brush our teeth, brush our teeth, brush our teeth.

Here we go 'round the mul-ber-ry bush, so ear-ly in the morn-ing.
This is the way we brush our teeth, so ear-ly in the morn-ing.

Brief Description

In a standing circle, students hold hands, sing, skip, and stop at the cadence. Then they offer ideas for what they do in the morning to get ready for school. When a child offers an idea and an action that pantomimes the idea, the class joins in singing the words and making the motion. The group alternates skipping and pantomiming for sections of the song. The person offering the idea may stay in his or her place in the circle or may stand in the center, twirling with a finger pointed to choose the child who will take the next turn at the cadence. Partners may offer ideas from the center of the circle. Younger children may be more successful walking than skipping in a circle. Version 2 uses the standard game to help students practice ideas for safety tips, hygiene habits, and helping behaviors.

Age Appropriateness

Version 1—Preschool through Grade 3 Circle Game

Version 2—Preschool through Grade 2 Helping Game

Degrees of Intensity

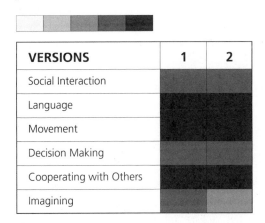

VERSIONS	1	2
Social Interaction		
Language		
Movement		
Decision Making		
Cooperating with Others		
Imagining		

Learning Opportunities

- *Coordinate movement* with beginning and ending of sound: Auditory-motor skills.
- *Locomotor movement* in a circle—skipping, walking: Motor skills.
- *Maintain pace and space* while moving in a circle: Auditory-visual-motor skills, spatial skills.
- *Pantomime movement* to language ideas: Drama skills.
- *Whole-group cooperation*: Social skills.
- *Word substitution:* Language skills, music skills.
- *Imitate* actions: Visual-motor coordination.
- Echo phrase *structure:* Music skills.
- *Melody* patterns of DO DO DO DO MI SO SO MI DO and DO | RE RE SO₁ SO₁ DO DO: Music skills.
- *Rhythm* patterns of ♪ | ♩ ♫ ♫. ♩. (DI DU DI DU DI DU DU) and ♪ | ♫♩ ♩ (DI DUDADI DU) and ♫♩ ♩ (DUDADI DU): Music skills.

Song and Activity Background

The earliest mention of it was in 1821 and over twenty-two versions existed in the 1890s, yet *Mulberry Bush* seems to be a later version of *Bramble Bush:* "Here we go 'round the bramble bush . . . on a cold and frosty morning" (Baring-Gould and Baring-Gould 1967, 251–252; Newell 1883; Opie and Opie 1988, 277). The melody of *Mulberry Bush* also matches a song that was a precursor, variously known as *Nuts in May, Nuts and May,* and *Knots of May:* "Here we go gathering nuts in May . . . on a summer's morning." Through its many evolutions, the song seems to celebrate the earth's flowering; it is a May game that depicts everything from the stages of getting married to roses gathering dew and flowering. The game format fits the traditional circle dance that is balanced by the participants standing still when there are actions to perform, then skipping in a circle again.

Script. Version 1: Circle Game

Teacher	Students
When students form a standing circle, set a storytelling mood by pretending: • *It's early in the morning and here we are, going around a bush.* • *Let's imagine that the bush is very large and that we must keep our circle round to avoid skipping into the branches. As we sing and skip, let's keep our circle big and round as we go around the mulberry bush. As we sing "so early in the morning," stop and face toward the mulberry bush.*	The group holds hands, sings, and skips in a circle around the mulberry bush. Imagining that they are avoiding the branches helps them to concentrate on keeping the circle round and full as they move.
After practicing several turns of keeping the circle round, encourage ideas for the next section of the song: • *When I get ready for school, I drink a glass of juice like this.* [Pantomime, then sing.] *"This is the way we drink our juice . . ."*	As you model an idea and appropriate actions, and as they sing and imitate, students are prompted to think of ideas for getting ready for school. As they sing "so early in the morning," all stretch arms above heads and down.
Taking the hands of students on either side of you, sing the first section, *"Here we go round . . ."* and skip around in a circle. Some students need reminders to hold their neighbors' hands lightly as they skip. Skipping can cause some children to hold very tightly for balance. At the cadence, ask, • *Who has another idea to share for what we do in the morning to get ready? Let's listen and watch as Manny tells us his idea.* • [Manny says, "Tie our shoes."] *Manny, show us how we'll look as we do that.* [All imitate.] *Let's put Manny's idea into the song.*	Students watch and listen to others as ideas are shared, then imitate the motions and sing.

Teacher	Students
• *Before our next turn, let's all stop for a moment and think about what our idea will be if we get a turn. Take some thinking time. Raise your hand when you have an idea. When most of us have our ideas ready, then we'll know we can begin the game and not need to stop to think of ideas.* • *I see most people had enough thinking time to get an idea. Carl will give us one this time. Here comes the song . . .* Play continues as students share and demonstrate ideas. At appropriate intervals, play can be vitalized by instructing the circle to "go the other way," "tiptoe," "march," and so on. The student sharing the idea can also be encouraged to speak in full sentences "This is the way we . . ." or to sing the idea with the group joining the singing as soon as they hear the idea.	 Skipping around the mulberry bush alternates with singing ideas for getting ready for school. Students can also create ideas and actions as small groups.

Additional Versions of Mulberry Bush

Version 2: Helping Game. The *Mulberry Bush* activity can be used to highlight students' ideas for how to help at home, how to practice safety tips, and how to demonstrate hygiene habits. Students can offer these ideas as part of whole-group activity, or they can create ideas and actions as small groups.

- *This is the way we make our beds . . .*
- *This is the way we buckle our seat belts . . .*
- *This is the way we floss our teeth . . .*

Old Dan Tucker

SCENARIO

PRINCIPLE 2

VERSION 1: FOLLOW-THE-LEADER GAME

"I'll begin," said the teacher to focus the group, seated in a circle. "Your challenge is to imitate the ways I am showing the beat, and to change the movement whenever I do. Listen to the song as you move." The teacher proceeded to sing *Old Dan Tucker* as he clapped, tapped, swayed, and snapped, changing movement with each phrase. Students did not know the song, so they listened and imitated the movements.

"You followed my movements very closely, so the next time I'll make them a little more challenging. What word or words did you hear in the song?" Students began to share their recollections of words or phrases that they had heard the teacher sing. The teacher greeted all ideas with acceptance but did not indicate whether they were accurate or inaccurate.

"For not knowing the song and for being busy with the motions, you remembered lots of the words. I'll sing again and you can check your observations." As the teacher began the song again, he demonstrated new movements, changing on each phrase. "Now tell us the words or phrases you heard."

Through collaborative recall, students pieced together the words of *Old Dan Tucker.* When most of the words were collected, the teacher spoke the words to the song, piquing students' interest by announcing, "This song is about a most unusual

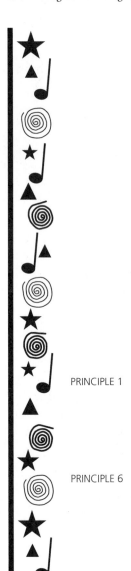

PRINCIPLE 1

PRINCIPLE 6

fellow. It may not make complete sense, but after I finish saying the words, I'd like you to tell me what you think about Old Dan Tucker and about the person singing the song."

Students were encouraged and guided to listen to each other as they shared their ideas about the song. Because class time was growing short, the teacher decided that they wouldn't be able to plumb the meanings or give the historical background of the song. "Do some thinking about this song, and we'll discuss it further the next time I see you. For now, let's sing, and I will give you more movements. There are two things for you to notice this time: How do I know when to change the movements, and how do I know how fast or slow my movements should be? Ponder those questions as we sing and move."

"What were my two questions?" Chester repeated the study questions before students began sharing their observations. Students were led to connect the movements and the changes of movement to their previous music study: moving to the beat and changing movements with each phrase. "Just so I can check your listening, place your palms up, and when you hear a new phrase, turn your hands over, palms down. Reverse your hands each time you hear a new phrase." The class got more practice with phrase changes by having designated students listen for and change movements on song words that signaled a new phrase.

"I think it's time to play follow-the-leader with Dana as our leader. We'll sing and match the movements that Dana selects. Dana, for now, don't worry if you miss a phrase change. It's just a structure you can use, but don't let it confuse your enjoyment of your turn. We'll follow you." Dana and other students took turns showing a variety of other movements to the beat, at times combining movement patterns and gestures.

As students' turns followed, their intensity in performing the beat made the song sound heavy and plodding. "Did anyone notice what is happening to our singing?" the teacher queried. Responses included "Yes, we're almost shouting," "We're singing like this [demonstrating accenting every beat]," "I didn't hear anything." The teacher shaped their movement and singing by giving information and making suggestions: "Musicians don't normally accent every beat, and when they do, it often sounds like a march or an exercise. Let's be careful in our singing. Maybe our next leader can experiment with movements that will challenge our voices to stay light and flowing. Who would like to try it? If no one volunteers, that means I get another turn!"

Old Dan Tucker

Brief Description

In a sitting circle, students imitate the leader and create ways of moving to the beat. Phrases or sections can signal a change in movements. In the Pass-the-Beat Game of Version 2, students hold both fists in front of them, and as their right hands receive the beat, their left hands pass the beat (or vice versa). Designated starters begin the song and pass the first beat, and the beat travels around the circle until the cadence. For added challenges, phrases or sections can signal a change in the beat direction, and two or more beats can be passed at a time. Version 3 challenges students to make a beat dot score to the song. After the beat dots are notated, students study them with the song to find where specific words occur in the score.

Age Appropriateness

Version 1—Grade 2 through Grade 6   Follow-the-Leader Game

Version 2—Grade 2 through Grade 6   Pass-the-Beat Game

Version 3—Grade 3 through Grade 6   Beat-Score Study

Degrees of Intensity

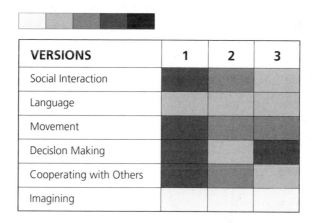

VERSIONS	1	2	3
Social Interaction			
Language			
Movement			
Decision Making			
Cooperating with Others			
Imagining			

Learning Opportunities

- *Coordinate movement* with beginning and ending of sound: Auditory-motor skills.
- Demonstrate the *steady beat:* Music skills.
- *Imitate movements:* Visual-motor skills (Versions 1, 2).
- *Move* to specific words: Auditory-motor skills, music skills (Versions 1, 2).
- Demonstrate *phrases* of the song through movement: Music skills (Versions 1, 2).
- *Notate sound* with beat dots: Music skills, motor skills (Version 3).
- *Read and study* a song score: Music skills, reading skills (Version 3).
- AB (binary) song *structure:* Music skills.

Song and Activity Background

According to Lomax and Lomax (1947, 77), the origins of this "darn fool ditty" lay in the blackface minstrel-show traditions of the mid-1800s in America. *Old Dan Tucker* is attributed to a famous minstrel performer, Dan Emmett, who was born in Southern Ohio of Irish heritage. The minstrel show was an important form of American entertainment until the end of the nineteenth century, and several songs were so well loved by the people that they were learned from the minstrel shows and transformed into folk songs by oral tradition.

One variant includes nine verses that tell the story of Old Dan Tucker coming to town and causing quite a stir as he rode a billy goat and led a hound. When the hound barked, the billy goat jumped and threw Dan Tucker "right straddle of a stump." Then Dan climbed a tree to see his "Lord and Master," but he fell when the limb broke. When he went to the mill to get some meal "for his swill," the miller swore he'd never seen anyone like Dan Tucker. Then Dan got drunk and fell in the fire, and as he was struggling, a chunk of fire fell in his shoe. Dan still had enough stamina left to go to town and dance with the ladies. But his partner, the one singing the song, said they had a "fallin' out." What do you think it was all about? Dan stepped on her corn and she kicked him in the shin. The ninth verse seems to indicate a warming of her heart as she tells that early in life he learned to play the banjo and fife, he'd play till the girls and boys went to sleep then creep into his own bunk. The tall-tale elements of *Old Dan Tucker* are found in many folk songs. Students may enjoy exploring what reasons there might be for those practices. The rousing spirit of this song lends itself well to beat activities such as those described here.

Script. Version 2: Pass-the-Beat Game

Teacher	Students
• *Let's sit close together and place both fists in front of us like this.* [Model the position of fists.] • *If I begin a beat by tapping my left fist on the right fist of the person to my left, he then must tap his left fist on the fist of the person to his left and so on.* • *I'll start the beat, and let's all watch it pass from person to person.* The group watches as the motion proceeds around the circle from fist to fist. Some groups work better with the motion passing to the right rather than the left. The right fist, therefore, could be the one to pass the beat.	Students observe the teacher's modeling, then tap their neighbor's fist as the motion is sent around the circle.
• *Now that we've practiced our movement, listen to the song.* • *The song is about a man who does some unusual things.* • *As you listen, practice the beat by tapping one of your fists on top of the other. You may alternate fists with each beat if you like.*	As students listen to the song, they practice demonstrating the beat by tapping their own fists. The teacher watches their movements to determine whether further practice in moving to the beat is necessary before proceeding with the activity.
• *What word or words did you hear?* Antiphonning can be used to help students learn the words. • *Let's antiphon the words. We'll speak rather than sing the song this time.* Begin the antiphonning activity by having students antiphon the phrase endings. For example, say "*Old Dan Tucker was*" and have students fill in "*a mighty man.*" Parts of the song where students are unsure of the words can be reviewed in repetitions of the antiphonning activity by the teacher speaking those parts.	Students collectively recall the song. As students antiphon, the teacher listens for the words they need to hear again, then speaks those parts during another turn of antiphonning.

Teacher	Students
Students predict where the beat will end, then sing and pass the beat with fists.	
• *Let's sing the song together now and pass the beat as we sing.*	
• *If I start the beat and it proceeds steadily as we sing the song, where do you think it will end?*	
• *I'm seeing some fists hitting a little hard as they pass the beat. Check with your neighbor right now to decide on a tap that is comfortable for both of you. Remember also that we want the beat to move smoothly and musically as we sing, so tapping too hard would work against that.*	Occasionally, students begin hitting fists too hard as they pass the beat. Students can further study by counting the number of beats in the song and comparing that with the number of people who passed the beat.
Repetitions of the song can involve predicting where the cadence beat will occur, letting the beat-starter decide which direction to send the beat and beginning two beats (or more) at the same time from different points in the circle.	Students are challenged to sing, watch, and perform the beat. They shape the activity by creating and meeting their own challenges.

Additional Versions of Old Dan Tucker

Version 3: Beat-Score Study. After students have had many opportunities to sing the song and move to the beat, they make individual beat scores of the song using the song-dotting technique. As they beat-dot, students coordinate their movements and dotting, not with the rhythm, but with the beat. (See "Song Dotting" in Chapter 5.) Students make scores, read scores, and circle the dots on which key words such as "man," "pan," "wheel," "heel," "supper," and "lookin'" occur.

Old Grumbler

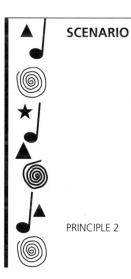

SCENARIO

PRINCIPLE 2

VERSION 1: IMAGINATION GAME

With a look of intrigue and mystery, the teacher sang the first verse of *Old Grumbler* to the students: "Old Grumbler was dead and lay under the ground, under the ground, under the ground. Old Grumbler was dead and lay under the ground, way high up." As she expected, the fifth-grade students looked at her first with puzzlement, then with disbelief when they heard the final phrase. "How could he be under the ground and be 'way high up'?" asked Zeke. "Good question," the teacher responded with a twinkle in her eye. "That's the riddle of this song. I will be *very* interested in how you solve it. First, though, get into groups of four sitting together on the floor, as I sing the song for you again. Your task is to listen for clues as you get into groups, and you have only until the song ends to be in your groups, ready to go on." As she sang the song and the students moved into circles of four, the teacher distributed one large sheet of paper to each group.

"You get to solve this puzzle as a group. After your group comes to a decision on what you believe this song is about, draw a picture describing your solution. I'll be

giving you some markers in a moment, but to get you ready for solving the mystery, consider these questions: Who is Old Grumbler? Is that a real name or a nickname? Where do you think he or she got that name? How did he die? And, as Zeke so clearly posed, how can he be under the ground 'way high up'?

"You will have several minutes to discuss and draw, so work as efficiently and co-operatively as possible. We will take time to hear your explanations of your ideas and your drawings, so keep that in mind as you work. You may want to designate someone to be the speaker for your group."

Students listened intently and with good-natured humor as their classmates shared their drawings and explanations of the first verse of *Old Grumbler*. The teacher purposely let the students themselves manage this time of sharing ideas and asking questions.

Old Grumbler

Old Grum-bler was dead and lay un-der the ground, un-der the ground, un-der the ground. Old Grum-bler was dead and lay un-der the ground, way high up.

Verse 2—*Three apple trees grew right over his head . . .*

Verse 3—*The apples were ripe and were ready to drop . . .*

Verse 4—*There came an east wind a-blowin' them off . . .*

Verse 5—*There came an old lady a-pickin' them up . . .*

Verse 6—*Old Grumbler jumped up and he gave her a knock . . .*

Verse 7—*Which made the old lady go hippety hop . . .*

Verse 8—*Old Grumbler lay down with a smile on his face . . .*

Brief Description

In Version 1, students initially hear only the first verse of the song; then, in small groups, they discuss and draw what they think the song is about. As students are seated in a circle or in a scatter formation for the Drama Game of Version 2, they listen to all the verses being sung, then act out the story that the song portrays. In Version 3, students create their own stories about what happened to Old Grumbler and compose new verses to tell their stories.

Age Appropriateness

Version 1—Grade 3 through Grade 6	Imagination Game
Version 2—Grade 4 through Grade 6	Drama Game
Version 3—Grade 4 through Grade 6	Composition Game

Degrees of Intensity

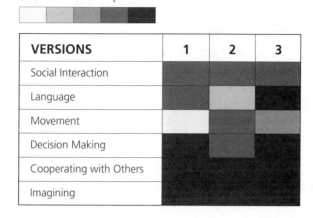

Learning Opportunities

- *Imagination* in exploring meaning: Thinking skills.
- *Role-playing* characters in the song: Drama skills (Versions 2, 3).
- *Word substitution* to create new verses: Language skills (Version 3).
- *Audience etiquette* for performances: Social skills (Version 2).
- *Creative writing* in preparing a story: Language skills (Version 3).
- Echo phrase *structure* and anacrusis: Music skills.
- *Melody* patterns of SO₁ | DO DO DO MI and SO₁ RE DO: Music skills.
- *Rhythm* patterns ♫ ♩. (DUDADI DU) and ♪ | ♫ ♪ (DI DUDADI DU): Music skills.

Song and Activity Background

As a song that begs to be dramatized, *Old Roger* is perhaps more well known than its cousin, *Old Grumbler*. The cadence chunk "way high up" has been sung as varying sorts of exclamations: Hee! Hi!, Heigh Ho, Hum ha, Hee haw, E I, and I O. In describing the drama that accompanies the song, Opie and Opie (1985, 252) suggested that the apple tree was part of Old Roger; therefore, he had good reason to get mad at the old woman for stealing part of his body—a theme common to other games in which the dead man jumps up and chases mourners or visitors *(Dead Man Arise, Jenny Jones)*. The Opies said of this play, "We can only feel that this dramatic comedy was a shout of laughter in the face of death, enacted by a whole community hand in hand and probably fortified by liquor. It may have been played at wakes" (p. 251).

There are many variants of the story of *Old Grumbler* and of the dead man's name. "Old John Rogers" was a 1907 poem from the United States that described the apple tree, the apples, the woman, and Old John Rogers, who gives the woman a whack—at which point she runs to the top of the hill, sits down, and makes her will. Perhaps because Roger was a popular Christian name during the Middle Ages, "Old Roger," "Poor Roger," and "Sir Roger" are the most common names among the more than seventy versions available. Yet, the name that occurs in a song may be the most unstable element of traditional lore, because people forget names or are tempted to insert names of local characters or a joke name. For the story of *Old Grumbler* and *Old Roger,* there is "Poor Tommy" in Edinburgh, "Poor Johnnie" in Norfolk, "Poor Toby" in Belfast, and "Poor Gracie" in North Shields (Opie and Opie). In 1883,

Newell reported "Old Cromwell" as the deceased, and because "Oliver Cromwell" is the bogeyman in a Liverpool version (about 1890), there is some speculation that Old Cromwell was mangled into "Old Crummle," "Old Grumble," or "Old Grumbler" (Opie and Opie, pp. 252–253). Whatever the origins and variants of this story, it provides a rich experience for students in storytelling, story making, and story acting. The story is acted out today in nearly exact replication of the play described by Gomme in 1894.

Version 1 developed in classes of Peggy Bennett at The University of Texas at Arlington in 1993. Version 3 was developed by Annette Coffin with her students in British Columbia, Canada, about 1993.

Script. Version 2: Drama Game

Teacher	Students
With facial expression and gestures that dramatize the song, begin singing *Old Grumbler* to the students. Interest and vocal participation can be elicited by brief questions or comments inserted between verses. Questions can be effective tools, even when they are not overtly answered by students.	
• *What do you think happens next?* • *You'll hear some words that repeat. Please join me in singing as you hear the repetitions.* • *Must have been a pretty strong wind!*	Students listen and join in singing during verses of the song.
As you sing "*way high up*" for each verse, you can add movement that provides closure. On "*way*," clap hands at waist level or lower; on "*high*," cross hands like an X at nose level; and on "*up*," make a fist with each hand about chin level. These hand movements approximate the Curwen hand signs for the melody of that song chunk, SO$_1$ RE DO.	Students imitate the teacher model for the hand movements.
• *If we were to act out this story, whom would we need for the first character? What other characters do we need for the play?*	Students recall the verses and collect the characters needed for the story. Volunteers are selected to dramatize the story: a Grumbler, three apple trees, an east wind, an old lady.
• *Let's arrange ourselves so that we can all see the play. Some characters are off stage when the curtain opens. Who are they?* • *Remember that the theater lights dim just before the curtain opens. Audience etiquette tells us that we applaud when the curtain opens—to give the cast our thanks for their efforts.* • *We'll all sing the song as we watch the characters explore their roles.*	Students sing for the play and applaud for the finish. Depending on time and inclination, curtain calls can be practiced as the audience continues to applaud.

Teacher	Students
Successive performances of *Old Grumbler* can occur with a new cast of characters or time can be taken for all students to rehearse all the parts of the story.	Students explore the many possibilities for and variations on the characters involved in the story.
• *Let's all sing as we play the part of Old Grumbler. Think about how you want the audience to see you. Will they see your face or not? If they do, what expression will you have?*	
• *If the verse portrays an apple tree growing, how will you express that? How will you show the gradual growth of a tree? What will you look like when you're grown?*	Some students can be designated mourners, wailing and sniffling as the scene opens, then joining the chorus after verse 1.

As they intially hear all verses of *Old Grumbler*, students can lie on the floor with their eyes closed and "see a movie" as the story unfolds. Then, in small groups, they can dramatize the play.

Sometimes it makes sense to have all students practice the roles in each verse as a way of preparing them for performing the roles individually.

Especially for Grades 5 and 6, creating a drama without previous modeling can lead to clever and unique interpretations of the song.

Additional Versions of Old Grumbler

Version 3: Composition Game. After learning the song and acting out the verses, students are challenged to create their own stories to answer the question "*How did Old Grumbler die?*" Students write their stories on paper and read their stories to the class; then the class chooses one story it enjoys. In small groups, students compose one verse to correlate with the new story. These verses can be the basis for further dramatization.

Old House

SCENARIO

PRINCIPLE 2

VERSION 1: IDENTIFYING REPETITIONS

"There is quite a bit of repetition in this song. What repetitions do you hear?" After this short introduction, the teacher sang the song, repeated the question, and looked with curiosity as many hands went up. The teacher called on all who had their hands up, listening to each one but making little or no comment. As she listened to individuals, other hands were raised. Students were clearly getting support from the fact that she was still calling on volunteers and had not yet given "the answer." Many students indicated that "tear it down" repeated, but the teacher did not react other than noting the response. "You heard 'tear it down' repeat," was a comment she made several times. The teacher was not concerned that some students might be getting answers from others who spoke first. Some of these students rarely spoke up, and that was what she was addressing at the moment, trying to encourage all of her students to share what they heard.

"The repetitions you heard have given us some ideas to check with the song. Here comes the song. Listen to see if we missed any repetitions. Do all of the ideas mentioned repeat in the song?" After singing, the teacher focused on "tear it down." "Many heard 'tear it down' repeat in the song. Now listen closely to see if all the 'tear

it down' phrases are exactly the same. Here comes the song." This time, the students were split in their answers. Some felt that every "tear it down" was the same; others felt that some phrases went up, some stayed even, and some went down. Still other students thought that the 'tear it down' phrases either went up or stayed the same.

"Show me with your hands when you think the melody of 'tear it down' goes up, stays the same, or goes down." With each option, the teacher simultaneously modeled actions with her hands. To illustrate the pitch going up, the teacher placed her hands at waist level so that each hand looked as if it was holding a baseball but was ready to drop it (LA), then lifted her hands and made them into fists at chest level (DO). To show the pitch staying the same, she repeated the same position for each syllable of "tear it down." To show the pitch going down, she let her hands drop lower, dropping the imaginary ball from her hands and her arms at the same time.

When several students suggested that there were only two types of "tear it down," one that went up and one that stayed the same, the teacher asked the class to check this observation as she sang the song and used her hands to indicate the melodic contour of each "tear it down." The teacher encouraged students to practice these actions as she sang the song again, and was careful to let students figure out the pattern by themselves. Before validating students' opinions, the teacher asked the class to check the patterns without seeing her hands do the actions. This strategy gave some of her slower students a chance to remember what the pattern was and to hear it for themselves. Meanwhile, the rhythmic energy of the song was taking over—some students were tapping their feet, and others were quietly bouncing with the song.

PRINCIPLE 4

"Let's all sing the song as we feel the 'tear it down' phrases with our actions." After the song, the teacher asked the students if there were any words or places they were unsure of, clarifying the sequence of hammer, saw, and wrecking machine. Watching students' movements as they sang, the teacher offered constructive feedback: "Kate, that took some listening." "Jerry, I could tell you heard the pattern too that time, because your hands moved right with the melody."

PRINCIPLE 6

Some were still struggling to hear the melody changes, but the teacher knew that varied repetition would help them feel more confident. "Turn to a partner and create two movements—one to show the melody going up and another to show the melody staying the same." By working with partners, students had additional help in coordinating their actions with the song. They were eager to share their creations, and the activity seemed to enliven the study as students actively sang the song and watched others' movements.

Old House

Old house, tear it down! Who's gon-na help me tear it down?

Bring me a ham-mer, tear it down! Bring me a saw, tear it down! The

next thing you bring me, tear it down, is a wreck-ing ma-chine. Tear it down!

Brief Description

In Version 1, students identify the pattern of contour and repetition in the "tear it down" phrases and incorporate movements that show this pattern. Movements are introduced that show the hand signs for solfa, as students sing LA₁ LA₁ DO when the phrase goes up and LA₁ LA₁ LA₁ when it stays the same. The beat activities described for *Old Dan Tucker* and the hand-jive activity described for *Hot Cross Buns* are also effective for *Old House*.

Age Appropriateness

    Version 1—Grade 3 through Grade 6   Identifying Repetitions

    Version 2—Grade 3 through Grade 6   Building a House

Degrees of Intensity

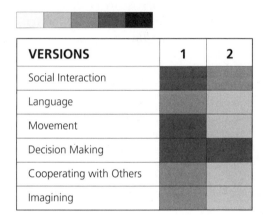

VERSIONS	1	2
Social Interaction		
Language		
Movement		
Decision Making		
Cooperating with Others		
Imagining		

Learning Opportunities

- *Coordinate movement* with specific sounds: Auditory-motor skills.
- Identify *repetition* through movement: Auditory-motor skills (Version 1).
- Use movement and *hand signs* to illustrate *melodic contour*: Auditory-motor skills, music skills (Version 1).
- *Pantomime* the words to a song: Drama skills (Version 2).
- *Melody* in minor mode and patterns of LA₁ DO LA₁ LA₁ DO and LA₁ LA₁ DO and LA₁ LA₁ LA₁: Music skills.
- *Rhythm* pattern of ♫♩. ♩ (DU TA DU): Music skills.

Song and Activity Background

Old House is a balanced call-and-response structure with spirited, **syncopated** rhythms. This appealing melody may have been an African American work song that accompanied tedious and strenuous tasks. A second verse suggests building the house up after tearing it down (*Making Music Your Own*, Book 2, Silver Burdett Company, 1971, p. 26).

Additional Versions of Old House

Version 2: Building a House.   By changing the words to describe building a house instead of tearing it down ("*New house, build it up, who's going to help me build it up?*"), students can enact the building of a house. One or two students are chosen to be the builders, and they, through pantomiming while all sing the song, enlist other students to be walls, doors, windows, fences, and so forth. The builders lead others to the appropriate places and have them bend over, raise arms, and generally take the shape the builder indicates. Once the house is built, the words can be changed back to the "tear it down" version, and the house can be carefully disassembled.

Paw-Paw Patch

SCENARIO

VERSION 1: WHO'S MISSING GAME

The preschool children were seated in a scatter formation on the floor with their eyes closed as they sang, "Where, oh, where is pretty little Susie? . . . Way down yonder in the paw-paw patch." During the song, the teacher gently tapped the head of Deidre, who hopped up quickly and went to hide behind the screen. Deidre knew she had a short amount of time until the song was over and the other children would be opening their eyes.

As all began singing "Come on, boys, let's go find her. Come on, girls, let's go find her. Come on, everyone, let's go find her, way down yonder in the paw-paw patch," the children stood and wandered around trying to discover who was missing. At the end of this verse, all sat down on their spaces.

"Were you able to decide who is missing from our group?" asked the teacher. Several children spoke out in their eagerness to guess. "So that we'll all be able to hear you, please raise your hand if you have a guess," the teacher prompted. "Jeremy, who is missing?" she asked. "Kelly," responded Jeremy; he looked around the group to check and discovered that Kelly was seated right behind him. All giggled as the teacher joined in their delight when they guessed someone who was clearly still in the room.

After a couple of guesses more and much looking around the room, the children finally agreed with Jon that Deidre was missing. "Well, let's see if Deidre is behind the screen. We'll call her by asking 'Oh, Deidre, are you there?' Let's ask the question together." As she modeled the question for her students, the teacher used a little voice play to insert a bit of humor and vocal exercise into this part of the game. She used exaggerated intonation and quizzical facial expressions as she posed the question to Deidre.

As the class focused on the edge of the screen, Deidre came out smiling. "Yes, I am," she replied, and the group welcomed her back by singing, "Come on Deidre, come on back again. . . . paw-paw patch."

As the group sang the first verse and covered their eyes, they shifted to singing about a missing boy: "Where, oh, where is handsome little Johnnie . . . paw-paw patch." Deidre then quickly and quietly tapped a boy to go hide behind the screen.

The delight and enjoyment this game gave the children always amazed their teacher. It seemed so simple and not very challenging for them. But the children were satisfied with the simple tasks of finding who was missing, calling for hidden children to identify themselves, and welcoming the child back to the group.

Paw-Paw Patch

Brief Description

In the Who's Missing Game of Version 1, children sit in a scatter formation on the floor with their eyes closed. The first verse is sung as one child is chosen to be Susie and to hide behind a partition. During the second verse, children wander around trying to discover what child is missing from the group. After children guess the missing child, the game begins again. In Version 2, a child is chosen to go hide, and the group tries to find the hiding spot.

Age Appropriateness

Version 1—Preschool through Grade 1   Who's Missing Game

Version 2—Preschool through Grade 1   Hiding Game

Degrees of Intensity

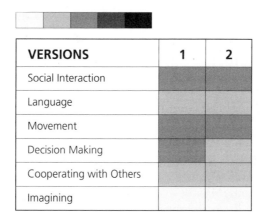

VERSIONS	1	2
Social Interaction		
Language		
Movement		
Decision Making		
Cooperating with Others		
Imagining		

Learning Opportunities

- *Scan* the group to look for the missing person: Visual skills, recall skills (Version 1).

- *Coordinate and pace movement* while moving in a scatter formation: Spatial skills, motor skills.

- *Voice play* to ask a question: Voice skills (Version 1).

- Balanced phrase *structure:* Music skills.

- *Melody* pattern of unisons (DO DO DO DO) and SO SO SO LA SO FA MI DO DO: Music skills.

- *Rhythm* patterns of ♪♪ ♫♫♫ ♪♪ ♩ (DU DE DUTADETA DU DE DU) and ♪♪ ♪♪ ♫♫♫ ♪♪ (DU DE DU DE DUTADETA DU DE): Music skills.

Song and Activity Background

With the exception of different cadence-phrase melodies, the melody of *Paw-Paw Patch* resembles that of a song known from the early 1900s in Britain, *Dusty Bluebells*, which is played similarly to the games known to many American children as *Bluebird* and *Ginger Snap*: "In and out the dusty bluebells . . . who shall be my master? Tippitty tappitty on your shoulder . . . You shall be my master." *Paw-Paw Patch* also has apparent connections in melody and words to *O Belinda* ("Right hand up, O Belinda . . . won't you be my darling?") and *Boston* ("Come on, girls, we're going to Boston") (Opie and Opie 1985, 367). *Paw-Paw Patch* also bears a similarity to *Where, O Where Is Old Elijah?* which loosely tells the biblical stories of Elijah and the chariot, Absalom and the spear of Joab, and Daniel in the lions' den: "Where, o where is Old Elijah? . . . Way over in the Promised Land" (Sandburg 1927, 92–93). According to Sandburg, the words and melody of *Where, O Where Is Old Elijah?* may have been borrowed from black Americans and could be considered a "white man's spiritual."

Version 1 was developed with Tony Williamson's Oregon preschool students in the mid-1980s. Version 2 resembles the game described in Seeger's 1948 book, *American Folksongs for Children.*

Additional Versions of Paw-Paw Patch

Version 2: Hiding Game.   One child is chosen to go hide while the others sing the first verse with their eyes closed. During the second verse ("Come on, girls, let's go find her . . ."), all search for "Susie." When Susie is found, she is welcomed back to the group with "Come on [insert child's name], come on back again . . . paw-paw patch." This game could be modified by challenging only one or two children to go find Susie or Johnny as the others watch and sing.

Punchinella

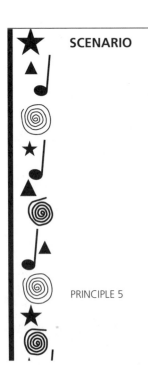

SCENARIO

PRINCIPLE 5

VERSION 2: SEATED GAME

"Only five minutes left, so we have time for about three turns of *Punchinella*. We'll play it right from our chairs, so all three ideas will need to be something we can each do from our spaces." The multiage class cheered at the thought of playing one of their favorite games, *Punchinella*.

Because so little time was left, the teacher knew that she must use the activity efficiently, so she modified the way the game was to be played. "Mikayla's our Punchinella. Let's sing to her." As the teacher began the song, she exaggerated the arm movement that gestured toward Mikayla on "Oh, look. . ." As the class joined the teacher on the gesture and continued to sing, all watched Mikayla as she pondered what movement she would demonstrate. "Oh, look who's here, Punchinella, Punchinella. Look who's here, Punchinella from the zoo."

As the class watched and sang the second verse, "Oh, what can you do . . . ?" Mikayla rapidly pounded on her desk with her hands. The teacher continued to sing as she watched but decided to intervene before the next verse. "As we perform Mikayla's idea, we will use our fingertips on our desks so that we don't lose the song. If you can't hear your own singing, your hands are too loud. [Singing] 'Oh, we can do it too. . .'"

"Two more turns," the teacher reminded the class as they sang the last verse, "Oh, who do you choose . . . ?" and Mikayla rotated with eyes closed and arm extended.

"Only one more turn after Rocky," the teacher prompted when Mikayla's finger pointed to Rocky at the cadence of the song. The song led Rocky's finger to Faith for the last turn, and rather than singing the verse of "Oh, who do you choose . . . ?" the teacher ended the game by singing, "And that's the last turn, Punchinella, Punchinella. That's the last turn, Punchinella from the zoo."

Punchinella

Oh, look who's here, Punch-i-nel-la, Punch-i-nel-la.

Look who's here, Punch-i-nel-la from the zoo!

Brief Description

With the class in a standing circle, one person is in the center as Punchinella. The song begins with an exaggerated arm gesture, moving from outside to inside the circle, directed toward Punchinella and coordinated with the anacrusis feeling of "Oh, LOOK." As students walk in a circle or stand still, they sing the first verse introducing Punchinella: "Oh, look who's here. . . ." Gesturing with arms extended and palms up, students ask Punchinella in the second verse what she or he can do for a motion, "Oh, what can you do?" During this verse, Punchinella demonstrates a motion, and students watch. During the third verse, "Oh, we can do it too, . . ." all, including Punchinella, perform Punchinella's motion. During the last verse, "Oh, who do you choose, . . ." all stand and clap while Punchinella closes eyes, spins with finger extended, and stops at the cadence to see whom the song chose for the next Punchinella.

Age Appropriateness

Version 1—Preschool through Grade 6	Circle Game
Version 2—Preschool through Grade 6	Seated Game
Version 3—Grade 3 through Grade 6	Partner Game

Degrees of Intensity

VERSIONS	1	2	3
Social Interaction			
Language			
Movement			
Decision Making			
Cooperating with Others			
Imagining			

Learning Opportunities

- *Coordinate movement* with beginning and ending of sound: Auditory-motor skills.
- *Move* to specific words and word phrases: Auditory-motor skills.
- *Imitate movement:* Auditory-visual-motor skills, motor figure-ground skills.
- *Work with a partner:* Social skills, motor skills (Version 3).
- *Anacrusis* and variant of echo phrase *structure:* Music skills.
- *Melody* patterns of SO₁ | DO DO DO and SO₁ SO₁ | LA₁ LA₁ TI₁ SO₁ DO: Music skills.

Song and Activity Background

Often known as *Punchinello,* this game is played in similar fashions throughout its many versions. One version solves the problem of "Who gets the next turn?" by having all children sit down after they imitate the person in the center. The last one to sit down is the next Punchinello. Of course, this idea does not work very well when children *want* the next turn!

The song text apparently originated around 1910 with the French "Polichinel" or "Polchinelle" and was created for use in kindergartens (Opie and Opie 1985, 412–413). The title is probably related also to the seventeenth-century commedia dell' arte stock character Pulcinella, who in turn is the model for Punch of the British Punch and Judy puppet plays. A version recorded in London in 1973 offers the words "What shall we do, Punchinello, little fellow? What shall we do, Punchinello, little dear?" and "We'll do the same, Punchinello . . . little dear." Though words and melody vary from place to place, Punchinello has been played since the 1940s, when New Zealand physical education specialists introduced it into their schools, and Brownie leaders taught it throughout the 1950s, 1960s, and 1970s (Mary Chater's *A Baker's Dozen: Singing Games for Brownies,* 1947). *Punchinella* is still a popular game and song today. The Opies comment that the song melody that is most commonly known lacks the verve of such games as *Okey Kokey (Hokey Pokey)* and *Lubin Loo (Looby Loo),* but the version presented here seems to remedy that. Capturing the swing rhythms of black American chants and melodies, this version was taught to Dr. Marty Richardson Stover by her inner-city children in Fort Wayne, Indiana, in the early 1970s.

Script. Version 1: Circle Game

Teacher	Students
Sing the first verse of the song for students.	
• *Let's pretend that Punchinella is standing in the middle of our circle.*	Students stand in a circle as they practice the gesture for beginning the song, "Oh, LOOK. . ."
• *As we sing "Oh, look who's here," we gesture to her or him as we sing. To make a big gesture, let's move our hand from outside the circle to inside the circle as we sing "Oh, LOOK."*	
Sing the melody of "*Oh, LOOK* . . ." as the gesture is practiced.	

Teacher	Students
• *That feeling of moving from a sound that's not so important to one that's important is sometimes called a pickup in music. Another term and the one that we'll use is anacrusis.* • *Get your arms ready for the anacrusis on "Oh, LOOK" as we walk and sing.*	Students gesture on the anacrusis, then walk in a circle as they sing the first verse. At this point, they are hearing the term "anacrusis" and feeling the anacrusis movement, but no detailed or technical definition is necessary.
• *Fred, will you be our first Punchinella? Step into the center, and the words we sing will help you know what to do.* • *As we sing and walk, Punchinella has some thinking time to decide what motion he will show us on the next verse.* • *OK, class, here comes the song. Be ready to sing, gesture, and walk until the cadence. Ready, "Oh look who's here . . . zoo."*	The circle of children walk and sing as Punchinella stands in the middle, thinking of a movement idea.
Model the actions for the second verse. As you lead the singing, sing loudly enough to support students' voices, but do not overpower them. • *This is Fred's turn all by himself, and it's our turn to observe.*	At the cadence, students stop walking and, following the lead of their teacher, face into the middle, looking at Fred and singing, "Oh, what can you do . . . zoo?" With open arms and palms up, students in the circle gesture with curiosity each time they sing "what." As he hears the second verse, Fred smiles and demonstrates a karate chop in the air. After watching for the entire verse, the class imitates Fred's motion as they sing, "Oh, we can do it too, Punchinella, Punchinella. We can do it too, Punchinella from the zoo!"
• *For the next verse, Fred, you'll need to cover your eyes with one hand and point the index finger of your other hand.* • *While we sing the song, you will turn slowly, listening for the cadence to tell you when to stop moving.* • *Your finger and the song's cadence will choose the next Punchinella.*	Students sing "Oh, who do you choose . . . zoo?" At the cadence, Fred opens his eyes.
To assist the auditory-motor coordination and integration necessitated by the final verse, you may briefly step in at times to guide younger students in having their fingers move and stop. This help can give them the sense of stopping with the cadence so that they can do so on their own for their next turn. • *Follow your finger to a student in the circle, Fred.*	Fred follows his finger to Barbara, takes her place in the circle, and the song begins again as Barbara enters the circle as the new Punchinella.

Additional Versions of Punchinella

Version 3: Partner Game.   Punchinella can be played with two people in the middle each time. Students in the circle quickly find a partner to imitate the Punchinella motions. Both Punchinellas cover their eyes and let the cadence choose the next two Punchinellas. This version seems to appeal especially to intermediate-age students.

Rig-A-Jig-Jig

Five versions of *Rig-a-Jig-Jig* are described in the section on "Making Activities Context Appropriate" at the beginning of this chapter.

Rig-a-Jig-Jig

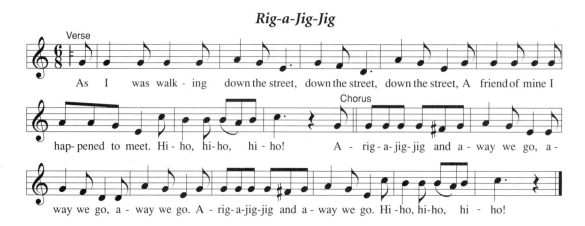

Age Appropriateness

Version 1—Grade 3 through Grade 6	Circle Game
Version 2—Grade 2 through Grade 4	Exchange Game
Version 3—Preschool through Grade 3	Imitation Game
Version 4—Preschool through Grade 3	Seated Game
Version 5—Grade 3 through Grade 6	Create-a-Game
Version 6—Grade 4 through Grade 6	Extension Game

Degrees of Intensity

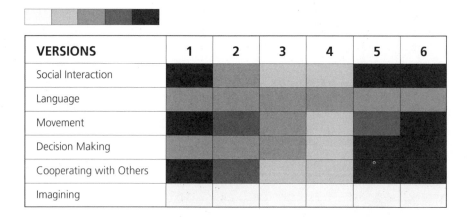

VERSIONS	1	2	3	4	5	6
Social Interaction						
Language						
Movement						
Decision Making						
Cooperating with Others						
Imagining						

Learning Opportunities

- *Coordinate movement* with beginning and ending of sound: Auditory-motor skills.
- *Move* to specific words: Auditory-motor skills.

- *Greet a partner* with a handshake: Social skills (Versions 1, 2, 4).
- *Observe and recall* movements: Visual-motor skills (Versions 3, 6).
- *Create a game* (Version 5).
- Echo phrase *structure* and AB (binary) song structure: Music skills.
- *Melody* patterns of unison (SO SO SO SO SO) and DO¹ | TI TI TI LA TI DO¹: Music skills.
- *Rhythm* patterns of ♪ | ♩ ♪ ♫ ♩. (DI DU DI DU DA DI DU) and ♪ | ♫ ♫ ♩ ♪♪ (DI DU DA DI DU DA DI DU DI DU) and ♪ | ♩ ♪ ♩ (DI DU DI DU): Music skills.

Song and Activity Background

Those who have seen the classic movie *It's a Wonderful Life* may hear the resemblance between *Rig-a-Jig-Jig* and the song that was featured in that movie, *Buffalo Gals*. The resemblance is so strong, with the lively melody and rollicking rhythms, that one wonders if *Rig-a-Jig-Jig* may be a variant. Labeled as an English dance song, *Rig-a-Jig-Jig* was found in *Women's Get Together Songs* (Lorenz 1942, 111). In this source, the song is given two additional verses: "Said I to her 'What is your trade . . . ?'" "Said she to me 'I'm a weaver's maid . . .'." *Rig-a-Jig-Jig* was a play party game in the southern United States in the early 1900s, and it is a common entry in music series textbooks and songbooks for teachers.

The games described in the several versions presented in this chapter developed in classrooms with varying contexts. Versions 1 and 2 were suggested in the Grade 4 book of the series *This Is Music* (Allyn and Bacon, 1962, p. 102), and Version 3 developed in the inner-city classroom of Peggy Bennett in the 1970s in Fort Wayne, Indiana.

Additional Versions of **Rig-a-Jig-Jig**

Version 6: Extension Game. The game consists of creating new actions on the words "a-rig-a-jig-jig" in the chorus, coordinating each action with the rhythm of these words, and adding them in sequence to extend the song. This version can be done with students in their seats or standing with partners in a scatter formation. If the students are standing, they can walk around the room during the verse and find a new partner at the cadence with whom to do the actions.

For the first turn, only one action is used and the song is not changed. For the second turn a new action is proposed. When "a-rig-a-jig-jig" is sung, the new action is performed; then "a-rig-a-jig-jig" is repeated and the previous action immediately follows. "A-rig-a-jig-jig" is sung twice because there are now two actions to perform. The expanding sequence of actions and the accompanying repetitions of "a-rig-a-jig-jig" cause the chorus to get successively longer.

With three actions, the chorus of the song will go like this:

- *A-rig-a-jig-jig* [hands], *a-rig-a-jig-jig* [feet], *a-rig-a-jig-jig* [shoulders], *and away we go, away we go, away we go.*
  A-rig-a-jig-jig [hands], *a-rig-a-jig-jig* [feet], *a-rig-a-jig-jig* [shoulders], *and away we go. Hi-ho, hi-ho, hi-ho.*

When there are three actions or more to remember, it can be important to review the sequence without the song before starting a turn. It is often valuable to repeat a turn before adding a new action, giving students a chance to practice the sequence. Remembering all the actions in correct order becomes especially difficult when there are six or more actions.

There are two ways to build the sequence. The first action can always be at the end of the sequence, so that the newest action will always be the first in the sequence. Or the first action can always be first in the sequence, in which case the newest action will take its place at the end of the sequence. Although having the first action anchor the sequence at its close has seemed the easier of the two alternatives, the important thing is to settle on one procedure or the other.

Ring Around the Rosy

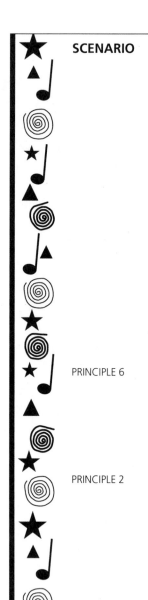

SCENARIO

VERSION 2: IMITATION GAME

A group of first-grade children were singing and playing *Ring Around the Rosy.* Tommy stood in the middle of the circle, awaiting the end of the song, when he would get to show the other children how he wanted them to fall. As the children sang and walked in a circle, some bumped into each other, some walked toward Tommy as they watched him closely, and some were so interested in how they would fall that they forgot to sing. Though the teacher was somewhat bothered by this untidy participation in the play, he understood that trying to fix all the behaviors at this point would interrupt the flow of the activity and detract from the sheer pleasure the children were experiencing.

Suddenly, all the voices joined in singing "we all fall down" with expectant looks at Tommy. At that point, Tommy leaped into the air and, with a look of wild delight, fell on his knees, arms extended high above his head, with thumbs up in each hand. Giggling, the other children jumped to do the same, checking to see that their statues looked just like Tommy's.

"Freeze so that we can see your statues," the teacher encouraged as he walked around the circle looking with curiosity at individual children's positions. As the children remained frozen, the teacher called attention to details of Tommy's statue and gave feedback on how children imitated his idea: "Many of you noticed his thumbs! Some of you even jumped the way Tommy did!" Occasionally, the teacher directed Tommy or the other children to look at an individual child: "Tommy, look whose hands (knees) look just like yours. Did you notice Valerie? Look at how Myron's facial expression is matching yours!"

PRINCIPLE 6

As the children prepared for another turn of *Ring Around the Rosy,* the teacher decided to have Tommy select who would be next in the center of the circle. "If you would like a turn to give us a statue, raise your hand. Tommy, look at each person who is volunteering for a turn and choose one of those people." As the next child moved to the center, the teacher decided to shape the way that children were moving to alleviate the crowding that had occurred earlier.

PRINCIPLE 2

"I have a challenge for you during Faith's turn. Let's hold hands and make a nice round circle. With your eyes, draw an imaginary line from one person's toe to another's. Do you see how that line makes a circle? Our challenge for Faith's turn is to keep that nice round circle as we sing and move. Do you think we can do it? Remember to have your statues freeze right on the last word of the song. Here comes the song . . ."

Ring Around the Rosy

Ring a-round the ros- y, a pock-et full of pos- y. Ash-es, ash-es, we all fall down.

Brief Description

In a standing circle, children hold hands and walk as they sing. At the cadence, they all fall down into a statue of their choice. The play is simple but appealing to young children as they repeat the sequence of walking and falling, walking and falling. In Version 2 (the Imitation Game), children are challenged to mimic the child in the center, who makes a statue at the end of the song. In Version 3, children focus closely on counting and body position as they are challenged to "fall on two points" or "fall on four points," allowing only that number of parts of the body to touch the floor.

Age Appropriateness

Version 1—Preschool through Grade 1   Falling Game

Version 2—Preschool through Grade 2   Imitation Game

Version 3—Grade 1 through Grade 2   Counting Game

Degrees of Intensity

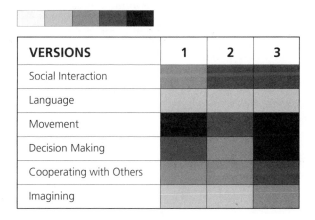

VERSIONS	1	2	3
Social Interaction			
Language			
Movement			
Decision Making			
Cooperating with Others			
Imagining			

Learning Opportunities

- *Coordinate movement* with beginning and ending of sound: Auditory-motor skills.
- *Imitate* body positions: Visual-motor skills (Version 2).
- *Maintain pace and space* while moving in a circle: Auditory-visual-motor skills, spatial skills.
- *Observe details* of body positions: Visual figure-ground skills (Version 2).
- *Count* points touching the floor: Cognitive skills, motor skills (Version 3).
- Short-short-long phrase *structure:* Music skills.
- *Melody* patterns of SO SO MI LA SO MI and SO MI SO MI and MI | SO SO DO: Music skills.
- *Rhythm* patterns of ♪ | ♩. ♩. ♩. (DI DU DU DU) and ♩ ♫ ♫. ♩ (DU DI DU DI DU DU): Music skills.

Song and Activity Background

Known variously as *Ring a Ring o' Roses, Ring a Ring a Rosie, Round the Ring of Roses, Ring a Ring a Row-o, Ring Around the Rosie, Ring Around the Rosey,* and *Ring Around the Rosy,* this may be the quintessential children's game—its appeal lies very simply in the act of falling down. At one time, the object of the game was apparently to choose the one who is liked the best, but most children play the game now as a challenge to see who is the last to fall down. Seven of the earliest versions known in Britain have been traced to the 1880s and 1890s, and Newell (1883) noted that the song may have been known in the United States from the 1790s. The German version of 1796 was a popular ring game that cadenced with "Sit you down!" Though the first two phrases are often similar, it is the third phrase that offers many variants: A tishoo a-tishoo, Atch chew! atch chew!, Hush! hush! hush! hush!, Ashem ashem, Husha husha, and Ashes, ashes (Opie and Opie 1985, 220–227).

The rather widespread rumor that the song reflected the horrors of the Great Plague of 1665 implies that the ring referred to the sore, the posies were herbs carried as protection, the "a-tishoo, a-tishoo" indicated the final symptom of the illness—a sneeze—and "we all fall down" reflected the deadly outcome. "This story has obtained such circulation in recent years it can itself be said to be epidemic" (Opie and Opie, 221). The Opies carefully discount and discredit such claims.

Versions 1 and 2 are traditional games, and Version 3 comes from *Let's Do It Again* (Richards 1985, 76).

Script. Version 1: Falling Game

Teacher	Students
Sing the song to the children. • *What does this song tell us to do?*	Students answer with various descriptions. "It tells us to fall." "It tells us to 'ring around the rosy.'"
• *How can we make a ring? What would you suggest?* • *How can we fall so that we will not get hurt?* • *What if I fall and accidentally kick Ryan? How can I be careful not to do that?*	Children are prompted to create a circle and to articulate ways to avoid injuries during the play.
• *Now that we've discussed ways to keep us safe, let's sing, walk, and fall at the cadence, right on the last word.* • *We'll be interested in seeing your statues, so be sure to freeze and let us see the position you've chosen.*	Children walk and sing. As they fall at the cadence, they are quickly reminded to freeze. Call attention to simple and elaborate statues as you direct children's attention and make observations (not evaluations): • *Eddie, you stopped moving right when the song stopped.* • *Look at the way Patty fell.* • *You look very relaxed, George.* • *That doesn't look very comfortable, Sally.* • *That position requires lots of balance, Janet.*
• *Choose a different way to fall this time. Maybe you got some ideas from seeing others, or maybe you still have some ideas of your own. Here comes the song. . .*	The song and the activity are repeated so that the children may have many opportunities to fall and to explore different ways of falling. Watching their responses will give ideas for shaping the play. • *What will we look like if we fall as fast as we can? As slow as we can? Like a feather?* • *What would we look like if we did the opposite of falling down?* • *How will you fall with only one hand and one leg touching the floor?*

Additional Versions of **Ring Around the Rosy**

Version 3: Counting Game. Teacher and children decide how many points they will allow to touch the floor when they fall. The group sings and walks in a circle; then each student makes a statue at the cadence. Teacher and children may count how many points are touching the floor for individuals in the group—children may work in partners for this version. The group may also decide before the song how many points all should have touching the floor for their statues at the cadence, or they can see who can have the most points touching the floor.

Row, Row, Row Your Boat

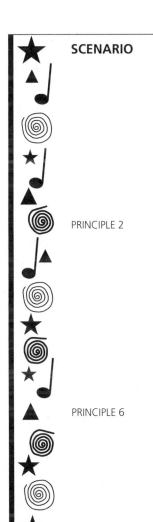

SCENARIO

PRINCIPLE 2

PRINCIPLE 6

VERSION 1: ROWING GAME

"Ike is rowing with his feet!" Gary said as he pointed and smiled. Quickly Ms. Lynn directed the attention of students in this multiage class to Ike. "I noticed your rowing, too, Ike," she said in a supporting tone, "and as I watched you, I imagined what kind of boat you were in. Tell us what kind of boat you were picturing." "Last summer, my family went to the park and rented a paddleboat. That's what I was rowing," Ike replied. "I think I've seen those," remarked Ms. Lynn. "What color is the boat you're in?" "Yellow." "And tell us where you are so that we know how to imagine you in your boat," encouraged the teacher. "I'm on the pond in King Arthur Park," answered Ike. "Is the pond very big? Are there trees around it? Are there any other boats on the pond that you must watch out for?" queried Ms. Lynn as she paused for Ike to answer each question and set the stage for triggering students' imaginations. "Let's sing for Ike as we watch and imagine his boat. Ike, will you be able to stop your boat at the end of the song?"

The class sang and watched Ike. "Now let's all get into a yellow paddleboat on the pond in King Arthur Park. Ike has shown us how to do it. Here we go. [Singing], 'Row row . . . dream.'"

Ms. Lynn was being careful not to hype students' ideas, because she wanted to show interest rather than approval. She knew that too much enthusiasm or approval could stimulate these students into competition for increasingly elaborate ideas, rather than simply having fun with the activity. The verbal and nonverbal reactions she used, therefore, were selected to communicate "Interesting imagery you have given us!" and "We can imagine you in that boat!" rather than "What a great idea!" or "I like the way you are doing that."

As the play activity continued, students shared their ideas and imaginings, Ms. Lynn's role was to show encouragement and delight in the imagining process; help students notice, listen to, and be interested in each other; join the spirit of imagination by asking questions and making connecting comments ("Darla's boat was in the river. Are we in the same river with your boat or a different one?"); and use the song as a backdrop and pacesetter for each idea.

Row, Row, Row Your Boat

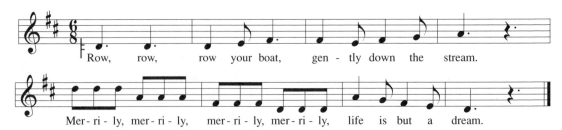

Row, row, row your boat, gen-tly down the stream.

Mer-ri-ly, mer-ri-ly, mer-ri-ly, mer-ri-ly, life is but a dream.

Brief Description

In the Rowing Game of Version 1, students create ways of rowing as they are seated in a circle or in rows. After a student demonstrates an idea, the class sings and imitates that student's movement. Version 2 asks students to create rowing motions with a partner. Version 3 challenges students to work in small groups to create a scene for the boat in which they are traveling. The Scene Development of Version 4 is a group creation of a spontaneous scene that is inspired by the boat-rowing activities. Although Version 4 does not require singing, it grows from the images that have been created in previous versions of the song activity. An outgrowth of Version 4, the Creative Writing of Version 5 asks students to imagine themselves as a character in the scene and to write about the scene from that character's perspective. Imagery of where students are, what kind of boat they are in, why they are rowing, and what the scenery looks like can be added to all versions of the activity.

Age Appropriateness

Version 1—Preschool through Grade 2 — Rowing Game

Version 2—Grade 1 through Grade 2 — Partner Game

Version 3—Grade 2 through Grade 4 — Small-Group Game

Version 4—Grade 3 through Grade 6 — Scene Development

Version 5—Grade 3 through Grade 6 — Creative Writing

Degrees of Intensity

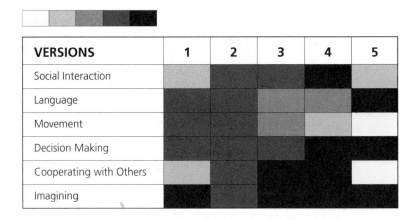

VERSIONS	1	2	3	4	5
Social Interaction					
Language					
Movement					
Decision Making					
Cooperating with Others					
Imagining					

Learning Opportunities

- *Coordinate movement* with beginning and ending of sound: Auditory-motor skills.

- *Create movement* for rowing: Visual-motor skills.

- *Imitate movements:* Visual-motor skills.

- Work with a *partner:* Social skills, motor skills (Version 2).

- *Group* collaboration and cooperation: Social skills (Versions 3, 4).

- *Verbalize* experiences and imaginations: Language skills (Versions 1, 2, 3, 5).

- *Pantomime ideas:* Drama skills (Versions 3, 4).

- *Creative writing:* Language skills, drama skills, writing skills (Version 5).

- *Share and read* creative writing (Version 5).

- Balanced phrase *structure:* Music skills.

- *Melody* patterns of DO DO DO RE MI and DO^I SO MI DO and SO FA MI RE DO: Music skills.

- *Rhythm* patterns of ♩ ♪♩ ♪♩. (DU DI DU DI DU) and ♩. ♩. ♩ ♪♩. (DU DU DU DI DU) and ♫♩ (DUDADI): Music skills.

Song and Activity Background

Row, Row, Row Your Boat is well known and often parodied around the world. A traditional round, *Row, Row, Row Your Boat* has possible origins as a minstrel song and was copyrighted in New York in 1852 (Fuld 1971; Opie and Opie 1985, 454).

The scene-development activity in Version 4 was inspired by presentations of Mary Opland Springer, a music and theater arts educator from Seattle. The creative-writing activity of Version 5 was inspired by presentations of Sandy Murray, a classroom and music educator in Abbottsford, British Columbia.

Script. Version 1: Rowing Game

Teacher	Students
• *Put yourself into a boat right where you're sitting, and as we sing the song, row your boat.* With little introduction, the song activity is begun. You may or may not want to model a rowing motion. Some students may rely too much on imitating your ideas.	Students row as they sit in their chairs or on the floor. Many remember to coordinate their rowing with the starting and stopping of the song.
• *I see lots of rowing going on. Use the same idea or think of a different way to row as we sing the song again. Here comes the song.* As students row, notice their ideas and show curiosity and interest in what they are doing. Focusing students to listen for the cadence and to coordinate their actions with the song challenges listening skills, introduces a controlling element, and identifies a moment in which the activity will stop. Then new directions, comments, and challenges can be made.	Students are given opportunities to repeat their movement ideas. Some students keep the same idea, some slightly change their ideas, some copy others' ideas, and some change to a completely different way of rowing. • *Sarah, you stopped rowing when the song stopped. So did Jim. Let's see who will stop with the cadence this time. Here comes the song.*

Teacher	Students
• *Did you see some interesting ideas in the ways people around you rowed? Whose idea did you notice?* • *Jeffrey, Donna wants us to see your idea. Will you please show us what you were doing?* Encourage students to notice and become intrigued with various ideas. Point out details and uniqueness by such comments as • *Look at how he is holding his hands.* • *I've never thought of rowing like that before.* • *That must be a strong current—look at how she is working to row!*	Students notice others' ideas and, as a result of the teacher modeling, develop a curiosity about the details of their movements. Students can be encouraged to articulate their observations by prompts such as • *What do you see in her rowing motion?* • *What do you notice about the way she is holding the oar?* • *What kind of boat do you imagine he is in?*
After viewing an individual's idea, the class can imitate that motion as they sing. • *Now that we've observed his strategy, let's row like George as we sing.*	Questions and comments help capture students' imaginations and set the tone for role playing, but too many questions of any individual may feel overwhelming. Try using different questions for various turns. • *What color is your boat? Why are you in it?* • *Are you fishing? Did you catch anything?* • *Is the water deep or shallow? You are wearing a life vest, aren't you?* • *Where are you?* • *What time of year is it? Tell us what the weather is.*

Additional Versions of Row, Row, Row, Your Boat

Note: To elicit imagery, the sample questions and comments offered in the script can continue with additional versions. Any version except 4 and 5 may be a good starting point for this imagery.

Version 2: Partner Game. Students join with a partner to figure out a way to row their boats. After watching students' boats, help students observe others by noticing and briefly commenting on what they see or imagine. Depending on the rowing of some partners, the speed (tempo) of the song may need to be adjusted for each turn.

> *Each of you get someone else in your boat. Together you are going to find a way to row your boat. You may be seated in a chair, seated on the floor, or standing as you row.*

Version 3: Small-Group Game. In small groups of four to seven, students imagine what kind of boat they are rowing. They decide how to portray this scene, dramatizing what they imagine so that others can observe what they are doing. Using a quiet sign or an attention-getting device is helpful to gain students' attention when their planning time is up (see Chapter 7). When a group presents their ideas to the class, the class practices audience etiquette: a hush falling over the audience when performers are ready, polite attentiveness, and enthusiastic applause. At the conclusion of a group's performance, the rest of the class observes and asks questions or makes comments about what they think the group was doing. Comments or questions are directed as observations, not as evaluations, of students' ideas.

Version 4: Scene Development.

■ *I am going to imagine myself in a scene. I will say just enough to give you an idea of where I am and what I'm doing. Then, when I stop speaking, you are invited to join me in this scene. You will be acting out your part and watching your classmates as you time your entry into the scene. When our scene seems complete for today, I will say "curtain" to signify that our activity is over.*

A variety of scenes is possible. One option is the swamp scene. The teacher moves onto the floor, sitting in an imaginary boat, rowing gently, lazily looking around the area.

■ *What a hot, muggy day it is! Most people wouldn't even come out here. They think this swamp is too hot, too frightening, and has too many insects. But maybe that's why I like it. There are so many things to see and listen to.*

Continue by pantomiming actions as students join the scene, one or two at a time, making appropriate noises or actions for their characters. Students step into the scene and become characters or a part of the scenery. When all students who plan to join have done so, call "curtain" to end the activity.

Version 5: Creative Writing.

■ *Now that we have had such rich experiences in our swamp scene, you will need to get a blank sheet of paper and a pen or pencil ready for the next activity.*

Students go to their chairs or desks and get paper and pencil ready.

■ *You will have five minutes. Decide which of the characters in our scene you would most like to be, and describe the scene or portions of the scene from your perspective as this character. Will you be the mosquito, the alligator, the sun, or something else? The only rule is to keep your pencil moving the entire time. When I say, "Time is up," finish the sentence you are on and lay your pencils down. We'll be so interested in where your imaginations take you in your story. Be ready to write.*

After the writing activity, students can volunteer to read their stories to the class. During this sharing, the teacher models acceptance of and interest in the writing, rather than evaluation or approval. Emphasis is on allowing the creation and being fascinated with ideas.

Scotland's Burning

SCENARIO

PRINCIPLE 2

VERSION 3: DRAMA GAME

"This is a song that takes place outside the United States. What place did you hear me sing about?" the teacher asked the fourth-grade students after she sang the song once. After the students answered, "Scotland," she asked them if Scotland is a country, a city, or a continent; if we would go east or west to get there most quickly; what other place is close to it; and if they could locate it on a map of the world. The uncertainty of their answers caused the teacher to give them an assignment: "For next

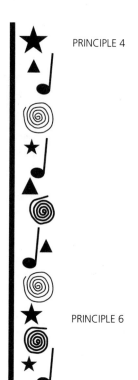

PRINCIPLE 4

class, do a little investigation. What can you find out about Scotland? We'll all be interested in what you find!

"Let's sing the song again, and after the song, I'll ask what you noticed about it," said the teacher to focus their attention. Students raised their hands to offer various ideas about what they heard: "It's about a fire." "Our voices sing pretty high on 'fire.'" "We sing everything twice, except 'fire.' We sing that four times."

Offering her observations, the teacher continued, "You gathered lots of information about the song, and some of your ideas caused me to think about what you were hearing. Rather than collect your ideas for the meaning of it now, let's take until the count of ten to get into small groups of four to seven people." After the students had gathered in groups, the teacher continued with directions. "How would you act out the song? Decide as a group; then be sure to practice with the song so that your actions coordinate with the singing. Let's sing the song once more before you begin working on your task."

Students took turns sharing their small-group creations with the class. Students in the class were encouraged to make observations and comparisons without making evaluations. The teacher set the tone for these observations and guided the interactions: "Tell us what you saw rather than whether or not you liked it. Offer us an observation rather than a criticism. For example, you might say 'Everyone in that group did the same actions' rather than 'They didn't come up with different ideas!' Or you might say 'Their actions were at lots of different speeds' or 'I didn't understand all the actions they were showing us. I need to see it again, please.' "

PRINCIPLE 6

Scotland's Burning

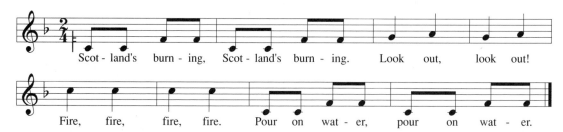

Brief Description

In Version 1, the Hand-Sign Game, students learn hand signs for the melody by echoing the teacher, phrase by phrase. Varied repetition helps them learn and practice coordinating hand signs with the melody. Version 2 introduces solfa syllables that correlate with the hand signs. Version 3 challenges students to think about the meaning of the song and create appropriate actions to dramatize the words.

Age Appropriateness

Version 1—Grade 1 through Grade 6   Hand-Sign Game

Version 2—Grade 1 through Grade 6   Solfa Syllables

Version 3—Grade 3 through Grade 6   Drama Game

2

Degrees of Intensity

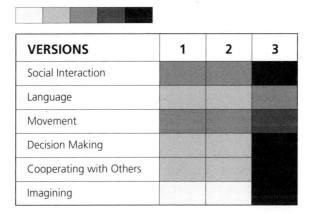

VERSIONS	1	2	3
Social Interaction			
Language			
Movement			
Decision Making			
Cooperating with Others			
Imagining			

Learning Opportunities

- *Imitate* actions: Visual-motor skills (Version 1).
- Perform Curwen *hand signs:* Auditory-motor skills, music skills (Version 1).
- Learn *solfa syllables:* Music skills (Version 3).
- *Pantomime* actions to depict meaning: Drama skills (Version 3).
- Small-group *cooperation* and *collaboration:* Social skills (Version 3).
- Balanced phrase *structure:* Music skills.
- Pentatonic *melody* and patterns of SO$_l$ SO$_l$ DO DO and unison (SO SO SO SO): Music skills.
- *Rhythm* patterns of quarter notes and eighth notes: Music skills.

Song and Activity Background

Sometimes found as *London's Burning,* this traditional round appears in many music series textbooks for children. The hand-sign activity presented here comes from Richards (1985, 83).

Script. Version 1: Hand-Sign Game

Teacher	Students
• *Echo my hands and my voice, please.* Show students the solfa arm signs for the tonal patterns of the song. Fingertips and heels of hands touch lightly about waist level for *"Scotland's"* and move up to chest level for *"burning"* as each hand forms a fist. Coordinate the hand signs with the singing of *"Scotland's Burning"*; then pause for students to echo.	Hesitantly and awkwardly at first, students sing and approximate the hand signs demonstrated by the teacher.
"Look" is sung with hands diagonally crossed at chin level; for *"out,"* lift elbows until hands are horizontal, beside each other. On *"fire,"* lift arms above your head with the same hand sign as *"Scotland's"*; for *"pour on water,"* hand signs are lowered and look exactly the same as *"Scotland's burning."* (See hand-sign chart in Chapter 6.)	Students imitate.

Teacher	Students
• *Let's do that again, now that you know how the song sounds and how your hands will move. Echo me.*	Multiple and varied repetitions help students gain confidence in performing the hand signs.
• *When we combine my part with your part, we will have the whole song. Let's sing both parts and use our hands.*	Teacher and students sing and perform hand signs, repeating each set of words to form the whole song.
Practice can be offered to older students by challenging them in various ways. • *Close your eyes as you sing and hand-sign the song.* • *Watch someone other than me as you sing and sign.* • *Put the song in your inner hearing as you sing and sign.* • *Sign and antiphon the song.*	Students can also work with partners to practice the song and hand signs. Partners can simply face each other and watch each others' hands, or they can put one hand behind their backs and use their partner's hand to form and perform hand signs.

Additional Versions of Scotland's Burning

Version 2: Solfa Introduction. When students are familiar with the song and the hand signs, they can be introduced to the solfa syllables that the hand signs represent. Solfa syllables can also be written on the board so that students can see the spelling and the relative vertical relationships of the syllables.

- *When our hands are in this position, we will sing SO. And each time they are in this position, we will sing DO. How will you sing the first words of the song— "Scotland's burning"? [SO₁ SO₁ DO DO] Let's sing the song with those two new syllables.*

- *Now we'll sing RE for this hand sign and MI for this one. We've already learned most of the new syllables!*

- *Here's "fire" that's high SO. Show me low SO then high SO. "Pour on water" sounds just like another part of the song and, therefore, has the same signs and syllables. What does it match? Let us see and hear the match you found.*

- *Let's sing the whole song in solfa syllables and show our hand signs:*
  SO₁ SO₁ DO DO SO₁ SO₁ DO DO   RE MI RE MI
  SO SO SO SO   SO₁ SO₁ DO DO SO₁ SO₁ DO DO

Antiphonning, inner hearing, and partner work can be used to give students varied practice as they learn solfa syllables. The teacher can lead singing by showing hand signs, using slight changes from the melody of *Scotland's Burning*. As they watch the pattern of the teacher's hand signs, students sing the tones and solfa syllables that the hand signs represent.

- *Watch my hands and sing what you see.*

  [Teacher hand-signs: S₁S₁DD S₁ D R S₁D R M S S S₁ D S₁D]

Sing with Me

SCENARIO

VERSION 1: MOVEMENT GAME

"Sing with me, all together. Sing with me, all together. Sing with me, all together. Won't you be my honey?" Ms. Suarez sang the entire song as a way of introducing it to her students. Students reacted to the last phrase with puzzled looks and giggles. "Isn't that a crazy way to end a song—'Won't you be my honey'?" the teacher noted. "I am surprised at how many songs from a long time ago end that way. Will you sing with me?" Ms. Suarez knew that when children are making fun of something, the teacher can often stop that behavior by quickly admitting that their perceptions have validity. The teacher sang again, communicating delight at and encouragement for students' participation in singing.

Without pausing between songs, Ms. Suarez led singing for two more turns, changing the words and actions to "Clap with me, all together...." and "Wiggle with me, all together." Students joined in the spirit of the song and added a dramatic gesture of their choosing for "Won't you be my honey?"—they placed their hands on their hearts. Ms. Suarez added just enough drama in her modeling to capture students' interest but was careful not to overstimulate their behaviors.

"We have sung, clapped, and wiggled. What would you have us do as we sing? Raise your hand if you have a suggestion." Several children spoke as they raised their hands. Natalie raised her hand quietly, and when Ms. Suarez called on her, Natalie offered, "Stomp our feet." The teacher began singing, "Here comes Natalie's song . . . 'Stomp your feet . . . honey?'" Several students continued stomping after the song ended. Ms. Suarez was concerned that the movements might get out of hand, especially with this class. "That was enthusiastic stomping, but did you notice where the song tells you to stomp? We'll stomp again but see if you can stomp only when the song tells you to."

PRINCIPLE 6

"Seth is raising his hand without letting us hear his voice. What's your idea, Seth?" the teacher asked. "Hop," answered Seth. "Before we can hop, Seth, we need more words to fill up the space in our song. Listen, 'Hop hmm hmm all together.' Did you hear the space that needs some words? What could we fill in there?" As Seth pondered the question, Ms. Suarez sensed he needed some guidance. Singing each example, Ms. Suarez offered, "We could sing 'Hop hop hop' or 'Hop like a frog' or 'Hop in a circle.' Which of those choices would you like?" Getting the idea, Seth beamed and said, "Hop up high!" "OK, we have our song. Remember to move only when the song tells you to. Let's sing," Ms. Suarez prompted as she led the children in the next turn.

Students continued to offer ideas, naming their movement ideas, and fitting their words into the flow of the song. After a few turns, the teacher added, "Let's remember who gave us this idea, by putting Maggie's name in the song. [Singing] 'Touch your wrist, just like Maggie . . . honey?'" Students were initially challenged to remember the name but soon enjoyed this way of having their verbal and movement contributions acknowledged through song.

Sing with Me

Sing with me, all to-geth-er. Sing with me, all to-geth-er.

Sing with me, all to-geth-er. Won't you be my hon - ey?

Brief Description

In a sitting circle or in a scatter formation, children offer movement ideas for the song. As ideas are verbalized and demonstrated, all imitate and sing. Version 2 challenges students to identify ways of greeting others.

Age Appropriateness

Version 1—Preschool through Grade 3   Movement Game

Version 2—Grade 1 through Grade 3   Greeting Game

Degrees of Intensity

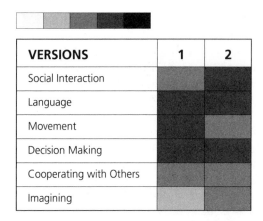

VERSIONS	1	2
Social Interaction		
Language		
Movement		
Decision Making		
Cooperating with Others		
Imagining		

Learning Opportunities

- *Move* to specific words: Auditory-motor skills.
- *Match movement* to language ideas: Auditory-motor skills (Versions 1, 2).
- Verbalize and demonstrate ways of *greeting* others: Social skills (Version 2).
- *Word substitution:* Language skills, music skills (Versions 1, 2).
- *Imitate* actions: Visual-motor coordination (Versions 1, 2).
- Balanced phrase *structure:* Music skills.
- Pentatonic *melody* and patterns of SO₁ SO₁ LA₁ DO and unisons (DO DO DO) and RE MI SO₁ LA₁ DO DO: Music skills.
- *Rhythm* patterns of ♩. ♪ ♫ ♩ ♩ (DU TA DU DE DU DU) and ♫ ♩ (DU DE DU) and ♩. ♪ ♫ (DU TA DU DE): Music skills.

Song and Activity Background

If the tune of *Sing with Me* sounds familiar, you probably know the song *The Old Brass Wagon:* Circle to the right, the old brass wagon . . . You're the one, my darling. *Sing with Me* is probably a variant of that play party song from the Indiana, Missouri, and Iowa pioneers in which the song gives "calls" to tell players which movement to do next (Sandburg 1927, 159). The *Sing with Me* activity described here functions in the same way but with individual movements rather than group, circle movements. Version 1 is from Richards (1985, 85), and Version 2 developed in the special education classes of Peggy Bennett in Fort Wayne, Indiana, in the mid-1970s.

Script. Version 1: Movement Game

Teacher	Students
Introduce the song by singing it. Gesture for students to join in as you sing the song again, communicating delight at and encouragement for their participation.	Students observe and begin to sing with the teacher during repetition of the song.
With little or no pause between songs, lead singing for a few more turns and change words and actions as you repeat the song. Students can suggest a movement or a gesture for the cadence phrase, *"Won't you be my honey?"* • *"Clap with me, all together . . ."* • *"Wiggle with me, all together . . ."* • *What shall we do when we sing "Won't you be my honey?" Can you think of a movement or a gesture that we could use to end the song for each turn?*	Students sing and imitate the motions of the teacher. If students have difficulty suggesting a movement or a gesture for the cadence phrase, prompts can help guide them: • *What gesture might suggest a question?* • *What movement could we make that is different from the rest of the song?* • *What movement or gesture could suggest that the turn is over?*
Encourage students to offer movement ideas for turns of the song. • *We have sung, clapped, and wiggled. Raise your hand if you have a suggestion for another idea we could show as we sing.*	Natalie raises her hand, and when the teacher calls on her, she offers, "Stomp our feet." Help students control their actions by challenging them to coordinate their movements with the song. Focusing their attention on the cadence lets students move continuously through the song but stop on the last word. • *Make sure your actions stop at the end of the song. Listen closely for the* cadence.
Instructions and song prompts can be sung on the starting pitch. • *Here comes Natalie's song . . . "Stomp your feet . . . honey."* After a few turns or on another day, add • *So that we remember who gave us this idea, let's put Maggie's name in the song.* [Sing.] *"Touch your wrist, just like Maggie . . . honey."*	Students continue to offer ideas, identify movements, and fit new words into the flow of the song. Through the song, students are acknowledged for their verbal and movement contributions.

Additional Versions of Sing with Me

Version 2: Greeting Game. Begin class with *"Wave to Florence, all together . . . honey?"* After all students greet Florence with a wave, guide further turns.

> *Florence, I hope you enjoyed getting all those waves! Whom do you want us to wave to this time?*

After several turns in which students decide who will receive a wave from the class, add more opportunities for making choices.

> *Patrick, whom would you like us to sing to this time?* [Patrick answers, "Larry."] *And, how would you like us to greet him? There are many other ways to show we're glad to see someone. How shall we greet Larry?*

After Patrick decides on "thumbs up," all join in singing and gesturing: *"Thumbs up to Larry, all together . . . honey?"* Use a moderate tempo so that students can adequately pronounce the words and perform the gestures. The activity evolves within a class and over several classes to be a way of greeting students.

Skip to My Lou

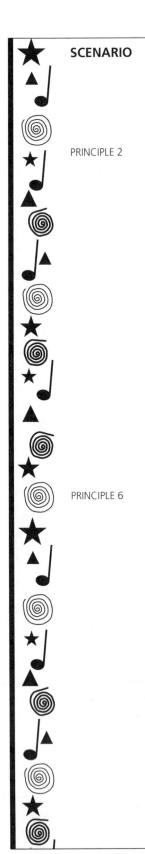

SCENARIO

PRINCIPLE 2

PRINCIPLE 6

VERSION 6: PHRASE GAME

"Watch what I do at the end of the song." The teacher sang "Round and round and round we go . . ." and when he came to the cadence phrase, "Skip to my lou, my darling," he tapped the words on his palm. "Raise your hand if you can tell us what you heard my hands do." Students raised their hands and responded with a variety of observations: "You clapped at the end of the song." "I heard your hands sing 'Skip to my lou, my darling.'" After listening to several answers, the teacher asked the students to join him in singing the song and tapping the words "Skip to my lou, my darling."

"You are listening to the words at the end of the song, but what do the words at the beginning of the song tell us to do?" "Go round and round!" answered the students. "Well, then, make up an action that you can do while in your seat that goes 'round.' Don't forget to have your hands sing 'Skip to my lou, my darling.' Take a moment to think of an action. [Pause.] Is your idea ready? Here comes the song." After the group practiced individual ideas, several students demonstrated their movements for the class to try.

"I noticed that most of these actions can go in two different directions. It would be interesting to change the direction of the actions while we are singing. Listen to the song this time, and see if the song tells you when you could change the directions."

Offering his observations the teacher continued, "Many of you were changing directions at the same time. You found a clue in the song to help you know when. Try it again. Everyone do your own action with the song and change directions when the song tells you to. [Singing the starting pitch] Ready, sing . . .' Round and round . . .'"

"Some of us forgot to tap the words 'Skip to my lou, my darling,' but we'll remember this time. Who will show us where the song tells you to change directions?" Several students showed their ideas as all sang the song. After each demonstration, the teacher made an observation or asked a question of the class. "Did your hands first go in a clockwise direction, then counterclockwise?" "How many times did Claude change directions?" "What surprised you about Emily's actions?" "Phoebe, you even remembered to tap 'Skip to my lou, my darling.' What listening!"

"Everybody try your own actions again as you listen for the clues in the song. What tells you to change direction?" After reflecting on how their movement coordinated with the song, students responded, "The pause," "The word 'go,'" "When the song goes up," "On the longer word," "On the higher tones." Some responses were clarified when needed: "What do you mean 'when the song stops'?" "I saw what your hand was doing. How would we put that in words?" "Oh yes, 'going up.' Are you sure it happens every time we sing 'go'?" The teacher led students to study their decisions about the song and check their responses by singing the song and listening for the clue. "Let's listen. Do you change every time we sing the 'go'?" "Listen for higher tones. Is that where the song tells us to change?"

After shaping students' discoveries of song parts by having them connect listening and moving, the teacher offered appropriate vocabulary so that students could identify what they had been studying. "Notice how the song has four parts. 'Skip to my lou my darling' is one part, and the three places where we sing 'Round and round and round we go' are the others. Each of these parts of the song is called a phrase, and the places where you wanted to change directions are called cadences or phrase endings. Phrases are parts or sections of music that feel complete. Sing the song again and snap your fingers at the end of each phrase. Remember, it's where you sensed a change of direction."

Skip to My Lou

Round and round and round we go.
Fly's in the butter-milk, shoo, fly, shoo!
Round and round and round we go.
Fly's in the butter-milk, shoo, fly, shoo!

Round and round and round we go. Skip to my lou, my dar - ling.
Fly's in the butter- milk, shoo, fly, shoo! Skip to my lou, my darl - ing.

Brief Description

In a seated circle or in a scatter formation for the Round Game of Version 1, students sing and observe the teacher as he or she makes a circular motion. The activity elicits movement ideas from the students to show what could go "round and round." Students offer ideas, imitate others' ideas, and coordinate movements with the song. The Partner Game of Version 2 challenges partners to create a movement that goes "round." The Name Game (Version 3) challenges students to sing names in order around a circle, and Version 4 challenges students to suggest patterns in which the names are sung. Version 5 greets each student with a handshake and eye contact, then three students and the greeter join hands to skip in a circle for section 2 of the song. Version 6 focuses on moving to the repetitions in the song, leading students to discover and explore song phrases.

Age Appropriateness

Version 1—Preschool through Grade 4	Round Game	
Version 2—Grade 1 through Grade 4	Partner Game	
Version 3—Grade 3 through Grade 6	Name Game	
Version 4—Grade 3 through Grade 6	Pattern Game	
Version 5—Preschool through Grade 2	Greeting Game	
Version 6—Grade 3 through Grade 6	Phrase Game	

Degrees of Intensity

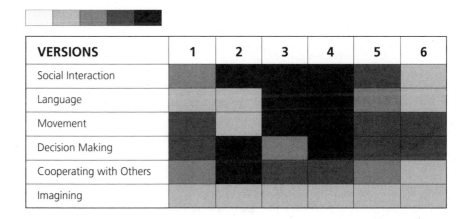

VERSIONS	1	2	3	4	5	6
Social Interaction						
Language						
Movement						
Decision Making						
Cooperating with Others						
Imagining						

Learning Opportunities

- *Coordinate movement* with beginning and ending of sound: Auditory-motor skills (Versions 1, 2).

- *Isolate a body part* for movement: Motor figure-ground skills (Versions 1, 2).

- *Cooperate with a partner:* Social skills, motor skills (Version 2).

- *Learn names:* Social skills (Versions 3, 4, 5).

- Sequence and sing *names* in varying patterns: Thinking skills (Versions 3, 4, 5).

- *Word substitution:* Language skills (Versions 3, 4, 5).

- Coordinate movement with *phrases:* Motor skills, music skills (Version 6).

- Balanced phrase *structure:* Music skills.

- *Melody* patterns of RE MI FA MI RE DO DO and MI MI DO DO MI MI SO: Music skills.

- *Rhythm* patterns of ♪♪♪ ♪♪ ♪ ♪ (DU DETA DU DE DU DU) and ♪♪ ♪♪ ♪♪ ♪ (DU DE DU DE DU DE DU): Music skills.

Song and Activity Background

"Skip-a to my lou," "skip to ma lou," "skip to my lula," "skip come a lou," "shoo li loo," and "shoo la lay" are just a few of the more than 175 variants of the popular play party song and game *Skip to My Lou* (Seeger 1948, 167). What is a "lou"? Though most of us have known this song for years, few of us know what "lou" or "loo" means. If Opie and Opie (1985, 320) are correct, "lou" is an old form of the word "love," and this would explain the bachelor game format of stealing partners: "Lost my pardner, what'll I do?" "I'll get another'n purtier'n you" (Lomax and Lomax 1947, 80).

One source, *The British Broadside Ballad,* traced the tune of *Skip to My Lou* to a sixteenth-century song called *Dargason.* In Porter's *Negro Folk Singing Games* (1914), *Skip to My Lou* was described as being played just like *The Jolly Miller,* with one person in the center as partners circled singing. At the cadence, each inside player tried to grasp the arm of the outside player of the couple in front, and the center person tried to grab any free arm.

Schoolchildren commonly add their own verses to those most widely known (and are encouraged to do so): "Fly's in the buttermilk, shoo, fly, shoo!" "Little red wagon, painted blue." "Loo loo skip to my (pronounced 'ma') loo." Twenty-five verses of *Skip to My Lou* appear in the *Handy Play Party Book* (Rohrbough 1940). The variant "round and round" is from Richards (1985, 86). Version 5 was developed in the special education classroom of Margaret Wharram in Ontario, Canada, in the 1970s.

Script. Version 1: Round Game

Teacher	Students
• *Do you see something going around?* Help students concentrate by beginning the song with no introduction. Sing and slightly move a toe in a circular motion. On the last phrase, tap the rhythm pattern as you sing "Skip to my lou, my darling."	Students offer a number of guesses about what you are making "go around." Right, wrong, and repeated answers are equally acceptable: "I think it was your eyes," "Your head was moving," and "You were making your breath go around."

Teacher	Students
• *Several different answers give us reason to check our observations. Keep watching, and I'll repeat my idea.* Repeat the motion so that students may check their ideas as time and interest allow.	Students sing and observe to check their ideas.
After students discover the teacher's secret motion, they try moving just their toes as they sing. Prompt them to come up with ideas of their own: • *What can you make go around?* • *Do you all see Rodney's idea? Notice how he is holding his arms. Let's sing the song and use Rodney's movement.* • *Can we do Joyce's idea and still remember to tap for the last phrase? Let's try it!*	Playing and sharing, students sing as they try their own ideas, try ideas of others, and observe others' ideas. Each turn of the song is closed by tapping the rhythm to the last phrase.

Additional Versions of Skip to My Lou

Version 2: Partner Game.   Students join with a partner to create a movement that goes around. Students also can organize into small groups to create ways to "go round" with the song. Students take turns observing partners, or groups share ideas; then other partners or groups can imitate. These observation times are good opportunities for helping students learn to observe without evaluation. Clapping "*Skip to my lou, my darling*" at the end of the song can help control movement by requiring students to shift from one activity (going around) to another (clapping) and by indicating when the movement needs to stop.

   ▪ *Let's sing and observe as Marcia and Pat show us their idea. What will you be able to describe about their idea when their turn is over?*

   ▪ *Now that we've noticed details of Marcia and Pat's movement idea, let's try it with our partners. Remember to tap the cadence phrase.*

Version 3: Name Game.   As a name activity, this melody can collect six names in each verse. Singing and gesturing in order around the circle, students track the names and tap for the cadence phrase: *"There's Jennie with Cecil, and Cecil with Roger, and Roger with George, and George with Devon, and Devon with Marsha, and Marsha with Vicki. Skip to my lou, my darling."*

Version 4: Pattern Game.   Once names are well known, students can challenge themselves by determining patterns for singing names. For each singing, names are repeated if necessary to complete the pattern and the song.

   ▪ *Let's sing only one-syllable names around the circle.*

   ▪ *Sing every third person, skipping two in between.*

   ▪ *Can we sing only the names of people wearing jeans? Let's try it!*

Students can be asked to assess their own abilities to sing and track the patterns of names.

- *How did you do with that challenge? On a scale of 1 to 5, with 5 being the highest, show me on your fingers how well you were able to sing every name with that pattern.*

- *I see some 4s, a couple 5s, and several 3s. Let's all aim for 4s and 5s this time in our self-assessments. Here's the song and pattern again.*

Version 5: Greeting Game.   As children sit or stand in a circle, the leader moves to eye level of a child and greets the child by singing and shaking his or her hand or waving. With each succeeding phrase, the teacher moves to the next child. The song phrases allow for greeting three children per verse; then all clap the word rhythms as they sing the cadence phrase: "*Skip to my lou, my darling.*"

- "*Hi, Patricia. How are you? Hi, Jody. How are you? Hi, Brandy. How are you? Skip to my lou my darling.*" ["I know you" may be used instead of "How are you?"]

An optional activity is for the leader and three children to join hands and skip in a circle as they sing the next verse: "*Skip with me, I'll skip with you. . . .*" After several repetitions of the game, children can suggest how the circle should move for the second verse: walk, jump, hop.

- "*Skip with me, I'll skip with you. Skip with me, I'll skip with you. Skip with me, I'll skip with you. Skip to my lou my darling.*"

Version 6: Phrase Game.   (See Scenario.)

Three Blind Mice

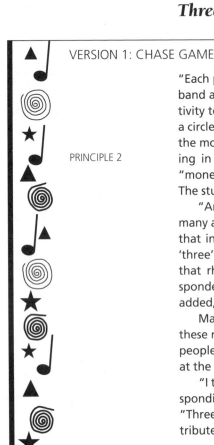

VERSION 1: CHASE GAME

PRINCIPLE 2

"Each person who received a mouse tail, please tuck it inside the back of your waistband and move over to the wall." Ms. Conrad was teaching the *Three Blind Mice* activity to her fifth-grade students for the first time as they were seated on the floor in a circle. To introduce the activity, the teacher had captured their attention by cupping the mouse tails inside her hands and asking secretively, "What do you think I'm holding in my hands?" After listening to several guesses ranging from "a spider" to "money," Ms. Conrad opened her hands and the braided yarn strips fell to the floor. The students looked puzzled.

"Any more guesses as to what these are?" "Yarn," a student replied. "Well, how many are there?" asked Ms. Conrad. "Three," responded several students. "You know that in music class, I probably have a song in mind. Do you know any songs about 'three' something?" "Three men in a tub!" Derrick shouted. "I don't know a song to that rhyme, but if that were the match, what would these be?" the teacher responded. Pondering, Derrick and a couple of his buddies said, "Oars?" and then added, "You wouldn't be able to paddle with those, though."

Marty guessed, "'Three in the Middle'?" "Oh, I do know that song! What would these represent in that song activity?" the teacher queried. "I don't know, maybe the people trying to get out of the middle of the circle?" She and her classmates chuckled at the image her answer created.

"I think it's 'Three Blind Mice,'" offered Jerry, "and those are the mouse tails!" Responding with a smile and a look of "you figured it out!" Ms. Conrad began to sing "Three blind mice. Three blind mice. See . . ." as she walked around the circle and distributed the three "mouse tails."

Three Blind Mice

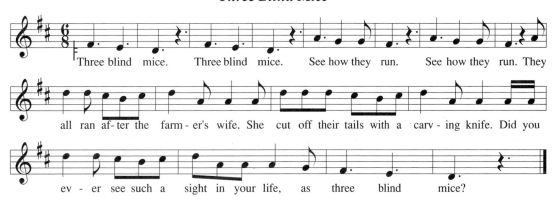

Three blind mice. Three blind mice. See how they run. See how they run. They all ran af-ter the farm-er's wife. She cut off their tails with a carv-ing knife. Did you ev-er see such a sight in your life, as three blind mice?

Brief Description

With the class in a seated circle, the teacher distributes one mouse tail (a long piece of cloth or yarn) to each of three students. The "mice" then go to the corner to hide their eyes, making them "blind." The leader silently designates someone in the circle as the farmer's wife, and the song begins. While the song is sung, the mice walk around the outside of the circle, and when the group sings "the farmer's wife," the designated person jumps up and runs after the mice, trying to grab their tails. The song is sung twice. At the end of the second song, the mice who have kept their tails get one more turn as mice. The farmer's wife gives away the tails she has collected to the students who become the new mice for the next turn. Once the new and returning mice have their backs to the group, the "wife" secretly designates a new wife and the game begins again.

Age Appropriateness

Version 1—Grade 3 through Grade 6   Chase Game

Degrees of Intensity

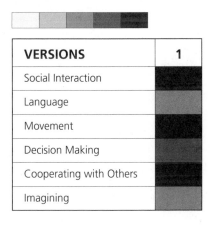

VERSIONS	1
Social Interaction	
Language	
Movement	
Decision Making	
Cooperating with Others	
Imagining	

Learning Opportunities

- *Coordinate movement* with beginning and ending of sound: Auditory-motor skills.
- *Manage movements* to catch and avoid getting caught: Motor skills.

- *Competition* with minimal emphasis on winners and losers: Social skills.
- *Phrases* with and without anacruses: Music skills.
- *Melody* patterns of MI RE DO and SO | DO¹: Music skills.
- *Rhythm* patterns of ♪ | ♩ ♪ ♫ ♩ ♪ ♩ (DI DU DI DUDADI DU DI DU) and ♪ | ♫ ♫ ♩ ♪ ♩ (DI DUDADI DUDADI DU DI DU): Music skills.

Song and Activity Background

Possibly three and a half centuries old, "[*Three Blind Mice*] is probably the best known round in the world" according to *The Oxford Dictionary of Nursery Rhymes*, but it made its appearance in children's literature only in 1842. According to *The Annotated Mother Goose*, a version of this traditional song was found in the 1609 edition of *Deuteromelia or The Seconde part of Musicks melodie*, which was likely written by Thomas Ravenscroft, a teenage chorister at the time (Baring-Gould and Baring-Gould 1967, 156). Like *Ring Around the Rosy*, *Three Blind Mice* has been absolved of continuing rumors of hidden, sinister meanings.

A favorite of intermediate-age students, this game was developed in the 1980s by Mary Opland Springer and her drama and music students in Seattle.

Script. Version 1: Chase Game

Teacher	Students
When the group is seated in a circle, give the mouse tails to three students. • *Each person who received a mouse tail, please tuck it inside the back of your waistband and move over to the wall. Turn your backs to the group.* • *For this game, we need to make a safety check of our room. Please look behind you. If you see any materials on the floor, if you're sitting too close to the wall, if you see a corner of a desk or a chair protruding near our circle, please fix those things.*	As the mice are getting ready, check that students are not tying or threading tails through belt loops, because clothing could be torn. Some teachers keep extra scarves, belts, or ties in their rooms to serve as a waistband for those students who are not wearing clothing with a place to hang the tail. Tails may be made of paper or cloth, and should be long enough and thick enough to handle (and grab!) easily.
When the mice are ready and the area has been checked for safety, explain the game as briefly as possible. Over-explaining rules and procedures before playing can add more confusion than it resolves. Also, students may be more intrigued by just a few clues about how to play than by long, detailed explanations. Often, clarity comes from doing the activity rather than from hearing about it. • *To make themselves temporarily blind, the mice will face away from the circle, and I will point to a person who will be the farmer's wife.* • *When we begin singing the song, the mice start walking around the outside of the circle.* • *As we sing "the farmer's wife," the mystery wife will jump up, chase the mice, and see how many tails she can get before the cadence of the next song.* • *Now, based on what I just explained, how many times through the song will constitute a turn?* ["Twice."]	During the first playing of *Three Blind Mice*, students may laugh and cheer so much that the song is continued only by the teacher and a few students. In play that involves a chase, adults and children often forget to sing or they sing in a quality that may be more raucous than usual. Be prepared to remind and challenge them: • *We can't play the game without the song.* • *Do you think you can keep the song going without my help?* • *Raise your hand if you think you can sing every word this time.* • *We may need to save this game for another day when we have more singers to support it.* • *How did you do in singing the song that time, on a scale of 1 to 5 with 5 being the highest? Let's all aim for 4s and 5s this time.*

Teacher	Students
• *Yes, let's go. Mice, turn around. You are the wife* [pointing silently to Jared], *and here comes the song.*	During his turn, Jared is able to take two tails.
• *Now that you have seen one turn, let's take stock of how we did or what questions you might have.*	
• *First, did you notice what happened to the song?* [Collect observations.]	
• *I helped continue it that time, but from now on, the song is your responsibility as well. Keep it going.*	Students are reminded that the activity needs their voices and that this is a good opportunity to practice healthy, energetic singing.
• *Also, some classes like to have the rule that the wife can cut through the circle but the mice can't. Let's try it.*	
• *Are there any other points we need to clarify now, or shall we continue with another turn?*	
• *If you still have a tail, you get another turn. Mice get a maximum of two consecutive turns.*	You may want to suggest that the mice who lost their tails give them to someone new rather than having the "wife" give them away.
• *Jared, your responsibility is to give the two tails away quickly and, after the mice are not looking, point to a new wife. The sooner we take care of all that, the sooner the song can begin for another turn.*	

Tideo

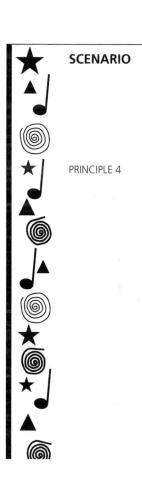

SCENARIO

PRINCIPLE 4

"Here is a new song. After I sing it, I'll ask you what you think it is about." The fourth-grade class listened as the teacher sang, "Pass one window, tideo. Pass two windows, tideo. Pass three windows, tideo. Jingle at the window, tideo. Tideo, tideo, jingle at the window, tideo." Then the teacher asked, "What do you think it's about?"

"Windows," Amy answered. "What else did you hear?" asked the teacher. "Something that sounded like tidy bowl," responded Wendell, with a puzzled look on his face. The fourth graders erupted into laughter. "Yes, you did hear a word that sounded like 'tidy bowl,' but I was singing 'tideo.' What do you think 'tideo' means? Any guesses?" None of the students ventured a guess.

"If I said to you, 'Tideo,' what region of the world do you think of?" After students offered their ideas, the teacher continued. "It sounds British to me. Can you imagine hearing someone say 'tideo'? How would you use a British accent to say 'tideo'? What do you think it would mean?" Students responded: "It sounds like 'hello.' " "I think it sounds like 'good-bye.' " The teacher replied, "I think it sounds like both 'hello' and 'good-bye.' Do you know any other languages that use the same word for hello and good-bye?" Some students suggested "aloha" and "shalom." "Let me sing the song again, join in for any sections you can sing, and then I'll tell you what I imagine when I hear this song." As the teacher repeated the song, the students listened and sang portions that they recalled.

"Have you ever been on an old, old street in a big city? Sometimes in older sections of the city, we can see the windows of houses right next to the sidewalk. Have any of you seen houses like that? Imagine a nice warm day and you are sitting by your open window watching people walk by. Your window is so close to the sidewalk that you are able to hear people if they greet you. What kind of greetings might you see?

Imagine them as we sing. 'Pass one window, tideo . . . tideo'." The teacher connected the song to the imagery by collecting students' responses for ways of greeting. As greetings were suggested, they were demonstrated and imitated by the group.

"We still need to solve the 'jingle at the window' section. What do you think that means? Why would we be jingling at the window?" Because students were gaining confidence in letting their imaginations suggest solutions, they offered a variety of possible explanations.

"This section tells us about something that we don't jingle these days, we push. Any guesses? Yes, it is an old-fashioned doorbell, which was actually a bell that was jingled by shaking the stem that hung down. [Use a shaking motion with the hand to demonstrate the jingle.] I'll take the first turn walking along to greet my neighbors. Sing with me, please."

Throughout this introduction to *Tideo*, students' ideas were collected and explored for their connection with words of the song. The teacher chose to take time to create and pursue images because she knew that such collaborative problem solving helps give the song meaning for students. As students shared and explained their ideas, they were encouraged to listen to each other: "Let's listen to what Amanda tells us." "All ears are on Arthur's voice." Gentle and curious probing to further understand students' ideas was projected through prompts such as "Amanda, what made you think of that?" "Tell us a little bit more about what you are imagining, Arthur." Though the discussion took time, the teacher felt a great deal of satisfaction when the students used the imagery they had created to provide a delightful context for their interaction as they played the game.

Tideo

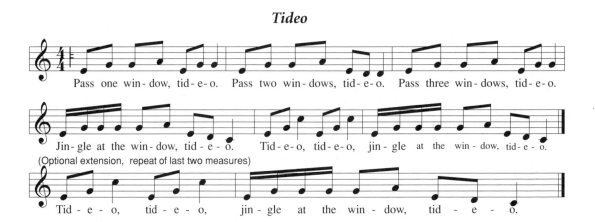

Pass one win-dow, tid-e-o. Pass two win-dows, tid-e-o. Pass three win-dows, tid-e-o.

Jin-gle at the win-dow, tid-e-o. Tid-e-o, tid-e-o, jin-gle at the win-dow, tid-e-o.

(Optional extension, repeat of last two measures)

Tid-e-o, tid-e-o, jin-gle at the win-dow, tid-e-o.

Brief Description

As the group stands in a circle, one person stands on the inside. When the song begins, the leader walks, passing a window and greeting a "person in the window" each time he or she hears "tideo." At the phrase "jingle at the window," the person in the center stops in front of a student and makes a jingling motion with a hand, ringing the doorbell. On the next "tideo," the two students mirror movements as they face each other: lightly slapping their thighs on "ti-," lightly clapping hands on "de-," and raising arms in the air to tap fists on "-o." After jingling again on "jingle at the window, tideo," the phrase "Tideo, tideo, jingle at the window, tideo" is repeated with the arm movements, but this time, on "jingle at the window, tideo," the partners link arms and trade places. The game now has a new leader for the next turn.

Age Appropriateness

Version 1—Grade 3 through Grade 5

Degrees of Intensity

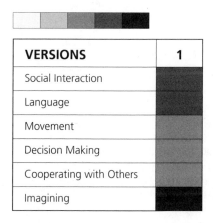

VERSIONS	1
Social Interaction	
Language	
Movement	
Decision Making	
Cooperating with Others	
Imagining	

Learning Opportunities

- *Coordinate movement* with beginning and ending of sound: Auditory-motor skills.
- *Move* to specific words: Auditory-motor skills.
- Demonstrate ways of *greeting:* Social skills.
- Movement to *melodic contour:* Music skills, auditory-visual-motor skills.
- Balanced phrase *structure:* Music skills.
- Pentatonic *melody* and patterns of MI SO SO LA MI SO SO and MI SO DO[I] and MI SO SO SO SO LA MI RE DO: Music skills.
- *Rhythm* patterns of ♫♫ ♫ ♫ ♩ (DUTADETA DU DE DU DE DU) and ♫ ♫ ♫ ♩ (DU DE DU DE DU DE DU): Music skills.

Song and Activity Background

Tideo was especially popular in Nebraska, Oklahoma, and Texas as a play party song in the early 1900s. Found in a number of current sources, it can be titled *Pass One Window, Toddy-o,* and *Jingle at the Windows,* and the first line has been found as "Skip one window" and "Pass one window." Seeger's version of 1948 is "Skip one window . . . Jingle at the windows, tideo. Jingling jingling jingling Jo, Jingle at the windows, Tideo." The game with motions that approximate the MI SO DO[I] hand signs can be found in Richards (1985). The need to help Japanese teachers understand the song created the imagery described in the scenario; it was developed in Tokyo by Peggy Bennett in 1991. With this imagery, the person walking inside the circle had a purpose and context for interacting with those standing in the circle.

Script. Tideo

Teacher	Students
This game may be presented without introduction or with the introduction described in the scenario. On the inside of a standing circle, walk, sing, and pause to greet a student with a wave, a nod, or a handshake on each "*tideo.*" Stop in front of one student and jingle an imaginary doorbell during "*jingle at the window, tideo.*" On "*Tideo, tideo,*" slap thighs for "*Ti-,*" clap hands for "*-de-,*" and tap fists overhead for "*-o.*" Each syllable raises the level of movement from low to high, and the hand motions give the partners a way to interact that performs a melodic pattern from the song. The "*Tideo*" movement in this part of the song approximates the direction the melody is moving and the solfa hand signs for MI SO DO^I. (See Chapter 6 for illustrations of hand signs.) Both partners do the jingling motion for "*jingle at the window, tideo.*" Repeat the phrase and the hand movements for "*Tideo, tideo*"; then hook elbows and exchange places during the last "*jingle at the window, tideo.*"	Students listen to the song and observe the motions of the leader.
• *Now that you've heard the song and have seen the activity, it's time to collect your observations. Describe the different motions you saw me do as I took a turn.*	Students answer with various descriptions of their observations. Further prompts can include • *Show me what you saw.* • *What was I singing when I did that? Do you remember?*
After the class has collected observations and sequenced the movements, it is the new person's turn to walk inside the circle, to "go visiting along the sidewalks." At this point, however, you might let the student decide whether she or he would like the next turn. • *Barry, it's your turn. Do you want to take it, or would you rather that I took another turn so you could observe again?*	You can help the students concentrate on the greeting by cueing: • *How will I [or Barry] greet people this time?* • *Will I [or Barry] greet everyone the same way, or will we vary our greetings?*
As the game progresses, students become more interactive within the roles they are playing. They try out various ways to greet people; they return greetings in the same ways they are greeted; and they walk with freedom and confidence around the circle as they coordinate movements with specific sections of the song. • *In what other ways do we show someone we're happy to see them?* • *How might we look if we don't know someone but we are saying "hello" to them without words?*	This activity comes alive when students' ideas are used. Greetings may include behaviors as diverse as nodding, waving, tipping the hat, bowing, "high fives," and "thumbs up." Students can also learn appropriate responses to greetings: • *Be sure you acknowledge someone's greeting. You may respond in the same way they greet you or in another way. But it is good manners to respond.*
After the activity is learned and played several times, a new variation can be introduced by challenging students: • *We have been jingling the doorbell with our hands. How else could we jingle as we play this time?* • *Let's watch Amanda on her turn and see what she shows us for a jingle.*	All students in the circle can be involved by holding up one, two, and three fingers when singing the numbers in the song; showing the jingling motion for those sections of the song; and doing the hand gestures as they watch the partners for the "Tideo, tideo" patterns.

Twinkle, Twinkle, Little Star

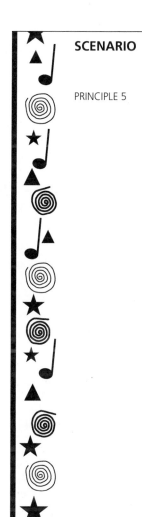

SCENARIO

PRINCIPLE 5

"This is such a lovely song, and it reminds us to appreciate beautiful things that we may not understand," the teacher began. Her second-grade students were all seated, facing her. "Let's sing the song together. [Singing] Ready, sing . . . 'Twinkle, twinkle . . . are.' " Students were accustomed to singing this song with a heavy beat and accenting every syllable. The teacher wanted to move them away from that habit. Her voice, words, and gestures communicated softness and fluidity.

"Have you ever wondered about stars?" the teacher asked quietly. "What makes them twinkle? How far away are they? If we were close enough, could we touch them? Show us how your hands would move if they were to look like a star twinkling." Students responded with a variety of hand movements, and the teacher noted, "Look at all those quietly twinkling stars! Veronica is giving us an idea. Let's let our fingers blink like Veronica's fingers. Here comes the song . . ." All sang and used Veronica's idea for finger movements.

"Follow my movements this time as our stars twinkle," the teacher prompted as all sang the song again. Gracefully moving her arms in an arc from one side of her body to the other, the teacher changed directions with the beginning of a new phrase. "Such lovely, slow movements we're seeing! It can be harder to move slowly than to move quickly. When we sing 'Up above the world so high, like a diamond in the sky,' it almost sounds as if we are trying to explain about stars to someone who may not have noticed them. What gesture could we use to show where those stars are?" Students offered gesture ideas.

"Oh, what a nice feeling that would give to our song, Carlos! Please show and describe your idea. [He was gesturing upward with one arm, then with the other.] We almost have a ballet with our hands and arms to perform with our song. Let's see how beautiful we can make it this time."

The activity continued for a couple of more repetitions of the song. Listening to the children's singing was so satisfying for their teacher. By changing the imagery and demonstrating musical movement, she had helped them change the way they were singing the song.

Twinkle, Twinkle, Little Star

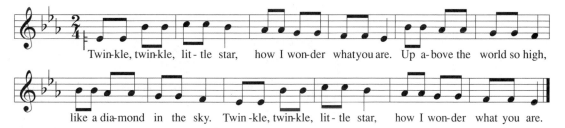

Twin-kle, twin-kle, lit-tle star, how I won-der what you are. Up a-bove the world so high,

like a dia-mond in the sky. Twin-kle, twin-kle, lit-tle star, how I won-der what you are.

Brief Description

Using imagery of stars and wonder, students create and imitate movements that correlate with the feeling of the song and the song phrases.

Age Appropriateness

Version 1—Preschool through Grade 2

Degrees of Intensity

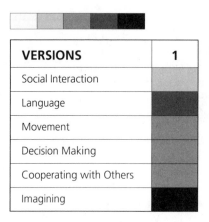

VERSIONS	1
Social Interaction	
Language	
Movement	
Decision Making	
Cooperating with Others	
Imagining	

Learning Opportunities

- *Coordinate movement* with beginning and ending of sound: Auditory-motor skills.
- *Imitate* movements: Visual-motor skills.
- *Musical movement* to *phrases:* Music skills.
- Balanced phrase *structure:* Music skills.
- *Melody* patterns of DO DO SO SO LA LA SO and FA FA MI MI RE RE DO: Music skills.
- *Rhythm* pattern of ♫ ♫ ♫ ♩ (DU DE DU DE DU DE DU): Music skills.

Song and Activity Background

A popular and well-known song for generations of children, *Twinkle, Twinkle, Little Star* has been parodied many times for various occasions. Its tune is a French folk song that Mozart used as the basis of a keyboard composition. Though the first verse is commonly known, the additional stanzas of the poem, listed in *The Annotated Mother Goose*, are not. Repeat the first two phrases of the first verse for the ending of each subsequent verse:

> *When the blazing sun is gone, when he nothing shines upon,*
> *then you show your little light, twinkle, twinkle all the night.*
>
> *When the traveler in the dark, thanks you for your tiny spark,*
> *he could not see which way to go, if you did not twinkle so.*
>
> *In the dark blue sky you keep, and often through my curtains peep,*
> *for you never shut your eye, till the sun is in the sky.*
>
> *As your bright and tiny spark lights the traveler in the dark,*
> *though I know not what you are, twinkle, twinkle little star.*

(Baring-Gould and Baring-Gould 1967, 125).

Uncle Joe

SCENARIO

PRINCIPLE 2

PRINCIPLE 7

VERSION 1: RACE GAME

Mrs. Roberts's students were seated in a circle. "Please listen to this song. After I sing it, tell me what you think it is about." After she sang the verse of the song ("Did you ever go to meetin', Uncle Joe? . . ."), students' comments came quickly. "It's about Uncle Joe." "He's going to a meeting." "My uncle goes to meetings in New York all the time. We get to go to the airport to see him come home sometimes." "There's no wind in this song."

Always delighted with the variety of responses such a question could stimulate, Mrs. Roberts said, "Listen to the song again. What kind of meeting do you think this Uncle Joe is going to? Does the song sound like a song about a business meeting?"

More discussion followed, and intermittently Mrs. Roberts would repeat the song, inviting students to sing along on any part they knew. "What is the weather like?" she asked. Discussion followed about the wind and its effect on people and the weather.

After the teacher repeated the verse, she added the chorus, "Hop up, my ladies, three in a row. . . ." Having already been stimulated to treat the song as a puzzle and verbalize their ideas, students wondered aloud about how the three ladies were connected to the meeting and why they were hopping. Johnnie thought that Uncle Joe had come late and three ladies had to stand to let him pass so he could get to the only empty seat. Eleanor said she thought that it was the women at the meeting who had the most to say, and they stood when they spoke. Mrs. Roberts commented that it was a good idea to stand when speaking to a group, because it let the listeners know who was speaking ("who had the floor") and it was easier to hear the speaker that way.

"Maybe that is a part of what this song is about," Mrs. Roberts added. "Before we take any more ideas, let's sing it again." After she sang the song once more, Mrs. Roberts described for the eager listeners some kinds of social gatherings that people in the American West would have, and suddenly the song had a context for the students. Students learned that people would look forward to all sorts of gatherings, because those events were chances to relieve the isolation that many early farmers and ranchers might have experienced.

Uncle Joe

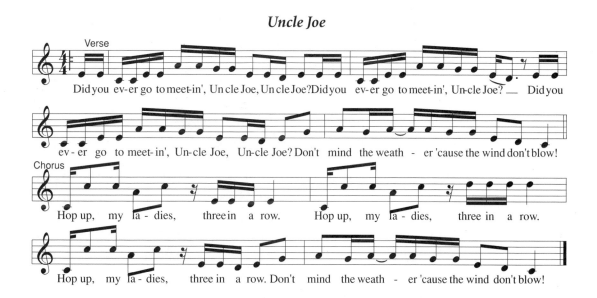

Brief Description

After being introduced to the song (see the Scenario), students are in a seated circle for Version 1. One student, who is chosen to be Uncle Joe, walks around the circle while the class sings the verse, "Did you ever go to meetin'. . . ?" On the chorus, Uncle Joe taps a student on the shoulder each time the word "hop" occurs, tapping a total of three students. When tapped, each student stands (or hops up), while Joe continues around the circle with the song. Joe should continue walking steadily around the circle until the cadence phrase of the chorus, "Don't mind the weather . . . !" At this point, the four students—Joe and the three he tapped—race to a new place in the circle. The three students who were tapped each vacate a spot, and it is getting into one of these three spots that is the objective of all four students. Students must move quickly because they have only the length of that last phrase to get to their new spot. The student who is unable to get to a vacant spot becomes the next Uncle Joe. An alternative ending repeats the last phrase until the students find their places. In Version 2, students create actions for the chorus to perform on the sixteenth note rests.

Age Appropriateness

Version 1—Grade 2 through Grade 5   Race Game

Version 2—Grade 2 through Grade 5   Finding the Rests

Degrees of Intensity

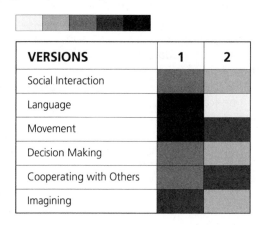

VERSIONS	1	2
Social Interaction		
Language		
Movement		
Decision Making		
Cooperating with Others		
Imagining		

Learning Opportunities

- *Coordinate movement* with beginning and ending of sound: Auditory-motor skills.

- *Move* to specific words: Auditory-motor skills.

- *Imagine* the social, geographical, and historical context of the song: Social studies skills.

- Balanced phrase *structure* and AB (binary) song structure: Music skills.

- *Melody* patterns of SO | LA SO LA LA SO SO MI RE DO and MI MI DO DO MI MI SO SO and DO DO¹ DO¹ LA DO¹: Music skills.

- *Rhythm* patterns of ♪ | ♫ ♬ ♫ ♩ (DE DU DETA TA DETA DU DE DU) and ♬ ♫ (DUTA TA DU DE): Music skills.

Song and Activity Background

First published in New York in 1829, *Uncle Joe* (also known as *Hop Up, My Ladies*) is based on a tune called *Miss McCloud's Reel* and apparently has links with *Jump, Jim Crow* (Lomax 1960, 228–229). As you consider the additional verses that are often included with the song, imagine people of long ago traveling by horseback to social gatherings, riding sometimes two or three to a horse: "Did you ever go to meetin'?" "Will your horse carry double?" "Is your horse a single-footer?" and "Would you rather ride a pacer?" Students can create rich images of the time, the place, and the conditions under which those questions might be asked, as well as thinking about the meanings of "hop up, my ladies, three in a row." The race game described here was created by a group of teachers in Betty Hoffmann's classes in Kalispell, Montana, in the 1980s.

Script. Version 1: Race Game

Teacher	Students
As students are sitting at their desks or on the floor, focus their attention on the word "hop" in the song:	
• *As you listen to this song, count the number of times I sing "hop." Check your answer by snapping your fingers each time this word occurs.*	Students suggest answers and count the number of snaps to check.
• *We snapped for each hop, now think of another action we can do every time we sing that word. Think of something we can do as we remain seated.*	Reagan suggests shrugging shoulders, and the group sings as they coordinate shrugging on each "hop." As more ideas are solicited, students suggest actions involving hands, fingers, shoulders, noses, and so on.
• *Now our challenge is to do a different action for each hop. How many different actions will we need? Which three will we start with? Here we go.*	Students suggest and perform three different actions for the song, timing them to coincide with each "hop."
	The varied repetitions, coordinating movement with specific words, help students focus on parts of the song and prepare for the timing of important actions in the race game.
• *The group activity for this song requires you to listen closely. One student will be Uncle Joe, and he will walk around the outside of the circle. Let's make a sitting circle. Etsuko, will you please select our Uncle Joe?*	Etsuko chooses Kenneth to be Uncle Joe.
• *Kenneth, you're our first Uncle Joe. You walk around the circle, going to your meetin'.*	Students listen to the instructions for the game.
• *When we get to the "Hop up" part of the song, you will gently tap the shoulder of the student you're closest to.*	
• *Class, if Uncle Joe taps your shoulder, stand on your space. Because there are three hops in the song, Uncle Joe will tap three students.*	
• *When we sing "Don't mind the weather 'cause the wind don't blow," all four students will try to find a new place to sit. If four of you are aiming for three spaces, what will happen?*	Students acknowledge that when each person scrambles for a space, one person will be left without a space in the circle.

Teacher	Students
• *The student left without a space will be our next Uncle Joe. We can help our Uncle Joe, Kenneth, by snapping our fingers on the word "hop." That way he'll have extra clues for when to tap a shoulder. Our Uncle Joe is ready, so here comes the song.*	The game continues as time and interest allow. For a slight change after several turns, students can be asked to guess what kind of meeting Uncle Joe might be attending. • *If we watch Uncle Joe, we may be able to tell by his actions what meeting he's going to.* • *Based on your observations, where do you think Uncle Joe was going?*

Additional Versions of Uncle Joe

Version 2: Finding the Rests.   To add more action and interest to the introduction described in the Scenario, the teacher can model a quick action on each of the three sixteenth rests in the chorus. Sing the chorus, "*Hop up my ladies, . . .*" and ask students to observe as you snap during each rest (after "ladies").

■ *Where in the song do the actions come? Do they happen on a word? How many actions are there?*

■ *Let's all do the actions this time.*

Students count the number of actions, notice where they occur, and imitate the teacher's movements. Some students may have difficulty identifying exactly when the actions occur, suggesting the words "three" and "row," or the second syllable of "ladies."

After providing thinking time, challenge students to suggest actions to perform on the rests. Students can work alone or with partners. If they are working with partners, they can sing the verse as they walk around and find a new partner at the cadence phrase.

■ *Each of these places is called a rest, because no sound occurs there. We are filling in the rests with actions, however. What other action could we use for this place in our song?*

Whistle, Daughter, Whistle

SCENARIO

PRINCIPLE 2

Ms. Appleton had sung *Whistle, Daughter, Whistle* several times with her Grade 6 class; they enjoyed making up rhymes and singing them. The teacher would often have individual students practice their conducting skills as the class sustained the "oh," and the student would indicate when the class was to continue the song.

On this day, however, the class seemed tired and uninterested in singing the song again. To offer them a somewhat different experience, Ms. Appleton divided the class into two groups, a North side and a South side. She turned to the South. "What animal will we sing about first?" she asked. "Turtle" was the response. She looked at the North group. "You get to figure out a rhyme for 'turtle,' but you also get to choose the animal the South group has to rhyme." As she had expected, the groups chose animal names that were difficult to rhyme—platypus, tiger, grizzly, and condor. The level of excitement in the class was high, however, and many of the rhymes were ingenious. The students sang the song with glee.

PRINCIPLE 5

On another day, Ms. Appleton had the class list six animals, which she wrote down on the board. She then placed the students in groups of four. Each group was to create a rhyme for each of the six animals on the list. "What is your rhyme for 'whale'?" Ms. Appleton asked one group. Eagerly awaiting their turn, the group responded enthusiastically, proud of their unique and clever rhyme: "I'm having sex with Dale." Quite an outburst from the class met the group's offering. Startled, Ms. Appleton responded quickly, with little expression of either surprise, humor, or displeasure, "We can't sing those words in class." Without waiting, she turned and asked another group for their rhyme, which was "I'm reading all my mail." "That fits the song. Let's sing the whole song with this rhyme."

After class, Ms. Appleton allowed herself to smile at the line about Dale, but she knew that it would not have been a good idea to show her amusement to the class. Although singing the rhyme might not have hurt anything, it could hardly have helped the rest of the period flow smoothly. Problems could easily have developed, from silliness that might be difficult to contain, to a phone call that night from a parent after an excited child had quite innocently shared this verse at home. At the time, Ms. Appleton's sense was to turn attention quickly to a more appropriate rhyme and to do so without exaggeration and emotion. "It worked this time," she thought to herself, and she was pleased that the enthusiasm of the class didn't seem to be dampened either by the inappropriate line or by her response. Students had continued to offer rhymes, and even the group with the offending line had participated with undiminished enjoyment in suggestions from other groups as well as their own subsequent contributions.

Whistle, Daughter, Whistle

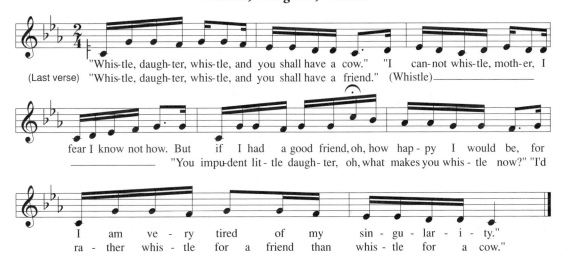

Brief Description

After suggesting various animals, students create verses that end with a word that rhymes with the animal chosen. The verses suggest reasons the daughter would not want to or be able to whistle for this animal. In the final verse, the mother proposes that the daughter whistle for a friend, at which point the daughter readily accepts.

Age Appropriateness

Version 1—Grade 3 through Grade 6

Degrees of Intensity

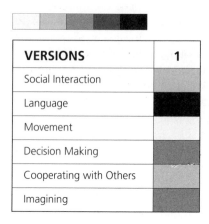

VERSIONS	1
Social Interaction	
Language	
Movement	
Decision Making	
Cooperating with Others	
Imagining	

Learning Opportunities

- *Create new verses* that *rhyme:* Language skills.

- *Cooperate with others* in creating new rhyming lines: Social skills.

- Short-short-long phrase *structure* and **fermata** symbol: Music skills.

- Minor mode and *melody* patterns of MI RE ❘ DO DO TI₁ TI₁ LA₁ and LA₁ MI MI RE MI MI: Music skills.

- *Rhythm* patterns of ♪ ❘ ♫♫ ♫♫ ♫♫ ♩ (TA DUTADETA DU DETA DUTADETA DU) and ♫♫ ♪ ♪ (DUTADETA DUTA): Music skills.

Song and Activity Background

The interchange between the mother and the daughter in *Whistle, Daughter, Whistle* parallels a showdown of wills between a cajoling mother and an obstinate daughter that can be found in *Lazy Mary, Will You Get Up?* The drama in both of these songs is similar to that in *Paper of Pins* and *Old Woman,* in which stories of pleading with women are resolved only when the women are offered a man. The most common version of *Whistle, Daughter, Whistle* includes the phrase "If I had a young man, oh, how happy I would be." This song and its reference to courtship may have French and German connections to a fifteenth- or sixteenth-century round in which a nun or a monk is tempted to dance by a variety of offers (Newell 1883). The song version presented here, however, adapts the words to sing about and yearn for a good friend rather than for a young man. These changes were made to broaden the appeal of the song. Without intending to lessen the importance of the courtship rituals to which this song may be related, the version appearing here highlights the importance of friendship.

Asking students to consider why the daughter is being asked to whistle in *Whistle, Daughter, Whistle* may yield some creative answers to this riddle.

Script. Whistle, Daughter, Whistle

Teacher	Students
Sing the song and ask, • *What animal was the daughter being asked to whistle for?* • *Why might the daughter need a cow?* • *What other animal could she whistle for?*	Students listen, answer, and suggest other common animals.
For the first few animals suggested, supply and sing a rhyming line: • *"Whistle, daughter, whistle, and you shall have a fish. I cannot whistle, mother, for that is not my wish."* • *"Whistle, daughter, whistle, and you shall have a pig. I cannot whistle, mother, my lips are not that big."* With each new rhyme, continue singing the song to the end.	Students suggest animals, challenging their teacher to create a rhyme.
Intermittently, ask students about the characters in the song, focusing their attention on each phrase: • *Who is singing the song first?* • *The daughter is the first person we sing about, but listen to the first line. Is it the daughter who is singing?* • *When does the daughter start singing? When does she stop?* • *Notice how the melody changes on the word "mother." Can you make your hand look like mine on that word, going down just a little, from a fist to the first finger pointing up. [The hand signs for DO and TI] Try it as we sing that verse again.*	Students begin to sing parts of the song with the teacher. As they listen closely for the stepwise changes in the melody, students can perform hand signs for any intervals that may be difficult. Students answer the questions and check their answers with the song. Students perform the hand signs on "mother," imitating the actions of the teacher.
As students begin to seek more difficult rhyming challenges, encourage them to help with the rhyming: • *Sherman has suggested we sing about a goat. Sing that first part with me and put "goat" in the song. [Singing the starting pitch] Ready, sing . . . "Whistle, daughter, whistle, and you shall have a goat." [Hum the next phrase.]* • *Now, what will come next?*	Students sing along, but when the teacher hums the rhyming line, they realize they don't have words to finish the phrase. "Something that rhymes with goat," reply the students, as they suggest throat, boat, or coat.
• *Offering one rhyming word isn't enough to complete the phrase, is it?* • *That's right. So what will it be? Start from the beginning and see what you get.* • *It fits easily, doesn't it. Let's use those words and sing the whole song.*	"We need more." "We have to work out a whole line." Students sing the first line together and fumble through the second. One student then suggests, " "I'll jump into a moat." The class laughs and hardly needs encouragement to try it in the song, singing it all the way to the end.

Teacher	Students
• *When you come to the "oh," make a check mark in the air with your finger. Notice how this changes the feeling and the sound of your voice.* • *This time, try waving at a friend on the "oh."* The class continues with various rhymes. Each time a line is suggested, it is put into the song and the whole song is sung. Commonly, several lines are suggested for each animal, and each is sung.	The higher tone in the middle, "oh," can be difficult for students to sing. As the rhyming continues, begin to include small actions on this word: making a check mark in the air, throwing a Frisbee, or waving at a friend. These gestures focus students' attention indirectly on this moment in the song, causing them to use a little more energy when they sing this tone.
When the time runs out, or when there are more lines to sing than make sense, students are invited to write their lines so they can be sung on another day.	Although some animals, such as giraffe and rhinoceros, are difficult to find rhymes for, support students in their attempts to work out solutions.
• *Did you notice how we hold the "oh" a little bit longer than the other words? In music we call this a* fermata. • *Conductors show performers with a gesture how long to hold a fermata. Josh, will you be the conductor? We'll watch your hands and you'll show us how long we should hold the "oh" this time.* • *Remember, you don't want the music to sound weak. Make sure you let us continue while we still have breath to energize our singing.*	Students get chances to conduct the "oh." Some have the class hold it for a long time, others for very short times, and some for a medium length. Continue to use and encourage students to use the term "fermata" as they participate in the conducting activity
The last verse of the song, which involves whistling the second phrase, can be used as a punch line to end the activity.	

Wild Birds

SCENARIO   "What is an enchanted forest like?" With that question, Ms. Snowdon quietly began class. A few hands went up as students eagerly offered their own perspectives: "Animals can talk." "It has a castle." "Mysterious things happen." "There is magic and magicians." Ms. Snowdon listened attentively to each comment and then continued.

"I have a song about an enchanted forest. It's a place where the animals are very special. There are birds in this forest, wild birds, that fly from tree to tree, singing to each other. One bird, with long, orange tail feathers, and a bright blue beak, sat on a branch of an old oak tree and sang to his friends in the forest." As the teacher quietly sang "oo" on the first phrase of the song *Wild Birds,* she began to paint a picture with her words, her voice, and her movements. A quiet, hushed setting was important for her story.

Descriptions of the birds and the forest included the coolness and fresh smells of the air, the colors of the trees and flowers, the flight of the birds, the play of light on the leaves and the rocks. Ms. Snowdon enjoyed inviting her students to add their own imaginative descriptions of the forest, so she would ask students to describe what a

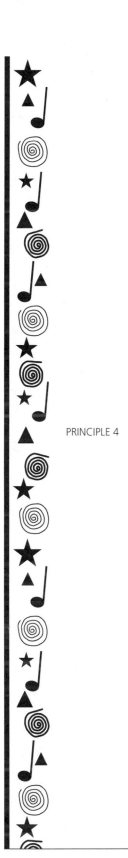

particular bird would look like, what kind of trees they thought were there, and what other animals would hear the birds sing to each other. With quiet energy in her voice, the teacher frequently sang the birdsongs, one of the phrases of *Wild Birds*, always singing it with an "oo" vowel and a sustained, energized, light vocal sound.

After students had heard one phrase several times, Ms. Snowdon had them echo her. "The bright blue bird in the tall pine sang to his friends and they would echo him. Listen to the song, and you be the echo for me."

As Ms. Snowdon continued to spin the story of the wild birds who live in an enchanted forest and the prince who lived in a castle in the middle of that forest, she moved quietly around the room, stopping near different students, to sing and have the class echo the phrases of the song. "This prince loved these birds. He would sit in an upper turret of his castle just listening to the birds call to one another." Here the teacher sang one of the phrases and had her students echo, establishing a pattern so that students would not need a prompt to echo each time. She repeated phrases with which students had difficulty, sometimes using her hands to gently sketch the contour while she sang and her students echoed.

"The prince loved listening to the birds sing so much that he had the windows of his bedroom opened so he could hear them in the evening. The birdsong would lull him to sleep at night and was the first thing he heard upon awakening in the morning. Sometimes he would awaken deep in the night, and he would hear the sound of one of the wild birds, floating on the cool, dark air of the forest."

Singing the phrases of the song inside the story was a way Ms. Snowdon was teaching the melody. She knew this was a difficult song to learn, and focusing on just the melody like this not only helped set the tone of the story but also was an effective introduction to the song. The vocal exercise students were getting by vocalizing on this open vowel was also a part of learning the song and practicing good vocal technique.

"The prince wanted to have these birds close to him all the time, so he built a cage that he could have in his bedroom. He caught one of the birds and put it in the cage, but their wildness was important to him. He didn't want to just own one of the wild birds, he wanted to be close to them. The birds, who could talk, sang this song to him. In their song, they described a way that a wild bird might be caged but wild at the same time. Listen to the song and tell me what the wild birds had in mind."

At that point, Ms. Snowdon sang the words to the whole song. When she finished, she took comments from the class about what the song suggested would happen.

Ms. Snowdon loved the quiet focus that this game established in her class. She didn't know whether it was the character of the song, the story, or maybe just that students had to close their eyes while they sang and played the game. Probably it was some of each. But it didn't matter. The softness of their voices, the hush just before singing the song and between clues, and the chance for students to sing by themselves when giving clues, all made the game quite worthwhile to her.

Another day she would have the students give the clues singing on the pure, sustained "oo" vowel she used when introducing the song. She had done this with last year's fourth graders, and it was a real challenge for them to identify each others' voices. She remembered how Jason's sweet boy-soprano sound had fooled so many students. Jason, who had always been in the middle of any mischief, had also been tickled and surprised that students could not guess him—and he got lots of turns that day. Ms. Snowdon thought this class would respond well to the challenge of giving the clue on "oo." But that would be for another day, she thought.

PRINCIPLE 4

Wild Birds

Round, round the wild birds fly. Poor lit-tle birds in a cage, don't cry.
Ka - go - me, Ka - go - me, Ka - go - no na - ka - no to - ri - wa,

Hide your eyes and soon you'll be with the wild birds fly - ing free. Who's stand-ing back of you,
I - tsu i - tsu de - ya - ru? Yo - a - ke - no ba - n - ni, Tsu - ru to ka - me to

can you say? If you guess my name you can fly a - way.
sub - be - ta. U - shi - ro - no sho - men——— da - re?

Brief Description

As students sing the song, seated in a circle or at desks with eyes closed for Version 1, four students ("birds") wander around the class. At the cadence, each bird stops behind a student, lightly touches that student's shoulder, then sings the cadence phrase: "If you guess my name you can fly away." Listening to the voice, the student guesses who is singing the clue, and if the guess is correct, the students change roles. If the guess is incorrect, the bird who gave the clue gets another turn. In Version 2, with students in a seated circle, one student sits with eyes closed in the center of the circle and another walks around the outside. At the cadence, the student on the outside stops behind a student in the circle, who then gives the singing clue for the student sitting inside to guess. The students in the circle for Version 2 can have eyes open or closed.

Age Appropriateness

Version 1—Grade 3 through Grade 6   Four-Bird Game

Version 2—Grade 1 through Grade 3   One-Bird Game

Degrees of Intensity

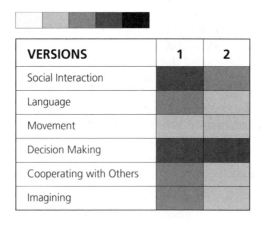

VERSIONS	1	2
Social Interaction		
Language		
Movement		
Decision Making		
Cooperating with Others		
Imagining		

Learning Opportunities

■ *Coordinate movement* with beginning and ending of sound: Auditory-motor skills.

■ Imagination for *storytelling:* Language skills.

■ Exploring *vocal production:* Vocal skills.

■ *Solo singing:* Vocal skills.

■ Combined short-short-long and balanced phrase *structure:* Music skills.

■ Minor mode and *melody* patterns of LA₁ LA₁ LA₁ LA₁ LA₁ TI₁ TI₁ LA₁ SO₁ LA₁ and LA₁ SO₁ LA₁ TI₁ LA₁ LA₁ LA₁: Music skills.

■ *Rhythm* patterns of ♫♫ ♫♫ ♫ ♩ (DUTADETA DU DETA DU DE DU) and ♩ ♫♫ ♫♫ ♩ (DU DU DE DU DE DU) and ♫♫ ♫♫ ♫♫ ♩ (DU DE DU DE DU DE DU): Music skills.

Song and Activity Background

Wild Birds is a Japanese folk song that is found in many music songbooks and series texts. The present version draws on these texts and Japanese teachers Sachiko Torikai, Aiko Iwashige, and Kenny Tanaka, all of whom sang to Douglas Bartholomew versions that they had learned as children. The games described in Versions 1 and 2 came from the classes of Gloria Nelson and Arva Frank, music teachers in Corvallis, Oregon.

Script. Version 1: Four-Bird Game

Teacher
• We will have four wild birds, who will fly smoothly and quietly around the room; the rest of us are the caged birds with our eyes closed. • At the end of the song, each wild bird will stop behind a student. The birds will then take turns, one at a time, singing the clue, [Singing] *"If you guess my name, you can fly away."*
• Just before singing the clue, the wild bird will put a hand on the shoulder of the student he or she is standing behind. This student then guesses the name of the wild bird who just sang. • All of us still keep our eyes closed. We can make mental guesses about who we think sang, but we keep our ideas in our inner hearing. • One at a time, the birds sing their clues. Each bird will touch a shoulder, sing his or her clue, and wait for the response before we hear the next bird's clue.
• I will be a wild bird for the first turn, and I need three others to join me. • OK, Jim, Sally, and Al, you can be wild birds with me. The rest of you will close your eyes, and some of you will be chosen to guess who you think it is that is singing the clue. Make sure you listen. • Jim, would you be the wild bird who indicates the order in which we should take our clue-giving turns? Here comes the song, close your eyes . . . *"Round, round the wild birds fly . . ."*
At the end of the song, touch a student's shoulder and sing, *"If you guess my name you can fly away."* After the student guesses, prompt Jim. • Jim, gesture silently to the bird who will sing next. [Jim gestures to Al.] • Remember to touch the shoulder before you sing. [Al sings his clue.]

Teacher

- *After all the guesses are made, students look up to see the person who sang to them.*
- *If you guessed correctly, trade places, and we'll have some new wild birds.*
- *Let's see who our new wild birds are. Samantha, Alison, Lone Wolf, and Fred. We'll close our eyes, and Alison, you choose the order in which the birds will sing at the end of the song. Remember how peaceful the forest is as we sing the song. Close your eyes. Here comes the song.*

Some students disguise their voices, which may tickle the class, but this doesn't necessarily keep others from identifying them. A surprisingly effective way of disguising voices is for students to sing the clue on "oo."

Additional Versions of Wild Birds

Version 2:. One-Bird Game.   After introducing the story and song about an enchanted forest, the teacher chooses a student to sit inside the circle. "*You will get to guess who is singing a clue later in the song.*" All students practice singing the clue so that they will know what to sing if chosen: "*If you guess my name, you can fly away.*"

The student in the circle is instructed to close her eyes and wait till she hears the clue, then she is to guess who she thinks sang the clue. The teacher walks on the outside of the circle as all sing the song and stops behind a student at the cadence. This student sings the clue, "If you guess my name you can fly away," and waits for the child sitting in the center to guess a name. Whether the guess is correct or not, the student in the center becomes the student to walk around the circle, and the student who sang the clue goes to the center of the circle.

Appendix A:
Children's Folk Song Collections

Adzinyah, A. K., D. Maraire, and J. C. Tucker. 1986. *Let your voice be heard: Songs from Ghana and Zimbabwe.* Rev. ed. Danbury, Conn.: World Music Press. With CD or audiocassette tape.

Baring-Gould, W. S., and C. Baring-Gould. 1967. *The annotated Mother Goose.* New York: New American Library.

Campbell, P. S., E. McCullough-Brabson, and J. C. Tucker. 1994. *Roots and branches: A legacy of multicultural music for children.* Danbury, Conn.: World Music Press. With CD or audiocassette tape.

DeCesare, R., ed. 1991. *Songs of Hispanic Americans.* Van Nuys, Calif.: Alfred Publishing. With audiocassette tape.

Gomme, A. B. 1894. *Children's singing games.* New York: Dover.

Locke, E. G., ed. 1988. *Sail away: 155 American folk songs to sing, read, and play.* Rev. ed. New York: Boosey & Hawkes, Inc.

Lomax, A. 1960. *Folk songs of North America.* Garden City, N.Y.: Doubleday.

Lomax, J., and A. Lomax. 1947. *Best loved American folk songs.* New York: Grosset & Dunlap.

Monsour, S. 1995. *Songs of the Middle East.* Miami: Warner Brothers Publishing.

Newell, W. W. 1883. *The games of American children.* New York: Harper & Brothers.

Opie, I., and P. Opie. 1985. *The singing game.* New York: Oxford University Press.

Richards, M. H. 1985. *Let's do it again: The songs of ETM.* Portola Valley, Calif.: Richards Institute.

Rohrbough, L. 1940. *Handy play party book.* Revised by C. Riddell, 1982. Burnsville, N.C: World Around Songs.

Sandburg, C. 1927. *The American songbag.* New York: Harcourt Brace Jovanovich.

Seeger, P. 1964. *Folk songs of Peggy Seeger.* New York: Oak Publications.

Seeger, R. C. 1948. *American folk songs for children.* New York: Doubleday.

Scott, J. W., J. A. Scott, and L. Seidman, eds. *Folksong in the Classroom* (periodical). P.O. Box 925, Sturbridge, MA 01566.

All past and current music series textbooks are excellent sources of song scores and recordings. Publishers include Allyn & Bacon; Follett; American Book Company; Ginn; Holt, Rinehart & Winston; Macmillan McGraw Hill; and Silver Burdett & Ginn.

Appendix B: Glossary

AB   A musical structure having two parts, the second part contrasting with the first. *See* Binary structure.

ABA   A musical structure having three parts, the first and the last being either identical or very similar. *See* Ternary structure.

Adagio   A tempo indication meaning slow.

Allegro   A tempo indication meaning fast, lively.

Anacrusis   Unaccented sound or sounds followed by an accent at the beginning of a phrase or a musical unit; also called a pickup.

Antiphonning   A manner of performing in which a leader and responders alternate singing successive parts of a song.

Balanced structure   A song or another musical work with phrases of equal length.

Bar line   A vertical line through a staff that separates music notation into measures; the first beat following a bar line is the first beat of a metric group.

Bass clef   A symbol that indicates that the fourth line of the staff is F.

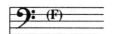

Beam   A broad horizontal or slightly slanted line that connects two or more note stems and indicates duration. *See also* Flag.

Beat   The feeling of a steady pulse; in a moderate tempo, it can be called a walking beat. The beat division (fast beat) and the meter (slow beat) are usually determined in relation to this moderate, walking beat.

Binary structure   A musical form having two parts, often contrasting (AB).

Cadence   The sound or series of sounds that brings closure to a phrase or a musical unit.

Canon   A piece of music in which two or more groups play exactly the same music but start at different times. It is similar to a round but has a formal ending.

Chest voice   The lower register of the voice, having a heavier quality than the head voice.

Chinning   Singing a song using neutral syllables, such as "doo" or "loo."

Chorus   (Musical structure) A section of a song that repeats both melody and words, usually between verses; sometimes used synonymously with "refrain."

Chunk   A group of sounds that are perceived and remembered as a cohesive, single unit; either a subdivision of a phrase or equal in length to a short phrase.

Clef   A sign indicating the position of a particular pitch on a staff.

Closure   A sense of musical completeness; the sense that the end of a phrase or a musical unit has arrived.

Coda   The ending section of a larger musical work, from the Italian word for "tail."

Contour   The general shape of a melodic line resulting from changes in pitch height.

Crescendo (<) The dynamic indication for getting louder. *See* Dynamics.

D.C. al Fine   Abbreviation of the Italian *Da Capo al Fine,* telling the reader to return to the beginning and to conclude when the word *fine* is reached.

Decrescendo (>) The dynamic indication for getting softer. *See* Dynamics.

Diatonic scale   A seven-tone scale, common in Western European musical cultures; often found in its major-scale format: DO RE MI FA SO LA TI and DO again.

DO   A solfa syllable indicating either the tonic of a major key (movable DO) or the note C (fixed DO).

DO sign (⊧) A sign that indicates the position of DO on a music staff.

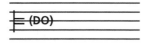

Double bar   Two parallel vertical lines indicating the division of music into sections, and also indicating the end of a piece of music.

Double bar   Final double bar

Downbeat   The first beat of a measure, usually with a feeling of emphasis or accent.

Duration   The length of time a musical tone is sustained.

Dynamics   The levels of loudness and softness of musical sounds. Specific dynamic indications:

   p = piano, soft; *mp* = mezzo piano, medium soft; *pp* = pianissimo, very soft

   f = forte, loud; *mf* = mezzo forte, medium loud; *ff* = fortissimo, very loud

Echo structure   A song structure in which the text matches the following pattern:

X   Y   Y   Y   X   Y   Z

Episode   (Musical structure) A section of music that separates main thematic material. Episodes are typically of looser organization than themes and are often performed only once in a piece.

Fermata (⌢) A sign indicating that a sound should be held longer than its notated or expected length.

Flag   A curved line extending from the tip of a note stem to indicate a shorter duration.

Flat (♭) A sign that lowers a note or tone by a half step.

Form   The overall organization of a piece of music, including its structure.

Form book   A series of song scores for a single song, each score reflecting different aspects of the song.

Glissando   An uninterrupted series of pitches steadily moving in one direction, usually performed very quickly, giving the impression of a gliding or sliding pitch.

Grand staff   A combination of two staves, one with a treble clef and the other with a bass clef, typically used to write music for the piano.

Half step   The smallest interval on the piano, from one piano key to the closest key in either direction.

Hand signs   Hand positions that represent solfa, a different position for each syllable.

Hand staff   An open hand, palm toward the face and thumb up, that represents a music staff.

Head voice   The higher register of the voice, in which the primary area of resonance is in the head cavities.

Ideograph   A pictograph of a piece of music using symbols or pictures to represent phrases or song chunks.

Inner hearing   The cognitive skill of forming mental images of aural phenomena such as words and melodies without sound being directly present. Hearing words, melodies, or sounds "inside the head."

Interval   The distance between two pitches.

Key signature   The arrangements of sharps or flats placed at the beginning of each line of a music staff to indicate the key of the composition.

Leger line   A small horizontal line used to extend the music staff to place a note either above or below the staff.

Lifted voice   Use of the voice well supported by breath energy and often using head resonance.

Major scale   A seven-tone scale with the following sequence of rising steps from the first tone: whole, whole, half, whole, whole, whole, half.

Map   A line, representing musical flow, that is followed or traced while singing or listening to a song or other musical work.

Measure   (Music notation) The space between bar lines, defined by the meter; sometimes called a bar.

Melodic contour   *See* Contour.

Melody   (1) The musical element that refers to a succession of pitches, described as going up and down. (2) An organized series of sounds combining pitch and duration, often referred to as the tune.

Melody graph   A depiction of melodic contour, either by a line or by a series of dots.

Meter   The grouping of beats, usually with a feeling of emphasis on the first of each group; often organized in groups of two or three.

Meter signature ($\frac{3}{4}$, $\frac{2}{4}$, $\frac{6}{8}$)   Two numbers, one above the other, placed at the beginning of a written piece of music to indicate the beat value and beat grouping for that piece.

Middle C   The note C found in the middle of the piano, and on a leger line below the treble clef and above the bass clef.

Minor scale   A seven-tone scale whose natural form consists of the following sequence of rising steps from the first tone: whole, half, whole, whole, half, whole, whole. In other forms (melodic and harmonic minor), the first four steps are the same but the final three are varied.

Moderato   A tempo indication meaning medium speed.

Natural sign   (♮) A sign that cancels a sharp or a flat.

Note   A written representation of a pitch and/or duration.

Notehead   The oval portion of a note, either solid or open, that indicates a pitch on the staff.

Octave   The interval in which two pitches are seven steps apart and share the same note name.

Ostinato   A repeated musical pattern, usually used as an accompaniment.

Partner songs   Two or more songs that can be performed together with a pleasing result.

Part singing   A manner of performing songs in which two or more groups sing different musical material at the same time, in contrast to unison singing; also called singing in harmony.

Pentatonic scale   A five-tone scale, most often consisting of the first, second, third, fifth, and sixth degrees of the major scale, or the tones DO, RE, MI, SO, and LA.

Phrase   A self-contained portion of a musical work, set off by a cadence and having a sense of closure.

Pitch   The "highness" or "lowness" of a tone, related to the frequency of vibration. Pitch can be indefinite—as in the roar of the surf or a cymbal crash—or definite—a specific frequency or note name.

Points of closure   The beginning and the ending of a musical unit.

Presto   A tempo indication meaning very fast.

Range   The distance from the lowest to the highest pitches in a song, or of a voice or an instrument.

Refrain   A section of music that repeats, often acting as an ending and separating multiple verses; sometimes used synonymously with "chorus."

Rest   A measured silence within a musical composition.

Rhythm   (1) The pattern of durations in a musical piece. (2) The musical element pertaining to the arrangement of durations.

Rhythm syllables   Syllables used to represent and sing rhythm patterns—for example, DU DE and DU DA DI.

Round   A song sung by two or more groups, all singing identical music but starting at different times. *See* Canon.

Scale   A sequence of tones arranged in a specific pattern of intervals, usually stepwise.

Sharp (♯)   A sign that raises a note or tone by a half step.

Short-short-long structure   A song structure with three phrases, two shorter phrases followed by a longer phrase.

Slur   One syllable set to two or more tones, indicated in notation by a curved line joining different notes.

Solfa   A system of teaching notation using syllables to represent relationships among the tones of the diatonic scale—for example, DO RE MI FA SO LA TI.

Solfège   *See* Solfa.

Solfeggio   *See* Solfa.

Song chunk   *See* Chunk.

Song dots   Music notation using dots to represent individual sounds of a song.

Staff   A five-line grid on which notes representing sounds or tones can be written.

Stem   A vertical line added to a notehead to indicate rhythmic value.

Stress pattern   A group of sounds or syllables in which one sound predominates.

Structure   The pattern or organization formed by repetitions and contrasts of phrases; also, the organization of tones and rhythm underlying a musical work or style.

Symphony   (1) A work for orchestra in multiple movements, usually four. (2) An orchestra or, less often, any large collection of musicians.

Syncopation   The placement of emphasis on normally weak beats or weak parts of beats.

Tempo   The relative speed of a beat.

Ternary structure   A musical form having three parts, the first and the third consisting of similar music (ABA).

Tie   A curved line connecting two notes of the same pitch; often used to connect notes over bar lines.

Timbre   The unique quality or tone color of a sound. Often used to refer to the characteristic sound produced by an instrument or voice.

Tone   Broadly, sound with definite pitch; also, the quality of a sound.

Tonic   The tone of central importance in a musical piece; also called the keynote. Example: DO in a major key.

Treble clef   A symbol indicating that the second line of the staff is G.

Unison   An interval of no distance; a repeated pitch.

Unison singing   Singing the same musical material, words and pitches, at the same time.

Verses   Multiple stanzas set to identical music, often separated by a repeating chorus or refrain.

Vocal folds   The tissues in the larynx whose vibrations, caused by breath passing between them, are the source of vocal sounds.

Whole step   An interval consisting of two consecutive half steps.

Appendix C:
References

Andre, T. 1979. Does answering higher-level questions while reading facilitate productive learning? *Review of Educational Research* 49:280–318.

Bamberger, J. 1991. *The mind behind the musical ear: How children develop musical intelligence.* Cambridge: Harvard University Press.

_____ . 1978. Intuitive and formal musical knowing: Parables of cognitive dissonance. In *The arts, cognition and basic skills,* edited by S. S. Madeja. St. Louis: CEMERL.

Baring-Gould, W. S., and C. Baring-Gould. 1967. *The annotated Mother Goose.* New York: New American Library.

Bartholomew, D. 1994a. Rote teaching and music meaning. *Cadenza* 39, no. 1:19–20.

_____ . 1994b. Fielding answers. *Cadenza* 38, no. 2:18–19.

_____ . 1993. Effective strategies for praising students. *Music Educators Journal* 80, no. 3:40–43.

_____ . 1991. Whole/part relations in music: An exploratory study. *Journal of Aesthetic Education* 25, no. 3:175–191.

_____ . (1985). A phenomenology of music: Themes concerning the musical object and implications for teaching and learning. Ph.D diss., Case Western Reserve University (University Microfilms, No. 8601937).

Baumeister, R. F., D. G. Hutton, and K. J. Cairns. 1990. Negative effects of praise on skilled performance. *Basic and Applied Social Psychology* 11:131–148.

Bennett, P. D. 1996. Introducing a song: Ways to capture attention. *EdVentures in Learning* 1, no. 1:20–22.

_____ . 1992a. On preparing classroom teachers to teach music: Rethinking expectations. *Journal of Music Teacher Education* 1, no. 2:22–27.

_____ . 1992b. A tribute to teachers. *Southwestern Musician* 60, no. 7:37, 39.

_____ . 1991a. Children's pattern perception, accuracy, and preference in three response modes. *Journal of Research in Music Education* 39, no. 1:74–85.

_____ . 1991b. I can sing! *Oregon Music Educator* 43, no. 2:9–13.

_____ . 1990a. Children's perceptions of anacrusis patterns within songs. In *Music Education Research Reports,* edited by T. Tunks. Austin: Texas Music Educators Association.

_____ . 1990b. Leading singing: Six simple suggestions. *ETM News* 7, no. 3.

_____ . 1989. Is praise always positive? *TMEC/MENC Connection* 3, no. 2:12–13.

_____ . 1988a. The perils and profits of praise. *Music Educators Journal* 75, no. 1:22–24.

_____ . 1988b. Making movement musical. *ETM News,* 6, no. 1.

_____ . 1987. From Hungary to America: The evolution of Education Through Music. *Music Educators Journal* 74, no. 1:37–45, 60.

_____ . 1986a. A responsibility to young voices. *Music Educators Journal* 73, no. 1:33–38.

_____ . 1986b. Confessions on classroom management. *ETM News* 3, no. 4.

_____ . 1985. Getting a turn in music class. *ETM News* 3, no. 1.

_____ . 1984. Starting a song. *ETM News,* 2, no. 1.

Bennett, P. D., and D. R. Bartholomew. 1997. *SongWorks 2: Studying and teaching music through song.* Belmont, Calif.: Wadsworth, forthcoming.

Brand, M. 1990. Master music teachers: What makes them great? *Music Educators Journal* 77, no. 2:22–25.

Brooks, J. G., and M. G. Brooks. 1993. *In search of understanding: A case for constructivist classrooms.* Alexandria, Va: Association for Supervision and Curriculum Development.

Brooks, M. 1984. A constructivist approach to staff development. *Educational Leadership,* 42, no. 3:23–27.

Brophy, J. 1981. Teacher praise: A functional analysis. *Review of Educational Research* 51:5–32.

Butler, R. 1987. Task-involving and ego-involving properties of evaluation: Effects of different feedback conditions on motivational perceptions, interest, and performance. *Journal of Educational Psychology* 79:474–482.

Cannella, B. 1986. Praise and concrete rewards: Concerns for childhood education. *Childhood Education,* March/April, 297–301.

Canter, L., and M. Canter. 1976. *Assertive discipline: A take-charge approach for today's educator.* Seal Beach, Calif.: Canter and Associates.

Cassidy, J. W. 1990. Effect of intensity training on preservice teachers' instruction accuracy and delivery effectiveness. *Journal of Research in Music Education* 38, no. 3:164–174.

Charles, C. M. 1985. *Building classroom discipline: From models to practice.* New York: Longman.

Chase, R. 1971. *American folk tales and songs.* New York: Dover.

Choksy, L. 1988. *The Kodály method.* 2nd ed. Englewood Cliffs, N.J.: Prentice Hall.

Chopra, D. 1993. *Ageless body, timeless mind.* New York: Harmony Books.

Cooper, M. 1984. *Change your voice, change your life.* New York: Macmillan.

Covey, S. R. 1989. *The seven habits of highly effective people: Restoring the character ethic.* New York: Simon & Schuster.

Creighton, H. 1962. *Maritime folk songs.* Ethnic Folkways Library Album #FE 4307. "Harbor Grace Diddling," p. 9.

Curwin, R. 1980. Are your students addicted to praise? *Instructor* 90 (October): 61–62.

Curwin, R. L., and A. N. Mendler. 1988. *Discipline with dignity.* Alexandria, Va.: Association for Supervision and Curriculum Development.

Deci, E. L. 1971. Effects of externally mediated rewards on intrinsic motivation. *Journal of Personality and Social Psychology* 18:105–115.

Deci, E. L., G. Betley, J. Kahle, L. Abrams, and J. Porac. 1981. When trying to win: Competition and intrinsic motivation. *Personality and Social Psychology Bulletin* 7:79–83.

Dewey, J. [1902] 1956. *The child and the curriculum.* Chicago: University of Chicago Press.

Dillon, J. T. 1981a. Duration of response to teacher questions and statements. *Contemporary Educational Psychology* 6:1–11.

_____ . 1981b. To question or not to question during discussions, II. Non-questioning techniques. *Journal of Teacher Education* 32:15–20.

_____ . 1978. Using questions to depress student thought. *School Review* 87:50–63.

Eisner, E. W. 1994. *Cognition and curriculum reconsidered.* 2nd ed. New York: Teachers College Press.

Elkind, D. 1976. *Child development and education.* New York: Oxford University Press.

Emmer, E., C. Evertson, and L. Anderson. 1980. Effective classroom management at the beginning of the school year. *The Elementary School Journal* 80:219–231.

Farnsworth, C. H. 1909. *Education through music.* New York: American Book.

Farson, R. 1968. Praise reappraised. In *Human dynamics in psychology and education.* Boston: Allyn & Bacon.

Flanders, N. 1970. *Analyzing teaching behavior.* Reading, Mass.: Addison-Wesley.

Fuld, J. J. 1971. *Book of world-famous music.* New York: Crown Publishers.

Gall, M. D. 1984. Synthesis of research on teachers' questioning. *Educational Leadership* 42, no.3:40–47.

———. 1970. The use of questions in teaching. *Review of Educational Research* 40: 707–721.

Gall, M. D., B. A. Ward, D. C. Berliner, L. S. Cahen, P. H. Winne, J. D. Elashoff, and G. D. Stanton. 1978. Effects of questioning techniques and recitation on student learning. *American Educational Research Journal* 15:175–199.

Gardner, H. 1991. *The unschooled mind: How children learn and how schools should teach.* New York: Basic Books.

———. 1981. *The quest for mind: Piaget, Levi-Strauss, and the structuralist movement.* 2nd ed. Chicago: University of Chicago Press.

Garvey, C. 1977. *Play.* Cambridge: Harvard University Press.

Ginott, H. 1971. *Teacher and child.* New York: Macmillan.

Goetze, M., and H. Yoshiyuki. 1988. A comparison of the pitch accuracy of group and individual singing in young children. *Bulletin of the Council for Research in Music Education* 99:57–74.

Gomme, A. B. 1894. *Children's singing games.* New York: Dover.

Gordon, E. E. 1984. *Learning sequences in music: Skill, content, and patterns.* Chicago: G.I.A. Publications.

Gordon, T. 1974. *Teacher effectiveness training.* New York: P. H. Wyden.

Green, G. A. 1990. The effect of vocal modelling on pitch-matching accuracy of elementary school children. *Journal of Research in Music Education* 38, no. 3: 225–231.

Hare, V. C., and C. A. Pulliam. 1980. Teacher questioning: A verification and an extension. *Journal of Reading Behavior* 12:69–72.

Harmin, M. 1994. *Inspiring active learning: A handbook for teachers.* Alexandria, Va.: Association for Supervision and Curriculum Development.

Hart, L. 1983. *Human brain and human learning.* New York: Longman.

Higgins, K. M. 1991. *The music of our lives.* Philadelphia: Temple University Press.

Hitchcock, H. W. 1974. *Music in the United States: A historical introduction.* 2nd ed. Englewood Cliffs, N.J.: Prentice Hall.

Hitz, R., and A. Driscoll. 1988. Praise or encouragement? New insights into praise: Implications for early childhood teachers. *Young Children,* July, 6–13.

Howard, V. A. 1992. *Learning by all means: Lessons from the arts.* New York: Peter Lang.

Hunt, M. 1982. *The universe within: A new science explores the human mind.* New York: Simon & Schuster.

Johnson, D. W., and R. T. Johnson. 1989/90. Social skills for successful group work. *Educational Leadership* 47, no. 4:29–32.

Jones, F. H. 1987a. *Positive classroom discipline.* New York: McGraw-Hill.

———. 1987b. *Positive classroom instruction.* New York: McGraw-Hill.

Jones, F. P. 1976. *Body awareness in action: A study of the Alexander Technique.* New York: Schocken Books.

Joyce, B., and M. Weil. 1986. *Models of teaching.* 3rd ed. Englewood Cliffs, N.J.: Prentice Hall.

Kamii, C. 1973. Pedagogical principle derived from Piaget's theory: Relevance for educational practice. In *Piaget in the classroom,* edited by Milton Schwebel and Jane Raph. New York: Basic Books.

Kidson, F. 1907. *Eighty singing games.* London: Bayley and Ferguson.

Kohn, A. 1993. *Punished by rewards: The trouble with gold stars, incentive plans, A's, praise, and other bribes.* New York: Houghton Mifflin Co.

_____ . 1992. *No contest: The case against competition* Rev. ed. New York: Houghton Mifflin.

_____ . 1986. How to succeed without even vying. *Psychology Today,* September, 22–28.

Kramer, J. 1988. *The time of music: New meaning, new temporalities, new listening strategies.* New York: Schirmer Books.

Langness, A. P. 1992. A descriptive study of teacher responses during the teaching of singing to children. Ph.D. diss., University of Colorado, Boulder.

_____ . 1991a. Voice discovery in a "safe" atmosphere: What every child needs. *Oregon Music Educator* 43, no. 2:42–46.

_____ . 1991b. Developing children's voices. In *Bodymind and voice: Foundations of voice education,* edited by L. Thurman & G. Welch. Minneapolis: The VoiceCare Network.

Lepper, M. R. 1983. Extrinsic reward and intrinsic motivation. In *Teacher and student perceptions: Implications for learning,* edited by J. M. Levine and M. C. Wang. Hillsdale, N.J.: Erlbaum.

Lomax, A. 1960. *Folk songs of North America.* Garden City, N.Y.: Doubleday.

Lomax, J., and A. Lomax. 1947. *Best loved American folk songs.* New York: Grosset & Dunlap.

Lorenz, E. J. 1942. *Women's get together songs: All the songs you love to sing.* Dayton, Ohio: Lorenz Publishing.

Madsen, C. H., Jr., and C. K. Madsen. 1983. *Teaching/Discipline: A positive approach for educational development* 3rd ed. Raleigh: Contemporary Publishing.

Madsen, C. K., and J. W. Cassidy. 1989. Demonstration and recognition of high and low contrasts in teacher intensity. *Journal of Research in Music Education,* 37, no. 2:85–92.

Madsen, C. K. and T. L. Kuhn. 1978. *Contemporary music education.* Arlington Heights, Ill.: AHS.

Marzano, R. J. 1992. *A different kind of classroom: Teaching with dimensions of learning.* Alexandria, Va.: Association for Supervision and Curriculum Development.

McAllester, D. 1985. Introduction. In *Becoming human through music,* edited by David McAllester. Reston, Va.: MENC.

McGinnis, A. L. 1985. *Bringing out the best in people.* Minneapolis: Augsburg.

Mills, S. R., C. T. Rice, D. C. Berliner, and E. W. Rousseau. 1980. The correspondence between teacher questions and student answers in classroom discourse. *Journal of Experimental Education* 48:194–204.

Mursell, J. L. 1956. *Music education: Principles and programs.* Morristown, N.J.: Silver Burdett.

Nelson, J. 1987. *Positive discipline.* New York: Ballantine.

Newell, W. W. 1883. *The games of American children.* New York: Harper & Brothers.

Norrick, N. R. 1993. *Conversational joking: Humor in everyday talk.* Bloomington: Indiana University Press.

Opie, I. and P. Opie. 1985. *The singing game.* New York: Oxford University Press.

Pater, R. 1988. *Martial arts and the art of management.* Rochester, Vt.: Destiny Books.

Patterson, J. L. 1993. *Leadership for tomorrow's schools.* Alexandria, Va.: Association for Supervision and Curriculum Development.

Piaget, J. 1973. *To understand is to invent.* Translated by George-Anne Roberts. New York: Viking.

Piers, M. W. 1972. *Play and development.* New York: W. W. Norton & Co., Inc.

Redfield, D. L., and E. W. Rousseau. 1983. Meta-analysis of experimental research of teacher questioning behavior. *Review of Educational Research* 51:237–245.

Richards, M. H. 1985. *Let's do it again: The songs of ETM.* Portola Valley, Calif.: Richards Institute.

_____ . 1984. *Aesthetic foundations for thinking, rethought, Part 1: Experience.* Portola Valley, Calif.: Richards Institute.

_____ . 1980. *Aesthetic foundations for thinking, Part 3: The ETM process.* Portola Valley, Calif.: Richards Institute.

Richards, M. H., and A. Langness. 1984. *Music language, Section 2.* Portola Valley, Calif.: Richards Institute.

_____ . 1982. *Music language, Section 1.* Portola Valley, Calif.: Richards Institute.

Rohrbough, L. 1940. *Handy play party book.* Revised by C. Riddell, 1982. Burnsville, N.C.: World Around Songs.

Rosenshine, B. 1976. Classroom instruction. In Psychology of teaching methods. *The Seventy-Fifth Yearbook of the National Society for the Study of Education,* Part I, edited by N. L. Gage. Chicago: University of Chicago Press.

Rubin, L. 1983. Artistry in teaching. *Educational Leadership* 40, no. 4:44–49.

Rusk, T. 1993. *The power of ethical persuasion.* New York: Penguin.

Sandburg, C. 1927. *The American songbag.* New York: Harcourt Brace Jovanovich.

Schutz, A. 1964. Making music together: A study in social relationship. In Schutz, *Collected papers II: Studies in social theory,* edited by Arrid Brodersen. The Hague: Martinus Nijhoff.

Seeger, P. 1964. *Folk songs of Peggy Seeger.* New York: Oak Publications.

Seeger, R. C. 1948. *American folk songs for children.* New York: Doubleday.

Selye, H. 1974. *Stress without distress.* New York: New American Library.

Simpson, G. G. 1949. *The meaning of evolution.* New Haven: Yale University Press.

Sloboda, J. A. 1985. *The musical mind: The cognitive psychology of music.* Oxford: Clarendon Press.

Small, C. 1977. *Music, society, education.* London: John Calder.

Swanwick, K. 1988. *Music, mind, and education.* New York: Routledge.

Swift, S. 1985. *Centered riding.* New York: St. Martin's/Marek.

Thurman, L. 1983. Putting horses before carts: When choral singing hurts voices. *The Choral Journal,* April, 23.

Thurman, L., and G. Welch, eds. 1991. *Bodymind and voice: Foundations of voice education.* Minneapolis: The VoiceCare Network.

Thurmond, J. M. 1982. *Note grouping: A method for achieving expression and style in musical performance.* Camp Hill, Pa.: JMT Publications.

Upitis, R. 1987. Toward a model for rhythmic development. In *Music and child development,* edited by J. C. Peery, I. W. Peery, and T. W. Draper. New York: Springer-Verlag.

Welch, G. 1985. Variability of practice and knowledge of results as factors in learning to sing in tune. *Bulletin of the Council for Research in Music Education* 85:238–247.

Williams, J. M. 1993. *Applied sports psychology: Personal growth to peak performance.* 2nd ed. Mountain View, Calif.: Mayfield.

Winne, P. H. 1979. Experiments relating teachers' use of higher cognitive questions to student achievement. *Review of Educational Research* 49:13–50.

Yarborough, C., S. J. Morrison, B. Karrick, and D. E. Dunn. 1995. The effect of male falsetto on the pitch-matching accuracy of uncertain boy singers, grades K–8. *Update* 14, no. 1:4–10.

Yoder-White, M. G. 1993. Effects of teaching intensity on sixth-grade students' general music achievements and attitudes. *Dissertation Abstracts International* 55, no. 2:237A–238A.

Subject Index

Name Index

Song Index